Trading Strategies Crash Course

4 books in 1

Technical Analysis for Beginners + Crypto Trading+Day Trading Strategies+Day Trading Options

Andrew Elder

Table of Contents

BOOK 1 Technical Analysis for Beginners 17

Introduction 18

Chapter 1 What Is Technical Analysis 20

Understanding Technical Analysis 20

How Technical Analysis Can Support Traders 21

Using Charts in Technical Analysis 22

A Brief History of Technical Analysis 23

Key Definitions and Philosophy of Technical Analysis 24

Chart Construction 25

The Underlying Assumptions of Technical Analysis 28

How Technical Analysis Is Used 29

Chapter 2 Basic Concept of Trend 30

The Trend Has 3 Directions 31

The Trend Has 3 Classifications 32

Support and Resistance 33

Trendlines 35

Trend Channel 39

Divergence 41

Chapter 3 Recognizing Breakout 44

Breakout 45

Breakdown 49

Short Selling 53

False Breakout 55

Stop-Losses 56

Chapter 4 The 4 Types of Indicators You Need to Know 57

Simple Moving Average (SMA) 58

Relative Strength Index (RSI) 61

MACD Indicator 63

On-Balance-Volume (OBV) 66

Chapter 5 Continuation Patterns 68

Pennants Pattern 69

Flag Pattern 70

Wedge Patterns 71

Triangles 72

Rounding Bottom..75

Gaps   76

Head and Shoulders Pattern 77

Double Bottom 78

Double Top..79

Chapter 6 Reversal Patterns **80**

The Head and Shoulders..80

Moving Average 88

In Summary..89

Chapter 7 24 Candlestick Patterns That Every Trader Should Know
....**90**

What Is a Candlestick? 90

Practice Reading Candlestick Patterns..............................91

6 Bullish Candlestick Patterns 91

6 Bearish Candlestick Patterns..95

4 Continuation Candlestick Patterns.................................99

Other Candlestick Patterns 101

Chapter 8 Avoid the Traps **110**

Fakeouts and Fake Head-and-Shoulders 111

No Trend at All..113

Adjust Your Moving Averages...114

Risky Symmetrical Triangle..115

Super Rocket Stock 117

Long Candles 119

Lack of Discipline 119

Chapter 9 Trading Psychology **121**

Trading with Emotions..121

Bias in Trading 123

Psychology Affecting Traders' Habits 125

Why Trading Psychology Is Important..............................131

Psychologically Approach Toward Success 133

Chapter 10 10 Top Tips for Each Aspect of Trading................**135**

1.   Research...135

2.   Stop-Loss/Take Loss 136

3.   No Planning... 136
4.   Over-Rely on a Broker 137
5.   Message Boards.. 137
6.   Calculate Wrong.. 137
7.   Copy Strategies... 138
8.   The Main Tools Used in Trading 138
9.   Market Data and Trading Platform 139
10. Stocks Scanner and Watch List 139

Chapter 11 Designing Your Trading Strategies............ 141
Where to Start? 141
What Is the Best Site? 141
What Broker Do I Use? 142

Chapter 12 Structuring Your Analysis Framework 145
What Is a Technical Analysis Framework..................... 145
Structuring Your Trend Analysis Framework 146
Structuring Your Support and Resistance Framework 148
Secondary Frameworks 151
Selecting Timeframes... 152
Putting It All Together... 153
Components of a Trading System................................ 154

Chapter 13 School of Indicators................................. 155
Choosing Indicators and Brokers for Forex 157
Moving Averages.. 158
Relative Strength Indicators (RSI)............................. 162
Stochastic Indicators 168
Bollinger Bands 174
Moving Average Convergence Divergence Indicator............ 177

Chapter 14 The Best Trades: Putting It All Together.................. 181
Examples of Best Trades.. 186
Top 10 Rules for Successful Trading........................... 189
How Much Do You Buy or Sell? 190

Conclusion 192
Glossary.. 195
BOOK 2   CRYPTO TRADING.. 206
Introduction 207
Chapter 1 What Is a Cryptocurrency? 211

Chapter 2 Why Make Trading in Crypto?........................**215**

Advantages..215

Disadvantages...216

Best Cryptocurrency to Invest 217

Chapter 3 Recognizing the Risks of Cryptocurrency..............**220**

Cryptocurrency Returns..220

Capital Gains… or Losses 221

Income 221

Risks   222

Types of Risks in the Cryptocurrency Business 222

Risk Management Methods 227

Chapter 4 Looking About the Hood: Blockchain Technology **232**

Transactions on the Blockchain System 234

How Is the Blockchain System Different?..................234

How Coins Are Formed 235

Factors Affecting the Cryptocurrency Market...........235

Chapter 5 How Does Cryptocurrency Work? **238**

Chapter 6 Crypto Exchange and Brokers.......................**242**

Moving Average (MA)..242

The Moving Average Convergence-Divergence (MACD)..........243

Bollinger Bands..244

Relative Strength Index (RSI)..245

Money Flow Index (MFI) 246

Fibonacci...247

Trend Lines and Trend Channel...................................248

Chapter 7 Trade in Crypto **250**

Chapter 8 Identifying Top Performing **254**

Ethereum 254

Litecoin 259

Bitcoin Cash..261

Iota   261

Chapter 9 Crypto Mining..**264**

Mining Cryptocurrencies 264

Mining and the Blockchain 265

Hash Function 265

Proof of Work..265

CPU vs. GPU Mining 266

Compare CPU vs. GPU Capacity 266

Functions of the GPU vs. the CPU 267

Chapter 10 Crypto Futures and Options 268

The Future of Cryptocurrency 268

The Outlook for Cryptocurrency 271

The Future of Cryptocurrency and Fiat Currency 273

Cryptocurrency Around the World 274

Regulations and Cryptocurrency 275

Institutional Investors and Cryptocurrency 277

Chapter 11 Using Technical Analysis 278

Types of Technical Analysis 279

Technical Indicators 279

Trend Analysis 281

Drawing Trend Lines 282

Trading Channels 285

Volume Analysis and Price Action 287

Chapter Summary 289

Chapter 12 Minimizing Losses and Maximizing Gains 290

Losses Are Inevitable in Crypto Trading 290

Chapter 13 Using Ichimoku and Fibonacci Techniques 294

Ichimoku Cloud and Fibonacci 295

Chapter 14 n.15 Considerations Before Getting Started with Crypto 298

1. The Difference Between ICOs and Cryptocurrencies 298

2. Understand the Source of Funds 299

3. Know the Product 299

4. Know the Team Behind the Product 299

5. Know the Competition 300

6. The Token's Value 300

7. Know the Type of Tokens 300

8. Know Your Customer (KYC) Laws and Regulations for ICOs 301

9. Know How the Token Will Be Used 301

10. Know the Company's Business Development Plan Before Investing 302

11. Know Project Code and Roadmap Prior to Investment........302
12. Know the Team Behind an ICO 302
13. Know Where to Buy ICOs 303
14. Know Where to Store Your ICOs..303
15. Know How to Protect Yourself From Scams 304

Chapter 15 n.15 Possible Moves When Your Portfolio Is Down.305
1. Stop and Reassess the State of Your Portfolio.......................305
2. Don't Trade When Your Portfolio Is Down 306
3. Stop Trading for a While if You're Scared...............................306
4. Don't Trade When Your Portfolio Is Low 306
5. Don't Trade Often or Frequently if You're Broke 307
6. Sell Into a Dip if You're Upside Down 307
7. Diversify Your Holdings 307
8. Stay Invested 308
9. Take Longer-Term Positions 308
10. Don't Expect Much...308
11. Set Your Margin for Success..308
12. Keep an Eye on Coins You're Not Trading 309
13. Don't Be Afraid to Change Your Strategy 309
14. Be Patient and Realistic...309
15. Don't Give Up...310

Chapter 16 n.15 Challenges and Opportunities for Crypto Investors
...311

Chapter 17 n.24 Signals That Every Trader Should Know..........315
When Trading too Much 315
When Trading too Little 315
Momentum Selling 316
Momentum Buying..316
Beware 317
Excessive Shorting 317
Spike Trading..317
Spike Selling 318
Dollar Trend 318
Price Trends..319
Dollar Selling..319
Price Selling..319

False Earnings Reports.. 320

Closed Trade.. 321

Flooding 321

Quick Changes in Price.. 321

Insider Buying 322

Earnings Surprises 322

Talk to the Management Team... 323

Information Overload 323

Analyst Issuance... 323

Upward Pressure.. 324

Earnings Reports 324

Stock Splits.. 325

Chapter 18 Resources for Personal Portfolio Management......... 326

What Is a Portfolio in Cryptocurrency?..................................... 326

What Are the Different Types of Cryptocurrency Portfolios?... 326

How to Build a Portfolio? 327

Where to Create an Account on an Exchange? 327

How to Use an Exchange? 327

Keeping Track of Your Portfolio Value and Profit/Loss 328

Chapter 19 Tips for Getting Started with Cryptocurrency.......... 329

Ignore Sources that Are Biased 329

Start Small... 329

Have Realistic Goals 330

Don't Try to Guess and Trade... 330

Be Patient and Don't Panic 330

Learn From Your Mistakes.. 331

Plan Ahead 332

Don't Trust Others Completely... 332

Pick Currencies that Have Huge Communities......................... 333

Don't Get Bored.. 334

Don't Forget to Have Fun!... 334

Chapter 20 n.5 Cryptocurrencies to Invest in 2021 336

Bitcoin (BTC)... 337

Ethereum (ETH) 338

Litecoin (LTC)... 338

Bitcoin Cash (BCH) 339

Binance Coin (BNB) 339
To Date the Not-So-Great Cryptocurrencies..................340
Chapter 21 Why the Interest in Cryptocurrency Is Growing? 341
How Much Bitcoin Is There?...................................341
Where Can I Buy Bitcoin? 342
How Much Money Is in Bitcoin? 342
What Are the Benefits of Cryptocurrency?.....................342
Is Bitcoin a Scam?...343
How Do I Get Hold of Bitcoin?................................343
Will This Affect Me When I Retire?...........................344
Are All Cryptocurrencies the Same? 345
Could the Value of Bitcoin Crash Again? 345
Why Is the Government Getting Involved?......................346
What Do Consumers Think?.....................................347
Chapter 22 Trading on Breakouts of Local Tops and Important Levels..349
Triple Taps Strategy...354
Homework...356
Chapter 23 Cryptocurrency Trading Mistakes to Avoid 357
Mistake #1: Using Real Money to Trade Instead of Practicing Paper Trading as a Beginner.......................................358
Mistake #2: Trading Without Any Stop Loss....................358
Mistake #3: Not Maintaining Balance Properly.................359
Mistake #4: Adding to Losing Trades..........................359
Mistake #5: Not Keeping a Journal Specifically for Trading 360
Mistake #6: Risking More Than You Can Afford to Lose 360
Mistake #7: Not Having Enough Capital 360
Mistake #8: Using Leverage 361
Mistake #9: Acting on Trading Indicators and Patterns That Are Not Very Clear to You..362
Mistake #10: Going With the Herd 362
Mistake #11: Bottom Trading 362
Mistake #12: Hodling...363
Mistake #13: Relying on Gut Instinct Alone 363
Mistake #14: Trading Worthless Cryptocurrencies 363
Mistake #15: Not Having Security 364

Mistake #16: Anthropomorphizing the Market 364

Mistake #17: Not Diversifying... 364

Mistake #18: Relying on Chance Instead of Skill 365

Mistake #19: Believing Other People Easily 365

Mistake #20: Panic Selling... 365

Mistake #21: Not Knowing How to Keep the Money and Then Make Some More... 366

Mistake #22: Committing the Sunk Cost Fallacy 366

Mistake #23: Being Envious... 366

Chapter 24 Innovative Cryptocurrencies..................................... **367**

Ripple 367

IOTA   369

Chapter 25 Principles of Crypto Trading **373**

Understanding the Ideas and Processes of Trading 373

Trading Rules that Guide You Through Creating Disciplines .. 375

Trading Strategies 376

Crypto Trading Tools... 377

Understanding Fundamental and Technical Analysis............... 379

Chapter 26 Creating a Personalized Trading Plan....................... **380**

Consider Trading Goals... 380

Consider Your Risk Tolerance.. 381

Consider Trading Limits.. 381

Consider Your Ideal Level of Involvement................................. 382

Consider Your Familiarity With Trading 382

Consider Your Strengths and Weaknesses.................................. 382

Consider the Other Challenges in Your Life at the Moment 383

Stick With It 383

Don't Be too Anxious to Get Started.. 384

Conclusion **385**

Glossary... **387**

Book 3 Day Trading Options: **393**

Introduction **395**

Day Trading's Historical Context:.. 396

Becoming a Day Trader: 397

CHAPTER 1: What Is Options Trading? **398**

Understanding Options Trading: A Beginner's Guide............... 398

CHAPTER 2: Understanding and Managing Risk in Options Trading.....................402

Managing Risk with Options Spreads..........................402

CHAPTER 3: Software Required Before Getting Started 405

Charts 407

CHAPTER 4: Platform and Tools for option Trading 408

CHAPTER 5: Understanding the Basic Techniques 412

Understanding Basic Techniques in Technical Analysis 412

The Importance of Technical Analysis in Options Trading........414

CHAPTER 6: Learn to Become a Day Trader...............................415

Becoming a Proficient Day Trader...............................415

Understanding Day Trading.......................................415

Intraday vs. Swing Trading.......................................417

CHAPTER 7: Fundamental Analysis 419

Fundamental Analysis Methodology.........................420

CHAPTER 8: Technical Analysis for Training Options..............422

Technical Analysis for Options Trading 422

Determining Trend or Range....................................423

Chart Patterns to Watch For.....................................423

CHAPTER 9: How to Find the Best Options to Get Started 425

Strategies for Adopting an Options Trader's Mindset...............425

The Crucial Role of Trading Psychology 426

Differentiating Between Losing and Bad Trades.......................427

CHAPTER 10: Theoretical and practical training of operational techniques 429

Bullish Trading Strategies 430

Risk/Reward Analysis for Long Call Options Strategy 431

CHAPTER 11: Psychology of An Option Trader..........................433

Greed   434

CHAPTER 12: What Kind of Trader Are You? 437

Day Trading 437

Options Trading..438

CHAPTER 13: Common Mistakes to Avoid in Day Trading.......440

Common Mistakes to Avoid in Day Trading 440

CHAPTER 14: Advanced Trading Strategies...............................443

Advanced Trading Strategies.......................................443

CHAPTER 15: Covered Call Strategy (or Protected Puts)............ 446

Covered Call Strategy (or Protected Puts) 446

CHAPTER 16: Brokers 450

Choosing the Right Broker 450

CHAPTER 17: Options Day Trading Styles 455

Resistance Trading Strategy with Options 456

Support and Resistance Breakouts: 456

Momentum Options Day Trading 458

Scalping Options Day Trading 460

CHAPTER 18: Historical Events in the FX Markets 464

History of Forex Trading: Origins 464

CHAPTER 19: Introduction to Candlestick 468

Introduction to Candlestick Patterns 468

Candle Patterns 470

CHAPTER 20: How to Trade Options on Robinhood 473

CHAPTER 21: Binary Trading Options 477

60-Second Binary Options 477

Understanding Trading Styles 480

CHAPTER 22: Options Day Trading Rules for Success 482

CHAPTER 23: Creating Your Own Day Trading Strategy 485

CHAPTER 24: How Options Prices are Determined 488

Intrinsic Value and Option Pricing 488

CHAPTER 25: Pro Tips for Day Trading Options 492

CHAPTER 26: Risk Management Strategies 496

Risk Management Strategies: Protecting Your Capital 496

CHAPTER 27: Advanced Technical Analysis 499

CHAPTER 28: Options Trading Strategies 502

CHAPTER 29: Options Greeks and Volatility 505

CHAPTER 30: Risk Assessment and Trade Selection 508

CHAPTER 31: Trading Psychology and Discipline 511

CHAPTER 32: Real-Life Case Studies 514

CHAPTER 33: Tax Implications and Record-Keeping 517

CHAPTER 34: Regulations and Compliance 520

CHAPTER 35: Options Trading Tools and Software 523

CHAPTER 36: Options Trading in Different Market Conditions 527

CHAPTER 37: International Options Markets 530
Legend of Terms...533
FAQ..542
Conclusion 545
Book 4 DAY TRADING STRATEGIES.....................................548
Introduction 549
Managing Your Day Trades...550
ABCD Pattern...552
Bull Flag Momentum..553
Chapter 1 Know the Market 555
Things to consider before getting started..................555
Choose a broker 556
Trading on the Stock Market.......................................556
Futures Markets 557
FOREX Markets..557
Why Day Trade Options 558
Things to watch day trading options 559
Chapter 2 How to Manage Risk in Day Trading: Stop Loss and
Take Profit 560
Step Risk Management..560
Chapter 3 Quantitative Risk and Qualitative Risk 566
Qualitative Risk..569
Chapter 4 Day Trading is Really Possibility to Business...........572
Trading Plans 572
Journals...575
Training 577
Chapter 5 Technical Analysis 578
Chart Patterns 583
Bollinger Bands...583
An Overview and Summary of Technical Analysis for the Stock
Investor...584
Chapter 6 Consolidation Chart Patterns to Know...........585
Chapter 7 Relationship with Fundamental Analysis 594
Chapter 8 Range Trading or Channel Trading.................599
Trading Strategy for Ranges 601
Chapter 9 News Trading 602

Chapter 10 Pairs Trading.. 606

Currency Pairs... 606

Asset Class.. 608

Chapter 11 Intraday Scalping.. 609

Chapter 12 Breakout... 612

Chapter 13 Application on the Options Market......................... 617

Chapter 14 Analyzing Mood Swing in the Market..................... 620

Chapter 15 Options Trading Strategies...................................... 626

Options Strategies... 626

Selling covered calls against LEAPS and other LEAPS Strategies
627

Buying Put Options as Insurance.. 628

Chapter 16 Application on the Futures Market.......................... 631

How Can We Make a Profit on the Futures Markets?............... 634

Chapter 17 Which Market to Trade and with which Broker....... 637

Chapter 18 Application on the Stocks Market............................ 642

Chapter 19 How Does The Stock Market Work?........................ 649

Stock Market Corrections and Crash.. 651

Fundamental Market Analysis... 652

Technical Market Analysis... 652

Chapter 20 Application on the Forex Market.............................. 655

Chapter 21 Application on the Commodities Market................. 661

Chapter 22 Application on the Crypto Value Market................. 666

Chapter 23 Top Day Trading Tools... 672

Stop Loss Management... 675

Penny Stock Level 2 Quotes 676

Chapter 24 Momentum Trading... 677

Chapter 25 Common Day Trading Mistakes to Avoid............... 683

Chapter 26 Portfolio Diversification.. 689

Introduction to Diversification.. 690

The Process of Asset Class Allocation 692

Chapter 27 Options Day Trading Rules for Success................... 697

Rule for Success #1 – Have Realistic Expectations.................... 698

Rule for Success #2 – Start Small to Grow a Big Portfolio.......... 698

Rule for Success #3 – Know Your Limits................................... 698

Rule for Success #4 – Be Mentally, Physically and Emotionally Prepared Every Day..699

Rule for Success #5 – Do Your Homework Daily 700

Rule for Success #6 – Analyze Your Daily Performance............700

Rule for Success #7 – Do Not Be Greedy 701

Rule for Success #8 – Pay Attention to Volatility.......................701

Rule for Success #9 – Use the Greeks...701

Chapter 28 Trading With the Trend..703

Market Awareness 704

Setting Profit Goals 706

Day Trading?..707

Trading Puts...707

Conclusion 708

BOOK 1
Technical Analysis for Beginners

Candlestick Trading, Charting, and Technical Analysis to Make Money with Financial Markets
Zero Trading Experience Required

Andrew Elder

Introduction

Technical analysis has some similarities to fundamental analysis but is different in its approach. It is important to understand both of these aspects of analyzing a stock. Technical analysts use charts, market indicators, and other tools to predict future price movements. They study the patterns of supply and demand over time or trade volume on a particular stock or index.

In contrast, fundamental analysts focus their attention on company finances and economic data about industries for which the stocks trade (also known as industries). They are concerned with factors like corporate earnings reports, profit margins, unemployment rates, and gross domestic product (GDP) growth rates. They examine these economic factors to determine how they will affect the demand and supply of a particular stock.

Technical analysis is more concerned with the price movements of a stock or an index by examining historical records of trading activity. A technical analyst looks at past data to predict future price movements. They believe that history tends to repeat itself in the stock market and that past performance is the best indicator of what will happen in the future.

The difference between these 2 approaches really boils down to who is in control, whether it be fundamental or technical.

Technical analysis is concerned with things that a company does not directly control. For example, stock prices constantly react to whether or not people are optimistic about the future of a stock. If lots of people are buying a certain stock, it will typically go up in price. People are optimistic about that stock because they think it has potential for future growth. Unfortunately, the characteristics of fundamental analysis do not directly affect how much people are interested in buying a stock or what their expectations for its future growth might be.

In order to provide this kind of insight into its performance, fundamental analysts turn to earnings reports and other data released by companies that provide some indication of how well or poorly they are performing. The fundamental analyst looks at how the company is doing as a whole and tries to get an overall grasp of how the market reacts to these reports.

The technical analyst, on the other hand, is more concerned with the stock's past performance and charts this data in order to predict its future movement.

This analysis uses many different tools and a variety of charts such as bar charts, line charts, and candlestick charts. These charts help traders identify things such as the strength or weakness of support or resistance levels, which can be identified by drawing trend lines through significant highs or lows in price movements on a chart. Trend lines are used to identify optimal entry and exit points in the market.

The actual tools used in charting may differ from one technical analysis tool to another, but they each provide some unique insight into history. Technical analysis can be a useful way for investors to decide whether or not an investment is worth their money. It can help determine the future value of a stock by looking at its past performance.

For example, if a stock has historically closed at $20 per share and it drops to $15 per share, then there may be some reason for investors to believe that the price will move back up again closer to $20 per share as opposed to breaking through the support level.

Chapter 1
What Is Technical Analysis

Technical analysis is turning into an inexorably famous way to deal with exchanging, thanks to some degree to the progression in charting bundles and trading platforms. In any case, for a beginner trader, understanding technical analysis—and how it can support foresee patterns on the lookout—can be overwhelming and testing.

Technical analysis analyzes price movements in a market, whereby traders utilize striking chart patterns and indicators to predict future patterns on the lookout. It is a visual representation of the execution at different times of a market. It permits the trader to utilize this data as price activity, indicators, and examples to direct and educate future patterns before entering a trade.

This guide, Technical Analysis for Beginners, will acquaint you with the essentials of this exchanging approach and how it may be used to trade the monetary business sectors.

Understanding Technical Analysis

Technical analysis includes the understanding of examples from charts. Traders utilize important information considering price and volume and use this data to distinguish exchanging openings dependent on basic examples on the lookout. Various indicators are applied to charts to decide section and leave focuses for traders to boost a trades potential at great danger reward proportions.

The underneath chart is an illustration of a diagram with the utilization of the MACD and RSI indicators.

While investors of technical analysis accept that financial variables are the primary supporters of movements in the market, technical analysis traders keep up those past patterns that can support anticipating future price movements. Albeit these exchanging styles can shift, understanding the contrasts among principal and technical analysis—and how to join them—can be very helpful.

Study consolidating key and technical analysis.

How Technical Analysis Can Support Traders

Numerous traders have discovered technical analysis to be a valuable apparatus for hazard the executives, which can be a key hindrance. When a trader comprehends the ideas and standards of technical analysis, it very well may be applied to any market, making it a versatile logical device. Where key analysis hopes to recognize characteristic worth in a market, technical analysis hopes to distinguish patterns, which helpfully can be brought about by the essentials.

Advantages of using technical analysis incorporate the accompanying:

- Can be applied to any market using any period.
- Technical analysis can be used as an independent technique.
- Allows traders to distinguish patterns on the lookout.

Using Charts in Technical Analysis

The beneath chart is an illustration of a candle chart for the EUR/USD cash pair.

Technical analysis was developed to figure future price patterns in different business sectors. It is the foundation of analysis for some traders in the present quickly evolving markets.

There are 2 analysis instruments that traders and financial backers use for anticipating future price patterns: Technical analysis and fundamental analysis. In this guide, we will examine the first of the 2. We will discuss a wide range of technical analysis metrics, which will be a somewhat expanded guide.

When all is said in done, numerous traders utilize both, technical and fundamental analysis consolidated. Be that as it may, some trust one is better than the other and works better. Whichever the case, regardless of whether you are a bad-to-the-bone fundamentalist, you can't ignore the way that numerous traders utilize technical analysis and follow through on regard for some key price levels. Furthermore, that can move the market the other way to that proposed by basic research alone. If enough individuals accept a specific technical highlight to be pertinent, it will undoubtedly be market-moving and represent the deciding moment of a trade. For this very point, it delivers profits to know about technical analysis in the business sectors, at any rate at a fundamental level.

A Brief History of Technical Analysis

A few parts of technical analysis started to show up in Amsterdam-based trader Joseph de la Vega's records of the Dutch monetary business sectors in the seventeenth century. Nonetheless, many credit technical analyses to Munehisa Homma (1724–1803), additionally alluded to as Sokyu Homma or Sokyu Honma. He was a well-off rice vendor and trader from Sakata, Japan, who lived during the Tokugawa Shogunate. He is credited as a pioneer of technical analysis because he developed Candlestick Charting, which is a spine of technical analysis right up 'til today.

At first, in Japan, just actual rice was traded, yet starting in 1710, a fates market was set up where coupons addressing future conveyance of rice were traded. Homma was a fruitful trader in this optional market of exchanging rice coupons. Famous for his capacity in exchanging the rice market, Homma turned into a monetary guide to the public authority and was even granted the position of privileged Samurai. In 1755, he composed *The Fountain of Gold: The 3 Monkey Record of Money*, a book zeroed in on market psychology research. Hundreds of years after the fact, the Candlestick Charting method has been brought toward the Western world and is presently used by numerous traders everywhere in the world.

The history of technical analysis in the US started a little while, in the late nineteenth/mid-twentieth century. The most credited work has come from the gathered compositions of Dow Jones prime supporter and supervisor Charles Dow, who was additionally the pioneer of the Dow Theory. A hypothesis that has been based on all through late many years and now frames the premise of current technical analysis.

Key Definitions and Philosophy of Technical Analysis

Before we get more inside and out of the technical analysis, we must characterize what is unmistakable. In this guide, we will hold that technical analysis is the analysis of market action, principally using charts to figure future price patterns. The expression "market activity" incorporates 3 principle wellsprings of data accessible to professionals: price, volume, and open interest (open interest is just used in futures and options markets).

There are 3 premises at which point technical analysis is based:

Market Action Limits Everything

The assertion "market action discounts everything" shapes the premise of technical analysis. Numerous different standards follow this thought. What it implies is essential that anything that can affect the market price (fundamentally, politically, psychologically, and otherwise) is reflected in the market price. For example, if a price rises, it should imply that the request exceeds supply at the end of the day. On the other hand, if the price falls, it should mean that supply exceeds demand. In this manner, an analysis of price action is always necessary.

An expert doesn't accept that knowing the reasons why the price rises or falls is fundamental. That may appear to be fairly outrageous, and this is the specific motivation behind why numerous traders like to utilize a mix of technical and fundamental analysis.

Technical experts accept everything from a company's fundamentals to broad market components to showcase brain research areas now evaluated into the stock. This perspective is consistent with the Efficient Markets Hypothesis (EMH), which accepts a comparable price decision. The solitary thing remaining is the analysis of price movements, which technical analysts see as the result of market interest for a specific stock in the market.

Prices Move in Trends

Another reason that is vital to technical analysis is that prices move in trends. That is, a price moving is bound to persevere than to switch—the whole movement following techniques predicated on riding a current trend until it gives indications of inversion. Assuming prices didn't move in directions, there would be no reason for examining price patterns by any stretch of the imagination. That is, as all price movements would be random and unpredictable.

Technical analysts anticipate that prices will display drifts, even in random market movements, paying little heed to the period being noticed. As such, a stock price is bound to proceed with a past trend than move unpredictably. Most technical trading strategies depend on this assumption.

History Repeats the Same Thing

Another supposition in technical analysis is that human instinct doesn't change. Along these lines, since market action depends on human psychology research, history will generally repeat the same thing. Thus, there is a lot of things we can gain from market history and analysis.

Technical analysts accept that set of experiences will, in general, repeat itself. The redundant idea of price movements is frequently ascribed to market psychology, which will be truly unsurprising depending on feelings like fear or excitement. Technical analysis uses chart patterns to analyze these feelings and ensuing business sector movements to get trends. While numerous types of technical analysis have been used for over 100 years, they are as yet accepted to be important because they delineate patterns in price movements that frequently repeat themselves.

Chart Construction

This part is intended for individuals who are new to chart movement. We will be looking at how 3 sorts of charts are developed and how they portray similar data. We will likewise examine volume and open interest.

The Line Chart

The most fundamental chart and quite possibly the most generally used one is the line chart. Since closing prices are of outrageous importance to chartists, the line chart associates closing prices and makes them into a continuous line. The line chart is one of the least demanding to understand charts.

In any case, it additionally does not have a ton of data. We just know where the price has closed, yet don't have a clue where it has gone. 2 other chart types assist us with getting this data. Those are the bar chart and the candle chart.

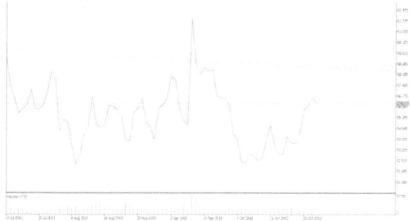

The Bar Chart

The bar chart passes on more data than the line chart. Notwithstanding, it is likewise more hard to peruse. The accompanying chart shows the critical metrics of a bar chart:

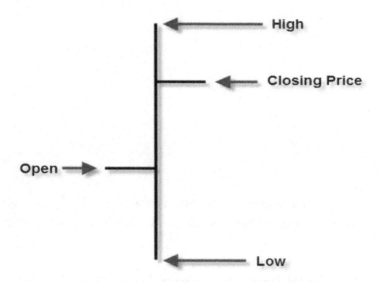

As should be obvious, the full scope of the price movement is the length of the upward line. The base mark of the upward line is the low of the reach, while the top is the high of the reach. Likewise, the flat left-pointing tick shows the initial price, while the right-pointing tick shows the end price. The open and closing prices show the everyday range without the spikes in prices. These are significant attributes because not the entirety of the time the end price of the last bar is the initial price of the following bar, as is with the line chart. Once in a while, there are gaps in charts and they portray that the price has opened at an unexpected price in comparison to the past closing price. The chart underneath shows the bar chart inside a similar time range for a similar instrument as in the past line chart.

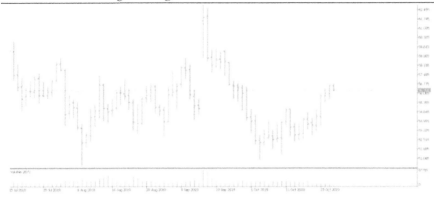

Notice how there is an enormous hole in the chart. That is something you would not see on a line chart since all price focuses are associated with a line.

The Underlying Assumptions of Technical Analysis

There are 2 basic techniques used to analyze securities and settle on investment decisions: fundamental analysis and technical analysis. Fundamental analysis includes analyzing a company's fiscal summaries to decide the reasonable worth of the business. In contrast, technical analysis expects that a security's price mirrors all openly accessible data and, therefore, centers around the measurable analysis of price movements. Technical analysis endeavors to understand the market estimation behind price patterns by searching for patterns instead of dissecting a security's fundamental attributes. Charles Dow delivered a series of publications discussing technical analysis hypotheses. His works included 2 fundamental presumptions that have kept on shaping the structure for technical analysis trading:

1. Markets are efficient with values representing factors that influence a security's price
2. Even random market price movements appear to move in identifiable patterns and trends that tend to repeat over time.

How Technical Analysis Is Used

Technical analysis endeavors to conjecture the price movement of for all intents and purposes any tradable tool that is for the most part subject to powers of market interest, including stocks, securities, fates, and money sets. Indeed, some view technical analysis as fundamentally the analysis of market interest powers as reflected in the market price movements of a security. Technical analysis most ordinarily applies to price changes. However, some experts track numbers other than price for pattern, trading volume, or open interest figures.

Across the business, many patterns and signals have been created by specialists to support technical analysis trading. Technical experts have additionally built up various trading frameworks to help them figure and trade on price movements. A few indicators are centered around distinguishing the current market pattern, including support and resistance zones. In contrast, others are centered around deciding the strength of a pattern and the probability of its continuation. Ordinarily used technical indicators and charting signals incorporate trendlines, channels, moving averages, and momentum indicators.

Chapter 2
Basic Concept of Trend

Traders often say, "the trend is your friend." If a given trend has become established, you can piggyback it in whatever direction it's going. And generally, traders only trade with the trend. So, if a trend is going up, you only trade bounces, and if it's going down, you'll generally trade it by going short (that is, selling stock to take advantage of the dips). The idea is that even if you don't execute your trade particularly well, the trend will help you out and usually ensure you don't make a thumping loss.

A trend is quite simply a direction of price movement. For instance, prices may be trending upwards. That doesn't mean you'll get a price rise every day, but it means that the price will tend to rise over time. For instance, in an upwards trend, you might have closing prices for a bit more than a couple of weeks that went something like; 50, 52, 51, 51, 54, 53, 56, 56, 57, 56, 59, 60, 59. You can see that sometimes prices are up, flat, or even down, but they are moving up on the whole. That's a trend—a general direction. There will be oscillations within the trend, but the trend itself remains unchanged. That means that you can trade these oscillations within the trend; as long as the trend continues, if you buy when prices are trading lower than the trendline, and sell when they're above the trendline, you'll make money. Trend trading strategies are very common and can be nicely profitable.

Trends often reflect a certain market sentiment—that is, if investors feel the economy is doing well, earnings are going up, the future will deliver better earnings still, there will probably also be an uptrend. But trust what you see on the chart, not what you see in the newspapers or on the bulletin boards.

I also need to give you a warning. Traders also sometimes say, "Is it a trend or will it bend?" That's why in the technical analysis we need to be able to recognize trends, but we also need to be able to recognize signals telling us that trends are about to end or even reverse.

The Trend Has 3 Directions

Okay, this is pretty simple. In the words of "those magnificent men in their flying machines," there are 3 directions:
- Up
- Down
- Flying around—or what traders call "sideways."

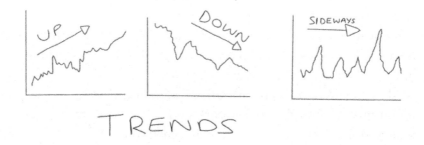

If you know the lyrics of the song, up and down are exciting—UP-tiddly-up-up and DOWN-tiddly-down-down—and the "flying around" or "sideways bit" is not really emphasized. It's the same on the stock market. Up and down will make you money. They're good strong trends. Sideways, also known as "ranging" or "consolidation," can be a big problem, and a market with a sideways trend is hard to make profits in. (On the other hand, when you get a breakout from a sideways trend, you'll notice!)

You'll see many times throughout the book some of my handout slides—yes, they're all drawn with my interactive whiteboard pen, but the good thing about the slides is that I've removed all the distractions that you get on a regular share price chart. No dates, prices, moving average lines, volume bars, whatever—just the trend! A proper uptrend has increasing highs, but it also has increasing lows. And while a downtrend will hit ever-increasing lows, it should also see each bounce achieving a lower and lower level. Sideways, on the other hand, price movement can be anywhere—sometimes within a really tight range, sometimes just looking chaotic on the chart with prices all over the place.

Technical analysis can help you identify trends and give you good reliable signals when a trend is coming to an end.

The Trend Has 3 Classifications

As well as 3 directions, the trend has 3 classifications or time zones:
- **Short-term trend:** Less than 3 weeks.
- **Medium-term trend:** A few months.
- **Long-term trend:** 6 months to 1 year.

Each market has its typical way of defining these 3-time classifications. Futures markets such as commodities futures tend to have shorter timescales, and equity investors have longer timescales, but you'll get the feel of whichever market you trade in after a while. A short-term trend can be part of a medium-term trend, and a medium-term trend can be part of a long-term trend—in other words, trends can come nested inside each other. Within a long-term bull market (a market in a long-term uptrend), for instance, the S&P may have shorter-term uptrends separated by short-term downtrends—rallies and dips. A longer-term investor who is a less active trader may see a continuing uptrend, where you, as a shorter-term trader, can see a pronounced short-term downtrend.

You might use different trends as different signals.
- **Long-term trend:** Okay, there's a trend here, so this is a stock I want to look at. And it's a long-term uptrend, so I will generally be buying stock when I think there's a medium-term uptrend.
- **Medium-term uptrend:** This gives me my profit expectation. Suppose we're trading low in the long-term trend, I can guess where the stock price should be headed within that trend. For instance, in a long-term trend where the recent high was around $62, and it looks like if it continues it would get to $65

quite easily, and the price is now $56, I have a $9 a share profit potential (and $6 profit potential if the trend fades).

- **Short-term uptrend:** This gives me my timing. So I've got that medium-term trend in mind, but when is the best time to get in? When I see a real short-term tick up that says to me this is the right time to initiate that short position.

Some people like to look at super long trends, like the idea of Kondratieff waves and 40-year cycles, but those are outside the scope of this book.

Support and Resistance

The trends we want to look at go up and down, and so do their trendlines. But we can also draw some really important straight lines on the chart, and these are called support and resistance lines.

You'll often see a share price exhibit a particular pattern of nearly getting to a price and then refusing to go any further. It's a bit like watching a child playing at the seaside, running down the beach towards the sea, but as soon as a wave comes, running back up the beach squealing happily so their toes don't get wet. Share prices behave just the same way!

A share price might keep falling to a particular price but then rising back again—that's a support line. It's likely that if the share price approaches that line, it will bounce off it again, so this supports the price. On the other hand, a share price might keep testing a high, but it never crosses that level—that's a resistance line, and the chances are, if it gets to it again, it'll not manage to maintain enough momentum to push its way through.

Here you can see my handouts. I promise you I had not been drinking when I made this one! See how the share prices just touch the resistance and support lines. (A channel has a resistance line at the top and a support level at the bottom—you can make some neat short-term trades inside a well-established channel, but the most profitable trades you'll make are on breakouts—which we'll talk about later.)

For instance, look at the way in the chart below. The AT&T share price in the second part of the chart keeps coming up to $29.50 and just falling back again. At the beginning of January 2021, it gets from $28–29.25, but it doesn't manage to stay there. Then it gets to $29.75 about 25th January, and then it falls off, then it gets there again about 17th February, and again, it falls off. That's a resistance line, a kind of tidemark. You could put a ruler on the chart and draw it across, and there you have your resistance line.

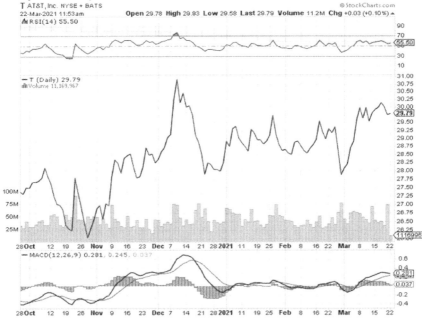

Now the stock has finally managed to push through to $30. It has actually gone through the resistance line… but I'm not sure I'm convinced. I'd want to see another indicator confirming that.

But there's another interesting thing; it does look as if the stock has formed a support line, too. Have a go at guessing where it is—and

I'm going to give you a clue, again you'll be looking at the more recent half of the time period. Can you draw a straight line which the price approaches, but won't go through? I reckon it's at about $28. Look, it's there just before that bit spikes up, then it falls back to it after the spike, then again at the beginning of March, and every time it bounces.

Now the support line is interesting because it says if I buy at $29, I probably only have 1 dollar downside, and I know that if the share price goes below $28, then it's time to take that loss and get out.

Why do support and resistance levels work? One reason is "anchoring," the way that certain information gets stuck in our minds. Investors and traders often remember the price they bought or sold at, and a lot of investors say, "I'm not going to sell till I get my money back." If a lot of them bought at $52 and the price went down temporarily to the mid $40 levels, then when they see $52 again, they'll sell—which by the rules of supply and demand, will cause the price to stop rising. That's a resistance level in action.

The more times a share price unsuccessfully tests a support or resistance line, the stronger that support or resistance becomes. Buying close to support or selling close to resistance makes a good trade, as you'll capitalize on the bounce. But you'll want to put a stop-loss just below a support line (or above resistance) to make sure that if there's a breakthrough, you cut your losses and make a quick exit. By the way, if a share price does break through a resistance line, that old resistance line will now become a support line. And if a share price breaks through a support line to the downside that support line will now function as a resistance line preventing the price from rising past it.

Trendlines

It's not always easy to see the market trend. If there's a lot of price movement, you may be able to see that the market's in an uptrend, but not how steep the slope is or how fast prices are rising. You're seeing all the noise, and that makes it difficult to see the signal—the real trend.

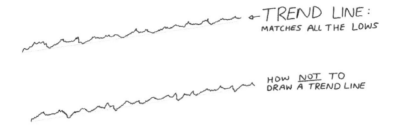

Drawing trendlines on the chart can help you visualize the trend. Basically, if the market's in an uptrend, then you're going to try to find a line that it keeps coming back to at the bottom. Find the lowest points that the price hits, and join them up. You are lucky. The software will do it for you—or at least help you do it—whereas this was a pencil-and-ruler job well into the 1980s. So, what you should have is a chart that now looks as if all the peaks are "sitting" on a line of support.

For a market in a downtrend, you're going to do things differently. You're going to draw a line that goes through the highest highs—the places that the price gets to when it bounces, but then runs out of steam and falls back.

Okay, with support and resistance, I showed you my hand-drawn pictures first. This time let's jump right into the real world and look at Amazon. I went on StockCharts and I just couldn't believe what a great example of a channel I'd got, so I stuck it into my drawing software and put in the trendlines—the real trendline is the straight one underneath, that's pushing it upwards, but you can also see there's a straight resistance trendline at the top. (The other 2 curvy lines are Moving Averages, which we'll cover later on.)

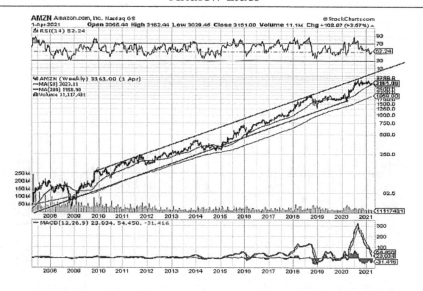

A trendline shows you very clearly the direction in which the market is moving and the speed of the move. It also acts as a support of the resistance line; for instance, in a downtrend, if the price goes towards the trendline (which is above the price bars), then you're getting to a decision point where it will either fall back again or make a breakthrough.

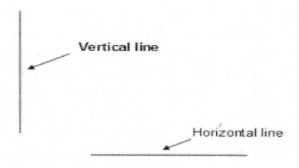

What you're doing is not very different from drawing support and resistance lines, but you're trying to get a slope instead of a horizontal line. The chart we just looked at is horrible for trying to draw a trendline, although it's got good support and resistance, so let's try something with an uptrend.

Here's Realty Income, where you have quite a lot going on, but I want you to look for one very clear uptrend. Just look at the candlesticks and ignore the other lines on the chart for the moment. But this is the kind of thing you'll see when you open a charting package—this one comes from StockCharts—and you need to get used to focusing on the lines that matter first, and then to look at the rest. Get some practice by grabbing a straight edge and trying to find the line of best fit—that's the trendline. (The trendline is not shown on this chart, you have to draw it yourself—but if you want to see a live visual demonstration on how to draw a trendline correctly, then I would recommend you watch my free bonus companion masterclass, as that covers this topic in a lot more detail to help your understanding.)

You see from the dip in the share price in early 2021 (down to 11th January) that it quickly establishes an uptrend, and if you draw a line under the lows, although it heads higher, and then back, it doesn't break the trendline, it keeps bouncing back from it and making higher highs (that is, every little spike goes higher even if it falls back a little in between) all the way through January and the first part of

February. Let's assume you got in around $58 in mid-January because you waited a little while to be sure it was a real uptrend; the stock would have gone to $63 (around 14th February) before finally breaking the uptrend by dipping to about $61 towards 18th February. That's $3 a stock profit, or 5% in about a month. You might have done a bit better than that, of course, if you didn't wait for the sell signal, but got out nearer to $63 a few days earlier.

One way of thinking of the share price is that it's connected to the trendline by a rubber band. It can get further and further away from the trend, but the stretchy rubber band will generally keep pulling it back. If it hits the trendline, it'll usually bounce. But as it gets close to that trendline, you're going to want to watch out—this is a dangerous time, and it's also, for some traders, an opportunity, as there could be a breakout.

Occasionally you might need to redraw a trendline. It may become steeper or it may, on the other hand, become less steep as price rises decelerate. That doesn't necessarily mean the trend has ended. However, when an uptrend becomes very steep, that could suggest the kind of manic frenzy that often accompanies a market top, so beware of trading in such conditions and keep an eye out for bearish signals (that is, signals telling you the price is going to fall) such as a drop in momentum or moving averages.

Trend Channel

We already saw how if you connect up the highs and the lows, you can create a wide bar with roughly parallel lines, as we did with Amazon. These 2 lines define the trend channel. I actually like trend channels a lot as a way to trade, but you do need practice in drawing them properly.

There are several things you need to know about trend channels:

- The longer a channel continues, the stronger the trend. (Remember that Amazon trend! Over a decade of it!)
- If a trend channel is combined with a strong trading volume, it's more reliable than if trading is weak.

- If the price breaks out of the channel, it is likely to move quite significantly in the direction it has now established.
- A narrow channel doesn't give you much room for trading — if a stock is always trading within about 2% of the trend that limits your potential profit. On the other hand, a wide channel, where the stock has some volatility within the overall trend, gives you a chance of larger profits.

If you get a good horizontal channel, running all the way across the page instead of up and down, this is one of the few times it's worth trading a stock that is not in an uptrend or a downtrend. You may have a stock where, for instance, a certain level of dividend yield means income investors tend to buy whenever it comes down to the bottom of the range, and sell when it gets to the top — you don't need to know the reason, just trade the channel. Buy at the bottom of the channel, sell at the top.

Channels are also really useful for setting your stop-losses and profit expectations. If you buy at the bottom, you're looking to exit at the top, but you should also set a stop-loss just below the bottom of the channel. If you've got it wrong, that stops you from being caught by an unexpected breakout.

By the way, you can even sometimes see from a channel how long the share price usually takes to move from bottom to top of the channel. That gives you a good idea of how long your trade will last so you can time it nicely!

Besides simple price channels, there are other kinds of channels, which use volatility rather than price indicators, such as Bollinger bands. But for the moment, let's just stick with the price channel; that's quite enough to get your head around!

Now go and find a few stock charts, and see if you can spot some price channels. See how many times the price bounced around within the channel and work out if you could have made a profit by trading it every time the price touched, or nearly touched, the bottom line.

Divergence

Remember, "Is it a trend or will it bend?" Divergence is one way to tell.

Now so far, we've talked about trends, channels, and support and resistance. You can make nice profitable trades by using them as your guide. But sometimes prices break out of their trends.

There are quite a few reasons that might happen. For instance, you sometimes see that if a stock gets promoted to a major market index, and big investment funds and Exchange Traded Funds have to buy the stock because it's in the index. Or a stock might have a profit warning which the market wasn't expecting, and the price goes way below the range. Or a war might break out, or there could be unexpected political news that drives the markets higher or lower. You might also see the end of a big investor exiting their position — for instance, with some IPOs, the end of a lock-in period may see some of the sponsors, founders, or management selling out. Or it may happen "for no reason."

Well, the reason is really that every time the trendline was tested before, there were buyers or sellers at the right price to send the stock back up. And this time, there weren't. And if that's the case, that quite likely reflects a slight change in market sentiment, and there are a few ways you could pick that up before the breakout. That's where divergence comes in.

When you're looking at your price chart, use a momentum or a trading volume indicator (like an oscillator) running beneath it. (We'll take a good look at those and the way they work later — for the moment, don't worry about what they mean, just look at the pictures.)

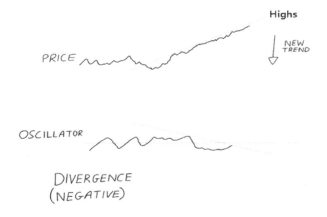

Usually, you'll see the 2 lines run pretty much in the same direction most of the time. But if you have an uptrend, and the oscillator is headed downwards, that's a negative divergence and it suggests that the uptrend might not continue.

On the other hand, if the price just made a new low, but the momentum indicator is headed up, that suggests prices might rise — positive divergence.

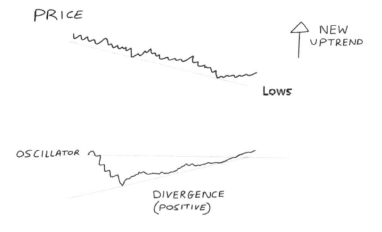

What you're seeing in the case of negative divergence is that while the price trend looks as if it's continuing, it is decelerating or falling behind the market. So, that's an indicator that your price trend isn't as strong as you think it is. But you don't need to pay attention to it all the time—just if:

- Your price is hitting new highs/lows
- You think you've got a double top or bottom forming (and we'll talk about those later).

To check if you really have divergence, connect up the highest highs, or lowest lows, and connect up the lines for the indicator for the same period—joining highs to go with price highs and lows to go with price lows. If the slopes are the same, great. If they're moving in opposite directions, you have divergence.

Divergence is not a signal—it doesn't tell you to trade. But it is an alert—that is, when you see divergence, if you're risk-averse, it's time to exit your position, and if you're a risk-on kind of person, it's time to stick close to your trading screen and watch that stock like a hawk.

Chapter 3
Recognizing Breakout

So far we have talked about trading within a range. That can be really profitable and it can also be quite a low-risk, low-effort form of trading if you identify the right stocks and keep an eye on the patterns.

But if you want to hit the big time, you want the runaway profits that come with a breakout. Remember that "ball on a rubber band" idea I used when I talked about the share price and the trendline? What happens when the rubber band breaks? The ball goes way, way up into the air (or, of course, if we're talking stocks, it could also go in the other direction)—that's a breakout! Compared to trading the range, trading a breakout is like jumping on a train when it's already started moving.

Just so you know: A breakout can happen in either direction, up or down—it's simply breaking out of a pattern.

A breakdown, on the other hand, only goes down.

Breakout

A more technical description of a breakout is that it's when a stock price moves outside an established channel, support, or resistance line, with increased volume. (The increased trading volume is required to show that it's a real breakout and not just a fluke.) Breakouts move to the upside, and they move fast.

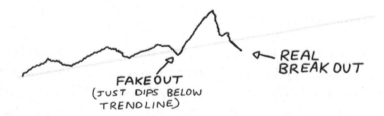

A genuine breakout is a big, bold move. If you're looking at a candlestick chart, you'll see a big-bodied candle closing well above the resistance level. If all you see is the price just poking over the edge of the resistance level, that's not a real breakout—it's a fakeout. If you see the price getting near to the resistance line, but it hasn't gone through it yet—it's a fakeout. Wait for the line to be broken before you trade.

Note by the way that a breakout can happen even in a bear market, that is, a market that is in a major downtrend—there won't be so many breakouts to trade, but stocks that have the strength to move against the market are stocks that should really get going once they start, so you will still get that speedy rise.

Your signal is simple—it's the first time that the price breaks out of the channel, or breaks the resistance line, and closes above it.

How do breakouts work? One way they work is what's called a lockout rally. Imagine you have a well-known stock that had bad results for a couple of years, it's taken a bit of action, and it's stopped going down but it hasn't begun to move up yet.

Everyone is thinking it will soon be time to buy it again, but they haven't bought it yet; they're waiting for something. And for whatever reason you get a little buying—maybe one brave fund manager, maybe a couple of brokers getting in—and it goes through the line, and now all those people who haven't bought it have a massive feeling of FOMO (which, as if you didn't know, means Fear of Missing Out). It's motoring, so it must be time to buy, so they buy, so it goes up a bit more, so more people buy…

At that point, of course, the short-term traders are already getting out with their profits!

How to Find Breakouts

If you're looking for breakouts, you won't find them. What you're looking for is the pre-breakout pattern. You're looking for stocks that are trading in a fairly narrow channel, that are trading in a really boring way—almost so the candlesticks fill the channel. You're looking for stocks that are range-bound. That is, stocks that are stuck in a range, which keep bouncing from top to bottom and back again without ever going anywhere. This kind of build-up is absolutely classic. It's like a pressure cooker—when it goes, it's going to explode. You can also look for stocks that are close to their 52–26-week highs—this information is easy to find on any finance site. If stocks are trading at a high for the period, they're also going to be close to a resistance level or close to the top of the trendline. That means they'll either be close to a fall back down again into the channel, or they'll be ready to break out. By looking for stocks that are close to a high, you've cut out all the stocks that are not really going anywhere much, so you've reduced the number of charts you need to look at before you find a good breakout pattern emerging.

Of course, you can also look for stocks close to 52–26-week lows. That might catch the "bouncers."

Draw your resistance lines on the chart—even if they were the last hit some time ago—and keep monitoring those stocks every time the price gets towards that resistance line. Use a volume indicator too—the best stocks for a breakout are those that haven't traded in great volume. You're looking for a market where investors have got bored, and they're not doing much—when you get the breakout, that's when they will get interested again! Then you will see the volume accompanying the share price move, which is how you know it's for real.

NARROW CHANNEL

Another good potential configuration is where you see a resistance level that has been repeatedly tested by sharp spikes. You're looking for the share price to make big spikes, to make a big jump to test the resistance level, and then for it to fall back really steeply. You don't want to see gentle waves; you want to see a spiky mountain landscape of strong rallies that quickly reversed. Or if you're a beach bum—you want to see big surf, not nice gentle waves. These spiky, punchy price movements show that the resistance level is a good strong one. It's as if the share price took a real run-up, but it still couldn't punch through the wall. So that's a tough wall, and any breakout that makes it through the resistance will be a massive one. The bigger the breakout, the more money you'll make on the trade. Further good signs that a breakout could be coming are:

- The channel grows narrower.

- A build-up period in which prices form a tight cluster.
- Trendlines which make an ascending triangle—the lows are getting higher, but the highs have been on the same trendline.
- The resistance level has been tested unsuccessfully several times.

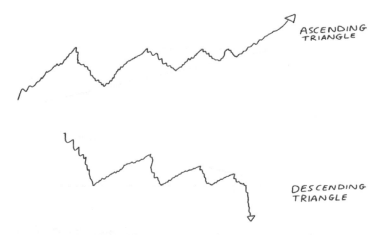

The longer the build-up, the bigger the breakout. Once you've found your targets, plan your trade in detail before any breakout. I'm going to talk about trading tips later—but you should always plan your trade so that when the breakout comes, you can act real fast. Remember, breakouts are fast.

What do you do if you miss a breakout? If it was preceded by a really good consolidation period (trading within a limited price range) and has made a definitive move to the upside, you should jump in even though you're a bit late. Or if it looks as if it's a pretty small breakout, you could wait for the price to test the line that was the old resistance level and has now become a support level, and you could buy it then. Happily, you do quite often get a second chance!

Breakdown

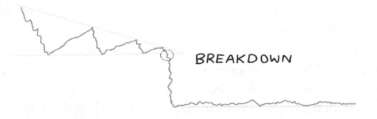

BREAKDOWN

What's a breakdown? It's just a breakout, except that the share price goes down instead of up. So it will usually be announced by a descending triangle in some cases—lower highs, but the lows are forming a horizontal line. Like a breakout, it's usually on high volume and will lead to a large price swing and, usually, into a new downtrend. It can often be very quick, which is why you need to set up your trendlines and then monitor them whenever you see a potential breakdown trade setting up.

Looking for a breakdown by just looking at loads of charts is like looking for a needle in a haystack. On the other hand, if you have collected half a dozen charts that show tight consolidation build-ups and descending triangle trendlines, you pretty much know that one is going to show up—but you have to be ready to act when it does. (That might mean actually watching your screens, but it could also mean setting up stop-limit orders with your broker and just letting them run.)

However, taking advantage of a breakdown isn't as easy as trading a breakout because you need to be able to short trade or trade options. Not everyone is happy trading short. (There's a subsection on this coming up.)

If you do go short, the best way to set up the trade is to put a sell stop-limit order just below the support level. That is an order, which specifies a price at which the order becomes valid, and a price limit after which it is no longer valid (e.g., "Sell 100 IBM if the stock price falls below 90 but not if it goes below 95). It's a good way of entering a breakout or breakdown trade. But if there is high volume and a lot of price action, you might not get your order filled. So waiting for a retest (or another chance) of the trendline that has now become a resistance level might give you a better price—if, of course, there is a retest. You can never be sure.

Think about that for a second; the moving average shows the average of prices for the last 20 days, let's say. As the share price falls quickly, it will fall below the moving average, because the moving average still has all the higher prices from previous trading days in it. As long as the price is still falling quickly, that will continue to be the case, but the moving average will eventually catch up once the fall decelerates. At this point, the stock might rebound, but even if it doesn't, the easy gains are gone and you can find a better trade elsewhere.

Channel Break—Some Trading Tips

Let's look at a typical channel break and see how to trade it. Technical analysis will give you good trading ideas, but you also need to learn how to trade. And if you haven't been involved in the stock market before, or if you've always been a buy-and-hold investor making simple market buy orders, you have a lot to learn.

First of all, you need to work out your profit target, and this will probably (though not always) also be your exit point. This is something buy-and-hold investors never bother with. It's easy with a channel break, though; look at the width of the channel, and if it's $6, then add $6 to the price at the resistance line, and that's your immediate profit target. If you're trading a round lot (100 shares), that's a total $600 profit.

Your goal should be to stack the odds in your favor, so usually, I like to see a stop-loss order that's half the size of the expected profit if the trade works. In this case, that would be $3. If the stock falls to $3 below the resistance line, you're out. You've lost $300. This seems like a reasonable balance to me, risking $300 against $600 with a good chart formation that has something like a 70% probability.

In fact, let's just multiply the probabilities to see how good it is:

- $600 x 70% = $420
- $300 x 30% = $90

So, if I'm right about that probability, then I have an expected value of $420 - $90 = $330. It's positive. But even if the probability was only half—now come on, do the numbers. It's still a good chunky positive number. What we calculated here was what statisticians call the expected value of all the probabilities, and you need this number to be a positive one. If it's negative, what you're making is not a trade but a gamble.

Don't just set the trade and run away. Keep monitoring it. In particular, you should be watching the volume indicator—if this is a genuine breakout, then you'll see the sellers coming in and the volume increasing. So you might get to your original exit point, and say that having reconsidered the situation, this looks like a massive breakout. In which case, set a new stop-loss order, and you might even decide to scale in, that is, increase your position by buying more shares.

But if you do scale-in, remember to reset your stop-loss order. With a breakout into a bullish trend, you may have this setup:

- You entered the position at $70
- Expected profit $6 (using the channel range) = $76 share price
- So, the stop-loss order is $3 = $70 - $3 = $67
- The price quickly gets to $73, you can see a lot of volume in the market, so you decide to scale in. If you keep your stop-loss order at $67, your potential extra profit is $3 (from $73–76), but your potential loss is now $6 ($73 all the way down to $67).
- So, you need to pull your stop-loss order up higher, to say $71, so your expected return is still greater than your possible loss.

Also, remember how we talked about different lengths of a trend? A breakout could just be one breakout in a series. Look at the chart of Mattel above, and you'll see that there are 3 series of consolidation/build-up phases, tight channels of trading, followed by breakouts. Can you draw the rough trendlines and work out the dates? (C'mon, this is what you're going to be doing every day as a trader.) Okay... Consolidation from late January to the middle of April, then a breakout (or breakdown); more consolidation till the middle of June when there's another breakout; then more consolidation through July, with a bit more volatile price action this time, and then a breakdown just before the beginning of August.

If you're a long-only trader, this chart is no good for you. But if you can go short, whether your broker lets you sell short (and effectively "lends" you the stock for the meantime), or whether you can take out options, then this is a great chart. It's particularly good because you have these short-term big steps down. Going short costs money, and options have expiry dates—so you're looking for shorter-term trades as well as simply going short.

The first breakout in mid-April went from $25 to $21, then the second one in June went from about $22 to $20. But the third one in late July started at $21, and the downtrend ran all the way to below $15 by mid-September. The final breakout in mid-November leads to a severe downtrend in December. If you'd made good money on the first breakout, you might have said, "Right, I'm done with that stock." You would have been wrong. There were another 2 good chances to make almost the same profitable trade, and the last was the best.

Hey, what was that gap up in November 2017 though? Apparently, the stock had got so low that there was talk of bigger toy company Hasbro buying it, and the stock jumped — but as you can see from the end of the chart, nothing happened.

The "gap" by the way is when prices open above the previous day's closing price, with nothing in between. You'll quite often find it relates to corporate news, whether that's a takeover rumor, as here, or an earnings surprise.

Short Selling

If you want to make the most of breakdowns, you're going to need to be happy short selling or using instruments that allow you to replicate a short sale.

Basically, short selling is selling a stock you don't own. It's as if you promised to deliver a new smartphone to a friend of yours, anticipating you can get it at money off on Black Friday. You charge your friends 10% less than the retail price, you get the phone at 40% off, and keep the change (though possibly not your friend). Short selling allows you to make money out of a forecast that a price is going down. If you'd shorted Nasdaq just before the tech crash, you'd have made a huge return, but a lot of traders just take 4–5% on each of their shorts.

The risk, of course, is if you'd sold your friend the smartphone at 10% below retail, then found out that the version they want has just had a price rise and isn't in the Black Friday sale, you'd lose money because you'll have to buy it at retail and they're still going to want that 10% off.

Shorting is not that easy to do as a retail investor—institutional investors like big mutual funds, pension funds, or hedge funds, and bank trading desks, make more use of it, often for portfolio protection rather than trading purposes. However, there are a few ways you can go short in the market.

If you have a margin account with your broker, and permission to short, your broker will "lend" you the shares in your margin account and then sell them on the market on your behalf. You will at some point either close the trade at a profit, close it at a loss, or possibly have to pay a margin call to keep your trade going if it's out of the money at the time (which is why you need a tight stop-loss order).

For the market as a whole or for individual sectors, you could buy an inverse ETF (exchange-traded fund). This kind of fund delivers the reverse of the market return, so if the market goes down, the ETF goes up. You buy and sell them just like you buy and sell a share, and they are low-cost funds, so you won't lose a load of entry commissions like you would with a mutual fund. This is my preferred choice if I see a good short trade in the S&P, for instance.

You can also use options. Frankly, there is a whole lot of very specific knowledge that you need to trade options—for instance, they come with expiry dates, so their value varies according to the time you have left as well as the price of the stock. Unless you are mathematically minded and willing to get to grips with the specifics (and take a look at the Black-Scholes formula if you're tempted), leave them alone.

Finally, you could use something called a Contract for Difference (CFD), unless you're in the US or Hong Kong. However, you may find in other jurisdictions they are only available to certain investors—professionals, high net worth individuals, and those who can display a high level of market expertise. Frankly, I would avoid them till you've got several years of profitable trading behind you. Even then—be careful. Please, let me emphasize that while stop-losses orders are important for all trading, they are especially important if you go short. If you buy a stock at $600 and it falls, the most you can ever lose is $600 a stock. That's it. Wipeout. But your house, your car, your collection of Pokémon cards, none of that's on the line. Nor are your other stock positions. I have been completely wiped out on 1–2 stocks (both, as it happens, involved corporate fraud), but I lived to tell the tale.

On the other hand, how high can a share price go? $100? Higher. $500? Higher. Tesla has been as high as $900. Want more? Berkshire Hathaway trades at $380,482.75. There is, effectively, no limit to how high a share price can go. That means if you go short, there is no limit to the amount you could potentially lose. You could lose your shirt — your house, your savings, the rest of your portfolio, the lot.

So, if you go short, make sure you have your trades thought through in advance, including your stop-loss order, and don't let anything prevent you from using that stop-loss. That stop-loss could just save your life.

False Breakout

This is the biggest problem with breakout trading — there are simply too many false breakouts. And that's one reason I've emphasized probabilities and stop-losses because not every breakout trade will work, so you need to minimize the impact of the fakeouts. That's in contrast to trading within a channel, where your profits will be more limited, but you have a slightly better probability.

This is why you need a good trading strategy — you'll need to maximize your profits and make sure that you control any losses very tightly, because the win/lose ratio is probably not going to be as good as with range trading.

One indicator you need to look at is volume, and there's actually one in particular, which is useful for breakouts — Volume Weighted Moving Average (VWMA). In the case of a fake breakout, it won't do much at all — in the case of a real breakout; it will accelerate upwards, giving you confirmation that you've made a good trade. VWMA also gives you your exit level, as once the price falls below the VWMA — indicating that the balance between buyers and sellers has tipped — you have exhausted the short-term profit potential of the trade.

It's worth keeping an eye on the news pages by the way. If a breakout happens along with fundamental news, such as a positive earnings surprise or a new product launch, it's probably a real breakout—and some serious institutional funds may back it.

Plus—don't give up! This could be part of the consolidation, the build-up—the last unsuccessful test of resistance before the real breakout. Patience is well rewarded.

Stop-Losses

Set your stop-losses tight for breakouts. If a breakout reverses, it could be fast and hard. The ideal for a breakout, though, is that if you've read the signals right, it should make money from the moment you enter the trade.

So, most traders put a stop-loss order just below the resistance line. If the price falls back here, it could fall away pretty sharply back into the old trading range, so stop yourself out of the trade. But remember that stocks will often retest the level they have just broken within the first few days, and then rise again—so don't set your stop-loss order at or above the resistance line, just a bit below. Only take your loss if the stock closes the day below the line.

Chapter 4
The 4 Types of Indicators You Need to Know

A n indicator is a mathematical computation based on a stock's price and/or volume. The outcome is utilized to forecast future prices. Technical indicators are used broadly in technical analysis to forecast changes in stock trends or price patterns in any traded asset.

Indicators are calculations based on the price and the volume of a stock (security) that gauge such things as money flow, trends, volatility, and momentum. Indicators are utilized as a secondary measure to the actual price movements and add extra information to the analysis of stocks. Indicators are utilized in 2 major ways: to validate price movement and the quality of price patterns and to create buy and sell signals.

There are 2 main sorts of indicators: leading and lagging. A leading indicator precedes price movements, giving them a prognostic quality, whereas a lagging indicator is a verification tool because it chases price movement. A leading indicator is believed to be the strongest in periods of non-trending trading ranges (sideways), whereas the lagging indicators are still helpful during trending periods.

There also are 2 kinds of indicators based on its construction: those that fall under a bounded range and those that don't. Those that are bound within a range are referred to as oscillators—these are the foremost common sort of indicators. Oscillator indicators have a range, for instance between 0–100, and signal periods where the stock is oversold (near zero) or overbought (near 100). Non-bounded indicators still form buy and sell signals in conjunction with showing weakness or strength, however, they vary in the manner they do this. The 2 major ways that indicators are utilized to form buy and sell signals in chart analysis are through divergence and crossovers. Crossovers are the most popular and are mirrored when either the price cross over the moving average or when 2 different moving averages cross over one another. The second way indicators are utilized is through divergence, which occurs when the price movement of an asset and the indicator are both moving in opposite directions. This hints to indicator users that the current price trend is weakening.

Indicators that are utilized in chart analysis provide an awfully helpful source of additional information. These indicators help out determine volatility, momentum, trends, and several other aspects in a security to aid in the chart analysis of trends. It is significant to note that while some traders use a single indicator exclusively for buy and sell signals, they are best employed in conjunction with chart patterns, price movement, and other indicators.

Simple Moving Average (SMA)

A simple moving average just takes several periods—say 10 days (which is 2 working weeks); it adds together the closing price for each day and divides by 10. So it's the average price of the stock over the last 10 days. You can calculate it over any period—20 days, 200 days, 1 year (though 1 year is probably not very useful for a trader). Or rather, you can get a chart package to calculate it for you, these days. Why do we use simple moving averages? We use them to take the "noise" out of the chart so that you can see the trend more easily. The idea is similar to trendlines, just a bit differently executed. But you should look at SMAs together with the price chart because it's when you put the 2 together that you get the best information—and when you use 2 SMAs together, you can also get some interesting information.

For instance, when the price dips below a moving average, that's a sign that the stock might be breaking downwards. In this sense, an

SMA can be treated a little like a resistance or support level. As a rule, in an uptrend, the price should be above the moving average—if it breaks down, this could be a strong signal that prices are shortly going to head downwards. But it's not got the best probability, so check with another indicator before you do anything about it.

Another way of using moving averages is to take 2 averages of different lengths and to look for a significant crossover. All technical traders have their favorites; some like to use the 10 and 20 days MAs, others prefer 50 and 200 days, longer-term averages.

When the shorter-term MA crosses over the longer term, it gives you a bullish signal—the "golden cross." It's telling you that over the shorter period, on average, share prices have been trending higher than over the longer term. You might not see that so clearly from the actual price line if the prices reported have been volatile. If the short-term MA crosses to the downside, you have a "death cross." Prices are trending lower. That could be a good sell signal.

The problem, of course, is that while moving averages clarify what's happening, because the majority of a moving average is made up of older price data, they have a built-in time lag. And if a stock is trading in a range, in a fairly choppy way, you may find that the averages keep crossing over without delivering you any real information.

Important points of simple moving average (SMA) are:

- It is a moving average of the stock price based on the time period and it acts as strong support and resistance.
- A buy signal is generated when the closing price of a candle moves above this moving average. A sell signal is generated when the closing price of a candle dips below the moving average.
- The most common SMA used are 20, 50, 100, and 200 time periods.

SPY   D

SPDR S&P 500 ETF TRUST   1D   Cboe BZX   O344.76 H347.86 L344

347.64   0.05   347.69

Vol 50.69M

SMAs 20 50 100 200 close close close close 335.80

The above figure shows 20 SMA, the average price movement of 20 days.

In order to access this indicator, a trader can go to the trading platform (example: Tradingview). Click "Indicators," and then type "Simple Moving Average."

Relative Strength Index (RSI)

The relative strength index (RSI) is a momentum indicator used to evaluate overbought or oversold conditions. It is perhaps one of the most well-known oscillators used by traders. Developed by Welles Wilder, the RSI is a momentum oscillator that measures the speed of the changes in price in any given timeframe. In plain English, the RSI tells us how quickly the price is changing at the moment. Just like the Stochastic oscillator, the RSI hovers between 0–100. Unlike the Stochastic though, there are clearly defined overbought and oversold levels. Generally, a reading above 70 is considered overbought and below 30 is oversold. These levels generate entry signals but, just like the Stochastic, divergences, centerline crossovers, and other types of divergences generate signals as well.

It is necessary to highlight here once again that this indicator is not infallible. It must be used in conjunction with other indicators, preferably those which measure trend strength and direction, to confirm readings. Many traders are quick to dismiss indicators because they do not understand this concept and instead expect the indicator to provide an infallible entry time after time. The markets do not work in this manner and if you let go of this expectation it will do wonders for your results as well as your peace of mind.

Now that that's out of the way, let's dig deeper into understanding how this number is calculated. The RSI has 3 basic components: the average gain, the average loss, and relative strength. The default lookback period of the RSI is 14 as recommended by Wilder but can be changed by the trader based on their needs. The RS component is calculated as follows:

- RS = Average gain / Average loss

The RSI itself is calculated as follows:

- RSI = 100 - (100/(1+RS))

Important characteristics of the RSI are:

- RSI is usually used on a 14-day timeframe with 70 and 30 as high and low levels respectively. The region above reference level 70 is considered as overbought and the region below reference level 30 is considered as oversold.
- If the RSI is in the overbought region, a correction or a pullback is likely to occur.
- If the RSI is in the oversold region, a bullish reversal is likely to occur.

Investors usually buy a stock when the RSI is in the oversold region and sell a stock when it is in the overbought region.

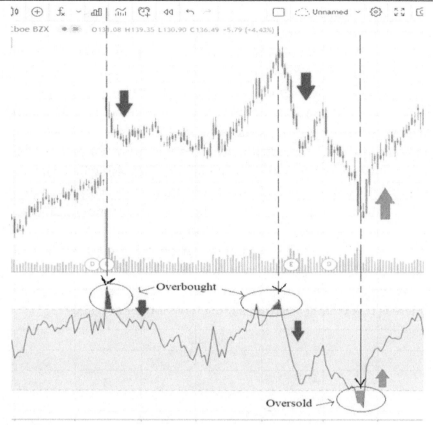

RSI is the curved line shown in the figure above.

Note: The RSI can sometimes stay oversold or overbought for days and it should only be used in conjunction with other indicators to determine the probability of a reversal in direction.

MACD Indicator

This is one of the most popular and used indicators in chart analysis. MACD is a trend-following momentum indicator that demonstrates the connection between 2 moving averages of prices. The MACD is merely the difference between these 2 moving averages plotted in opposition to a centerline. The centerline is the point at which the 2 moving averages are equal. Together with the MACD and the centerline, the EMA of the MACD itself is plotted on the chart. The thought behind this momentum indicator is to gauge short-term momentum compared to long-term momentum to assist signal the present direction of momentum.

MACD = Shorter run moving average - Longer run moving average When the MACD is positive, it indicates that the short-run moving average is higher than the long-run moving average and recommends upward momentum. The opposite holds true once the MACD is negative—this indicates that the short-run is below the long-run and recommends downward momentum. Once the MACD line crosses above the centerline, it indicates a crossing in the moving averages. The most general moving average values employed in the computation are the 12-day and 26-day exponential moving averages (EMA). The signal line is generally formed by using a 9-day EMA of the MACD values. These values can be adjusted to satisfy the requirements of the technical trader and the security (stock). For more volatile securities, shorter-term averages are employed whereas less volatile securities must have longer averages.

MACD

Daily Chart - Nasdaq 100 ETF (QQQQ)

Another side to the MACD indicator that's usually found on charts is the MACD histogram. The histogram is drawn on the centerline and delineated by bars. Every bar is the difference between the MACD and the signal line or, in most cases, the 9-day EMA. The longer the bars are in either direction, the more momentum behind the direction during which the bars point (see the figure above).

Interpretation

There are 3 general methods employed to interpret the MACD:

1. **Crossovers:** As shown in the chart above, once the MACD falls below the signal line, it's a bearish signal, which signifies that it may be time to sell. On the other hand, once the MACD rises higher than the signal line, the indicator offers a bullish signal, which recommends that the price of the security is probably going to experience upside momentum. Several traders wait for a confirmed cross higher than the signal line before stepping into a position to evade getting faked out (stepping into a position too early on), as shown by the primary arrow.

2. **Divergence:** When the stock price diverges from the MACD. It indicates the end of the present trend (see the figure below).

3. **Dramatic rise:** Once the MACD increases severely—that's, the shorter moving average pulls far away from the longer-run moving average—it's an indication that the stock is overbought and will shortly come back to normal levels.

Traders as well watch for a move below or higher than the zero line because this indicates the position of the short-run moving average in relation to the long-run average. Once the MACD is higher than zero, the short-run average is higher than the long-run average, which indicates upside momentum. The opposite holds true once the MACD is lower than zero. As you can see from the chart above, the zero line usually acts as an area of resistance and support for the indicator.

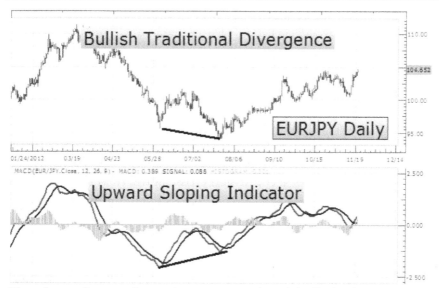

The chart shown above is an example of bullish divergence in MACD.

On-Balance-Volume (OBV)

This is a momentum indicator that utilizes volume flow to forecast changes in the security price. The OBV metric was developed by Joseph Granville in the 1960s. He considered that, once volume raises sharply without a major change in the security's price, the price will sooner or later jump upside and vice versa. It's also one of the simplest volume indicators to calculate and understand.

The OBV is computed by taking the entire volume for the trading period and allotting it a negative or positive value based on whether or not the price is down or up throughout the trading period. Once the price is up throughout the trading period, the volume is allocated a positive value, whereas a negative value is allocated once the price is down for the period. The negative or positive volume sum for the period is then added to a sum that is accumulated from the beginning of the measure.

It is significant to focus on the trend in the on-balance volume (OBV)—this is more vital than the actual value of the OBV measure.

This measure enlarges the fundamental volume measure by joining volume and price movement.

Interpretation

The theory behind OBV is relied on the difference between smart money—specifically, institutional investors—and less complicated retail investors. As pension funds and mutual funds begin to buy into an issue that retail investors are selling, the volume could increase even as the price remains comparatively level. Finally, volume drives the price upside. At that time, bigger investors start to sell, and smaller investors start buying.

The OBV is a running total of volume (negative and positive). There are 3 rules employed when computing the OBV. They are:

1. If today's closing price is less than yesterday's price, then: Current OBV = Prior OBV—Today's volume
2. If today's closing price equals yesterday's price, then: Current OBV = Prior OBV
3. If today's closing price is more than yesterday's price, then: Current OBV = Prior OBV + Today's volume

Chapter 5
Continuation Patterns

A t some times during a particular trend, the most predominant movement pauses for so many reasons. One of such reasons is that as the trend continues, long buyers will begin to sell with the mindset of making a profit. With this, there is bound to be buying pressure which causes the price to drop.

A synth of this selling and buying pressure leads to sideways price action. Contrarily, a chunk of downward movement sparks short selling to take over, thereby causing buying pressure to counter the downtrend. Note that market trends happen all the time in all markets to create recurrent patterns on charts.

This pattern can, therefore, be defined as a pause in the middle of a predominant trend when the bulls gather momentum in an uptrend or when the bears catch their breath for a while amid a downtrend. As a price pattern forms, traders can't possibly tell whether this is going to be a continuation or reversal so they must pay keen attention to the trendlines. This is to understand the price pattern to know if the price falls below or above the continuation line. The best practice that has worked for me so far is to assume that the trend is going to continue until a reversal is confirmed.

Generally, when a price pattern takes longer to form, the price movement within such a pattern will also take a long time to take shape, the movement is bound to be a significant one once the price breaks either below or above the continuation zone.

Pennants Pattern

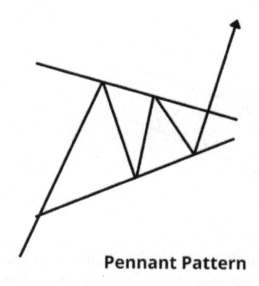

Pennant Pattern

A pennant pattern is typically forecasted by a sudden price rise. It is an almost vertical rise in prices that is also known as the flagpole or the mast. The 2 trend lines that come together to form the pennants pattern are down trend lines which stand for the no-so-highs. They can also be upward trend lines that stand for the lesser lows.

A pennant pattern that forms after a sharp downward move tends to keep sliding downwards and can be seen as a bearish pennant, while the pennant that forms after a sharp upward trend will be taken as a bullish pennant.

It is important to note that pennants usually appear around midway through the whole price movement so any move that follows the breakout of the pennant will carry the same weight as the flagpole.

Flag Pattern

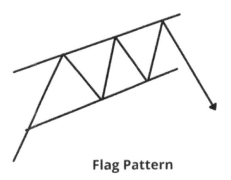

Flag Pattern

Flags come to life after 2 parallel slopy parallel trend lines come together in either an upward, downward, or sideways/horizontal movement. Generally, when a flag is in an upward slope, it shows as a pause in a market downtrend. This means that a flag that aligns itself downwards portrays a break in a market uptrend. In most cases, when the flag forms, it is followed by a decline in volume which picks up as soon as the price breaks away from the flag formation.

The flag pattern in a market chart has the shape of a sloping rectangle which has support and resistance lines that are parallel until a breakout happens. The breakout typically comes in the opposite direction of the trendlines. This means that the flag pattern is a reversal pattern.

Wedge Patterns

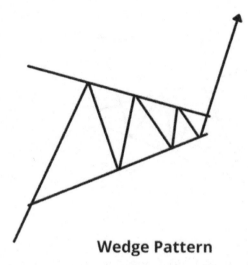

Wedge Pattern

The wedge pattern stands for the tight price movement that stands within the support and resistance lines which may either be a rising or falling wedge. Unlike what is obtainable with the triangle pattern, the wedge pattern does not include a horizontal trend line, but it is either marked by a couple of upward or downward trend lines.

When the wedge is a downward one, it means that there will be a price break in the resistance line. An upward wedge, however, indicates that the price will break from the support line. This, however, proves that the wedge is a reversal pattern because its breakout is in contrast to the general trend.

Triangles

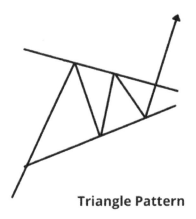

Triangle Pattern

Triangles are some of the most popular price patterns you'll come across in technical analysis because you are likely to come across them more than every other pattern. The most popular triangles are the ascending, symmetrical, and descending triangles. These patterns can stay for as long as weeks to many months.

For triangles like symmetrical triangles, they happen when 2 trend lines come together facing each other to indicate that a breakout is about to happen. It doesn't show direction. Ascending triangles on the other hand can be identified by their flat-up trend line and their rising low-trend lines which indicates that a high breakout may happen. The up-trend lines in descending triangles indicate that there might be either breakouts or breakdowns. The weight of either the breakdowns or the breakouts usually stands at the same height as the triangle's left vertical side.

Let's go deeper into understanding the 3 types of triangles one after the other:

Symmetric Triangles

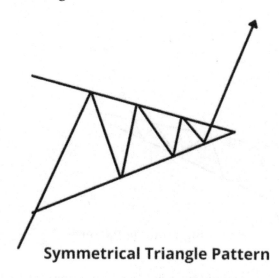

Symmetrical Triangle Pattern

Symmetric triangles come to life following the meeting of the connecting lines of the highs with the trendline that links the lows, such that it forms a triangle. These patterns are marked by a down trendline as well as an up trendline that comes together.

Because the 2 lines of the ascending triangle are marked by the same slope, it isn't quite possible to predict its direction. In most cases, there is a possibility of a breakout from one direction or the other. One can't tell which direction it will be. The direction of the triangle is also neither upward nor downward and this is because the slope of the 2 lines reflects one another.

The role of this pattern is to tell traders that the existing trend before the formation of the pattern will continue even after the price breaks away from the triangle.

Ascending Triangle

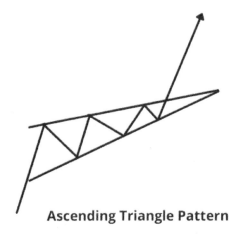

Ascending Triangle Pattern

This pattern is characterized by a flat line that accompanies the highs that remains at almost the same price as well as an up-trend line that follows the higher lows. In a nutshell, this trend indicates that the highs will remain the same while the lows increase.

When this pattern appears, it means that buying pressure is more than the selling pressure which will eventually end in a breakout at the upside.

Descending Triangle

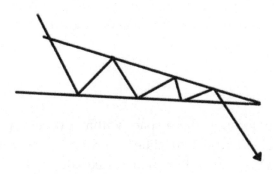

Descending Triangle Pattern

The descending triangle pattern can be likened to an upturned ascending triangle. This means that rather than facing up, it faces down.

This pattern is birthed by a flat slope at the base of the trendline as well as a sharp downward slope above the trendline. The descending triangle pattern indicates that sellers are taking over from buyers and forcing prices to decline. It is a bearish continuation pattern that forecasts a downward breakdown as soon as the pattern breaks.

Rounding Bottom

The rounding bottom pattern, which is also known as the cup, forecasts a bullish uptrend. The middle of the U shape presents traders with the opportunity to buy by taking advantage of the bullish trend that comes after the breakthrough from the resistance levels.

Gaps

Gaps are usually formed after a space within 2 trading periods as a result of a notable boost or decline in prices. A security can, for example, close at $10.00 and open at $12.00 after some earnings or other contributors.

Gaps are categorized into 3 distinct types which are the runaway, breakaway, and exhaustion gaps. While runaway gaps are formed at the middle of a trend, breakaway gaps form at the beginning of the trend. Exhaustion gaps on the other hand form somewhere close to the end of the trend.

Head and Shoulders Pattern

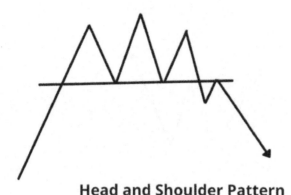

Head and Shoulder Pattern

The head and shoulders pattern forms to forecast the transition from bull to bear market reversal. This pattern is marked by a big peak which has 2 other small peaks at both sides. The 3 levels in this pattern drop to the same support level after which it is expected to break out in a downward movement.

This pattern may form at the top or bottom of the market in a series of 3 different pushes. The first is known as the initial peak or tough, while the second one is the larger one. The third push takes the form of the first one.

When there is an interruption in an uptrend by the head and shoulders pattern, it is most likely followed by a trend reversal which eventually leads to a downtrend. Contrarily, when a downtrend leads to the heads and shoulders bottom, it is likely to culminate in an upward trend reversal.

It is not unusual for horizontal or sloppy trendlines to form, then connect the peaks and the troughs which reflect within both the head and shoulders. There may be a decline in volume as the pattern is formed. The volume, however, springs up as soon as the price breaks above the head and shoulders bottom or below the top of the head and shoulders on the trendline.

Double Bottom

Double Bottom Pattern

This pattern is the reverse of the double top pattern. It takes the shape of the letter "W" and shows that the price has tried to break through the support level at 2 different times. This is a reversal chart pattern because it indicates a price reversal. After the 2 unsuccessful attempts at breaking through the support line, the market moves towards an upward trend.

Double Top

Double Top Pattern

This is the opposite of the double bottom pattern. It takes the shape of the letter "M" and falls into the reversal trend after 2 failed attempts at pushing through the resistance level. The trend eventually falls back to the support base, then begins a downward trend which pushes through the support line.

Both the double tops and bottom patterns signal at the points where the market tried to push through the support or resistance level twice without any success. The double top on the other hand is marked by the previous push up to the resistance level which precedes a second failed attempt then culminates in a trend reversal.

Summarily, price patterns form after prices take a pause. They point towards those areas where there may be a consolidation that would either result in a reversal or a continuation of a dominant trend. Trendlines are particularly important aspects of understanding these price patterns as they can appear in different forms like double tops, flags, cups, or pennants.

Volume is also another especially important aspect of this pattern. They usually decline as the pattern forms, then increase when there is a price breakout from the pattern. As a technical analyst, you should be able to use price patterns to predict future price trends which would include both continuations and reversals.

Chapter 6
Reversal Patterns

The Head and Shoulders

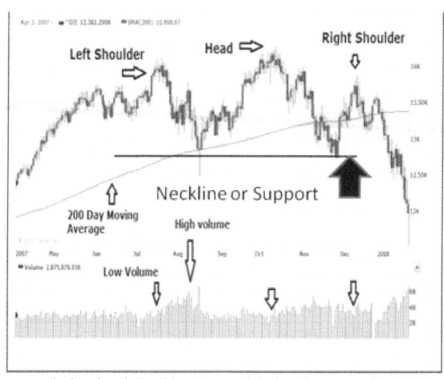

The head and shoulders is one of the best known and probably the most reliable of the reversal patterns. A head and shoulders top is characterized by 3 prominent market peaks. While the peak, or the head, is higher than the 2 surrounding peaks (the shoulders), as this pattern was forming, your original trend and/or channel line would have been headed upward and would have been on the low after the first shoulder was formed. That trend line would have been broken after the head was formed and the ensuing low was reached. A new trend line would have had to be drawn that now is actually the neckline, which is drawn below the 2 intervening reaction lows. Remember, the preceding upward trend was already broken when the second low was reached, and now a close below the neckline completes the pattern and signals an important market reversal. Let's take a look at a head and shoulders reversal that started a bear market which led to a severe market decline. See the figure below.

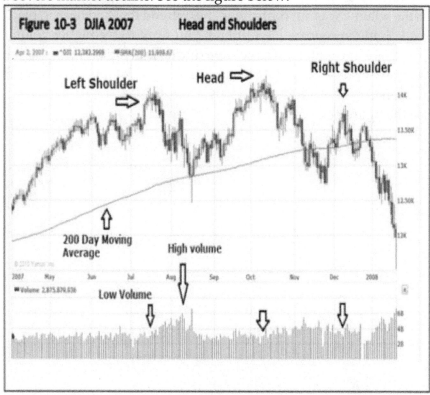

By the way... Does the above chart look familiar? Yes, this is a chart of the Dow Jones Industrial Average during the all-time-high set in October of 2007. And as you remember—that was the beginning of a major bear market. First of all—Look at the clear head and shoulders pattern. The left shoulder was the first high. Then the head is the all-time-high. Then the right shoulder is the third high, also called the third "peak." This is a classic head and shoulders pattern.

When you see one of these forming whether it is on an individual stock, index fund, or in this case, the Dow Jones Industrial Average, it is time to "sit up and pay attention!" This formation is one of the most reliable chart patterns you will see.

How do we know that distribution was underway after the first peak? Volume. The heavy volume during the pullback after the high on the left shoulder is our first clue. Look at the increased volume during that pullback. It tells us there was heavy selling, and, it tells us the volume was not confirming the uptrend that had been in place. For volume to confirm the uptrend, you want to see higher volume during advances and lower volume during pullbacks.

Let's take a closer look at the volume, and how volume must confirm the trend.

See the figure below.

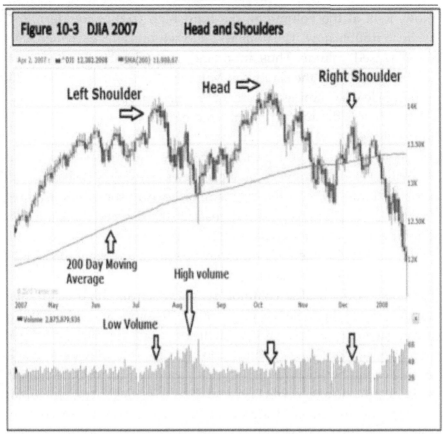

When looking at the volume across the bottom of the chart, as the first high formed (left shoulder), the volume was a little higher. Normally that is good. It is nice to see a stock, or in this case, the market, make a higher high on increased volume. But during the sell-off after the first high, the volume was higher than the volume of the advance while making the high. Thus, distribution…

Now, notice the volume on the all-time-high (head) is decreased volume. This is more distribution. The volume is not confirming the trend. The volume then increases on the next pullback. Inexperienced buyers are scooping up the stock and the pros are happy to sell. Make no mistake, distribution is always a result of the pros selling (distributing) their shares to the uninformed, the novices, the unsuspecting, and yes, the pigs that are greedy and hoping for more of an advance.

Now, look at the volume on the third high (right shoulder). Yep, we're in trouble now! The pullbacks and sell-offs after each high were on increased volume. Thus, more and more distribution, and more lambs being led to the slaughter. More dumb money listening to TV Talking Heads claiming all sorts of brainless prophecies.

At this point, the market is still trading above support levels. No major concerns, right?

At about this time you probably became dreadfully tired of the "Talking Heads" on every financial news network proclaiming all sorts of things. Personally, I remember hearing some who claimed that the DOW could, and should, reach 20,000. Do you think the ones claiming this had just purchased stocks "hoping" for further advance in the market? Maybe... Or they may be selling and want to keep the buyers coming so they can unload.

Let's also apply a little common sense. When the high at the first shoulder is reached, the DJIA is about 1,000 points above the 200-day moving average. Once again, when the head (all-time high) is formed the DJIA is about 1,000 points above the 200-day moving average. Who sees this and realizes at the very least there is most likely going to be a pullback or correction and begins selling? Yes, the smart money, the experienced traders. Sure, some might not sell out completely, but will certainly cut back and/or go to cash to preserve most of their profits. At the very minimum, tightening up the stop loss would be the smart thing to do. Simply, a stock, or the market, will normally not trade too far above the 200-day moving average for a long period of time before declining back closer to the moving average. In this instance, the market is 1,000 points above the moving average, so a decline should be expected.

Now, think risk vs. reward. Would a seasoned investor be buying a top? Would a smart investor be chasing the market, realizing there has been a long-term advance, buying in, and hoping it will go higher? No! The risk of a correction is too high, and, the chance the market is going very much higher is very low.

As a chartist, you can apply this knowledge to every investing and trading decision you make. For instance, before entering the market, you have to ask yourself:

- What is the market currently doing?
- Where is the market in relation to the moving averages?
- What does the volume tell you?
- What is the risk/reward?
- Are you buying a bottom or are you chasing the market?
- How do you protect your investment capital?

Every time you purchase an investment, your money is at risk. Therefore you must always make sure you are purchasing at a time when the risk is low, the reward is high, and your money is protected. Let's look at support levels. Support levels are very important. We always want to know where support may be in case of a decline. (See the figure below.)

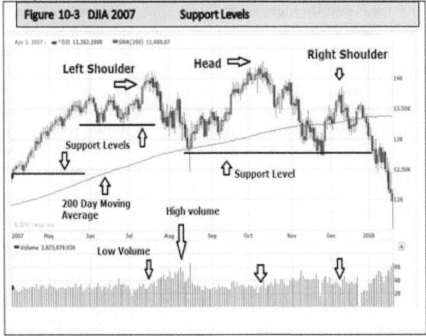

We see that there were only 2 support levels of any significance during this distribution phase. One was minor support just prior to the left shoulder and then there is the more significant support where the pullback landed on the 200-day moving average. The next significant support is found after the all-time high. These 2 significant support levels are what is considered the "neckline" on this pattern. The decline following the left shoulder top took about 30 days to find support and move higher to eventually form the highest peak, the head. That support level was tested and held prior to the right shoulder formation. But once that second support level was broken, a dramatic decline ensued. This is because the break below the neckline is a confirmation of the head and shoulders pattern.

Note again, the volume increased as the market moved past the all-time-high and then past the right shoulder. See the increase in volume on the declines compared to the volume leading up to the highs? What does that tell you?

For one, increased volume certainly tells us that more stocks are changing hands, more buyers, more sellers, but the increased volume is happening during declines. The volume must confirm the trend. And in this case, the highs are on low volume and the sell-offs are on high volume. Thus indicating further advance is not likely, and, the volume is confirming the developing trend, a new downward trend. Historically, every market top has experienced the very same signals, warnings, and told the investors what it was about to do. There is always low volume on advances, higher volume on declines, along with trend lines and support broken. This scenario always leads to a new trend with lower highs and then lower lows. The right shoulder in this pattern is the first "lower high." Let's look at one more thing using the very same chart. This time I added a trend line.

See the figure below.

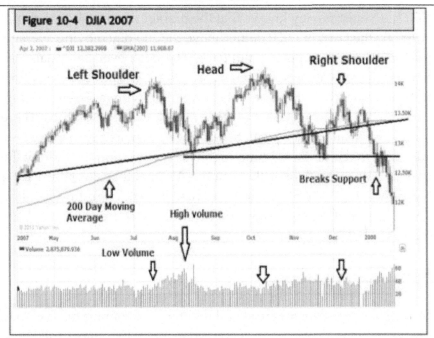

Figure 10-4 DJIA 2007

As we learned earlier, by connecting 2 or more lows, we can draw a trend line. The 200-day moving average is a trend line that can be added to any chart, and it is about as good as it gets, so to speak. The 200 DMA is also shown on the above chart. Now take note of the volume when the market broke below the support line. Yes, it was increased volume. Once the market closed below the support, panic ensued. Short sellers piled on.

Yes, a dramatic decline hit. But that can be expected once support is broken. When you think about every decline during the distribution phase for the 6-months prior to breaking support, yes, the pros were selling continually. Not so much to cause panic, but very methodically, and constantly selling. That is why the volume is low on advances when the market is topping out. The big money is not buying, they are gradually unloading. They wait for a little bounce and then sell into the strength. They are taking their profits. Many have been holding the stocks since they purchased them at the bottom during the previous "accumulation phase." In this case, that may have been in 2003 after the previous bear market when the Internet bubble burst.

You see, smart money knows that the market doesn't always go up. Anytime the DJIA is 1,000 points above the 200-day moving average, the smart money expects a pullback. There is never any guarantee that a pullback will be just a small correction. Any pullback may turn into a major correction or a bear market with a 30–50% drop. Experienced traders take some money off the table at the tops. There is no sense in allowing a profit to disappear, or worse, turn into a loss. Also note that after the all-time-high was reached and the head of the pattern was formed, over the ensuing 45 days there were at least 4 big down days where the sell-off created dark engulfing candles. These are very telling! They are your early warning signs. They indicate what is to come.

Moving Average

Moving averages are a very useful tool for determining trends. They can be applied to any chart. When displaying a chart, most will allow you to choose a 10-day moving average, a 20, 50, 100, or a 200-day moving average. The 200-day moving average is the most powerful of all. Whether you are dealing with an individual stock or a market index, when buying, your investment should be above the 200-day moving average (200 DMA). This average historically acts as both support and resistance. Meaning, if the stock or index is above the average, there should be support at or near the 200 DMA. If the stock or index falls below it, then the 200 DMA will usually act as resistance when the stock is trying to advance.

Notice in the above chart, in July of 2007 the first shoulder (peak) was formed, and then the market retreated to support right on the 200 DMA. Then after hitting the all-time-high, it fell through the 200 DMA.

Something significant—Take a look at the candle that formed when reaching the 200 DMA the second time. Do you see how it fell below the 200 DMA then traded higher to close above it? Yes, the following candle was a bearish engulfing candle that clearly fell through the support of the 200 DMA. But think of the psychology of the traders and investors. Many obviously believed there would be support at the 200 DMA and started buying. This buying provided a close above the average. The support of the 200 DMA didn't last, but traders were obviously buying in hopes the support would hold.

The 200 DMA is historically a great tool for the long-term investor. It can be used to signal buy and sell points. Meaning, the investor simply sells out when the security falls below the 200 DMA and waits for the security to cross back above the 200 DMA to reenter the position.

In Summary

Any way you look at the above charts of the head and shoulders formation—any way you analyze it—even pretend that 2008 has not arrived yet, and you are looking at these charts as they form on a daily or weekly basis.

Whether you would have drawn a trend line on the lows leading up to the very first peak (left shoulder), or drawn a support line, or drawn a channel line, used a 100 DMA or a 200 DMA, the result would have been the same.

Once the market broke below the first line of support and then broke the second line of support (neckline), the head and shoulders pattern was formed.

Chapter 7
24 Candlestick Patterns That Every Trader Should Know

andlestick patterns are used to forecast the future course of price movement. Find 24 of the most widely recognized candlestick patterns and how you can use them to distinguish trading opportunities.

What Is a Candlestick?

A candlestick is a method of showing data about an asset's price movement. Candle charts are quite possibly the most mainstream parts of technical analysis, empowering traders to decipher price data rapidly and from only a couple of price bars.

It has 3 fundamental highlights:

- The body, which addresses the open-to-close range
- The wick, or shadow, that shows the intra-day high and low
- The color, which uncovers the course of market movement— a green (or white) body demonstrates a price increase, while a red (or dark) body shows a price decline

Over the long run, singular candlestick from patterns that traders can use to perceive significant support and resistance levels. There are a considerable number of candlestick patterns that demonstrate a chance inside a market – some give understanding into the harmony among buying and selling pressures, while others recognize continuation patterns or market hesitation.

Before you begin trading, it's critical to acquaint yourself with the nuts and bolts of candlestick patterns and how they can advise your decisions.

Practice Reading Candlestick Patterns

The most ideal approach to figure out how to peruse candlestick patterns is to work on entering and leaving trades from the signals they give. You can build up your abilities in a danger-free climate by opening an IG demo account, or on the off chance that you feel adequately sure to begin trading, you can open a live record today. When using any candlestick pattern, it is critical to recall that in spite of the fact that they are extraordinary for rapidly anticipating patterns, they ought to be used close by different types of technical analysis to affirm the general pattern.

6 Bullish Candlestick Patterns

Bullish patterns may frame after a market downtrend, and signal a reversal of price movement. They are an indicator for traders to think about opening a long situation to profit from any upward direction.

Hammer

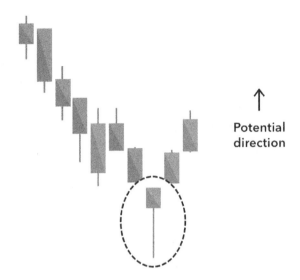

The hammer candle chart is shaped of a short body with a long lower wick and is found at the lower part of a descending pattern.

A hammer shows that despite the fact that there were selling pressures during the day, eventually, a strong buying pressure drove the price back up. The shade of the body can shift, however, green hammers show a more grounded positively trending market than red hammers.

Inverse Hammer

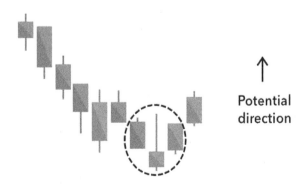

A comparatively bullish pattern is the inverse hammer. The only contrast being that the upper wick is long, while the lower wick is short.

It shows a buying pressure, trailed by a selling pressure that was not sufficiently able to drive the market price down. The converse hammer proposes that purchasers will before long have control of the market.

Bullish Engulfing

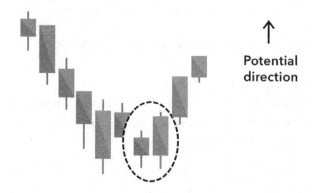

Potential direction

The bullish engulfing pattern is framed by 2 candlesticks. The main light is a short red body that is totally immersed by a bigger green candle.

Despite the fact that the subsequent day opens lower than the main, the bullish market pushes the price up, coming full circle in an undeniable win for buyers.

Piercing Line

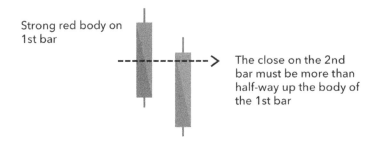

Strong red body on 1st bar

The close on the 2nd bar must be more than half-way up the body of the 1st bar

Reversal signal after a down-trend

The piercing line is likewise a 2-stick chart, comprised of a long red candle, trailed by a long green candle.

There is typically a huge gap down between the primary candlestick's closing price, and the green candlestick's opening. It shows a strong buying pressure, as the price is pushed up to or over the mid-price of the previous day.

Morning Star

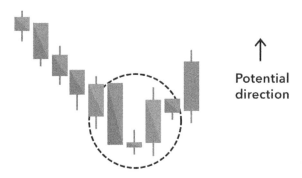

Potential direction

The morning star candlestick chart is viewed as an indication of expectation in a disheartening market downtrend. It is a 3-stick chart: one short-bodied candlestick between a long red and a long green. Customarily, the "star" will have no cover with the more extended bodies, as the market holes both on open and close.

It flags that the selling pressing factor of the principal day is dying down, and a positively trending market is not too far off.

3 White Soldiers

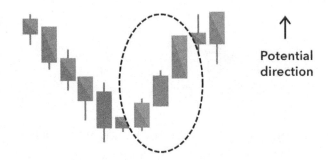

Potential direction

The 3 white soldiers' pattern happens more than 3 days. It comprises sequential long green (or white) candlestick with little wicks, which open and close logically higher than the earlier day. It is an extremely strong bullish sign that happens after a downtrend and shows a consistent movement of buying pressure.

6 Bearish Candlestick Patterns

Bearish candlestick patterns as a rule structure after an uptrend, and sign a state of resistance. Substantial negativity about the market price frequently makes traders close their long positions and open a short situation to exploit the falling price.

Hanging Man

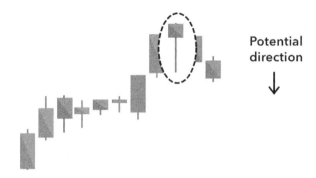

The hanging man is what could be compared to a hammer pattern; it has a similar shape, however, frames toward the finish of an uptrend. It shows that there was a critical auction during the day, however, that buyers had the option to push the price up once more. The huge auction is frequently seen as a sign that the bulls are failing to keep a grip available.

Shooting Star

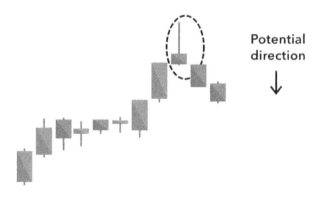

The shooting star is a similar shape as the inverse hammer, yet is framed in an uptrend; it has a little lower body and a long upper wick.

Typically, the market will gap somewhat higher on opening and rally to an intra-day high prior to shutting at a price simply over the open—like a star falling to the ground.

Bearish Engulfing

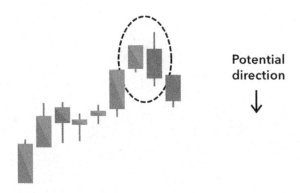

A bearish engulfing pattern happens toward the finish of an uptrend. The main candle has a little green body that is immersed by a resulting long red light.

It means a peak or lull of price movement and is an indication of a coming market slump. The lower the subsequent candlestick goes, the more critical the pattern is probably going to be.

Evening Star

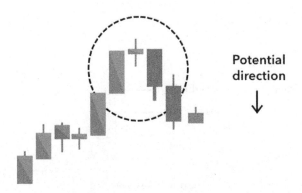

The evening star is a 3-candlestick pattern that is what could be compared to the bullish morning star. It is shaped of a short light sandwiched between a long green candle and an enormous red candlestick.

It shows the reversal of an uptrend and is especially solid when the third candle deletes the increases of the main light.

3 Black Crows

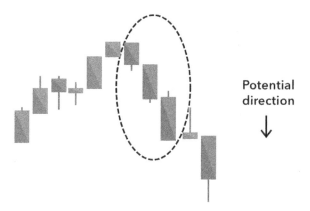

Potential direction ↓

The 3 black crows' candlestick pattern involves 3 successive long red candlesticks with short or non-existent wicks. Every meeting opens at a comparative price to the previous day, yet selling pressures push the price lower and lower with each nearby.

Traders decipher this pattern as the beginning of a bearish downtrend, as the traders have overwhelmed the buyers during 3 progressive trading days.

Dark Cloud Cover

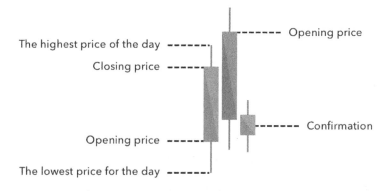

The dark cloud cover candlestick pattern shows a bearish reversal — a dark cover over the earlier day's confidence. It involves 2 candlesticks: a red candle that opens over the past green body and closes beneath its average.

It flags that the bears have assumed control over the meeting, pushing the price strongly lower. On the off chance that the wicks of the candlestick are short, it proposes that the downtrend was incredibly definitive.

4 Continuation Candlestick Patterns

If a candlestick pattern doesn't demonstrate a shift in market bearing, it is the thing that is known as a continuation chart. These can assist traders with distinguishing a time of rest on the lookout when there is market hesitation or nonpartisan price movement.

Doji

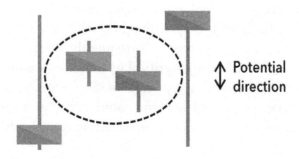

At the point when a market's open and close are nearly at a similar price point, the candle takes after a cross or in addition to sign—traders should pay special mind to a short to the non-existent body, with wicks of changing length. This present doji's pattern passes on a battle among buyers and traders that outcome in no net addition for one or the other side. Alone a doji is an impartial sign, yet it tends to be found in reverse patterns, for pattern, the bullish morning star and bearish evening star.

Spinning Top

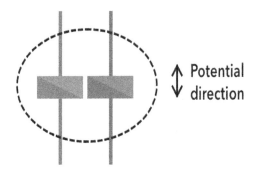

The spinning top candlestick pattern has a short body, focused between wicks of equivalent length. The pattern demonstrates uncertainty on the lookout, bringing about no significant change in price: the bulls sent the price higher, while the bears pushed it low once more. Spinning tops are frequently deciphered as a time of union, or rest, following a critical uptrend or downtrend.

On its own the spinning top is a generally considerate sign, however, they can be deciphered as an indication of things to come as it implies that the current market pressure is letting completely go.

Falling 3 Methods

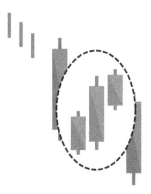

A 3-method arrangement pattern is used to forecast the continuation of the latest thing, be it bearish or bullish.

The bearish pattern is known as the "falling 3 methods." It is shaped of a long red body, trailed by 3 little green bodies, and another red body—the green candlestick are completely contained inside the scope of the bearish bodies. It shows traders that the bulls need more strength to alter the course.

Rising 3 Methods

The inverse is valid for the bullish pattern, called the "rising 3 methods" candlestick pattern. It includes 3 short reds sandwiched inside the scope of 2 long greens. The pattern shows traders that, in spite of some selling pressure, purchasers are holding control of the market.

Other Candlestick Patterns

Blue Sky Breakout

Generally, it's a good idea to wait for consolidation before taking out a long position on a security that has been ascending on the price charts. But sometimes it continues to move up for several days or more, causing the traders who are waiting for an entry on the sidelines to feel like they are missing out on the big move. In a relentless bull market, sometimes a trader is left with little choice but to jump into a security without waiting for it to dip a little bit.

A regular breakout is when a stock breaks above a resistance level, but there are still more resistance levels up ahead. A blue sky breakout is when the stock breaks through the final resistance level, leaving no other resistance points up ahead. A resistance level is a zone that a security commonly gets rejected at, indicating that supply has exceeded demand. During a blue sky breakout, you might see a series of green candles consecutively after resistance has been broken. The trouble with blue sky breakouts is that by the time the stock takes out the final resistance zone, it is usually already overextended, which could lead to a significant pullback.

If you decide to jump into a blue sky breakout, it's important to watch the trade closely, and not to hold onto it for longer than a few days. One way of knowing if the security will continue to go up is by assessing how much follow-through the stock has after it breaks resistance. If it breaks resistance, but only by a few cents, that's not a very good follow-through.

Cup and Handle

As the name implies, the candlesticks on the chart will resemble a cup and handle. The cup will be on the left side of the handle and it will be in the shape of the letter "U," while the handle will have a slight downward trend. As long as the bottom has a "U" shape, it is considered bullish, so it presents a buying opportunity. If the bottom has more of a "V" shape, it is best avoided, as the technical analysis indicates.

The candlesticks travel in a "U" formation. After making the "U" shaped recovery, they will start trending slightly downward again. Picture a downward slope at the top-right corner of the "U." The buy signal is presented during the consolidation period of the slight downtrend after the "U" shaped recovery. A realistic profit target can be assessed by measuring the distance between the bottom of the "U" and the top of the "U."

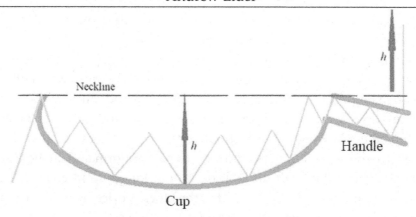

Neckline

Handle

Cup

If the move from the bottom of the cup to the top was 20%, the profit target could be 20%, with a stop-loss placed slightly below the handle formation. One of the drawbacks to playing a cup and handle pattern is that it can be difficult to tell if the cup is truly presenting a "U" or if it is actually a "V." Sometimes a sharp, V-looking bottom actually plays out quite well. Another drawback is that the cup sometimes forms without the handle.

The Bearish Abandoned Baby

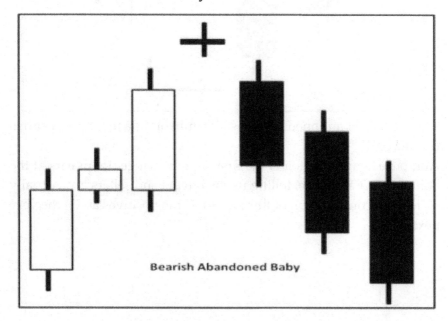

Bearish Abandoned Baby

The bearish abandoned baby is a candlestick pattern that usually tells us a reversal in the current uptrend is on its way.

First of all, the previous advance is eclipsed by a doji. That in itself is our first signal, but the confirmation comes the next day with a bearish engulfing candle. When you look at an advance at a stock's price while viewing a chart and see the doji and then see heavy selling the following day that should be enough to get your attention. In fact, experienced traders who see this pattern form and are holding the stock, usually begin to look back on a longer-term chart to see where support might be found for the stock's price. If it is very far below the current price, they would exit the trade.

The Bullish Abandoned Baby

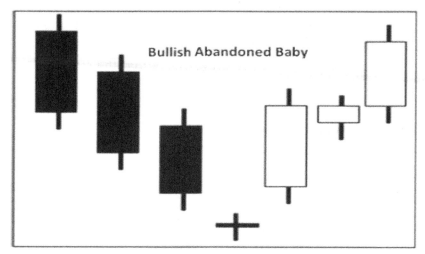

Bullish Abandoned Baby

The bullish abandoned baby is the mirror image of the bearish counterpart.

And once again, the doji is the first sign of change. It appears at the bottom, after a decline, telling us the buyers and sellers are virtually equal. The confirmation of this pattern is the positive candle the very next day.

The TRI Star

The tri-star is another type of candlestick pattern that signals a reversal in the current trend. This pattern is formed when 3 consecutive doji candlesticks appear after the stock has experienced an advance in price.

The above chart illustrates a bearish tri-star pattern at the top of the uptrend and is used to mark the beginning of a shift in momentum. A seasoned trader would be thinking, "Look out below!"

Keep in mind that even though the tri-star in this chart is clearly formed, many times there may only be 2 stars. Also note that these "stars" are actually doji candles, signifying that neither the buyers nor the sellers have any control since the stock opened and closed at virtually the same price on all 3 days. When you think about neither the buyers nor sellers having control and the doji forms at the end of an uptrend or a down-trend, then many times a change in direction is likely. In this case, 3 dojis were formed. But the important thing is what had previously happened.

The point is a trend in a particular stock or the overall market takes time. We are always looking for recognizable candles, patterns, or formations to appear at the end of an advance or decline. I would prefer to see a stock advance or decline a minimum of 5 days and then see a bottom or top forming. This lets us ignore small candles that appear a day or 2 after a change in trend has happened.

The Bearish Harami

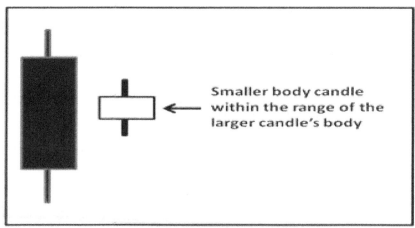

Smaller body candle within the range of the larger candle's body

The bearish harami is a pattern that forms at the top after an advance. It is indicated by a large dark candlestick that forms on a negative trading day signaling a change may be in store. Then there's a much smaller candlestick with a body that fits inside the vertical range of the larger candle's body. A pattern like this indicates that the preceding rising trend is ending.

When you think about it, the lower close of the bearish candle is an early warning sign. When this candle forms after an advance, you know the sellers have stepped in. Even before the next candle forms, you should be on high alert if you are holding this stock. Then when the next candle is formed showing the price cannot penetrate the upper area of the previous candle, this sometimes indicates a top has been reached and often reverse in direction will soon take place.

The Bullish Harami

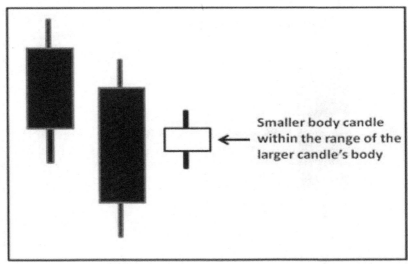

Smaller body candle within the range of the larger candle's body

The bullish harami pattern may look very close to the same as the bearish harami, but it forms at the bottom after a decline in the stock's price.

The bullish harami is a candlestick chart pattern in which a large candlestick is followed by a smaller candlestick whose body is located within the vertical range of the larger body candle on the previous day. In terms of candlestick colors, the bullish harami is a downtrend of negative-colored candlesticks engulfing a small positive (white) candlestick, giving a sign of a reversal of the downward trend.

The Harami Cross

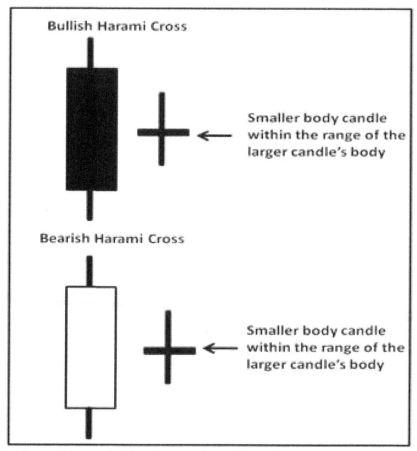

The harami cross is like the previous Harami formations except the small body candle is a doji. This indicates that the previous trend is about to reverse.

Think trader psychology for a moment. With the bearish harami cross, what might have happened in the trading that formed this particular pattern?

Obviously, the large white candle was formed with the market opening and the stock trading higher to the close that day. But on the following day, there are a couple of things we need to mention about the doji:

- The stock could not trade above the previous day's range

- No one had control. It was an even match between the buyers and the sellers.

Now, think about it a little further. If on this day when the doji is formed there are no longer enough buyers to push the price higher, and the sellers continue to sell at this price preventing an advance, the doji tells us that when the buyers and sellers are equal, then further advance may be unlikely.

The bullish harami is just the opposite. There were not enough sellers to push the price lower, meaning, the buyers stepped in after a decline in price and began buying at that level. So, once again, the doji tells the story and indicates a change in direction.

Chapter 8
Avoid the Traps

T rading chart patterns always sound so easy to do. Websites show you successful and profitable trades, and you look at the pattern and say, "oh yes, of course, anybody could have spotted that," and it looks so easy.

It's not. First of all, you have to kiss a lot of frogs—that is, for every chart that shows you a meaningful pattern, you're going to see an awful lot of charts where there's no clear trend at all. Secondly, some patterns can be deceptive and set traps for the unwary trader. For instance, "headfakes" often happen when you were expecting a proper breakout. And thirdly… some traders make life awfully difficult for themselves, whether through being too emotional, not setting stop-losses, not considering risk, or not knowing what some of the bad patterns look like.

Fakeouts and Fake Head-and-Shoulders

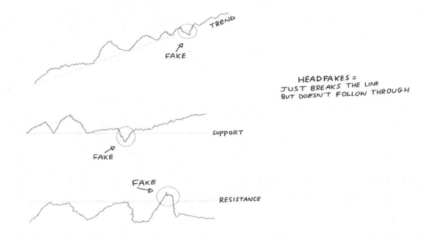

Sometimes the set-up looks great... but then the expected price movement fails to emerge. Prices move the "wrong" way for your trade. These are like a "headfake." But there are ways to check them out and avoid a few of the fakes.

You may fall into the trap of looking at a head and shoulders formation without realizing that it's actually just a blip in a bigger trend. Always check your chart for a longer time period before acting on some trade.

By the way, remember to check the pattern against the big picture. In the chart below, you think you see a head and shoulders formation, but actually, it's happening within a major trend and the trendline, not the neckline, is what matters. Always remember to look at several different time periods—I always look at 1 month, 6 months, 1 year, and 5 years, which may be overdoing it—so you don't get caught by a pattern that doesn't work.

THIS LOOKS LIKE
A HEAD & SHOULDERS
BUT WHEN YOU LOOK
AT THE BIG PICTURE
ITS STILL IN A BIG
DOWNTREND

Even if the price here had broken through the neckline, the top line of the downtrend channel would probably put up resistance, and that would limit your likely profits.

Or you may see the price come down to the neckline of the right shoulder, but not actually break through it. It might just dip below it in intra-day trading but still close above it. This isn't a proper breakout—wait for the price to close below the neckline before you buy.

In many head and shoulders patterns, there's a false breakout with a retracement before the real one. Sometimes, market practitioners are just trying to ensure traders with tight stop-losses are "stopped out" before the price really moves. So, don't put your stop too tight, and be ready even if it's activated to jump back into the next breakout.

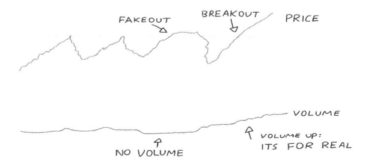

You also get fakeouts—for example, the price breaks the trendline to the upside, but then it falls back again, instead of giving you the expected breakout. You'll probably fall into that trap a few times, but some confirmations can help you avoid it:

- If there's a low volume of trading, it's probably a fakeout; breakouts have high volume.
- If the price is headed very slowly towards the trendline, it's probably a fakeout; breakouts have real momentum and tend to start with a really big move.
- A fakeout from a double top or double bottom is one that doesn't lead to the expected reversal—instead, you get a continuation. If you recognize it, you can simply reverse your trade—if you expected a double top to lead to a fall, and the price starts heading up, then stop the short and go long.
- Try placing your stops just short of the "expected" price or just a little more. Double bottoms, for instance, are well-known patterns, and lots of traders will have stop-losses at exactly the same price, often a round number. If you stay away from that level, you may not get faked out if the market-makers try to "shake the tree."

No Trend at All

Almost every good chart pattern needs a good strong trend established for it to work. It is really, really difficult to make money trading when there's no trend. And the market can be trendless for 60–70% of the time. If you don't trade for nearly 3-quarters of the year, how on earth can you make money?

Mind you, if you don't see any good trades in a sideways market, don't force the issue. It's always better to have cash sitting in your account than to waste it trading for the sake of trading. Taking a risk when you haven't identified a return is one of the dumbest things you can do.

Mean-reversion trades are probably your best bet. The concept of mean reversion is that statistical probabilities group towards the mean (average) so that if a price goes to an extreme high, it will probably fall back; if it goes to an extreme low, it will probably rise again. Even sideways markets have a range, though they don't have a trend, so identify that range and you've got a trading strategy.

But to carry out these trades, you need to get 4 things right:

- Detect oversold/overbought stocks using momentum and volume indicators, not just price charts.
- Buy stocks when they are trading on the low side of the range. It may be profitable to wait for a slight bounce so you know you're not going to get stuck in a downwards breakout that could cost you money. Your target price is not the other side of the range, but the middle (so your profit is half the width of the range).
- Be careful with your stop-losses. If there's a breakout, you do not want to get hit.
- If there is a breakout, it may be worth joining it. Again, be careful; set a tight stop-loss.

You will not make big money in sideways markets. You can make a little. If markets are range-bound for a long time then you may need to consider trading them, but to be honest, the risk-reward ratio is not that good, so I prefer to sit them out. Or you might look at another market to trade—foreign exchange, commodity ETFs, or futures; but to do that, you really should have already at least paper-traded these markets, or you could be jumping out of the frying pan into the fire.

Adjust Your Moving Averages

Most chart packages have already decided which moving averages to display. These are often, for instance, the 9 and 18-day averages, or 9 and 26-day, or 50 and 200.

But these might not be the best averages for you. Don't fall into the trap of letting a charting site decide which moving averages you should use.

For instance, if you've decided to become a day trader, you'll want to get something like 5-8-13 bar averages. You can get price bars for every hour, every 5 minutes, or every minute even, so you might have a 5-8-13 minute average instead of 5-8-13 days. Watch out though, because though in a good trend, they'll give you great signals; in choppy trading, they can be all over the place, and you're best declaring time out, going flat (closing all your positions), and going to get a coffee.

If you trade longer term, you'll want to look at longer-term averages such as the 26 and 50-day SMAs or EMAs. 20/21 are good for swing traders together with the 50-day; the 200 and 250-period MAs go well as the slower average.

Remember, the EMA moves faster than the SMA, so it will flag up trades more quickly—but you pay a price for this because it will give you more false signals than the SMA. If you're happy making a lot of trades and closing the bad ones quickly, use the EMA, as it will get you into a price swing more quickly; but if you want to trade longer-term, and keep your positions longer, then SMAs will give you winning trades that are slightly less profitable, but fewer stopped-out trades and fewer trades overall.

One of the reasons MAs work is that nearly everyone uses them. So, while you might think it's fun to create a 34-day moving average, it might not give you any useful, actionable information. You can try it, backtest it on a few charts and see. But I doubt you'll actually find that it's a secret weapon. I've tried a few and they've never worked out.

And lastly, moving averages just don't work in trendless markets. When the market is ranging, don't try to use the MAs for trading ideas—they're going to be all over the place and will only get you into trouble. Wait till you can see a clear trend again.

Risky Symmetrical Triangle

We've looked at ascending and descending triangles, which can give you a great trading signal. But sometimes the trendlines form a symmetrical triangle. The highs are getting lower, and the lows are getting higher, and when the 2 lines meet, something has got to happen. The trouble with this formation is that it's super risky. The chances are 50% it'll be up, and 50% it'll be down, and at a guess about 90% that it'll be fast and furious.

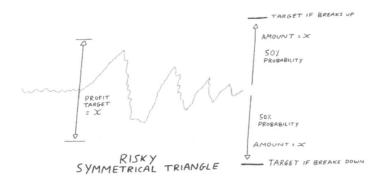

As I've stressed repeatedly, the trend is your friend, and trading a market that's not got a clear trend is tricky. And by definition, with one trendline going up and one coming down, with the symmetrical triangle, you have a trendless market—unless there's a really good strong moving average line, for instance, in which case you have a 50–60% chance that the breakout will be in the same direction. But there's also a good chance that there will be a fakeout first (usually with low volume while the real breakout will see an increase in trading volume).

So if you're risking on one of these triangles, it may be better to wait till the breakout and new trend are clear—and keep your stop-losses tight or the price could run away from you in the wrong direction. In fact, prices quite often gap-up (or down) from these formations, so even your stop-loss may not help you.

Your profit target can be measured by taking the depth of the triangle when it began to form and adding that to the breakout point. Your stop-loss should be at the last point at which the price touched the bottom line of the triangle. Since this is a 50–60% probable pattern, you're going to want a better than 2:1 risk/reward ratio for it to be potentially profitable. I wouldn't take it on much below 4:1, personally.

But you can ride the trend if you look at the moving average. As long as the price stays above the 20–50-day MA, you can keep your trade moving and bring your stop-loss up to date with the moving average every day. That way, you'll be stopped out automatically if the trend changes. A trailing stop like this is a great way to run a longer-term position.

Super Rocket Stock

One of the big dreams of the stock market is the one stock that will make you your fortune. "If I'd put every penny in my IRA into this stock... if I'd mortgaged my house and bought this stock... If I'd maxed out my credit card to buy this stock..."

Point one: Do not trade anything other than risk capital. That is money that you know you could afford to lose. If you lost your house and your pension and owed the credit card company $50,000, you would be in dire straits. Don't go there.

But secondly, this dream is exactly that—a dream. Shares do not go up and up and up. They go all around the houses.

Let's look at Cisco—a "rocket" of the tech boom. If you bought and held Cisco at $1.92 in 1994, you would have made a load of money. If you'd bought it at $15 towards the end of 1998, you would have seen it soar to over $80—and then fall back to below the price you paid for it by the end of 2002. Now, it would be worth $50. (This chart is from Bigcharts. Their data goes way, way back. Not all chart sites have such good long-term data.)

Plenty of gurus are keen to sell you their "rocket stocks." They'll use a combination of different approaches—analyst upgrades, earnings surprises, charting, trade volume. And they perform okay—for a while. But the problem with analyst upgrades is that analysts usually base their estimates on what the company tells them, and few analysts want to get out of step with a rising market—they fear if they call the top and the market keeps going up, they'll be fired. And the problem with "rocket stocks" is that there are many other people who have got in at the same time, and the same price, as you. If things go wrong, they'll chicken out.

These stocks are often really speculative, like GameStop, for instance. I'd call Tesla a super-rocket—it's been driven by having a great story and a charismatic CEO, but it hardly makes any money, and competition from companies like Toyota, Volkswagen, and Renault is heating up. (Incidentally, Volkswagen is up 62% from its lows. Good money for those who caught it.)

That means there's nothing to keep the share price from falling off a cliff. I know that we're talking about technical analysis and not fundamentals, but with stocks like this, I worry that the market is full of people who've heard the story but don't really understand the numbers. That pushes the stock up, and up, and up—and if you remember the parabolic rise? That's the trap.

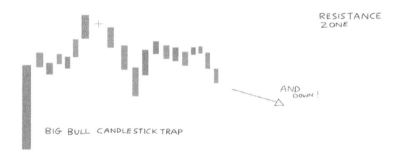

Long Candles

But sometimes, a super-long candlestick can be a trap. It looks like a bullish signal—and for a little while, it is. But while the share price may test resistance above this long candle, it's usually a bull trap and the share price will, after a while, come back to earth. And it can hit the ground hard.

Why does this big candle happen? New buyers are coming into the stock thinking that it's making a breakout. Maybe some big players are pushing the price up. What's important is that this long candle doesn't sit nicely among the other candlesticks—it's isolated. There may even be 2 big candlesticks.

Maybe you missed that signal, and you're sitting in the trading range on top. You'll often get another chance because a huge candlestick with a big upside shadow or wick will fake a breakout from the trading range. Novice traders will look at a big white or green candle and say, "Yay! Breakout!" Experienced traders will look at the big shadow on the upside, and they know that it means the market was trying to push prices higher and higher, but it wasn't working.

However, you should always check signals in a longer or shorter timeframe. For instance, a green/white weekly candle with a huge upper shadow looks as if the market tested the highs and couldn't sustain them. If you look at the daily candles, though, you may find that you have a pattern that is trading within the expected channel—up to the topside trendline and then just a small correction. In that case, don't get suckered—if you are long on the stock, it's still on course.

Lack of Discipline

The worst trap that most traders face is a lack of discipline. That might mean not getting up to catch the market open, not setting stop-losses, or not taking a trade where all the signals look good because you don't like the stock. Once you've decided on a trading strategy and on which signals are the ones you're going to trade, stick to your strategy and system. Chopping and changing lose trader's money...

It's about trading psychology—the psychology of other traders, but most importantly, your own.

Chapter 9
Trading Psychology

Trading with Emotions

I t is common for traders to have their emotions and feelings jumbled up when day trading, from the highs and the lows they experience from the market. This is a far outcry from the confident self that a trader usually poses before the markets open, bubbling up with excitement over the money and profits that they intend to make. Emotions in trading can mess up and impair your judgment and your ability to make wise decisions. Day trading is not to be carried out without emotions, but rather as a trader. You should know how to work your way around them, making them work for your good. A clear level headed and stable mind should be kept at all times, whether your profits are on the rise, or whether you are on a losing streak. This does not mean that as a trader, you are supposed to disconnect from your emotions. A person cannot avoid emotions, but in the face of real market scenarios, you have to learn how to work on and around them. The personality type of a trader plays a huge role in determining which kind of a trader they are. The cautious traders are mostly controlled by fear when opening up trades, while the risky type is in the greed-motivated bandwagon. Fear and greed are such huge motivators that they go a long way in the layout of losses and profits.

Greed

A trader may be fueled to earn more money by checking their balances in their accounts and seeing it be as of a low level. While this may be a motivator to work hard, some traders take it too far, wanting to earn a lot of money right there and then. They make mistakes while trading that has reverse effects than the intended ones. Such mistakes include an overtrade, taking unnecessary risks, among others.

Taking Unnecessary Risks

Greed for more money will seek to convince the trader to take risks that are not worth it to achieve a certain financial threshold in the trading account. These will most likely end up in losses. The risky traders may take risks such as high leverage, that they hope will work in their favor, but at the same time may have them making huge losses.

Making an Overtrade

Due to the urge to make more and more money, a trader may extend trading over long periods of time. Commonly these efforts are futile because the overtrading through market highs and lows put a trader in a position where their accounts can be wiped out due to greed. Disregarding the fact, time to trade and dive into opening trades without having done an analysis will most likely result in a loss.

Improper Profit and Loss Comprehension

Wanting to earn a lot of money within a short period of time, a trader will not close a losing trade, maintaining the losses, and on the other hand, overriding on profit-making trade until a reverse in the market happens, canceling out all the gains made. It is advisable to maximize and specialize in a successful trade and close a losing trade early enough, avoiding major losses.

Fear

Fear can work in both directions, as a limit to an overtrade, or also as a limit to making profits. A trader may close a trade so as to avert a loss, the action motivated by fear. A trader may also close a trade too early, even when on a winning streak in making gains, in fear that the market will reverse and that there will be losses. In both scenarios, fear is the motivator, working in avoiding failure a success at the same time.

The Fear to Fail

The fear to fail in trading may inhibit a trader from opening up trades, and just watch as the market changes and goes in cycles when doing nothing. The fear of failing in trading is an inhibitor to success. It prevents a trader from executing what could have been a successful trade.

The Fear to Succeed

This type of fear in trading psychology will make a trader lose out their profits to the market when there was an opportunity to do otherwise. It works in a self-harming way in market scenarios. Such traders in this category fear to have too much profit and allow losses to run, all the while aware of their activities and the losses they are going to make.

Bias in Trading

There are several market biases that a trader may tend to make that may be as a result of the emotions play, which traders are advised against. In the psychology of trading, these biases may influence a trader to make unwise and uncalculated trading decisions that may prove to be loss-making ones. Even when the trading biases are in focus, as a trader, you have to be aware of the emotions in you and come up with ways to keep them under control and maintain a cool head in your trading window. They include the bias of overconfidence, confirmation, anchoring, and loss.

Bias in Overconfidence

It is a common occurrence with traders, especially new traders, that when you make a trade with huge profits, you get in euphoria in the state of winning. You want to go on opening up trades, with the belief that your analysis cannot go wrong, boiling down to the profits and gains you've made. This should not be the case. You as a trader cannot be too overexcited and overconfident in the analysis skills that you believe you cannot make a loss. The market is a volatile one, and therefore, the cards can change at any given time, and when they do, the overexcited and overconfident trader now turns into a disappointed one. Get your analysis of the market right before opening up any trade, regardless of the previous trades, whether they were a loss or gain.

Bias in Confirming Trades

In trading psychology, the bias in confirmation of a trade you have already made, justifying it, is one of the factors that waste a lot of time and money for traders. This type of bias is mostly associated with professional traders. After making a trade, they go back in evaluating and analyzing the trade they just made, trying to prove that it was the correct one, whether they sailed according to the market. They waste a lot of time digging for information that they are already aware of. They could also be proving that the mistake they did in opening a wrong trade and making a wrong move was a correct one. Nevertheless, the bias in confirmation occurs when a trade they made turns out to be correct, and this strengthens their determination in their researching skills, further pushing them in wasting time in proving to themselves already known facts. They could also lose money in the process, and it is, thus, advisable against this form of bias in trading.

Bias in Anchoring on Obsolete Strategies

This type of bias in the psychology of trading applies to the traders that rely so much on outdated information and obsolete strategies that do more harm than good to their trading success. Anchoring on the correct but irrelevant information when trading might make the trader susceptible to making losses, a blow to the traders who are always lazy to dig up new information on the market. Keeping up with the current events and factors that may have an impact on the market is one of the key aspects of having a successful trading career. Lazy traders will tire of keeping tabs with the ongoing economic and even political situations whose influence is exerted on the foreign exchange market. An example of this is that some traders will have a losing trade, but they hope that the markets will reverse their assumptions based on obsolete information and strategies. Carry out extensive research, mindful not to be too time-consuming, to ensure you make trades in accordance with the right data.

Bias in Avoiding Losses

Trading with the motive to avert losses usually boils down to the factor of fear. There are some traders whose trading patterns and their trading windows are controlled by fear of making losses. Having gains and making profits is not a motivation to them when fear hinders them from opening trades that could have otherwise been profitable. They also close pas trade too early, even when making profits in a bid to avert the losses, their imaginable losses. After carrying out a proper and detailed analysis on the market, go for making profits without being deterred with the bias of avoiding to make a loss, for that just holds many traders. Come up with a plan for your day trading to deal with doubts about the trades you are to make.

Psychology Affecting Traders' Habits

Psychological aspects affect habits in trading, the mistakes, and the winning strategies that a trader comes up with. Explained below are the negative habits that many traders make, with the influence of psychology on their habits.

Trading Without a Strategy

With no trading strategy and plan, a trader will face challenges with no place to refer to the anticipated end result. A proper strategy should be drawn by a trader to be a referencing point when facing a problem in trading in the market. It should be a clearly constructed plan, detailing what to do in certain situations and which type of trading patterns to employ in different case scenarios. Trading without a strategy is akin to trading to lose your money.

Lack of Money Management Plans

Money management plans are one of the main aspects of trading, and without solid strategies in this, it is difficult to make progress in making gains in the trades opened. As a trader, you have to abide by certain principles that will guide you in how to spend your money in the account in opening up trades and ensuring that profits ensue from that. Without money management plans, a trader would be trading blindly with no end goal in mind, risking the money in non-profitable trades.

Wanting to Be Always Right

Some traders always go against the market, placing their desire of what manner they would like the market to behave in. They do not follow the sign that the market points to, but rather they follow their own philosophy, not doing proper analysis and always wanting to be right. Losses ensue from such psychological habits. When the trading window closes, the market will always overrule the traders. Thus, a trader's want to be always right against the market is overruled.

Looking at the Analysis

It's important to understand how to perform a proper technical analysis not just to determine the value of a certain option but also to make sure you don't scare yourself away with any certain number.

You might see a dip in a chart, or a price projection lower than you hoped, immediately becoming fearful and avoiding a certain option. Remember not to let yourself get too afraid of all the things you might come across on any given trading chart. You might see scary projections that show a particular stock crashing, or maybe you see that it's projected to decrease by half.

Make sure before you trust a certain trading chart that you understand how it was developed. Someone that wasn't sure what they were doing might have created the display, or there's a chance that it was even dramatized as a method of convincing others not to invest. Always check sources, and if something is particularly concerning or confusing, don't be afraid to run your own analysis as well.

Hearing Rumors

If you are someone that hangs around with other traders, maybe even going to the New York Stock Exchange daily, there's a good chance you are talking stocks with others. Make sure that any "tips" or "predictions" you hear are all taken with a grain of salt. Tricking others into believing a certain thing is true about different stocks and options can sometimes dapple into an area of legal morality, but it's important to make still sure you don't get caught up with some facts or rumors that have been twisted.

You should only base your purchases on solid facts, never just something you heard from your friend's boyfriend's sister's ex-broker. While they might have the legitimate inside scoop, they could also be completely misunderstanding something that they heard. Before you go fearfully selling all your investments from the whisper of a stranger, make sure you do your research and make an educated guess.

Accepting Change

As animals, we humans are constantly looking for a constant. We appreciate the steadiness that comes along with some aspects of life because it's insurance that things will remain the same. Sometimes, we might avoid doing something we know is right just because we are too afraid to get out of our comfort zone. Make sure that you never allow your fear of change to hold you back.

Sometimes, you might just have to sell an old stock that has been gradually plummeting. Maybe you have to accept that an option is no longer worth anything, even though it's been your constant for years. Ask yourself if you are afraid of losing money or just dealing with the fear.

Know When to Stop

For you to know when to stop can be the most challenging part of life. It's so hard to say no to another episode when your streaming service starts playing the next one. How are we supposed to say no to another chip when there are so many in the bag? Sometimes, if you see your price rising, you might just want to stay in it as long as you can. In reality, you have to make sure that you know when it's time just to pull out and say no.

If you wait too long, you could end up losing twice as much money as you were expecting to make. This is when the gambling part comes in, and things can get tricky. Make sure you are well-versed in your limits and that you are not putting yourself in a dangerous position if you don't trust your own self-control.

Accept Responsibility

Sometimes, we don't want to have to admit that we're wrong, so we'll end up putting ourselves in a bad position just to try to prove to someone, even just ourselves, that we were right. For example, maybe you told everyone about this great investment you were going to make, sharing tips and secrets with other trader friends about a price you were expecting to rise.

Then, maybe that price never rises, and you are left with just the same amount that you originally invested. You were wrong, but you are not ready to give up yet. Then, the price starts rapidly dropping, but you are still not ready to admit you are wrong, so you don't sell even though you start losing money. You have to know when just to accept responsibility and admit that you might have been wrong about a certain decision.

Discipline

Having a good knowledge and understanding of different stocks and options is important, but discipline might be the most crucial quality for a trader to have. Not only do you have to avoid fear and greed, but you have to make sure to stay disciplined in every other area.

On one level, this means keeping up with stocks and staying organized. You don't want just to check things every few days. Even if you plan on implementing a longer strategy for your returns, you should still keep up with what's happening in the market daily to make sure that nothing is overlooked.

On a different level, you have to stay disciplined with your strategy. Decide where personal rules might bend and how willing you are to go outside your comfort zone. While you have to plan for risk management, you should also plan that things might go well. If the price moves higher than you expected, are you going to hold out, or are you going to stay strict with your strategy?

Stick to Your Plan

If you don't stick to the right plan, you might end up derailing the entire thing. You can remember this element in other areas of your life. You can be a little loose with the plan, but if you go off track too much, what's the point of having it in the first place? If you are too rigid, you could potentially lose out on some great opportunities, but too loose can make everything fall apart.

Prepare for Risk Management

Aside from just knowing when to pull out to avoid being greedy, you also need to make sure that you are doing it so you don't end up losing money. Have plans in place for risk management, and make sure that you stick to these to ensure you won't be losing money in the end.

Determine What Works Best

The most important aspect of a trading mindset is remembering that everyone is different. What works best for you could be someone else's downfall and vice versa. Practice different methods, and if something works for you, don't be afraid to stick to that. Allow variety into your strategies, but be knowledgeable and strict with what you cut out and what you let in. Identify your strengths and weaknesses so that you can continually grow your strategies and always determine how you can improve and how you can cut out unnecessary losses.

Exercise Patience

In the world of investing, patience is the greatest virtue you can exercise. Most folks who venture into the world of investing in financial markets are hopeful they can make a good amount of money quickly. However, like anything in life, it takes time before you can become good at it.

This is why professional investors always preach patience.

If you go to your local bank right now and talk to an investment advisor, they will tell you to be patient, especially if it is going through a rough patch. They will tell you that you can make good returns, but you need to stay in the market long enough to see the results. They may even show you calculations of how your money compounds over time, thus giving you fabulous returns after 10–20 years.

Now, you surely don't have 20 years to make money at the moment. Well, it might be a good secondary investment, but certainly not something that you'd be betting on. Nevertheless, being patient is essential to making money in any type of investment.

You are only risking a small portion of your overall investment. This means that you can start small, but due to the power of compounding, you can make a serious amount of money.

This strategy has been successful for plenty of investors. But it takes time and study before you can make this strategy work. You need to keep in mind that rolling over money like this requires you to go on a winning streak. Therefore, you must have the right tools and information before making it big.

Why Trading Psychology Is Important

Most people fail in day trading because they start at the wrong end. They start by learning trading skills first, then move on to money and risk management techniques, and the last stop is to learn, superficially, about trading psychology.

In fact, the right sequence of learning day trading should be learning the trading psychology first, then money and risk management techniques, and the last part should constitute learning the trading skills.

It is very easy to learn technical analysis and how to use technical indicators. But it is very difficult to control one's emotions like fear and greed while trading or astutely manage money while day trading.

If you look at people in different fields, you will find the mindset is the main difference between those who reach the pinnacle of their chosen career and those who remain mediocre. Be it business, science, technology, sports, or any other creative pursuit; people who train their minds for success are the ones who win the race.

In intra-day trading also, hundreds and thousands of day traders use the same methods of technical analysis; however, only a few of them succeed in making profitable trades, and others go home with losses. It is the trading psychology that makes the difference between successful traders and those who failed.

Every trader, who tries to learn day trading, knows that there are certain rules to be followed, and still, the majority of them fail to do so; therefore, if you want to succeed in day trading, you must pay attention to how you react to markets. Stock trading is nothing but watching the price rise and fall and trading off with the trend. But still, traders fail to follow this simple method of trading.

Day trading happens 90% in the mind of a day trader, and only 10% in what happens in markets. A day trader takes decisions based on what they think is going to happen in stock markets and not on what is happening. This is the biggest mistake day traders make, and the reason is their emotions.

To overcome this psychological hurdle, day traders must learn how to manage their trades without emotions. They can do so only with the help of technology and self-discipline. If they do not have self-control or do not follow a disciplined trading plan, they cannot make profits in stock markets.

At a fundamental level, traders' emotions usually drive markets across the globe.

There are essentially 2 sentiments and states of mind that determine failure or success in stock trading: greed and fear. A trader's emotional nature largely establishes if they are going to be successful in stock trading. In establishing trading success, any trader's trading psychology can be as crucial as some other qualities, like knowledge, skill, and experience. Self-discipline, as well as risk-taking, are 2 extremely crucial parts of trading psychology. For the success of one's trading plan, following these factors is very important. Although fear and greed are definitely the 2 common emotions related to trading psychology, some other emotions also generate trading habits, such as hope and regret.

To have an understanding of trading psychology, just think about a few examples of the emotions connected with it.

Greed is usually an extreme wish for riches. Greed frequently motivates traders to remain in a profitable trade more than is sensible, in an attempt to get more profits from that trade, or even undertake big risky positions. Greed can be most evident in the last stage of bull markets, where speculation operates on a wider level, and traders and investors become careless.

On the other hand, fear makes traders exit positions too early or even stay away from tasking risk due to anxiety about big losses. Fear can be prevalent in the times of bear markets, which, as a powerful emotion, can induce traders and investors to do something irrational in their rush to close the trade. Fear usually turns into panic, which usually provokes markets to fall at a considerably faster pace compared to their upward trend.

Regret is another emotion that could cause a trader to enter a trade after originally missing it, as the stock changes too quickly. It is against trading wisdom and quite often leads to the trader entering way too late in the trade.

Successful traders follow some common psychological rules that add to their success. These include:

- They do not overtrade. They know their limits.
- They preserve their trading capital through risk management to gain trading success.
- They maintain their trading discipline at all times.
- They know the difference between not going against the trend and following the herd.

Psychologically Approach Toward Success

It may not seem to be a significant factor on the surface. However, psychology plays a huge role in the way investors conduct their trades. Psychology is arguable the most important aspect when investing. The fact of the matter is that for all of the analysis and research that you can conduct, you may find yourself falling victim to some of the most common issues that occur to traders. When an investor can control their emotional responses to the way trades are conducted, there is a greater possibility of success.

The most important factor you can put into practice when it comes to devising your investment approach is realistic expectations. This means that you are aware of the fact that investing takes time and effort. Of course, you're not expecting to take years before making a profit. However, you should keep in mind that starting small can ultimately pay off in droves later on.

When you start small, you can build momentum. When you build momentum, there is a snowball effect that makes you make more money. Sure, it's tempting to think that you could make 1 year's salary when in a single trade. Still, then again, you will eventually reach that level after gaining the experience that top traders have gained.

It's like pilots; as they accumulate flight hours, they can fly without instrumentation, relying on their experience and better judgment. Now, that doesn't mean that the pilot no longer needs the plane's instrumentation. It just means that they can use their judgment, especially when unexpected circumstances arise.

Also, having realistic expectations is vital to ensure that greed doesn't get the better of you. You see, greed is a very powerful force, particularly when you are good at investing. There is a temptation to take greater and greater risks. Eventually, though, you make one mistake that can derail a long time's worth of success. So, having realistic expectations is a great way of curbing the temptation to take unnecessary risks.

Chapter 10
10 Top Tips for Each Aspect of Trading

Y ou have to understand that the stock market is a very volatile place, and anything can happen within a matter of a few seconds. You have to be prepared for anything that it throws at you. In order to prepare for it, you have to make use of risk capital. Risk capital refers to money that you are willing to risk. You have to convince yourself that even if you lose the money that you have invested, then it will not be a big deal for you. For that, you have to make use of your own money and not borrow from anyone, as you will start feeling guilty about investing it. Decide on a set number and invest it.

1. Research

You have to conduct thorough research on the market before investing in it. Don't think you will learn as you go. That is only possible if you at least know the basics. You have to remain interested in gathering information that is crucial for your investments, and it will only come about if you put in some hard work towards it. Nobody is asking you to stay up and go through thick textbooks. All you have to do is go through books and websites and gather enough information to help you get started on the right foot.

2. Stop-Loss/Take Loss

You have to understand the importance of a stop-loss mechanism. A stop-loss technique is used to safeguard investment. Now say, for example, you invest $100 and buy shares priced at $5 each. You have to place a stop-loss at around $4 in order to stop it from going down any further. Now you will wonder as to why you have to place the stop-loss and undergo one, well, by doing so, you will actually be saving your money to a large extent.

Take a Loss

It is fine to take a loss from time to time. Don't think of it as a big hurdle. You will have the chance to convert the loss into a profit. You have to remain confident and invested.

You can take a loss on a bad investment that was anyway not going your way. You can also take a loss on an investment that you think is a long hold and will not work for you in the short term. Taking a few losses is the only way in which you can learn to trade well in the market.

These form the different "do" of the stock market that will help you with your intra-day trades.

Below are the "don'ts" of day trading.

3. No Planning

Do not make the mistake of going about investing in the market without a plan in tow. You have to plan out the different things that you will do in the market and go about it the right way. This plan should include how much you will invest in the market, where you will invest, how you will go about it, etc. No planning will translate to getting lost in the stock market, which is not a good sign for any investor.

4. Over-Rely on a Broker

You must never over-rely on a broker. You have to make your own decisions and know what to do and when.

The broker will not know whether an investment is good for you. They will only be bothered about their profits. If they are suggesting something, then you should do your own research before investing in the stock. The same extends to emails that you might receive through certain sources. These emails are spam and meant to dupe you. So, don't make the mistake of trusting everything that you read.

5. Message Boards

You have to not care about message boards. These will be available on the Internet and are mostly meant to help people gather information. But there will be pumpers and bashers present there. Pumpers will force people to buy a stock just to increase its value, and bashers will force people to sell all their stocks just because they want the value to go down. Both these types are risky, as they will abandon the investors just as soon as their motive is fulfilled. So, you have to be quite careful with it.

6. Calculate Wrong

Some people make the mistake of calculating wrong. They will not be adept at math and will end up with wrong figures. This is a potential danger to all those looking to increase their wealth potential.

If you are not good at calculating, then download an app that will do it for you or carry a calculator around to do the correct calculations. The reason is to make the right calculations and increase your wealth potential.

7. Copy Strategies

Do not make the mistake of copying someone else's strategies. You have to come up with something that is your own and not borrowed from someone else. If you end up borrowing, then you will not be able to attain the desired results. You have to sit with your broker and come up with a custom strategy that you can employ and win big.

These form the different "don't" of the stock market that will help you keep troubles at bay.

8. The Main Tools Used in Trading

Just like starting any other business or profession, you need a few important tools to begin day trading. Basically, you need a broker and a platform to execute your orders. These are the tools that you will certainly need to function as a day trader.

As explained, you also need a stock scanner to help you find a watch list and look for potential setups in real-time. On top of a stock scanner, it is ideal to be part of a trading community.

For you to carry out day trading successfully, there are several tools that you need. Some of these tools are freely available, while others must be purchased. Modern trading is not like the traditional version. This means that you need to get online to access day trading opportunities.

Therefore, the number one tool you need is a laptop or computer with an internet connection. The computer you use must have sufficient memory for it to process your requests fast enough. If your computer keeps crashing or stalling all the time, you will miss out on some lucrative opportunities. There are trading platforms that need a lot of memory to work, and you must always take this into consideration.

Your internet connection must also be fast enough. This will ensure that your trading platform loads in real-time. Ensure that you get an internet speed that processes data instantaneously to avoid experiencing any data lag. Due to some outages that occur with most internet providers, you may also need to invest in a backup internet device such as a smartphone hotspot or modem.

9. Market Data and Trading Platform

You can be successful in your trades if you know how to execute your trades in a jiffy. You must be able to move in and out of the trades easily.

It can be a challenge to perform trades fast enough if your broker doesn't use a platform or software with hotkeys.

You need to make fast decisions so you can make extra dollars when the stock suddenly spikes. If the stock rises, you need to be able to place money in your account and make money from it fast. You certainly don't want to be bumbling with your orders. You need fast executions, which is why you really need to use a good broker as well as a platform for quick order execution.

10. Stocks Scanner and Watch List

One of the common concerns among new traders is that they do not know the stocks to trade. Every day, thousands of stocks move in the market. However, looking for a setup that is an excellent fit for your risk tolerance and consistent with your day trading strategy can be difficult.

You need to use a scanner to browse the market and look for good trades.

The most popular stock scanners for day traders are the following:
- Stock Rover
- Cartmill
- Finviz
- Stock Fetcher

Community of Traders

Even though day trading can be really exciting, it is also quite tricky and can be emotionally overwhelming.

It is best to join a community of retail traders and ask them questions. Consult them whenever necessary, learn new strategies, and receive some expert insights and alerts about the stock market. But don't forget that you also need to contribute to the community.

You can also talk to each other and share screens and platforms so you can watch each other as you trade. It can be a fun, interactive environment, and you can learn from each other. Through this, you can gain more knowledge and experience in day trading.

You will meet experienced traders in an online community from whom you can learn much, and you can also help other newbie traders in exploring this lucrative business.

If you join an online community, you will see that other day traders lose money often. It can make you feel good to see that losing trades is quite common in this area, and everyone, including seasoned traders, still loses money in the process.

Bear in mind that you need to be an independent thinker. Basically, people may change when they join groups. They become more impulsive and unquestioning, nervously looking for a leader whose trades they can mimic. They respond with the crowd rather than using their own minds.

Members of the online community may be influenced by some trends, but they could lose a lot of money if the trends suddenly reverse. Don't forget that successful traders are usually independent thinkers.

You must develop good judgment so you can decide when to trade and when not to trade.

Chapter 11
Designing Your Trading Strategies

Imagine you just started your own business and want to branch out into an entirely new market. What do you do? First, you need a strategy. But where do you start designing your trading strategies?

Where to Start?

The answer is to start looking for the best site for your research. You will then have a place to go back whenever you want to re-do the research or go in a new direction. Without this, all of your efforts are wasted; you'll be starting from scratch each and every time. However, with a choice location that contains all of your accumulated data and notes in one spot, when you get an idea, it's just a single step away from putting it into action!

What Is the Best Site?

There are dozens of sites out there that present market information in different ways. Finding the best one for you will depend on what information you want and how it's presented. Find the best site for you by focusing on the following:

- All of the data you're interested in is presented in an easy-to-use format. Keep track of a lot of different information? Make sure that you can get all of it quickly and easily.

- The site is well organized and its data is presented in a clear manner. If everything isn't there, it's easy to find what is missing and add it to your list of what's needed.
- The site has a good selection of tools for analyzing the data, like charts, indicators, drawing tools, etc. These can help you see the information and draw conclusions that might not be obvious at first glance.
- The site is easy to use so you aren't wasting a lot of time getting started. It should also have good options for keeping your information private; you don't want everyone else on the Web knowing what your plans are!

What Broker Do I Use?

Your broker is just as important as your research site, if not more so. If you open an account with the wrong one, the problems probably won't stop at just trading issues either. Here's an introduction to some of the things that you need to find out about any broker before committing:

- **Regulation.** You need to know if your broker is regulated by any of the banking or regulatory agencies in your country. This shows that they have to follow strict guidelines and provide assistance to you when you have a problem.
- **Regulation compliance.** If they aren't regulated, it doesn't mean that they can't be trustworthy. Just make sure that their registration is current and contact them to see what kind of assistance they provide for new traders.
- **Licensing status.** If asked for proof of licensure, the firm should be able to confirm it immediately and without any trouble whatsoever because it should be on file with them as well as with the financial authority where the firm is located.
- **The broker should have an active online presence.** This way you can contact them whenever you need to instead of waiting for a response during regular business hours.
- **Leverage.** Make sure that your account has the available leverage that you want. This will help make trading easier

and less costly when profits are made, but it also has the opposite effect when losses are suffered.

- **Fees and commissions.** Brokers typically charge either fees or commissions on every trade, or both, so find out how much each one is. Also find out how they handle any additional costs such as exchange rates when international trades are made and extra fees for electronic payments like credit cards or debit cards, etc...

- **Binaries.** Look at how the broker handles the buying and selling of options, futures, and spot metals, and other instruments. Sometimes there are restrictions to what you can trade with one particular broker; it's a good idea to find out which ones work best for your needs, as well as costs.

- **Order flow.** The order flow will show you how much liquidity each broker has available at any given time so that you don't have to worry about getting filled or left out of a trade on your way up or down in a market.

- **Risk/reward ratio.** This is the amount of money you can expect to make per unit of risk involved when trading with the broker. The higher the number, the better; anything above 1.00 is considered a good risk/reward ratio.

- **Deposit and withdrawal methods.** Each broker has its own method of handling deposits and withdrawals; you need to find out what is available to you so that there are no delays or surprises when you either deposit money or want it back!

- **Online trading tools.** Different brokers will offer different things on their online trading platforms, so you need to see what's available and how easy it is to use. Some of these might include charting programs, research tools, or other things that help with your analysis.

- **Trading restrictions.** Some brokers are limited as to which instruments or strategies you can trade. This will vary and be based on your location, so look for something that fits your needs.

Your research and broker will help you make sound decisions when choosing to get involved in foreign currency trading where you can plan and execute trades more easily than ever before. Don't take any shortcuts and don't settle for anything less than the best when it comes to these 2 important aspects of Forex trading.

Chapter 12
Structuring Your Analysis Framework

What Is a Technical Analysis Framework

Our technical analysis framework is our personal set of rules and guidelines for analyzing the market. Personal is a keyword here. What I'm going to present to you is my personal guidelines on how to structure a good framework, from that you can take what works for you and ignore what doesn't.

Here are the different components of my technical analysis framework:

- Trend analysis framework
- Support and resistance framework
- Secondary frameworks
- Selecting timeframes

First, I like to create a trend analysis framework, this gives me the ability to consistently determine the state of the market. Every single time I open a chart, I will use the same strategies to determine what the trend is doing. Then, we're going to talk about creating a support and resistance framework, when I select a level as a support and resistance I want to be randomly assigning value to it every single time. I want to be able to value these levels in a consistent manner. Then, I'm going to go over potential secondary frameworks you can use in conjunction with the core trend analysis and support and resistance frameworks I like to use. And then, finally, we'll talk about selecting timeframes.

Structuring Your Trend Analysis Framework

Step 1. Select Your Primary Tools

- **Moving averages – Which moving averages? How many?** Moving averages are one of my favorite tools for analyzing trends and I did a very in-depth lesson explaining how to use these tools so if you wish to include moving averages in your trend analysis framework you need to select which moving averages you want to use and how many.
- **Candlestick analysis.** Those of you who are a bit more discretionary as traders may want to incorporate candlestick analysis in your framework.
- **Fibonacci retracements.** Fibonacci retracements are very useful in conjunction with moving averages and candlestick analysis.
- **Volume and open interest.** Volume and open interest can be useful tools as well.
- **Any other tool you enjoy using for trend analysis.** Finally, do not forget you can use any other tool you enjoy using for trend analysis, even ones I have not covered in this book. There is no right or wrong way to do this, initially, we want to build consistency above everything.

Step 2. Create Your Frameworks

Once we've chosen the tools we're going to use, we're going to create the framework itself. In example 1, I'm going to present to you a very simple framework using only moving averages.

Example 1: Simple moving average framework. I'll be using MA20, MA50, and MA100.

Moving Averages	20>50>100	20~50>100	20~50~100	20~50<100	20<50<100
Trend	Bullish	Bullish-Neutral	Neutral	Bearish-Neutral	Bearish

I've selected 3 moving averages: the 20, the 50, and the 100. Now every single time I open the chart I will have a consistent way of determining the market conditions. I will know if the 20 is above the 50 and it's above the 100 that the trend is bullish. I'll know if the 20 and 50 are crisscrossing or there isn't much distance between them but they're both above the 100, the trend is a rather weak bullish trend, so bullish-neutral bias. In an instance where the 20, the 50, and the 100 are crisscrossing and there's no clear trend I'll know it's neutral. In an instance where the 20 and the 50 are crisscrossing below the 100, I'll know there's a bearish-neutral trend. And if the 100 is above the 50 and the 20 is below the 50, I'll know there is a strong bearish trend. This would make it extremely easy for me to record trades, it'll make it extremely easy for me to backtest trades because it's consistent and I can do the same thing every single time.

Now, let's take a slightly more complicated example. Say your system is extremely sensitive to the current market conditions, you may want to introduce more variables.

Example 2: Moving averages + Open interest framework. I'll be using the MA20, MA50, and MA100.

Moving Averages	20>50>100	20~50>100	20~50~100	20~50<100	20<50<100
Open Interest Increasing	Strong-Bullish	Bullish	Neutral	Bearish	Strong-Bearish
Open Interest Decreasing	Bullish	Bullish-Neutral	Neutral	Bearish-Neutral	Bearish

Last time we had 5 different market conditions. By adding open interest alongside moving averages, we now have 10 different market conditions. When open interest is confluent with our moving averages, we assign more strength to the argument. I hope you can see how this framework allows us to be consistent.

Here are a few more possible combinations you can play around with to decide which ones you want to use:

- Moving Averages + Fibonacci (+ Open Interest/Volume)
- Candlestick Analysis + Fibonacci (+ Open Interest/Volume)
- Moving Average + Candlestick Analysis

You can combine moving averages with the Fibonacci retracement tool if you want even more complexity, add open interest and volume on top of that. You can combine candlestick analysis with the Fibonacci retracement tool. You can even combine moving averages with candlestick analysis. Your only limitations are your creativity and your understanding of the tools themselves.

Structuring Your Support and Resistance Framework

This is going to be a bit more difficult than our trend analysis framework because there is a lot more discretion when it comes to this.

Step 1. Select your Value System

I like to go about a support and resistance framework by creating a value system, so I use different things such as the number of data points, quality of data points, the length of time of an argument, psychological levels, and you can use any other factors you deem important to create a value system.

In an example now I'll show you how this value system would work in practice. We're going to analyze the $9,500 to $9,300 support area marked out over here:

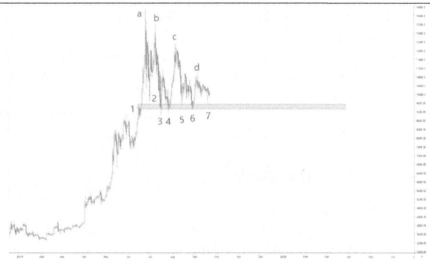

First, we're going to calculate the number of data points. I'm going to add one point for every data point there is then I'm going to subtract one point for every deviation.

Number of Data Points (Max 10)

- +1 for Data Point
- -1 for Deviation

Let's look at the data points in the picture (8.1), we have point (1) where it acted as a resistance before it flipped, then we have points (2), (3), (4), (5), (6), and (7); seven data points. I don't see any data points which disagree with this level so no points are taken away for deviation. That leaves us with +7 points for seven data points. Next, quality of data points, I'm going to subtract 1 for a messy point and I'm going to subtract 1 for weak context.

Quality of Data Points

- -1 for Messy Point
- -1 for Weak Context

(2), (3), (4), (7), these 4 points are messy in my opinion because these don't quite reach the support area and the points (3) and (4), while they didn't close below our region the wicks did go through. We're going to subtract 4 points because they aren't clean data points. Next, we're going to subtract some points for weak context, if you remember it's what happens after we interact with our level, at points (a), (b), (c), (d) the price is progressively getting lower and lower every time. These data points are quite significant for me I'm going to use my discretion, subtract an extra 1 point for weak context. That puts us at -5. Next, the length of time of an argument.

Length of Time of Argument (Max 3)

- Discretionary point

I'm going to set the max for 3 points and it's going to be discretionary. This support area is held for several months, it's longer than the average support area I tend to analyze so I'll be giving 2 discretionary points for the length of time of argument. That puts us at +2. Then psychological levels.

Psychological Levels (Max 2)

- Discretionary points

I don't see $9,500 and $9,300 as a key psychological level, so I won't be adding any points for that.

So, that leaves us with a final score = 4/10. This is without a doubt an area of support but it is below average in strength. This is an example I've come up with to show you guys how you can create a value system. By this point in the book, hopefully, your intuitive understanding of the data will let you create your own value system and through this, we have a consistent method of assigning value to our support and resistance arguments.

Step 2. Select Your Confluence Indicators and Assign a Value System to Them

Now that we have our base value system, we can expand it a bit more. We can use certain indicators that can be confluent with our support or resistance levels and incorporate them as complementary parts of the value system.

- Moving averages
- Fibonacci
- Anything else you'd like to include

Step 3. Select your Invalidation and Break Conditions

Now, we have our base value system, we need to determine our invalidation and breaking conditions. Under what conditions will we consider a support or resistance level broken?

- 1–2 candles close above your level?
- Candle close with increasing open interest/volume?
- Candle close and moving average cross?
- Candle close and without a retrace greater than 0.238?

You can see now why there's a lot of work to be done in this lesson. You need to sit down and create your own framework and if you don't understand the tools well enough to come up with your own then you're not ready to create your framework yet. Do not build your trading on a weak foundation, take the time to understand what you're doing.

Next, under what conditions do you no longer consider a support or resistance level significant? Will it be a failure to retest after it's broken or would it be when your value system drops to 0 so when your argument drops to 0 you no longer consider that level significant?

- Failure to retest after being broken?
- When does the value system drop to 0?

I'm just giving you ideas here, the end result has to be something you've come up with yourselves. With that, you will have a framework for analyzing support and resistance levels.

Secondary Frameworks

Let's cover some secondary frameworks you can use alongside your primary ones. For those who wish to complicate their analysis further. You could include a framework using oscillators like the relative strength index or Bollinger bands. You can use Elliott Wave theory if that appeals to you. Some traders like to study statistics on certain months of the year, days of the week, or times of the day and incorporate that into their systems. Also, if you're trading multiple similarly behaving assets you should have a system for analyzing liquidity to make sure the market has enough liquidity for your orders.

Selecting Timeframes

Next, we're going to talk about selecting our time frames. While this is important for our analysis framework, it's something I'd like to cover in a lot more detail in a future psychology book because your personal psychology and lifestyle is a huge factor when deciding which time frames to trade on.

Primary Timeframe

What type of trader do you want to be?
- Day trader: 1 hour
- Swing trader: 1 hour to 1 day

I've explained to you multiple times throughout this book the difference between time frames, when you go to higher timeframes data becomes more significant, volatility decreases. At lower timeframes data is less significant and volatility increases so you're going to have a lot more opportunities on lower timeframes and you're going to have a lot fewer opportunities on higher time frames. Personally, I like to trade on lower timeframes, I'll get into positions multiple times a day. I don't like waiting extended periods of time for positions to close because I cannot stop thinking about a position once I am in it. This is why psychology is extremely important when trying to select your time frame but for the purpose of this book, you can select what timeframes you like based on what type of trader you want to be. Do you want to be a day trader and trade timeframes under 1 hour? Do you want to be a swing trader trade timeframes from the 1 hour to say the 1 day or do you want to be an even longer time frame trader and trade weekly and monthly charts? That's up to you.

Experiment with both and decide which one you want to use and then I'd recommend selecting 2 complementary timeframes.

Complementary Timeframes

- Higher timeframes for trend analysis
- Lower timeframes for pinpointing support and resistance invalidations/breaks

Now a higher timeframe can be extremely useful for trend analysis and also pinpointing significant support and resistance levels. Then you also want a lower timeframe to complement this help and help pinpoint support on resistance and validations and breaks.

Putting It All Together

Now, we put it all together, here's your checklist:
- Analysis timeframes
- Trend analysis
- Support and resistance analysis
- Secondary analysis

You want to select your analysis timeframes. You want to have a trend analysis framework that you can perform on these timeframes. You want to have a support and resistance analysis framework. A value system in which you can assess the importance of different support and resistance levels and you can accompany this with any secondary analysis tools you want and you will go through this checklist every single time you analyze the market. This is a complete technical analysis framework.

Once you have built your technical analysis framework, congratulations! You have completed my technical analysis foundation book. Your next task is to translate your technical analysis framework into a trading system. You will use your framework to come up with a hypothesis for entry and exit strategies. You will then test these in the markets and attach correct risk management to them. Once your data shows that you are profitable you can then enter the market with your strategy.

Components of a Trading System

- **Psychology:** Without the metal framework to execute your trades, even the best system in the world is useless.
- **Risk management:** Every system is vulnerable to failure. A system will most likely be wiped out before it can earn money if it does not have long-term risk management.
- **Entry:** The least important part of a system. Choosing the best market circumstances to enter a trade.
- **Exit:** Exits are used to maximize winners and minimize losses. Often overlooked and far more important than specific entries.

Chapter 13
School of Indicators

orex indicators are frequently used by traders to increase their chances of profiting on the foreign exchange market while trading. Indicators, like other types of data and analysis, can influence trading decisions and serve as the foundation for Forex trading strategies. By analyzing historical market behavior and patterns, traders may be able to use the best Forex indicators to forecast how the market will behave in the future and, consequently, which trades are likely to be profitable.

What are currency market indicators? Before trading on a platform, Forex traders analyze a variety of data points to determine how the market is performing and how it is likely to change in the future. Traders should be able to employ more effective trading strategies and earn a higher return with detailed market analysis.

Indicators for Forex trading are one method of examining market data. Indicators use historical data, such as currency prices, volume, and market performance, to forecast how the market will behave in the future and which patterns are likely to repeat. Once traders have access to this information, they can make more informed trading decisions and potentially earn a higher return.

There are numerous different types of Forex indicators, and it's beneficial to understand what each one does before trading. The most frequently used Forex indicators are as follows:

Trend indicators:

- Average directional indicators
- Moving averages
- Parabolic

Momentum indicators:

- Relative strength index

- Moving average convergence divergence

Volatility indicators:

- Bollinger Band strategy
- Average true range
- Volume indicators

With so many different types of Forex indicators available, you may be unsure where to begin. This book can assist you in mastering the more technical aspects of trading. The best Forex indicators operate on the premise that historical patterns are likely to repeat themselves when similar circumstances arise. Rather than viewing the foreign exchange market as a random series of events, Forex indicators look for patterns in the market's specific behavior.

If a currency fell immediately following a political crisis, for example, this could have occurred as a result of repeated episodes of political instability. If this is the case, Forex indicators will record this information and use it to forecast whether or not the same behavior will occur in the future. By gaining access to this data, traders can gain insight into the factors that influence currency prices and the market as a whole and trade accordingly.

Forex indicators can be used to:

- Conduct technical analyses
- Contribute to risk minimization
- Establish a foundation for your trading strategies

Is it necessary to use Forex indicators? Technical instruments and sophisticated data are not only for seasoned traders and professional analysts. Indeed, indicators serve as a means of simplifying extremely complex and voluminous data, and anyone can benefit from their use. These indicators are an integral part of forex traders' daily routines while trading and play a significant role in their decision-making process. The more knowledge you have about the market, its operation, and the variables that influence it, the more informed you will be. By making trading decisions based on historical market activity and informing your trading strategy with previous currency patterns, you can increase your returns and profits.

How do you gain access to foreign exchange trading indicators? With so many indicators available, it can be difficult to determine which indicator is the best or most important for your trading needs. While a variety of indicators can be used to examine market behavior and forecast future market events, you may not want to use every Forex indicator when you first begin. By working with the best Forex broker, you can ensure that you have access to a variety of resources, including Forex indicators, Forex signals, and a Forex calendar. When you use multiple tools to develop a trading strategy, you take into account more variables, which may provide you with a more accurate picture of how the market will perform.

Access to Forex indicators is critical to trading success, so you'll want to ensure that your chosen broker offers in-depth market analysis and a variety of tools. Similarly, you may wish to choose a broker that offers a variety of potentially beneficial trading features, such as Forex signals and the best Forex trading app.

Along with access to Forex indicators and market data, the best Forex broker for you may offer Forex glossaries, coaching, and curated investments, as well as support during both Forex trading hours and non-trading hours.

Forex technical indicators are classified into 4 broad categories: trend, momentum, volatility, and volume, and are used to generate a technical analysis of the foreign exchange market. Technical indicators make quick calculations and then plot the results on a convenient graph. You can avoid time-consuming, complex mathematical calculations by utilizing these technical indicators, such as the moving average convergence divergence indicator, the relative strength index, or the Bollinger Bands.

Forex technical indicators generate simple-to-understand data that serves as a great visual guideline for past trends and potential future market activity, making it easier for traders to take action.

Choosing Indicators and Brokers for Forex

Choosing the right Forex indicators is just as critical as choosing the right broker. By incorporating various indicators into your trading strategy, you can increase your chances of success, and by carefully selecting Forex indicators and brokers, you can practice risk management and maximize your potential returns. For instance, choose a broker that offers all the tools and functionalities you require.

PayPal Forex brokers may make it simple to fund your account, and brokers that offer 24-hour support may provide you with the reassurance you require when you begin trading. Many people want to know what Forex leading indicators are, as they can appear quite complicated at first glance. However, the rationale for using Forex indicators is quite straightforward. Prior to making any trading decisions or transactions, you should gather as much information as possible. Knowing which events impacted the market in the past and the magnitude of their impact can aid in forecasting future market behavior. If you have a crystal-clear picture of what will happen to currency prices and the FX market in general, you should have a better chance of selecting the optimal entry and exit points and executing profitable trades.

Moving Averages

Moving averages are a widely used technical indicator in the Forex market. As popular as moving averages are, one question remains at the top of the list for the majority of traders — "How to make the most of moving averages?"

We will discuss what moving averages are and how to use them effectively. Additionally, we will discuss some of the drawbacks to moving averages that all traders should consider before incorporating them into their trading strategy.

Let's begin with answering the question, what is a moving average calculator?

To begin, it's worth noting that the moving average is a lagging indicator. This indicates that it is based on previous price movements. Moving averages are classified into 2 types: simple moving averages (SMA) and exponential moving averages (EMA). The simple moving average, as the name implies, is a simple average of a currency pair's movement over time. On the other hand, the exponential moving average gives greater weight to recent price action.

I prefer exponential over simply because I believe it provides a more accurate picture of what is occurring rather than what has occurred. Moving averages can be used in a variety of ways, but the 3 methods below are my personal favorites. Because the moving average is a lagging indicator, it should always be used in conjunction with other price action patterns and signals to help you improve your odds.

Analyze Trends

Moving averages are arguably the most frequently used indicator for trend analysis. There are numerous moving average combinations that a trader can use to analyze a trend, but my favorite is the 10 EMA and the 20 EMA.

As is the case with the majority of things in the Forex market, using moving averages to analyze trends is not an exact science. Nor is it something on which you want to rely solely. However, when used properly, these 2 moving averages can significantly simplify the process of identifying a trend. Consider the following example.

Observe how we are only looking for buying opportunities in the AUDUSD daily chart above when the 10 EMA is above the 20 EMA.

Because the 10 EMA is more closely related to price action than the 20 EMA, when it is on top, it indicates that the market is in an uptrend.

On the other hand, when the 10 EMA is below the 20 EMA, we want to look for selling opportunities only, as this frequently indicates the start of a downtrend.

Support and Resistance in Dynamic Modes

Additionally, these 2 moving averages can act as dynamic support and resistance. Several moving averages carry more weight in the market than others, including the 10 and 20 period moving averages. The following is a list of the 5 most frequently used moving averages by Forex traders:

- 10
- 20
- 50
- 100
- 200

Due to the frequency with which the periods above are used, the market tends to respect them more than others. That is why support and resistance levels work in the market—if a sufficient number of traders use the same level to buy or sell a market, the market is likely to react accordingly. Consider the 10 and 20 EMAs as dynamic resistance levels during a downtrend.

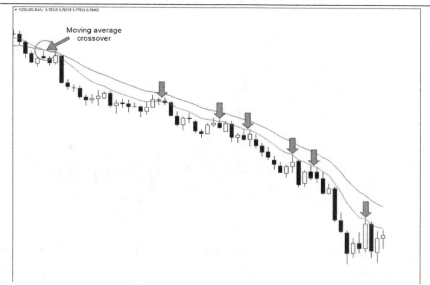

Take note of how the 10 EMA began to act as dynamic resistance once it crossed below the 20 EMA. When combined with a price action sell signal, this type of dynamic resistance can be extremely powerful.

Identifying Excessively Extended Markets

Finally, but certainly not least, moving averages can be used to determine whether a market is overextended. Forex traders frequently make the error of buying or selling too late. We want to avoid investing in overbought markets, and moving averages can assist us in determining whether this is the case.

It's worth noting that this method is complementary to the use of moving averages as dynamic support and resistance. This is an illustration of how to use moving averages to avoid selling into an overbought market.

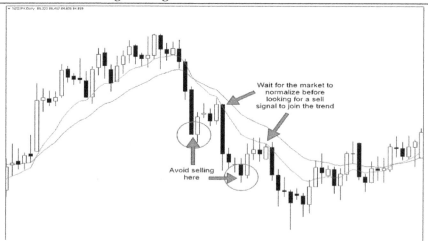

On the daily chart of the NZDJPY, the market made 2 extended declines away from the 10 and 20 EMAs. As price action traders, our objective is to avoid entering a market that has moved significantly away from our moving averages. Rather than that, we'd like to wait for the market to normalize and return to its moving averages before looking for a sell signal to join the trend.

Relative Strength Indicators (RSI)

Additionally, we'll discuss RSI trendlines and how to trade the RSI with various strategies such as the RSI 2 Period Divergence and more. I'll then assist you in identifying additional indicators to pair with the RSI indicator in order to enhance your trading performance.

How to Trade the Relative Strength Index (RSI) Indicator

Before we discuss the best strategies and settings for day trading and intraday trading with the RSI indicator, we should review some fundamentals. Technical analysis is a technique for predicting future market trends and price movements by studying historical market charts and comparing them to current charts. Technical analysis is concerned with what has occurred in the market and what may occur in the future. It takes the price of security into account and generates charts for use as the primary tool.

One significant advantage of technical analysis is that skilled analysts can monitor multiple markets and market instruments concurrently. Before delving into the details of the RSI indicator, it is necessary to review 3 fundamental principles of technical analysis:

- The trend is your friend. Technical analysis is used to identify market behavior patterns that have been recognized as significant for a long period.
- There is a high probability that many given patterns will produce the expected results. Additionally, there are recognized patterns that are consistently repeated.
- History tends to repeat itself. For more than a century, Forex chart patterns have been recognized and classified, and the frequency with which many patterns recur suggests that human psychology has remained relatively stable over time. Price Action offers substantial savings on everything.

This means that the current price reflects everything the market is aware of that could affect it, such as supply and demand, political factors, and market sentiment. Technical analysts, on the other hand, are only interested in price movements and not the reasons for any potential changes.

RSI—the Relative Strength Index Indicator—is one of the indicators heavily used in technical analysis. Due to the strength of its formula and the possibility of utilizing RSI divergence, RSI indicator trading has grown in popularity.

What Is the Relative Strength Index (RSI)?

The RSI calculates the ratio of upward to downward movement and normalizes the result to a range of 0–100. J. Welles Wilder invented it. The security is considered if the RSI is greater than 70. An RSI of less than 30 is interpreted as indicating that the instrument may be oversold (a situation in which prices have fallen more than the market expectations).

Contrary to popular belief, the relative strength index (RSI) is a leading indicator. 2 equations must be solved to calculate the RSI indicator. The first component equation determines the initial

Relative Strength (RS) value, which is defined as the ratio of the average "Up" closes to the average "Down" closes over "N" periods, as illustrated in the following RSI formula example:

RS = Average of "N" day's positive closes / Average of "N" day's negative closes

The actual RSI value is determined by indexing the indicator to 100 using the RSI formula example below:

RSI = 100 - (100 / 1 + RS).

How to trade the RSI in the short term. Many traders find that employing the RSI indicator in their day trading strategy is extremely beneficial. The default RSI period setting is 14, which is suitable for most traders, especially swing traders. However, some intraday traders use a different setting when trading the RSI indicator. They dislike the 14-setting because it produces infrequent trading signals. As a result, some traders choose to reduce their time frame, while others choose to decrease the RSI period to increase the oscillator's sensitivity.

Generally, intraday traders (day traders) frequently use lower settings with periods ranging from 9–11 hours. Swing traders who trade on a medium-term basis frequently use the default period setting of 14. Longer-term position traders frequently set it to a higher period, between 20 and 30 days. Which settings to use when trading with the RSI indicator depends on your trading strategy.

Setting the RSI Indicator for an Intraday Trading Strategy

Determine the most effective settings for your trading style by determining the amount of noise you are willing to process with the data you receive. Keep in mind that as you acquire experience with this indicator, regardless of the level you select, your ability to detect trustworthy signals will increase.

In the case of day trading and intraday trading with the RSI indicator, you will be making short-term trades. Traders frequently choose lower settings for all variables in this environment due to the earlier signals generated. As previously stated, short-term intraday traders typically trade with lower settings and periods ranging from 9–11.

Trading Strategies Using the RSI Indicator

You have now mastered the RSI indicator. However, you must understand how to use the RSI indicator effectively. It is now time to examine how to trade the RSI. The following are some examples of RSI indicator settings that can be used in conjunction with various trading strategies:

Levels of RSI and OBOS

With this strategy, you can predict when the price will bounce off the trendline, indicating an entry opportunity. If the RSI drops below 30, the market is oversold and may rise. A buy trade can be entered once the reversal is confirmed. If the RSI exceeds 70, the market is overbought and the price may soon fall. After confirmation of the reversal, sell. Bullish (upper) and bearish (lower) zones meet at the RSI 50 level. If the RSI is above 50, the trend is up. If it is below, the trend is down.

RSI 2-Period Divergence

This strategy is also known as an RSI 14 trading strategy. Compare the 5-period RSI to the default 14 period RSI. When using the RSI 14 trading strategy, the market may not reach oversold or overbought levels before turning. With a shorter period RSI, reversals can be detected earlier. When the RSI 5 exceeds the RSI 14, prices are rising.

When the 5-period (blue) is oversold, a buy signal is generated, and a 5 vs. 14 cross should occur (below 30). When the RSI 5 falls below and then becomes equal to the RSI 14, it indicates that recent prices are declining. This is a signal to sell. When the 5-period (blue) is overbought, a 5 vs. 14 cross should occur (above 80). Experienced traders may find that combining an RSI trading strategy with Pivot Points significantly improves their trading performance.

Trend Lines of the RSI

Trade the trendline break on the RSI chart. Create an RSI uptrend line by connecting 3 or more points on the rising RSI line. A trendline is formed when 3 or more points on the RSI line fall together. Price trends may continue or reverse after an RSI trendline break. Remember that an RSI trendline break typically occurs before a price chart trendline break, providing an early warning and trading opportunity.

Divergence of the RSI Classic

RSI bearish divergence occurs when the price makes a higher high while the RSI falls and makes a lower high. RSI divergence typically forms at the peak of a bullish market, and this is referred to as a reversal pattern. When the RSI divergence forms, traders anticipate a reversal. It is a forewarning of impending reversal, as it appears in several candlesticks before the uptrend reverses and breaks below its support line.

When the price makes a lower low and the RSI makes a higher low, this is known as a bullish RSI divergence. This is a signal that the trend may be changing from down to up.

The RSI divergence indicator is frequently used in technical analysis of the Forex market. Certain traders prefer to trade RSI divergence on higher time frames (H4, Daily). You can use these strategies to generate a variety of RSI indicator buy and sell signals.

Stochastic Indicators

I'm constantly amazed at how few traders truly understand the indicators they're using. Or, even worse, many traders misuse their indicators because they never took the time to learn them.

What Is a Stochastic Indicator (Stochastic)?

The Stochastic indicator provides insight into the momentum and strength of a trend. As we will see shortly, the indicator analyzes price movements and informs us of their speed and strength. George Lane, the inventor of the Stochastic indicator, stated that Stochastics is used to determine the price's momentum. Consider a rocket ascending into the air—before it can turn down, it must first slow down. Momentum always shifts in the opposite direction of price.

What Exactly Is Momentum?

Before we begin using Stochastic, it is necessary to understand what momentum is. Momentum is the rate at which the price of a security increases. I've always been a fan of delving into how an indicator analyzes price, and without getting too technical, this is how the indicator analyzes price:

The Stochastic indicator analyzes a price range over a specified period or number of price candles; the Stochastic indicator is typically set to 5–14 periods/price candles. This means that the Stochastic indicator compares the period's absolute high and low to the closing price. We'll see how this works with the following 2 examples. I've chosen a 5-period Stochastic, which means that the Stochastic will only look at the previous 5 candlesticks.

When the Stochastic indicator is high, it indicates that the price closed near the top of the range for a specified time period or number of price candles.

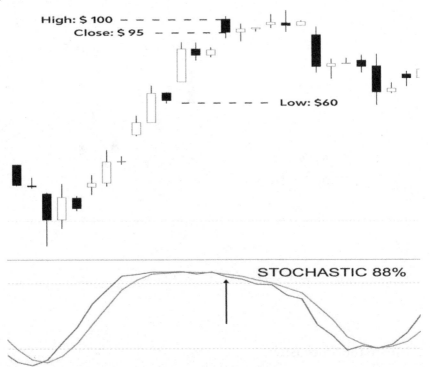

The graph indicates that the low was $60, the high was $100 (a $40 range), and the price closed almost exactly at the top, at $95. The Stochastic indicator is at 88%, indicating that the price closed only 12% (100% - 88%) below the absolute top.

How to calculate a high Stochastic:

- The 5 candles' lowest low: $ 60.
- The 5 candles' highest point: $ 100.

- The previous candle's close: $95

The Stochastic indicator's value is [(95 - 60) / (100 - 60)] 88% x 100

As you can see, the high Stochastic indicates that the price was extremely strong over the previous 5 candles and that recent candles are pushing higher. In contrast, a low Stochastic value indicates that the downside momentum is strong. As shown in the graph, the price closed only $5 above the range's low of $50.

Calculate the Stochastic

- The 5 candles' lowest low: $ 50.
- The 5 candles' highest point: $ 80.
- The previous candle's close: $55
- The stochastic indicator's value is [(55 – 50) / (80 – 50)] * 100 = 17%

Stochastic of 17% indicates that price closed only 17% above the range low, indicating that downside momentum is very strong.

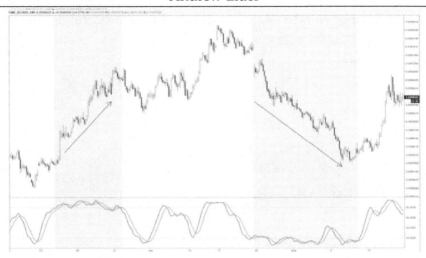

Stochastic Signal

Finally, I'd like to outline the most frequently used signals and strategies for traders to employ the Stochastic indicator:

When the Stochastic suddenly accelerates in one direction and the 2 Stochastic bands widen, this can indicate the start of a new trend. Even better if you can also identify a breakout from a sideways range.

- **Following the trend:** As long as the Stochastic remains crossed in one direction, the trend is still valid. When the Stochastic oscillates between oversold and overbought levels, avoid fighting the trend and instead attempt to hold onto your trades and ride the trend.

- **Strong trends:** At this point, the Stochastic is in the overbought/oversold area, at this point try to stick to the trend.

Overbought and Oversold can be used as trendfollowing signals.

- **Trend reversals:** When the Stochastic oscillates in a new direction and moves away from the overbought/oversold areas, this may indicate a trend reversal. As we shall see, the Stochastic can also be used effectively in conjunction with a moving average or trendlines. In order to identify a bullish reversal, the green Stochastic line must cross above the red one and exit the overbought-oversold area.
- **Divergences:** As with any momentum indicator, divergences can be a critical signal, in this case, indicating potential trend reversals or, at the very least, the end of a trend.

Using the Stochastic in Conjunction with Other Tools

As with any other trading concept or tool, the Stochastic indicator should not be used in isolation. To obtain meaningful signals and to enhance the quality of your trades, you can combine the Stochastic indicator with the following 3 tools:

- **Moving averages:** They are an excellent addition to this strategy because they act as filters for your signals. Always trade in the direction of your moving averages and look for longs only when the price is above the moving average and vice versa.

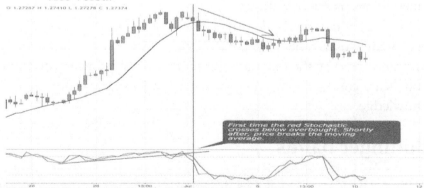

- **Price formations:** As a breakout or reversal trader, you should search for wedges, triangles, and rectangles. It may suggest a good breakout if the price breaks out of this pattern with an accelerating Stochastic.

- **Trendlines:** Stochastic divergence and reversal, in particular, can be traded effectively with trendlines. You must first identify an established trend with a valid trendline and then wait for the price to break it with Stochastic confirmation.

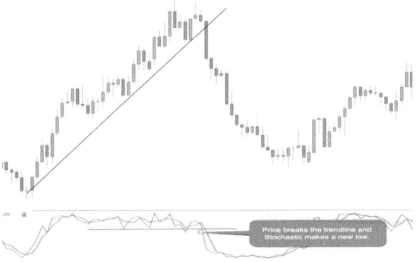

Price breaks the trendline and Stochastic makes a new low.

While you may not require the Stochastic indicator if you are able to read the momentum of your charts simply by looking at the candles, it certainly does not hurt to have it on your charts if the Stochastic is your preferred tool (this goes without a judgment whether the Stochastic is useful or not).

Additionally, traders share a great deal of incorrect information, and even widely used tools such as the Stochastic indicator are frequently misinterpreted by the majority of traders. Do not believe everything you hear; conduct your own research and expand your trading knowledge.

Bollinger Bands

Bollinger Bands are envelopes drawn at a standard deviation above and below the price's simple moving average. Because the bands' distances are based on standard deviation, they adjust to changes in the underlying price's volatility.

These bands are defined by period and standard deviation (StdDev). The default values for a period and standard deviation are 20 and 2, respectively.

Bollinger Bands assist in determining whether prices are relatively high or low. They are used in pairs, with upper and lower bands, and with a moving average. Additionally, the pair of bands is not intended to be used independently. Utilize the pair to validate signals generated by other indicators.

The likelihood of a significant price movement in either direction increases when the bands compress during a time of low volatility. Volatility rises when the bands grow exceptionally wide apart, and any current trend may come to an end. Prices have a tendency to bounce around within the bands' envelopes, touching one and then going to the other. These fluctuations can be utilized to help locate possible profit targets. The upper band becomes the profit objective if the price rebounds off the lower band and subsequently crosses above the moving average.

Price can stretch beyond or hug the band envelope for lengthy periods of time during strong trends. When a momentum oscillator reveals divergence, you may want to do further study to see if taking extra profits is a good idea for you. A significant trend continuation is anticipated if the price breaks out of the bands. If prices quickly return back within the range, however, the indicated strength is lost. Calculate a simple moving average first. Calculate the standard deviation across the same number of periods as the simple moving average. For the upper band, multiply the moving average by the standard deviation. The lower band is obtained by subtracting the standard deviation from the moving average. Typical values include the following:

- **In the short term:** We use a 10-day moving average with bands of 1.5 standard deviations. (1.5 times the standard deviation plus or minus the SMA). In the medium term, a 20-day moving average with bands of 2 standard deviations is used.
- **In the long term:** 50-day moving average, 2.5-standard deviation bands.

Moving Average Convergence Divergence Indicator

The MACD formula is as follows:
- MACD Line: (12-day exponential moving average - 26-day exponential moving average)
- MACD Line's 9-day EMA serves as the signal line.
- Histogram of MACD Lines: MACD Line - Signal Line

You're most likely thinking, "It's far too complicated, and I have no idea what it means." Avoid fleeing. Because I'm about to deconstruct the MACD formula into manageable chunks that even a 10-year-old can comprehend. That sounds reasonable? Then continue reading...

Step by Step De-Mystification of the MACD Indicator

You may now be wondering: "What are the optimal MACD settings?" To be honest, there is no optimal setting because it does not exist. And for this book, I'm going to use MACD's default settings. With that in mind, let us dissect the MACD indicator (step by step). It'll be simple, I assure you.

1. MACD Line

Simply subtract the 12-day EMA from the 26-day EMA (you can find it on your charts with zero calculations). Additionally, poof! This is the MACD Line. Here is an illustration:

MACD Line = 12 EMA - 26 EMA

I told you it was simple, correct?

2. The Signal Line

This becomes even simpler. Simply divide the MACD Line's historical value by nine. That's it; you now have your Signal Line.
Assume you have a MACD Line with these values, a, b, c, d, e, f, g, h, add the numbers together (which equals 45), and divide by nine. As a result, you'll obtain 45/9 = 5.

3. Histogram of the MACD

This is ridiculously simple (to the point of being comical). Simply subtract the MACD Line's value from the Signal Line.

Histogram = MACD Line - Signal Line

That is the MACD Histogram for you. This is what I mean. You may now be wondering, "So, which MACD indicator settings are optimal?" There is no such thing as the optimal MACD settings due to the market's constant movement. What works best at the moment is unlikely to continue to work in the future.
Thus, the critical point is not to optimize for the optimal MACD indicator settings—such a thing does not exist. Rather than that, you should understand the MACD concept in order to apply it to your trading needs.

Frequently Made Errors: How NOT to Use the MACD Indicator

Allow me to share 2 common errors traders make when utilizing the MACD indicator. They are as follows:

MACD Crossover Trading

This technique may be effective in markets that are strongly trending. However, bear in mind that the markets spend the majority of their time in a range. This implies that the MACD crossover will generate numerous false signals, resulting in "death by a thousand cuts."

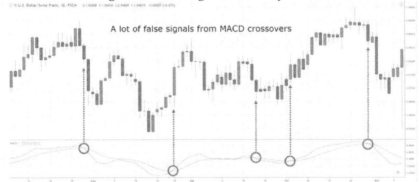

There are now more effective ways to employ the MACD crossover (but more on that later).

MACD Histogram Misinterpretation

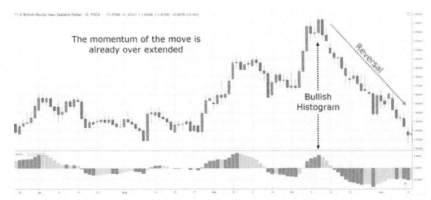

You're most likely thinking: "There is considerable momentum behind the movement. It is time to purchase!" Wrong! Because when such a move occurs, it is frequently too late to enter, and the market will almost certainly reverse. Rather than that, a better strategy is to trade against the trend — and profit from the reversal.

How to Interpret the MACD Histogram and Spot Momentum Reversals

When I first began trading, I enjoyed "chasing" breakouts. The more bullish the candles, the more likely it is that I will purchase the breakout. However, I was hemorrhaging money from my account. That's when I realized I'd entered my trades "late." I purchased when the price was on the verge of reversing direction. This resulted in an AHA moment.

I was curious. "What if I abandoned my pursuit of breakouts?" "How about I took the other side of the trade?" "What if I look for opportunities to short during periods of strong bullish momentum?" It worked significantly better! However, I had difficulty explaining what strong momentum is to traders. So, this is where the MACD histogram is useful.

- Allow time for the price to enter the market structure (like SR, trendline, etc.)
- The MACD histogram demonstrates significant momentum (you want to see a high peak/trough).
- Prior to trading in the opposite direction, wait for price rejection.

Chapter 14
The Best Trades: Putting It All Together

The market is linear—it can only go up or down. When you plot it on a conventional chart with time on the horizontal axis, you add a second dimension, but the market itself is the only price, which means that it has only one dimension. You can make bull and bear bodies have different colors, incorporate volume into the widths of the bodies, or add all kinds of indicators, increasing the number of dimensions, but the market itself is one-dimensional. The recurring theme of these books is that the market is basically simple. It moves up or down because it is constantly searching for the best price, which changes constantly because of unending changes in countless fundamentals. The fundamentals are anything that traders feel is important and include data on every stock, the overall market, politics, natural and manmade events from earthquakes to wars, and international factors. This results in the market always trying to break out from a trading range (its current area of agreement on the value of the market) into a trend, as it searches for the appropriate instantaneous value for the market. If the breakout is to the upside, the bulls are momentarily successfully asserting their opinion that the market is too cheap. If there is instead a downside breakout, then the bears at least briefly are winning their argument that the market is too expensive. Every breakout attempt is met by traders holding the opposite belief, and they will try to make the breakout fail and the market reverse. This is true on every time frame and on every bar and series of bars. The trading range can be a single bar or a hundred bars, and the breakout can last 1 bar or many bars. The key to trading is developing the ability to assess whether the bulls or bears are stronger. When a trader believes that the odds favor one side over the other, they have an edge. The "odds" refers to the trader's equation. An edge (positive trader's equation) exists if the probability of trade reaching their profit target before hitting their protective stop is greater than the probability of the market hitting their stop before reaching their target.

Having an edge allows them to make money by placing a trade. Every type of market does something to make trading difficult. The market is filled with very smart people who are trying as hard to take money from your account as you are trying to take money from theirs, so nothing is ever easy. This even includes making profits in a strong trend. When the market is trending strongly with large trend bars, the risk is great because the protective stop often belongs beyond the start of the spike. Also, the spike grows quickly, and many traders are so shocked by the size and speed of the breakout that they are unable to quickly reduce their position size and increase their stop size, and instead watch the trend move rapidly as they hope for a pullback. Swing traders are often uncomfortable entering on the spike because they prefer trades where the reward is 2 or more times the size of the risk. They are willing to miss a high-probability trade where the reward is only equal to the size of the risk.

Once the trend enters its channel phase, it always looks like it is reversing. For example, in a bull trend, there will be many reversal attempts, but almost all quickly evolve into bull flags. Most bull channels will have weak buy signal bars and the signals will force those bulls who prefer stop entries to buy at the top of the weak channel. This is a low-probability long trade, even though the market is continuing up. Swing traders who are comfortable taking low-probability buy setups near the top of weak bull channels love this kind of price action because they can make many times what they are risking and this more than makes up for the relatively low probability of success.

However, it is difficult for most traders to buy low-probability setups near the top of a weak bull channel. Traders who only want to take high-probability trades often sit back and watch the trend grind higher for many bars, because there may not be a high-probability entry for 20 or more bars. The result is that they see the market going up and want to be long, but miss the entire trend. They only want a high-probability trade, like a high 2 pullback to the moving average. If they do not get an acceptable pullback, they will continue to wait and miss the trend. This is acceptable because traders should always stay in their comfort zone. If they are only comfortable taking high-probability stop entries, then they are correct in waiting. The channel will not last forever, and they will soon find acceptable setups. Experienced traders buy on limit orders around and below the lows of prior bars, and they will sometimes take some short scalps during the bull channel. Both can be high-probability trades, including the shorts if there is a strong bear reversal bar at a resistance level, and some reason to think that a pullback is imminent.

Once the channel phase ends, the market enters a trading range, where there are many strong bull spikes that race to the top and strong bear spikes that race to the bottom. Traders often focus on the strong spike and assume that the breakout will succeed. They end up buying high and selling low, which is the exact opposite of what profitable traders do. Also, the reversals down from the top and up from the bottom usually have weak signal bars, and traders find it hard to take the entries that they have to take if they expect to make money in a trading range. Within a trading range, the probability for most trades hovers around 50%, and only occasionally gets to around 60%. This means that there are few high-probability setups. Also, lots of low-probability events happen, like reversals that don't look good but still lead to big swings and no follow-through after strong spikes. All of this makes it sound impossible to make money as a trader, but if you go back to each relevant section, you will remember that there are profitable ways to trade the market, no matter how it is behaving. Your edge is always going to be small, but if you are a careful, unemotional, and objective reader of the chart in front of you, and only look to take the best trades, you are in a position to make a living as a trader.

There are traders trading for every reason and on all time frames at every second on every chart. What generalities can be made about how discretionary traders, whether institutional or individual, will trade a bull trend? A bull trend begins with a breakout, which is a spike up and can contain one or many bull trend bars. If the breakout fails, the market will fall back into the trading range, and traders will fade the breakout (it will be a final flag reversal) and continue to trade the trading range. When a breakout is strong and successful, most discretionary traders will buy with a sense of urgency. They will buy at the market, on small pullbacks, at the close of the bar, and above each prior bar. Once the market transitions into a channel, they will buy below the low of the prior bar, like below low 1 and low 2 signal bars, expecting reversal attempts to fail (in a trend, most reversal attempts fail), and above the high of the prior bar, like above high 1, high 2, and triangle buy setups. They will then buy pullbacks from the breakouts of these small bull flags. They will even buy the first breakout of a bear microchannel in a strong bull trend, knowing that there might not be a breakout pullback setup until after the market has rallied many bars.

Early on, when the trend is strong, they will buy on new breakouts above prior swing highs, but as the 2-sided trading (selling pressure) increases, as seen by more and larger bear trend bars and more bars with tails on their top, traders will begin to sell above prior swing highs. Most will be selling to take profits on their longs, but as the slope of the channel becomes flatter and the pullbacks become deeper, more traders will start to short above swing highs, looking for scalps.

When the 2-sided trading increases to the point that the bears are about as strong as the bulls, traders will see the market as having entered a trading range. This means that they are much less certain that the trend will resume on each rally attempt (they no longer are looking for pullbacks in a strong bull trend, where the breakout usually quickly tests the old high). They will buy low, sell high, and most will scalp. They will look for high 1 and high 2 buy setups near the top of the range and will short above the signal bars, instead of buying up there. At first, they will only look for scalps, like pullbacks to the moving average, the bottom of the trading range, or the bottom of the bull channel. Once they see increasing selling pressure, they will begin to swing some and eventually all of their shorts, and will only look to buy deep pullbacks, lasting 10 or more bars and having 2 or more legs.

After there have been one or more pullbacks where the selling was strong enough to break below the trend line and below the moving average, some bears will look to short the test of the bull trend high, expecting a major trend reversal. They will short a reversal setup at a lower high, a double top, or a higher high, even though they realize that the chance of a swing down might be 40% or less. As long as the reward is much larger than the risk, they have a positive trader's equation, even though the chance of success is relatively low. Bulls will buy reasonable setups at the bottom of the trading range, like on larger high 2 buy setups, wedge bull flags, higher timeframe trend lines, and measured move targets. Traders realize that a trading range is simply a pullback on a higher timeframe chart. When the spike and channel are steep on a 5-minute chart, they together form a simple spike on a higher timeframe chart, like a 15–60-minute chart. The trading range on the 5-minute chart is usually just a pullback on a 15–60-minute chart. When bulls buy near the bottom of a 5-minute trading range, many will hold for a swing up, a breakout to a new high, and a measured move up, even though the probability may be less than 50%. This relatively low-probability swing long has a positive trader's equation because the reward is much larger than the risk.

While in the trading range phase, signals are often unclear, and there is a sense of uncertainty. Most of the signals will be micro double bottoms and tops, and small final flag reversals. This is lower probability trading, and traders have to be careful and quick to take profits (scalp). They must force themselves to buy low and sell high, not buy strong bull spikes near the top of the range and short strong bear spikes near the bottom. Invariably, the spikes look strong, but don't overlook all of the bars before them — in a trading range, most breakout attempts fail. Once the market has entered a trading range, if a leg is in a strong microchannel, lasting 4 or more bars, don't enter on the breakout. Wait to see if the breakout is strong. If so, enter on the pullback from the breakout. If there is a bear microchannel down to the bottom of the range, wait for the bull breakout and look to buy the pullback, whether it forms a higher low, a micro double bottom, or a lower low. If there is a bull microchannel up to the top of the range, wait to sell a lower high, micro double top, or higher high pullback. As with all trades, always make sure that there is an appropriate signal bar.

If the market enters a tight trading range, wait for the breakout, because tight trading ranges trump everything, including every logical reason to take a trade. Using stop entries in a tight trading range is a losing strategy, but the setups always look worthwhile. Instead, patiently wait for the breakout and then decide if it is likely to succeed or fail.

If there is a successful breakout of the top of the entire trading range, the process starts all over again. Traders will see the breakout as a spike and they will look for at least a measured move up. If there is an upside breakout, but it fails and the market reverses, traders will view the trading range as the final flag in the bull trend. If there is then a breakout below the trading range, traders will evaluate the strength of the breakout, and if it is strong, they will repeat the entire process in the opposite direction. The downside breakout from the trading range can occur without first having a failed upside breakout. Instead of a final flag reversal, the trading range can be some other kind of reversal setup, like a double top, a triple top, a head and shoulders top, or a triangle. All that matters is that there is a strong downside breakout, and traders will then expect pullbacks and a bear channel to follow the bear breakout, and then the market to evolve into a trading range, which can be then followed by a bull or bear breakout.

Examples of Best Trades

- Opening reversals where the setup is strong
- Swing for a reward that is at least twice the risk: The probability of success is 50–60%.
- Scalp for a reward that is at least as large as the risk: The probability is about 60–70%.

- Strong reversals, where the reward is at least twice the risk and the probability is 50–60%.
- Major trend reversal: Following a strong break of the trend line, look for a weak trend resumption to fail on a test of the trend's extreme; the reversal signal bar should be strong. After a bear trend, look to buy a higher low, double bottom, or lower low. After a bull trend, look to short a higher high, double top, or lower high.
- Strong final flag reversal after a swing up or down in a trading range or weak channel.
- Buying a third or fourth push down in a bear stairs pattern for a test of the low of the prior push down.
- Selling a third or fourth push-up in a bull stairs pattern for a test of the high of the prior push-up.
- Trading when the channel in a spike and channel day or the breakout in a trending trading range day reaches a measured move target and the move is weakening.
- Buying a high 2 pullback to the moving average in a bull trend.
- Selling a low 2 pullback to the moving average in a bear trend.
- Buying a wedge bull flag pullback in a bull trend.
- Selling a wedge bear flag pullback in a bear trend.
- Buying a breakout pullback after a breakout from a bull flag in a bull trend.
- Selling a breakout pullback after a breakout from a bear flag in a bear trend.
- Buying a high 1 pullback in a strong bull spike in a bull trend, but not after a strong buy climax.
- Selling a low 1 pullback in a strong bear spike in a bear trend, but not after a strong sell climax.
- Shorting at the top of a trading range, especially if it is a second entry.
- Buying at the bottom of a trading range, especially if it is a second entry.

Entering using limit orders requires more experience reading charts because the traders are entering a market that is going in the opposite direction to their trade. Traders should only use the limit orders to trade in the direction of the trend. For example, if a trader is thinking about using a limit order to buy at the low of the prior bar, they should only do so if the market is always in long, or they think that it is likely to immediately switch to always in long. They should never buy with the intention of scalping the long and then shorting once the low 2 sell setup forms if they believe that the market is still always in short and is likely to have only one smaller push-up. The probability of success is simply too low when using limit orders to trade countertrend. The low probability results in a losing trader's equation and you will lose money unless you are an exceptionally profitable and experienced scalper.

Surprises in trends are usually in the direction of the trend, so when you think that the low 1 in a bear trend is weak and that the market should have one more push-up, the odds are too great that it will not. However, experienced traders can reliably use limit or market orders with these potential best trade setups:

- Buying a bull spike in a strong bull breakout at the market or on a limit order at or below the low of the prior bar (entering in spikes requires a wider stop and the spike happens quickly; this combination is difficult for many traders).
- Selling a bear spike in a strong bear breakout at the market or on a limit order at or above the high of the prior bar (entering in spikes requires a wider stop and the spike happens quickly; this combination is difficult for many traders).
- Buying at or below a low 1–2 weak signal bar on a limit order in a possible new bull trend after a strong reversal up or at the bottom of a trading range.
- Shorting at or above a high 1–2 weak signal bar on a limit order in a possible new bear trend after a strong reversal down or at the top of a trading range.
- Buying at or below the prior bar on a limit order in a quiet bull flag at the moving average.
- Shorting at or above the prior bar on a limit order in a quiet bear flag at the moving average.

- Buying below a bull bar that breaks above a bull flag, anticipating a breakout pullback.
- Selling above a bear bar that breaks below a bear flag, anticipating a breakout pullback.
- When trying for a swing in a bull trend, buying or buying more on a breakout test, which is an attempt to run breakeven stops from an earlier long entry.
- When trying for a swing in a bear trend, selling or selling more on a breakout test, which is an attempt to hit breakeven stops from an earlier short entry.
- Buying a pullback in a strong bull trend at a fixed number of ticks down equal to or slightly less than the average prior pullbacks.
- Selling a pullback in a strong bear trend at a fixed number of ticks up equal to or slightly less than the average prior pullbacks.
- When a bear trend is about to break into a bull trend and needs one more bull trend bar to confirm the always in reversal, and the breakout does not look strong, sell the close of the bull breakout bar, expecting the follow-through bar not to confirm the always in flip and the bear trend to resume.
- When a bull trend is about to break into a bear trend and needs one more bear trend bar to confirm the always in reversal, and the breakout does not look strong, buy the close of the bear breakout bar, expecting the follow-through bar not to confirm the always in flip and the bull trend to resume.

Top 10 Rules for Successful Trading

Here are some guidelines that beginners should consider following until they are consistently profitable (at that point, they can expand their repertoire):

1. Take a trade only where you are going for a reward that is at least as large as your risk. When starting out, focus on trades where the reward is at least twice as large as the risk.

2. Take trades only if you think they probably will work. Don't even worry about how far the move might go. You have to simply ask yourself if the setup looks good. If so, you should assume that the probability is at least 60%. With the potential reward at least as large as the risk, this creates a positive trader's equation.
3. Enter only on stops.
4. Always have a protective stop in the market, because belief and hope will not protect against a premise that is failing.
5. Have a profit-taking limit order in the market so that you will not get greedy and watch your profit disappear as you hope for more.
6. Buy only above bull bars and short below bear bars.
7. Trade only a small position size. If you think that you can trade 300 shares, you should trade only 100 shares so that you are in "I don't care" mode. This will allow you to be more objective and less easily swayed by emotions.
8. Look for only 3–5 reasonable trades a day. If in doubt, stay out.
9. Look for simple strategies. If something is not clear, wait.
10. The best choices for a trader starting out are trends that develop in the opening range, strong trend reversals, and pullbacks in strong trends.

How Much Do You Buy or Sell?

Many traders try as much as possible to avoid the reality of this question. This question clearly explains money management. It's quite critical to the success of a trader. Let's explain the concept better using an example:

Hypothetically, you've got a certain amount of cash, at this point, you get to ask yourself the question of "how much is best to trade?" being more practical, let's say you've $10,000, how much of this total amount would you want to trade? Will you be smart to ask yourself this question or you will just decide to trade all you've? If you decide to trade all you've, what if you lose all $10,000?

Well, making the best decisions in this kind of situation means investing only about 2% of your capital. 2% of $10,000 means investing only $200. At the point of making this decision, you might as well say to yourself "What is the deal? I have got $10,000 why invest $200? Isn't that too small?" Well, that's not the point.

Conclusion

Technical analysis (TA) is a method of trading based on patterns and trends that emerges from charting stocks and other assets over time. These patterns form trends which are then used to make predictions about stock prices.

Technical traders do this through what are called indicators.

An indicator is a mathematical calculation based on price and volume which generates a signal which can be used to determine trends. Indicators are by no means a modern invention but the use of indicators such as the MACD is relatively new to mainstream traders, having been developed in the 1960s.

This method of trading has become increasingly popular as computers have become more advanced and more people have started using them to look at charts and make decisions about when they should buy/sell assets. This is known as algorithmic trading where traders program computer algorithms to automatically make trades for them based on conditions they have specified in their algorithm. Computer trading is also known as high-frequency trading where traders use computer algorithms to buy and sell assets within nanoseconds, separated by fractions of a second.

Traders do this by using indicators on their charts in order to decide when things are likely to change or whether there will be a big change in direction at all. These changes in direction can either be stops or targets and these are decided based on how well the traders' indicators are performing. Traders can then use the information they have gained from this method to make decisions about what to buy and how to sell, if at all.

The idea behind technical analysis is that the stronger the asset's performance is over a longer time period, the more likely it is to continue that movement for a little while longer and vice versa. So, if an asset has been going up for a long time, traders will want to take advantage of what they think will happen next and vice versa. Over time, this method can make profits from the stock market if things pan out as traders expect them to.

However, just because there is a strong uptrend in place doesn't mean that this uptrend will end tomorrow. Traders can take advantage of this by buying an asset and selling it when its price reaches their target or stop loss. Some traders may even wait until the price goes higher, taking profit along the way. Technical analysis does not guarantee that you will make a profit, though, so traders need to be careful when they use it and must expect to need to take losses if things do not go as planned.

Technical analysis is also known as charting or technical trading because traders rely on charts of assets in order to make their decisions. These charts track changes in prices over time and can give valuable information about how well indicators are performing which can be used to decide on targets or stops.

Technical analysis can also be used to help traders plan for future events in the market such as news or a company announcing its earnings. Technical traders would then try to read through the news and understand how it might affect the asset they are trading. This could then be added to their charts and used as a reference for what is likely to happen next. As a result of this, some traders will chart up-to-date news events and use them as indicators by which they will make their decisions about what to buy or sell.

Technical analysis is not always successful, however. If a trader's analysis is wrong or the asset moves in an unexpected way, the price may move up and down before moving back in the direction of the trader's analysis. This can either cause a loss or make a trader miss out on profits that they could get if they weren't trading based on their analysis.

There are also many different indicators and ways to use technical analysis which can cause traders problems such as getting too caught up in the analysis rather than trading. Trading is important because you need to move fast when prices are changing, but you also need to have a plan first so you know what your next move will be when an opportunity arises. There are so many different aspects to trading that you need to have a plan for what your next move will be before you start. Otherwise, it can be hard to make good decisions.

Glossary

AI/machine learning: Artificial intelligence or machine learning is giving a computer the ability to reprogram itself in the light of the information it has handled—basically, to learn. Computers can be taught to "recognize" chart patterns and will then refine their definition of the pattern by the results.

Algorithm: An algorithm is a mathematical process, or set of rules to be followed in a calculation. Algorithmic trading uses a computer program that places trades according to the rules that have been set.

AMA: Adaptive moving average: Different types include KAMA, JAMA, and HMA, after their inventors Kaufman, Jurik, and Hull. For technical analysis, they work in a similar way to the normal moving averages and EMA.

Ascending Triangle: A formation where the highs and lows form a triangle with the point on the top edge. The price is expected to break out in an upwards direction.

ATR: Average true range: Average trading range, including the averaging out of all gaps.

Backtesting: Running a test of a chart pattern against historical data to see how often a given trade rule would have been successful.

Bar: Shows the open, high, low, and closing price (OHLC) of a stock for a given period in the form of a bar (high/low) with 2 "tabs" showing the open and close.

Bear: Someone who thinks the market or a stock will go down. They are "bearish," that word also describes a chart formation that is likely to lead to a downwards price move.

Behavioral economics: Looking at economics as the sum total of individual actions, and bringing psychology to bear on why participants in an economic market behave the way they do.

Bollinger bands: Bands that are placed one standard deviation above and below the moving average. They're useful because they show the volatility of the price—how much it's likely to swing.

Bond: A kind of security that pays a "coupon" at a given rate of interest, issued by a government or corporation to raise debt funding.

Breakaway gap: A movement through support or resistance which is so strong that the stock "gaps" through the line—that is, opening a trading session above resistance, or below support, leaving a "gap" in the price chart.

Breakout: When a price breaks through a support or resistance line, or out of a chart pattern.

Bull: Someone who thinks the stock market or a particular stock will go up. "Bullish" might describe such a person or a chart formation that suggests the price will go up.

Bull/bear ratio: A market indicator published each week that shows the number of advisors who are bullish against the number who are bearish.

Candlestick: An alternative to the bar, the candlestick draws a box between the opening and closing prices, with a "wick" or "shadow" to show the high and low of the trading session. It is colored white/green if the price went up, black/red if the price went down.

CBOE: Chicago Board Options Exchange, the largest US options exchange.

Change momentum indicator: A technical indicator that uses momentum to identify relative strength or weakness in a market. Similar to the Stochastic indicator.

Channel: The band within which a stock is trading. In a typical chart, if the stock is trading in a horizontal range, you can draw one line joining all the "tops" and one line joining all the "bottoms," and this defines the channel.

Chart: A graphical representation of a stock's price movement.

Close: The closing price of a trading session.

Confirmation bias: When we believe more strongly things that happen to coincide with our existing beliefs.

Congestion: When a stock trades within a very narrow range of prices, showing that buyers and sellers are evenly balanced. It often happens after a major move in the share price.

Consolidation: A stock or security that is neither continuing nor reversing a larger price trend.

Continuation: When a chart pattern shows the share price should break out in the same direction as the existing trend.

Correction: When a share price falls because it has become overbought, but the overall uptrend is not broken.

Crossover line: when the price and an indicator (e.g., a moving average) or 2 indicators (e.g., 2 moving averages) cross each other.

Dead cat bounce: A sharp bounce within a major downtrend. Often, a market crash has a dead cat bounce that can look like recovery but very quickly fails.

Death cross: When the 50-day moving average crosses below the 200-day MA. A bearish indicator.

Derivative: Any security whose price depends on that of another security (e.g., an option, whose price depends on the underlying share).

Descending triangle: A formation where the highs and lows form a triangle with the point at the bottom. The price is expected to break out in a downwards direction.

Dividend: Some shares make a cash payment to their shareholders every quarter (usual in the USA), half-year (in the UK), or sometimes, monthly. This is paid out of the company's profits and is called the dividend. Calculate the dividend as a percentage of the share price and you have the dividend yield, which you can compare with the bank interest rate—it's the money you will be paid on your investment. But of course, in the case of shares, the price can also move up or down, whereas the cash in your bank account, if you put $100 in, stays $100—it's not going to turn into $50 or $125.

Donchian rule: Buying when a stock reaches a 4-week high and selling when it reaches a 4-week low. The Donchian rule relies on momentum—the idea that if the stock has reached a 4-week high it has established an uptrend that ought to continue.

Double bottom: A chart formation where the stock in a downtrend hits a support line twice and bounces off it both times; a breakout into an uptrend is likely.

Elliott Wave: The Elliott Wave principle attempts to identify long-term "waves" based on investor behavior, sometimes using the Fibonacci series.

EMA: Exponential moving average. This attempts to refine the ordinary moving average by giving more weight to more recent price moves.

ETF: An exchange-traded fund, also known as a "tracker," is a fund that replicates an index like the S&P500, Russell 1000, or Dow Jones Industrial Average. It's bought and sold like a normal stock, through a broker, and the big ETFs have tight spreads and low costs so they're a good way to trade the market.

Exhaustion gap: When a stock that has been rising fast gaps down. This shows that the price is no longer being driven by buyers — they are "exhausted."

False breakout/fakeout: When a share price crosses a resistance or support line, but then after a very small movement reverses the move. It's easy to fall into a trap here so make sure your stop-losses are good.

False signal: When a chart appears to be giving a signal, but in fact, it's just "noise." You can help avoid false signals by checking the signal with a second indicator.

Flag: A short-term rectangular trading channel running in the opposite direction to the main trend. You are looking for a signal when the price breaks out of the flag.

FTSE: The FTSE group runs a number of indexes, of which the best known is the FTSE 100, the UK stock market's biggest 100 stocks.

Fundamentals: The business realities behind the share, such as its earnings, assets, brand names, and operations.

Gap: When a share opens a trading session above or below the previous session's closing price and leaves a gap visible on the chart. This can be a strong signal.

Golden cross: 50-day moving average crossing above the 200-day MA. This is a bullish signal.

Guerrilla trading: Very short-term trading which aims for a low profit on each trade but making multiple trades within a trading session, often closing trades within just a few minutes.

Head and shoulders: A chart formation that forms 3 "peaks" with the largest in the middle. It is generally completed by a breakdown from the third peak, signaled by the price closing below the "neckline" joining the lowest prices in the series.

Heiken Ashi bar: Heiken Ashi takes candlesticks and uses an averaging formula to attempt to remove the "noise" from the chart, minimizing false signals.

HFT: High-frequency trading, using computerized orders based on algorithms; can trade many times a second.

High: The highest price reached by a share during any particular formation. Also, 52-week highs, which are reported on financial news pages and websites.

Ichimoku indicators: This is a relatively new technique we have not covered, which attempts to forecast potential price ranges as "clouds." It's based on candlestick charting but tries to extrapolate it forwards.

Index: A "bundle" of shares created by mathematical means (e.g., the S&P 500). The index reflects the aggregate performance of all the component shares.

Indicator: An indicator is based on an arithmetic manipulation of the raw price data. Examples would be a moving average, RSI, Stochastic, or Price by Volume.

Island reversal: A candlestick pattern in which the stock price creates an "island" top or bottom separated by gaps from the "mainland" trends.

Kondratieff wave: Kondratieff waves are very, very long-term waves. Personally, I am not willing to wait 40–60 years to see if my trades work out. Many academic economists don't believe in these waves, either.

Limit order: An order where you state a limit above which you are unwilling to buy, or below which you are unwilling to sell, a stock.

Linear regression line: The "line of best fit" allows all data points to be equally distributed around the line.

Liquidity: The ease with which a given security can be traded. More generally, the volume of trading in the stock market.

Long: To "go long" is to buy and hold shares.

Low: The low point in any given price pattern or formation. 52-week lows can be informative and are found on financial websites alongside other basic price information.

MACD: Moving average convergence divergence indicator. It shows the relationship between 2 moving averages and can show changes in the momentum of the stock price.

Margin: If you trade on margin, you are borrowing money from your broker to buy the stock. I do not advise you do this. It is an easy way to ruin yourself.

Market indicators: These are used to forecast trends for the market as a whole, such as the market breadth index (the ratio between stocks which closed up, and stocks that closed down).

Market order: An order to buy stock "at-the-market," that is, at the best price your broker can get.

Market timing: Trying to buy the market at the bottom and sell at the top. An impossible dream. Good traders are happy with getting 80% of the price action.

Maximum adverse excursion: The largest loss a single trade can suffer while it is open.

MBar or momentum bar (constant range bar): These charts, unlike conventional share price charts, do not show time. A bar is created for each move of a given amount, e.g., 10 cents. Some traders like these because they cut out a lot of "noise."

Mean reversion: The statistical likelihood that eventually extreme values will revert to the mean.

Momentum: The rate of change in prices.

NASDAQ: The second US stock exchange. It is all-electronic trading and has a higher percentage of tech stocks than the New York Stock Exchange.

Noise to signal: "Signal" is what we are looking for, something that tells us when a stock is going to go up or down. "Noise" is all the other stuff. It's like listening to old vinyl—the music is signal, the crackle and scratches are "noise."

NYSE: The New York Stock Exchange.

OBV: On balance volume, an indicator that shows up volume and down volume, giving a feel for how much of the trading volume relates to purchasers/bullish action and how much to sellers/bearish action.

Open: The share price at the opening of a trading session.

Option: A derivative that gives you the right to buy a share at a given price before a given date. It could simply be a private agreement, but most options are standardized and traded. Options are potentially useful because (1) they give you leverage, going up or down more than the share price, and (2) put options enable you to trade downtrends and breakdowns.

Oscillator: An indicator that shows values oscillating in a band between 2 extreme values, e.g., price acceleration between 0–100. RSI, Chaikin, and ROC are all types of oscillators.

Overbought/oversold: When a stock is "overbought," all the interested buyers have already bought it, and it is exposed if any of them decide to sell. Indicators such as RSI and OBV attempt to show when stocks are overbought or oversold.

Pennant: A short-term triangular formation within a defined up or downtrend. It is a continuation pattern, meaning that you'd expect to see the price break out in the same direction as the main trend.

Point-and-figure chart: These charts don't take account of the passage of time but create columns of price rises of a certain magnitude, reversing direction when the price direction changes. So, if a stock price went up to $10 every day for a week, and you had a $10 unit, you would end up with a column of 5 X's (or O's if the price were to go down). They are not much used these days, but the MBar is a more modern version of the same idea.

Put/call ratio: The proportion between put and call options purchased on a given day. It's a good way to measure whether the market is bearish (more puts) or bullish (more calls).

Pyramiding: Involves adding to a winning position as the price moves in the desired direction. It can be a good way to make more profit from a really strong breakout, but the stop-loss for the whole position needs to be reassessed to take account of the higher average purchase price.

Quant: Basically any individual in the investment community who bases their work on mathematics rather than gut feel, fundamentals, philosophy, or hype.

Range contraction: When the range within which the share price varies becomes smaller.

Range expansion: When the range within which the share price varies becomes larger.

Range trading: Identifying the range within which the share price trades, and aiming to buy towards the bottom of the range and sell towards the top of it, again, and again, and again.

Resistance: The concept that a stock will have a certain price level that it has touched several times but never exceeded, and that this forms a "resistance" to a move upwards. Drawing a resistance line is often a useful way of showing this.

Retracement: The amount that a stock "gives back" from a rise (or fall) in the share price before the uptrend (or downtrend) resumes.

Reversal: A change in the overall share price trend.

Risk appetite/risk aversion: A trader's desire to take on more risk, or desire to avoid risk. Risk is a spectrum, and not all traders have the same appetite for risk.

Risk reward ratio: The ratio between the risk you run and the reward you expect. For an individual trade, the ratio between the profit target and the stop-loss.

RSI: Relative strength index. An oscillator that displays bullish and bearish price momentum.

Runaway gap: A gap in the direction of the trend, usually associated with high volume. A bullish indicator.

Security: Any form of negotiable instrument representing financial value (e.g., a stock, bond, or option).

Share: A security entitling the holder to a share in the earnings and assets of a business.

Short: To "go short" is to sell shares you do not own. You will consequently profit if the share price goes down, as you can "cover your short" by buying the shares at a lower price.

Slippage: When your order is executed for a worse price than you expected.

SMA: Simple moving average. The average of the share's price over the last X time periods.

Spike: A sudden and large move in the share price.

Spread: When you buy stocks you pay a higher price than you'd get if you sold—the difference is the "spread" and it's how market makers and specialists make their money. Spread is one of the costs you need to allow for as a trader.

Standard deviation: A measure of how far values differ from the mean. For instance, a class of 10-year-olds probably has a low standard deviation in height; they will all be roughly as tall as each other. SD is one way to measure the volatility of a share price.

Standard error channel: Parallel lines drawn equidistant from the linear regression trend line to form a channel.

Stochastic oscillator: An indicator that shows momentum based on the price history of the asset.

Stop-limit order: An order which specifies a price at which the order becomes valid, and a price limit after which it is no longer valid, e.g., "Sell 100 IBM if the stock price falls below 90 but not if it goes below 95." It's a good way of entering a breakout or breakdown trade.

Stop-loss: The price at which you will close a trade if it goes in the wrong direction. You should always set a stop-loss at the same time as you make your original trade.

Support: A line which the share price repeatedly hits and then bounces. If a stock falls, it will usually stop at the support line, either temporarily, or before returning to higher levels. If a stock falls through the support line, it may well fall all the way to the next support line.

Swing trader: Traders are aiming to make gains by trading a stock and holding it for just a few days. They almost always use technical analysis.

Technical analysis: Reading patterns in the movement of the share price to ascertain the probability of the share price behaving in a particular way in the future.

Tick bars: Tick bars show price movement only if there has been a minimum number of trades.

Tracker: A fund that represents an index that is automatically created and traded on a stock exchange in the same way as a share.

Trailing stop: A stop-loss that is increased as the price of the share goes up so that you can't lose all your gains.

Trend: The general movement in a share price, either upwards, downwards, or sideways.

Trendline: A line that can be drawn to show the trend.

Triple top: Where the share price forms 3 peaks all hitting the same resistance level. The third time, it is likely to break downwards.

VIX index: An index that measures share price volatility.

Volatility: The amount of change in a share price. A share price that tends to move 1% a day is much less volatile than one that swings by 5–10% some days.

Volume: The amount of shares traded on a single day.

Wedge: A chart formation in which the share price forms a wedge that is pointing up or down in the opposite direction to the trend. The price should break out in the direction of the trend.

Whipsaw: A sudden change in the direction of the share price. Sometimes a whipsaw happens before a real breakout, which can be deceptive.

WMA: Weighted moving average.

Create Automatic Income for Life Immediately!

Forex Signals.

High Conversions Verified Forex Results.

https://1e503-r5sjod5kcm4z3ggybs8j.hop.clickbank.net

OR

BOTS Live Trading Room

https://db240ys-r9r60z39q8rgnkuklg.hop.clickbank.net

BOOK 2

CRYPTO TRADING

A Guide for Beginners to Know About Cryptocurrency Market, Crypto Investing, and Cryptocurrency Mining

Introduction

C rypto trading is a term often used when referring to the buying and selling of cryptocurrencies. This includes coins such as Bitcoin, Ethereum, Litecoin, Tether, and many more. Crypto trading can be done by opening an account with a crypto exchange like GDAX or Bitstamp.

With over 700 cryptocurrencies in existence today it's hard to keep up with them all on your own. There are quite a few exchanges that offer this service for traders who want to buy and sell cryptocurrencies on their trading platforms such as Coinbase and Poloniex. You need to know which exchanges support your desired coin.

Some trading sites have very advanced trading features, while some are still quite basic. The main differences between them are how they handle depositing, withdrawing, and storing of funds as well as different fees and charges for each exchange.

As someone new to crypto trading you may not want to jump into the deep end without any knowledge. You should learn as much as you can about the coins you're interested in before you start trading them. Investing in something means a bet on its future developments and potential earning that future stream of income based on your prediction of its success. The more informed you are about the market and your investment, the better decisions you'll make. You can discover useful information about any digital currency by researching them. Research can be done on Coin Market Cap or Reddit. There are also many crypto trading guides available online, which can help you to know more about the coins and trade them safely. The crypto trading guides are taught for all novice traders and novices in order to provide useful information that is easy to understand and implement.

Another easy way to learn about the coins is just by reading their whitepapers. This way you will gather knowledge about their goals and objectives based on technology, development team as well as their current state of development.

Know your investment. Before you start trading, it is important to have a good understanding of blockchain technology and the coin you are investing in. This is where most new traders fail, as they rush into trading without first considering if the coin has a future, if it is active, and what features does it offer. All these need to be carefully considered before deciding whether to invest or not.

Don't just rely on one exchange for all your coins' needs either (although you can do that too). If one goes down for whatever reason, you'll have a backup option for all of your coins. Having many exchanges also means fewer fees directly from the original exchange itself.

If you are trading large amounts of money each month, it is vital to pick a crypto exchange with low fees. Therefore, if you are trading for less than $10,000 you should choose a platform that charges a 0.10% fee per transaction. Be aware that most platforms offer discounts for using bank accounts when withdrawing and depositing money.

If your crypto exchange doesn't give you the option to toggle between fiat and cryptocurrencies easily enough then it's time to move on. While the number of digital currencies continues to increase so does their usefulness as a form of payment. A good example of this is Monero, which has been designed for exactly this purpose—transactions that cannot be linked to an individual user. Therefore, only trade on exchanges that allow you to easily toggle between cryptocurrencies and fiat.

Always double-check before you hit that buy or sell button. Once you have confirmed the trade of your coin it is then processed quite quickly, but if you don't check it properly and make a mistake, you will end up losing your valuable coins. So it's always best that once you are done with the confirmation of the transaction then don't move away from your computer. If this is not possible, make sure that someone else checks for mistakes before they go through with a transaction, if this is not possible then write down your order's details and leave it near to your computer for someone to spot any mistake.

The beginners are often also confused about what is the best exchange platform for them. There are many options available and they all vary depending on the fees, features, and locations of each platform. For instance, a discount platform in India will not allow you to trade in crypto coins as well as fiat currency due to its rules. Moreover, some exchanges offer free trading while others charge a commission fee of around 1% which is quite a big amount that you should not be charged on your first transaction with the exchange. However, before opting to join an exchange it is important to consider the factors below:

Decide if you want an exchange that has advanced trading features or one that offers better security.

Does the exchange support your currency? If it doesn't support your desired coin, then do not use that exchange.

Choose a platform that offers the lowest transaction fees and the highest level of security. This is quite hard as crypto exchanges often offer different features and trade volumes based on fees per transaction. So you would have to find the right balance in this regard.

Consider where the trading platform is located as some countries will not allow you to trade in their currency for legal reasons. Choose an exchange that allows access to a wide variety of coins and fiat currencies such as USD, GBP, EUR, etc.

Some investors have successfully used Coinmama to purchase bitcoins and other crypto coins. Coinmama is a UK-based cryptocurrency broker that promises to provide you with all the necessary information for purchasing Bitcoin or any other coin. If you are a beginner, then you definitely want to consider this option as it will be quite easy for you.

The popularity of Bitcoin has led many startups to create their own cryptocurrencies in the hope of gaining market share. You can buy these tokens from sites such as AirBitz, Bittrex, and Poloniex. Some of these exchanges offer no-fee trading while some charge a small percentage fee for every trade made. The fee structure often depends on how much traffic the exchange receives.

Hence, if you are a beginner, you should be careful about using these platforms to purchase your coins. But if you have enough experience and knowledge of the crypto market, then you can take advantage of this option which will allow you to buy your coins in less than five minutes.

Once you have started investing in cryptos, don't invest more than what you can afford to lose. If things go wrong then don't blame yourself or anyone else; instead just move on. Remember that investing in cryptos is not for the faint-hearted.

Now that you know the basics you should now be able to decide whether it is worth buying an alt-coin on the exchange or you should wait for its value to grow on its own. But don't keep it all to yourself as sharing is caring and it makes things more fun too!

Chapter 1
What Is a Cryptocurrency?

Cryptocurrencies, or cryptos, are peer-to-peer digital forms of monetary transactions that are decentralized. In that respect, it functions like cash, allowing you to give it to anybody who takes it in return for products or services. You may also trade it for another cryptocurrency or fiat cash.

Cryptocurrency is a word that combines two terms: one mathematical and one financial. Cryptology is the term used to describe almost impenetrable codes and ciphers. It's the stuff of espionage movies and suspense. But, at the end of the day, it's all about arithmetic. Cryptography is a difficult subject because of specific mathematical principles. In essence, it's about encoding anything for transmission that can't be decoded if intercepted, and it can't be changed or duplicated. It's almost as if it's a thumbprint of the element, message, or underlying material it's transporting.

Cryptography comes in a variety of forms. If you're using a computer that interacts securely online, the message is encrypted so that only the sender and receiver know the code to decode the data. To ensure this, the encryption employs cryptography.

The term's second element is currency. Currency has only recently come to signify the notion of fungible exchange. That is to say, you may trade it for anything. You may use it to purchase a car one day and donate the next. Currency is the most effective means to conduct transactions since it is used in nearly every aspect of human life. People continue to use the barter system, in which one set of products is swapped for another, but they eventually return to utilizing the value of the transaction in currency. Apart from the ease of being written on paper and carried or held as the value on a debit or credit card, cash may be used to give value to everything from vehicles to bridges, services to ice cream.

When you put them all together, you have a system that employs cryptography to encrypt and value a transaction. It may be broadly distributed for consumption by encapsulating it and assigning it a value, making the effort to sell or acquire it much easier. However, the previous model of money was discovered to be deficient in the implementation of this reality, in that the value of that currency could be controlled by governments. Because the government producing the currency has opted to issue additional money and dilute the value, what might purchase one ream of paper today may only be able to buy half a ream tomorrow. One of the things we needed was a mechanism to ensure that no single authority could manipulate the world's currencies, ensuring that everything remained stable and based entirely on supply and demand.

There are arbitrary pegs and movements in today's currency market to hold a currency at artificial levels. One country's monetary and fiscal policies may have an impact on someone on the other side of the world. This is not a disadvantage of decentralized currencies, which are utilized to do business all around the world. Bitcoins cannot be printed, nor can their circulation be expanded just because some government requires it.

Another characteristic of the cryptocurrency is that it was meant to not be raised beyond a specific amount in circulation, based on the principles and procedures established by the inventor and developers of Bitcoin (who we still don't know who they are).

Consider it for a moment. You have a currency in which the number of coins in circulation will never rise. The only thing that can happen to it is that it disintegrates into little pieces. So, if 1 BTC is worth $10,000 today, 0.1 BTC is worth $1000. This has two consequences. The first is that no one can influence the value of BTC by injecting additional BTC into the system. The second possibility is that demand for BTC will eventually outstrip supply, resulting in BTC's value rising in lockstep over time and fractioning lower and lower.

So, for example, we may end up dividing 1 BTC into a thousand parts, with each fraction valued at $10. This sounds eerily similar to a stock split. When you think about it, that's precisely what it is. The price of the underlying asset may change to reflect the new reality at that time. The lowest fraction or unit of Bitcoin ever transacted is 100,000,000th of a BTC, or 0.00000001 BTC, at the time of writing. At a $10,000 conversion rate, that equates to .01 cents in equal dollar worth.

However, because fractionating the currency is the same as creating additional money, the gain you may have realized is gone. It isn't the case. A sovereign decides whether or not to print new money. BTC's price is entirely determined by the market. It is impossible to sway the market once it has become large enough unless there is a coordinated, worldwide effort to do so.

All of these characteristics combine to make cryptocurrencies, such as Bitcoin, ideal assets for speculative trading. For the reasons we mentioned before, the speculative trading market, whether it is for FX or cryptocurrencies, is a mutually advantageous scenario. Speculative players provide the market with the liquidity it needs to function as a strong basis, while simultaneously providing liquidity to transactional users.

Things appear to be hazardous and risky without a central authority and the power of law to protect the transactions. But that's precisely what Satoshi had in mind when he created the money. The Bitcoin market is unaffected by short-term and shortsighted manipulation since it is free of influence by agencies and central banks, as well as treasury departments that are generally held to political vagrancies.

This calls into doubt the requirement for records to be preserved. There is no need for trust because the faith that is normally placed in public authorities to do the right thing is usually backed up by legislation. All of these consequences, however, appear after the crime, when it is too late. As a result, the Bitcoin system does not involve trust as a component. Instead, everything is controlled by records. Each transaction's history is recorded, from the initial block of BTC to the most recent one transacted just a few minutes ago.

What is the location of its preservation? Every bitcoin transaction is saved on every node. Every computer that connects to the BTC network is referred to as a node. It is based on the peer-to-peer (P2P) model. Everyone on the network or utilizing the service is considered a member of the P2P system (peer-to-peer system). Every node in this scenario is a computer that is logged into the system. A client is installed on each computer, which creates a network channel and turns the machine into a node.

Chapter 2
Why Make Trading in Crypto?

Nowadays, various people are deciding to contribute with advanced cash. This is because there is no vital total or paper to take care of a segment of your money. Any aggregate will achieve for the endeavor, except if you need to contribute a more prominent total to have two-fold or triple profit. Shooting graphs of computerized types of cash costs attract various individuals to risk everything.

Computerized types of cash rise and drop every so often, if you contributed thousands at this moment and have it in millions in the accompanying 4–5years. There is in like manner a possibility of losing the money you have contributed, so attempt to contribute what you can lose.

Bitcoin, quite possibly the most standard cryptographic cash on earth, has driven various examiners and sellers in the earlier years. Various dealers add to this coin, not because it's the top crypto of the thousand years, yet it is the most gainful one. If you decide to add to such an industry, know the benefits and inconveniences first before doing accordingly.

Advantages

- **Easy access:** Cryptocurrency is open with no attempt at being subtle and can be utilized by everyone. Monetary experts wherever on the planet can, without a doubt, get to because of the decentralized action. Portion trades have been simplified, while there is reliably a specialist adding costs for each trade you make in a regular portion system.

- **Private:** With advanced cash, you don't need to divide your information or each trade's nuances, besides the beneficiary. The whole of the trades is ensured about the use of "Cryptography." When a cryptographic cash move has been affirmed, it can't be upsets or charge-back, this shields the customers from coercion and hacking.

- **Lower fees:** Unlike while using a Visa, you need to pay for revenue, with cryptographic cash charges and costs won't ever be an issue. You ought to just investigate what is the best wallet to use that arranges such a Cryptocurrency you are using. This can moreover be a critical good situation for pioneers.

- **Mobile payments:** If you are struggling with revealing the whole of your ID when purchasing web using your cards, and monetary adjust, well Cryptocurrency just made it ideal for you. You can do portions and purchase to online stores without giving any near and dear information through the web or recipient, simply your wallet address will be observable to them. You can do these trades using your wireless.

Disadvantages

- **Price volatility:** The shakiness of computerized cash is the central obstacle you to must consider. The unusualness is the peril level of the instrument where cost is assessed. Thusly, placing assets into Bitcoin or some other online financial principles is hazardous, because the assessment of your money exchanged with them has no affirmation. It can climb to millions or perhaps billion anyway it can moreover go to nothing, no one can tell since no one controls it.

- **Possible government interface:** The public authority can't take your coins; notwithstanding, they can do such exercises on the off chance that they will decide to blacklist every single one of those computerized monetary forms in a particular country. In case the public position determination online wallets and associations to shut down the whole of your Bitcoins, etc., will be freeze and it will be a troublesome chance to get to them.

- **No refunds:** Refund is a No while using cryptographic cash, especially Bitcoins, for instance, you get something on the web, and the vendor fails to pass on your purchased things, you can't demand a rebate box Bitcoins. Some cryptographic types of cash, for instance, Ripple, have given chargeback decisions; notwithstanding, this won't ever exist on Bitcoins.

Best Cryptocurrency to Invest

- **Bitcoin:** Despite all the issues experienced by Bitcoin really remains the number 1 choice for placing assets into computerized cash. With a market cap of $134 billion, Bitcoin stays the best cryptocurrency on earth. This cryptocurrency fills in as a store and portion system all the while, allowing customers successfully to send and got portions on the web. Bitcoin has been keeping watch for quite a while, and no one can, without a doubt, break the weakness of this shrewd creation.
- **Ethereum:** Ethereum has set up itself as the second greater cryptographic cash on the planet lately. There are right now countless people who are holding such virtual cash. The limit of Ethereum to be second in the overview can be its quality for bringing a higher motivating force up shortly.
- **Litecoin:** This coin is quite possibly the most settled cryptographic cash streaming in the market now. It has a genuine component of security, taking care of data, and trade time. Litecoin shows a magnificent improvement like Bitcoin, no one knows, perhaps in a couple of years, this cryptographic cash will pull in an outstandingly high worth the market.

Chapter 3
Recognizing the Risks of Cryptocurrency

efore you begin the cryptocurrency business, you have to ensure that you consider the risks attached to it. This risk is defined by the ungrounded things that surround the profit that you will eventually make. When approaching an opportunity, we have to do it individually. The things that appear as high risks before you may not be the same for another person since we all have different lifestyles and financial states. And due to the volatility of the cryptocurrency business, we have seen several investors make millions of dollars, while the rest end up making little to no profit. Sometimes, it's even huge losses some of these people come out with. So, yes, learning about the risks attached is highly important.

Cryptocurrency Returns

There are several assets out there that generate different kinds of returns. For instance, one source of recovery could be the change in the value of an investment. You could also create an income in the form of dividends or interests when you invest in stock markets or forex markets. The investors would usually refer to these interests as capital gains and current income, respectively. Most people would invest in the crypto market for capital gains, but then, other people would invest for the current income opportunities.

Capital Gains... or Losses

One common reason that people invest in the crypto business is to get gains in the coins' value. They'd link the coins with precious metals such as gold because only a limited amount of it is available in the crypto market. So, if you want to extract many of these precious metals, you'd have to mine. The art of currency mining would be discussed later in this book. With that technique, most of the investors out there usually regard cryptocurrencies as assets even though they are basically assets employed for transaction purposes. So, when people buy them, they buy them with the mindset that they'd sell them once the prices rise to a large extent. If one is lucky enough it gets the value of the asset rise higher from the time it was purchased, one could get capital gains on selling the token. However, if the prices fall, you end up with a capital loss.

Income

Income is a type of return that falls in the lower cadre. An income is usually gotten from crypto dividends. These dividends occur when the public companies share a portion of their earnings to the shareholders. The types of dividends include cash payments, shares of stock, or some other asset. Earning dividends in the crypto market can be complicated because different currencies have different operating systems bound by different rules and regulations. However, the concept remains the same. When selecting a cryptocurrency for your portfolio, you have to ensure that you look into the crypto dividends and the potential of the capital gains. Some ways by which you can earn crypto dividends include the following:

- **Staking:** This involves you holding a proof-of-stake coin in a unique wallet.
- **Holding:** This involves you buying and holding crypto in any wallet you have.

Risks

Now, this is the stage where you get to realize that even though investments are great, you'd still have to consider the risks. The greater the investments you make, the greater the risks involved. And since cryptocurrencies are even riskier than other assets, they will fetch higher returns. The tie between a risk and a return is called the risk-return take-off. One mistake that most people make is thinking that the cryptocurrency business is a get-rich-quickly scheme. You should ensure that you do not invest your life savings or take out loans just to invest in it. You have to first understand what it means to be tolerant of risks before you sketch out an investment strategy suitable for you. You also have to bear in mind that those who made severe returns waited years before they got to such levels.

Types of Risks in the Cryptocurrency Business

1. Crypto Hype Risk

This refers to the hype that surrounds the cryptocurrency trade. The main reason that most people lose in this business is that they don't have full knowledge of what they are pouring their investments into. So, most times, they just operate in the market based on what they are told. The hype of the crypto business was one of the things that contributed to the market becoming hot at some moments. However, the moment the hype dies, the prices would immediately crash. Here are a few terminologies that are tied to this kind of risk.

FOMO

This term stands for "Fear of Missing Out." This is the kind of risk that plays out when you lay your fingers in a cryptocurrency that you don't have access to just because you notice an immediate boost in its value. You have to ensure that you stay away from such careless moves! If the price rises, it indeed would eventually crash one day or the other. So, it would be better if you allowed the hype to die down before buying. At least, then, you'd get it at low prices.

FUD

This term stands for "Fear, uncertainty, and doubt." It is what you want to use when you hear someone talking down the market. In September 2017, Jamie Damon, who is JPMorgan Chase's CEO, spread one of the biggest FUDs by calling the business of Crypto "fraud." In January 2018, he faced the consequences of him saying those words.

ATH

This term stands for "All-Time-High." You make use of it when you notice that the price of an asset has reached the highest point.

Bag Holder

In this business, bag holders are bought out of the FOMO at an ATH, and after that, lost the opportunity to sell. After that, they were left with wallets of valueless coins.

BTFD

This term stands for "Buy the fucking dip." If you want to escape being a bag holder, you have to ensure that you do as this term says!

Before purchasing any crypto asset, you have to ensure that you equip yourself with as much knowledge as you can lay your hands upon. Patience and understanding are some of the few things that contribute to an excellent business strategy.

2. Security Risk

This kind of risk has a lot of things to do with theft and scams. And unfortunately, this issue has been one of the most prevalent issues in the business. With every occurrence of theft, it was noticed that the value of the currencies dropped by certain levels. To prevent issues, a few things will be discussed here.

The Cryptocurrency

As mentioned earlier, hundreds of cryptocurrencies have been made available for investment purposes. However, you have to ensure that you plan on investing in choosing the cryptocurrency that you acquaint yourself with every detail on the protocols surrounding the blockchain network. You should also ensure that there are no bugs that could affect your investments. For this step, too, you might need to take note of the company's protocols.

These protocols are defined as rules and regulations that a specific blockchain network has agreed upon. To find out the nature of these protocols, you can check the website's white paper. The paper is a document that the crypto founders assemble to know more about a particular cryptocurrency. Most of the crypto issuers that can be trusted would correct issues the moment a bug is found. If they fail to do that, immediately cut off any ties you have with their coins.

The Exchange

Exchanges are platforms where you can trade cryptocurrency tokens. So, you have to ensure that whoever hosts your trading is of high integrity and credibility. The exchanges that are the most susceptible to attacks are the ones that are exchanged. Before you choose an exchange, you have to ensure that you look at the section for securities on the website. You should also ensure that there are no bug programs attached too.

Your Wallet

The last round of a security check is something that you need to do yourself as it involves you knowing what kind of crypto wallet you use. Even though these coins are usually not taken from one place to another, you could easily keep them in safe physical wallets. The private and public keys that you use for transacting with your altcoins can also be stored in these wallets.

3. Volatility Risk

This is the kind of risk that comes up in unexpected market movements. The volatility can sometimes be favorable, but then, most times, it catches a person off guard. Sometimes, the crypto market could move in directions opposite what you expected. So, consequently, you could end up losing the money you invest in the markets. Several factors contribute to the volatility of a call, and among them include the inception of technologies such as the Internet.

The best way by which you can ward off a volatility issue is by seeing things as they are. IF you have short-term investments, you should be able to find indicators as to how much money you can make or lose over a while. However, for long-term investments, volatility can turn into a very significant opportunity for you. To offer offset volatility risks, you could use automated trading algorithms on various exchanges. This technique will help you to reduce the risk of volatility to a large extent.

4. Liquidity Risk

This kind of risk involves you not being able to sell an investment in a short enough time to make a decent profit. It is an essential factor to be considered for every tradable asset. The forex market is seen as one of the most liquid markets in the whole world. When you trade currencies with meager volumes, you may not close your trade because of static prices. That is where the lack of liquidity can be a huge problem.

The issue of liquidity was one factor that led to the high volatility in cryptocurrencies like Bitcoin. When the liquidity is low, the risk of price manipulations would then come to play. Consequently, you would see a trader move the market in their favor by placing massive orders. These kinds of traders are usually referred to as "whales" in the crypto market. As crypto investments become more available, the market would usually become even more liquid. The rise in the number of trusted crypto exchanges will only offer opportunities for more people to trade.

One more key thing that certifies a cryptocurrency's liquidity is countries' take on the crypto regulations. Once the authorities can explain issues such as the ones relating to consumer protection and crypto taxes, more people would end up being comfortable with the trading of cryptocurrencies. That usually would lead to the liquidity of the currencies being affected. So, before you choose crypto to trade with, ensure that you check for its liquidity, check out its degree of acceptance, popularity, and the number of exchanges that it has been sold on.

5. Vanishing Risk

An example of a vanishing chance is the dot-com bubble. In the nineteenth century, several people worldwide usually planned businesses built on the internet's popularity. This way, sites like Amazon were able to rise to very high levels. Some others weren't that lucky and ended up crashing. To minimize the effect of a vanishing risk, you may need to sort out the fundamentals of the cryptocurrencies you decide to invest in.

- Do their goals capture you?
- Are they tackling issues that will continue even on the close dates?
- Who are the people partnering with them?

6. Regulation Risk

This issue is one of the things that attract people to the business of cryptocurrency. Since there were practically no rules in the olden days, the traders did not have to worry about being hunted down by the government. All they had with them were the sheets of white paper and sweet words. However, as the demand for cryptocurrencies grew, regulators worldwide began to scratch their heads on how they could keep up with the speed of the business. Most of the digital currencies out there aren't backed up by the central governments, which only means that each country has different standards.

You could also get to divide the cryptocurrency regulation risk into two different components. One is the regulation event risk, and the second is the regulation's nature. The first one may not mean that the crypto market is performing poorly. Sometimes, it could mean that the members of the market responded to an unexpected announcement. Most of the seemingly small regulations usually drove the price of the majority of the cryptocurrencies to a high level. There were no global crypto regulators for the latter, so most of the regulations were over the board. In some countries like Japan, though, the cryptocurrency exchanges were legally registered. Some other countries like China have been a bit stricter on cryptocurrencies, with a bit of leniency on the blockchain industries.

7. **Tax Risk**

This is a type of risk that involves the payment of taxes. At the inception of this trade, people weren't made to pay taxes from their returns. However, as more regulation policies began to rise, the authorities got a lot stricter with the taxation policies. In 2018, the U.S Internal Revenue Service perused the cryptocurrency trading systems. Although almost all of the investments made into the crypto trading business are prone to increases in the tax rate, the industry remained a fuzzy area.

Risk Management Methods

The only way anyone could achieve their investment goals is by investing at a consistent level with their view on risk tolerance. You can measure your tolerance to risks by weighing options like your investment goals, the time you have allotted to each of the plans, and so many other factors. You could also increase your tolerance to risks by setting goals that last for more extended periods and adding to your savings with methods like online investments and your current liquidity.

To measure your risk tolerance, we would go through a few points. First, you need to know that the subjects have two major components. One is your willingness to take risks, while the other is your ability to risk something. If you met a financial planner, you might be asked to fill forms that adequately measure your willingness to take risks. The records usually would contain questions on issues on risk-taking. The result determines whether or not you are averse to risks or tolerant of them.

A risk-averse investor would require that they have more returns before they can think of investing in higher-risk investments. A risk-tolerant investor, on the other hand, would need that they are willing to accept risks for small increments in returns. So, to get a proper understanding of the amount you are eager to invest in a market, you must find out your ability to take risks based on your financial situation. Some factors used to analyze your risk tolerance include the following:

- **Your emergency fund ratio:** This ratio can be calculated by dividing the cash available to you at the end of a month by the amount of money you spend monthly. A good result is given by a figure that is greater than six.
- **Your housing ratio:** To get this ratio, you should divide your housing costs by your gross pay. For people living in the U.S, they must get a figure that is lower than 28%.
- **Your debt ratio:** This ratio will help estimate your total debt divided by the total number of assets you own. The benchmark varies depending on your age and financial aims.
- **Your net worth ratio:** To get this figure, you would need to divide the net worth by the worth of all of your assets. To know your net worth, you could just subtract your debt from the value of all of your assets.

Now, how can one manage one's risks in a crypto trade?

- **Start by building up your emergency funds:** You can calculate your emergency funds by dividing the value of all the cash accessible to you by your monthly expenses. These steps will give you a rough estimate of the number of months you can go on without an additional cash flow. Ensure that in all you do, that the result is more significant than six months. You have to have an emergency fund before getting an investment portfolio.

- **Exercise a lot of patience:** The risks tied to one crypto business may differ slightly from the ones affecting the other more grounded markets such as equities and precious metals. However, you could execute similar techniques in the management of your portfolio risks regardless of your investments. The reason most traders lose a lot of money is that they can't exercise enough patience. The critical value is profitable for the long-term investors as it also helps traders and speculators.

- **Diversify outside and inside your cryptocurrency portfolio:** There are several ways by which you can diversify your portfolio, and here, a few of them would be discussed.

  o **Cryptocurrencies by market cap:** This category usually includes the top ten currencies like Bitcoin, Ethereum, and Ripple.

  o **Transactional cryptocurrencies:** This group contains the original content of cryptocurrencies. They are designed to be used as money and usually are exchanged for goods and services. Examples of these kinds of cryptocurrencies include Bitcoin and Litecoin.

  o **Platform cryptocurrencies:** These cryptocurrencies are usually designed to eliminate middlemen and create markets for other cryptocurrencies. Cryptocurrencies that fall into this category are usually considered suitable for long-term investments as they usually would appreciate as more applications are created on their blockchain.

  o **Privacy cryptocurrencies:** This type of cryptocurrency is very similar to the usual transactional cryptocurrencies, but they are usually focused heavily on transaction security and anonymity.

o **Application-specific cryptocurrencies:** This type of Crypto is application-specific in that it serves only a few functions, with it still being able to solve the majority of the world's problems. Some examples of cryptos that fall into this category include the Vechain used for the supply of chain applications.

Chapter 4
Looking About the Hood:
Blockchain Technology

I f you have been conscious about online activities, you must have heard the term "Blockchain" or "Blockchain Technology" one time or the other.

Trading crypto coins requires a deep understanding of Blockchain technology and how it works. Blockchain is an I.T, computing technology that makes the existence of digital coins possible.

Think of Blockchain as the operating system of a computer. Without an operating system, you can't install software or other programs on your computer. The computer will be blank and useless without an OS.

Blockchain is the operating network behind digital currencies. According to market reports globally, the demand for crypto coins has risen by over 35% since 2016. It's hard to trust anything digital, but Blockchain technology has consistently proven to be valuable, reliable, and secured.

Many digital agencies and companies around the world are beginning to integrate blockchain networks into their daily activities. Although there are certain aspects of the Blockchain that are still mystified, time will certainly expose the unknown benefits of the system and how it can be harnessed.

A block is a unit or structure containing transactional data. Thousands of blocks containing a history of transactional data are linked together to form a chain. The result is a system known as the

Blockchain system. This block can be likened to a digital ledger containing all the transactions carried out on the platform. The ledger is such that it records all transactions, debit, or credit that occur digitally, working like a highly organized financial system.

To start a transaction, a block must be created to kickstart the process. There must also be authorization from the sender before any transaction can take place digitally. This makes the Blockchain system a very safe and secure platform for transacting.

There are millions of blocks containing transactional data. As transactions continue to take place, more and more blocks are created. The Blockchain ledger is similar to a google spreadsheet that contains an unending array of blocks or linked computers.

It means anyone can view a transaction history but cannot alter, change, or copy it. How cool is that?

Yes, Bitcoin and altcoins rely on the system to function. However, Blockchain isn't just a complex system supporting digital transactions. Blockchain has multiple other uses, some of which have not been discovered yet. Industries like: manufacturing, production, finance can also use the Blockchain system.

According to some sources, Blockchain is capable of replacing the internet. The possibility of this happening is not known for now. The advances of the system are still young.

Transactions on the Blockchain System

In the physical world, transferring funds requires having the recipient's bank details, routing, ABA, account number, and other private details before you could send funds. Once you send funds successfully, a transaction ID is generated. This ID contains all the necessary details of the transaction. However, this system has a particular flaw. The security system cannot be trusted, especially when dealing with huge amounts. The system can also be tampered with and influenced.

The most frustrating of all is that...

This system can be manipulated by governmental bodies involved and can also be hijacked by fraudsters. This flaw is one of the reasons the Blockchain system of the transaction was established.

How Is the Blockchain System Different?

100% Security

The Blockchain system uses a secure and incorruptible algorithm to transact. You can view a user's data, but you can't make changes to it. To send funds, you need the authorized signature of the sender.

Decentralization

The Blockchain features a 100% decentralized system. The Government, bank, or financial bodies cannot interfere with the system. The transaction is based on mutual agreement between the sender and the recipient. The decentralization of this system means unrestricted, free, and unlimited transactions.

Automation

Going to the bank, standing queues are tiring. On the blockchain system, transactions can be automated. What this means is that you can trigger and program transactions to operate according to specific rules under certain requirements.

How Coins Are Formed

There are hundreds of digital coins in the market, with only a few in the front line, such as Bitcoin, Ethereum, and Litecoin. Coins are shared digital records or assets that have a digital value. What this means is they exist virtually as a record or data.

Coins are formed through a process called "mining." To get the picture clearly, juxtapose mining to minting, the production of hard currency. Only the Central Bank of a Nation is licensed to produce hard currency. In the digital world, coins are produced by a technical computing method known as mining. Anyone with the resources and skill can mine coins.

Factors Affecting the Cryptocurrency Market

The crypto market, like every other market, dances to the tune of supply and demand. However, this market is not lopsided like the usual traditional market. Economic activities, political operations tend to influence traditional markets. The factors altering the crypto market are different.

Below are some factors that influence the price of coins in the market:

- **Availability and supply of crypto coins.** The total coins available daily affects the market. The rate of mining and creating coins (pump rate) and the rate at which they are lost and destroyed (dip rate) affect the market.
- **Capitalization of the market.** This is simply all the accumulation of crypto coins in the system, the total accumulated value daily. The capitalization of the market; the value of the coin at certain periods affects trading.
- **The media and press.** Whatever the media portrays to the public becomes the major opinion. This also can influence the price of coins.

For example, Bitcoin spiked 20% after Elon Musk added #bitcoin to his Twitter bio (https://www.cnbc.com/2021/01/29/bitcoin-spikes-20%-after-elon-musk-adds-bitcoin-to-his-twitter-bio.html).

- **Crypto integration systems.** Sometimes, crypto demand becomes so high. Other times, it could become low. Some vendors require crypto coins to transact physically. For instance, in e-commerce, you can make payments using Crypto. Integration of crypto coins into existing infrastructure also influences the market.
- **Actions within the system.** Many things happen within the crypto space. Whatever it may be, it somehow affects the market. Security updates, coin exchange, etc., all influence the crypto market.

Blockchains are built from 3 technologies		
1. Private Key Cryptography	2. P2P Network	3. Program (the blockchain's protocol)
Cash vs. Plastic	Tree falls in a forest	Tragedy of the commons
Identity	System of Record	Platform

Chapter 5
How Does Cryptocurrency Work?

T he biggest reason why cryptographic forms of money are so popular right now is that Satoshi Nakamoto effectively figured out how to assemble an advanced decentralized money framework, called a decentralized cash system. But what exactly is a decentralized cash system?

A decentralized system means the network is powered by its users w/o having any third party, central authority, or middleman controlling it. No bank or government has power over this system.

~~Central authority~~

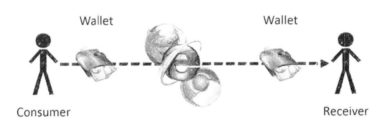

Wallet   Wallet

Consumer   Receiver

Decentralised

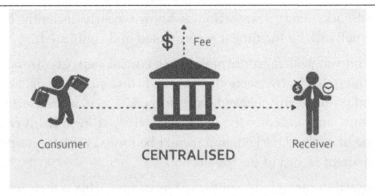

One problem with a decentralized network in a payment system is the so-called "double spending" attack. Double spending refers to a transaction that uses the exact same parameters as another transaction that has been previously validated by the network. In a centralized system, the bank can easily spot this type of attack and protect the affected account. Usually, this is done by a central server that keeps track of your balances. However, a decentralized system doesn't have the benefit of an agency actively safeguarding the network. So how do cryptocurrency networks protect themselves from these attacks?

The solution is most commonly known as "Blockchain Technology." Blockchain technology manages a growing set of data blocks by using the decentralized network, also known as the Peer-to-Peer (P2P) network. The blockchain is similar to an online ledger in that all transactions are recorded and made public to the whole network. Once a piece of data is stored on the blockchain, it cannot be altered or modified. The P2P network functions as a consensus network, which allows a new payment system and records the transactions of new digital money.

Let's illustrate an example. A cryptocurrency, such as Bitcoin, has its own peer-to-peer network. Every peer possesses a copy of the whole history of all network transactions, as well as the balance of each account on the network.

A transaction includes a process where A gives X amount of Bitcoins to B and is signed by A's private key. After signing, a transaction is broadcasted across the network from one peer to every other peer on the network. Every transaction is known nearly instantly by the whole network by the time it is completed and confirmed.

In the bitcoin system, confirmation is a crucial step. Confirmation is everything. If a transaction were left unconfirmed, it has the possibility of being hacked and forged. Once a transaction is confirmed and added to the blockchain, it is set in stone. It can't be undone, it can't be hacked, and it can't be forged because it's part of a permanent record of the transaction.

A transaction can only be confirmed by miners. This is their function in the bitcoin ecosystem. They keep track of transactions, validate them, and disseminate the data across the network. Miners are compensated with a cryptocurrency token, such as Bitcoins, for each successful transaction that they monitor and assist.

Chapter 6
Crypto Exchange and Brokers

R elatively, these tools will tell us when to enter or exit a trade. However, it is not a magic stick that helps traders win every single business; this only helps with showing actual data, reflecting how the market is doing. Therefore, traders should only use them as a reference to make a better trading decision.

Please practice trading with every indicator and tool mentioned in the section to get a sense of how they work. Of course, only practice with a small amount of money.

Moving Average (MA)

This is one of the most popular tools used by many traders. This helps in smoothing out the price movement of the financial asset from the past to the present point.

Ideally, as a trader, you can use the following tools in your favor to increase your winning trades.

SMA and EMA are the most popular ones of all.

The MA you choose to use will be best in your style. For example, SMA will be less sensitive to price fluctuation compared to ema. EMA can be used in a shorter time interval (minutes-hours) to get a grip on a quick change in price action. On the other hand, SMA can be used in a longer time interval (days-weeks) to see the overall trend in the longer term. Since it is more sensitive to price action, EMA responds quicker to price moves and gives out more signals to traders. However, more doesn't mean better. This can result in a lower accuracy level of the messages. SMA is less sensitive to price action. Therefore, its level of accuracy is higher. As a new trader, it is best to try different types of MAs, and later on, choose the one that best suits your trading style.

Again, choosing which MA to use will depend on the trading style of each trader. The longer-term MAs (such as weeks, months, or days) will give a bigger and better picture of the whole market. The longer-term MAs will also be more trustworthy and reliable when this comes to support and resistance level. Short-term traders often use shorter-term MAs (such as in 1 minute, 5 minutes, or 15 minutes, etc.). These traders usually use indicators with shorter periods (minutes to hours) to make multiple trades within a day. Shorter-term MAs can give more information about the market within a short period but will be less accurate and less reliable compared to the longer-term ones. This holds true for every indicator and tool in the financial market. Signs with a more extended time frame will be generally more accurate and more reliable compared to ones which a shorter time frame. MAs of 200 days, 150 days, and 50 days are most used by traders when it comes to measuring overall market trends and identifying reliable support and resistance levels.

So the question is, how do you trade using the moving average tool?

First, use MA to find out the current trend of one particular coin that you are trading. If the MA line stays below the candles, use this as a support level to buy. On the other hand, the MA line will be the resistance point if it is above the price line. Sell some of your holdings if the price gets closer to the MA.

The Moving Average Convergence-Divergence (MACD)

This is another one of the popular indicators that traders use to identify trends. The MACD can give out the exact signals to confirm whether the market is bullish or bearish. The MACD indicators are more potent if used on longer time-frame charts (month, week, or daily). The MACD consists of 3 parts: the MACD line, the signal line, and the histogram. This is stated in Investopedia.

When the MACD lines cross above the zero lines of the histogram, the market is considered to be an uptrend. Conversely, if the lines break below the zero lines of the histogram, the market is in a downtrend. Pay attention to this information for your trading decision.

When the signal line crosses the MACD line either from above or below, the price can be reversed to the other direction. Usually, the MACD line is on top of the signal line when the trend is bullish. If the MACD line crosses the signal line and gets to the bottom, that's a bearish signal, which means this is time to sell. Use this information as buy and sell signals.

The divergence between the price line and MACD lines can also predict a change in price movement. It would be a little advanced to recognize this as a beginner, but with practice, you will be able to spot them easily. When this happens, it can forecast the end of the current trend and a reverse.

Bottom line: To use the MACD indicator effectively:

- Identify the overall trend of the market by seeing whether the MACD lines are above or below the histogram.
- Look for buying signals when the MACD line starts to rise above the signal line. In reverse, consider selling when MACD falls below the signal line.
- Spot the divergence between the price and the MACD line. This will be a sign of a trend reversal.

Bollinger Bands

Another popular technical analysis tool we will discuss is Bollinger Bands. Bollinger bands are often used to measure the volatility of the market. There are three parts to the Bollinger bands: the upper band, the lower band, and the middle line (this line is also known as moving average 20).

It is considered an uptrend when the price movement is held above the middle line (ma20). On the other hand, a downtrend happens when the price movement keeps running below the middle path.

If all bands point upward, the chances are that the market is going bullish. And if all three bands indicate downward, this is a bearish signal.

It is more effective to trade with Bollinger bands when the market is in high volatility (bands widen) versus a low volatility market (bands contract). However, when the bands contract and keep getting narrower after a decent period due to low volatility, do expect a sharp and dramatic move in either direction. This can be the beginning of a new trend.

In conclusion, a Bollinger band is a tool used to measure market volatility. The price movement usually happens within the bands. For that reason, the upper band can act as a robust, resistance level, while the lower groups can be an excellent supporting point. Bollinger bands can also indicate overbought or oversold by seeing whether the price went outside of the upper band or lower band.

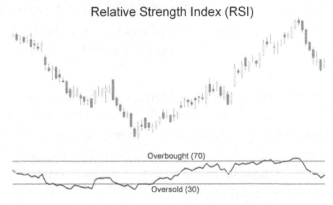

Relative Strength Index (RSI)

Relative Strength Index (RSI)

This is another indicator that is used to point out whether the market is overbought or oversold. RSI is relatively simple to use and can be useful if traders can use it the right way. The RSI oscillates between

0–100. This is considered overbought if RSI rises above 70 or oversold if RSI falls below 30.

By using level 55 as the centerline, the market can be considered up-trending if the RSI> 55 or down-trending if the RSI< 55.

A straightforward strategy to use RSI is to buy when the RSI goes below 30 and sell when it reaches 70. For a short position, sell when the RSI>70 and buy again when it is <30.

Money Flow Index (MFI)

This is another technical indicator used to determine the oversold or overbought condition of a security or a currency. Unlike RSI, which is only associated with the price, MFI combines data of both cost and volume and shows the market condition on a scale of 0 to 100. The market is overbought when the MFI is over 80 and considered oversold when it falls below 20.

Similar to RSI, traders can consider buying when the MFI is oversold (under 20) or be ready to sell when the MFI is overbought (over 80). Additionally, level 50 (the middle line) is a crucial point to watch. When the MFI starts to cross 50 headings upward, this indicates that money begins to pour into the market. We can also see this as a signal to buy.

In another scenario, if the direction (cost) goes up but the force behind it decreases (money flows out), chances are that the price cannot keep going up for long before changing direction. Using the same concept, when the price goes down, but the MFI starts to increase (money begins to flow in), the price might soon start changing direction and increase.

To sum this up if:

- The price goes up to and the MFI goes up: Buy signal
- The price goes up to and the MFI goes down: Sell signal
- The price goes down and the MFI goes up: Buy signal

• The price goes down and the MFI goes down: Best to do nothing and keep watching the market closely.

Fibonacci

Fibonacci is the most reliable technical analysis indicator for entry and exit points on a trade position. Leonardo Fibonacci first introduced Fibonacci (he was a mathematician). He came up with a sequence of numbers, beginning with 0 and 1, where the next number was created by the sum of the two previous numbers. This goes like this... 0,1,1,2,3,5,8,13,21,34,55,89,144...and so on. These numbers are significant because they generated a so-called golden ratio of 1.618 (by dividing any given number to the smaller number before this). This golden ratio is also known as "nature's secret code" or "the universal code." In finance, the series of Fibonacci also plays a big role. Traders use mainly the three percentages based on the golden ratio of 38.2%, 50%, 61.8%, and 100% to calculate and identify the supporting and resistant point of a price line.

Support and resistance points tend to bounce between Fibonacci lines (those lines going across the chart). In order from the bottom to the top: 0, 0.382, 0.5, 0.618, 1.

There are a few different Fibonacci tools used for various purposes. To draw a Fibonacci retracement, first, we need to determine the current trend of the market. If an exchange is in an uptrend, we will start from the lowest price point of the chart from the lower left and drag the Fibonacci to the upper right direction toward the highest price point of the table and connect them. On the other hand, if the market is in a downtrend, we start the Fibonacci tool from the highest price point from the upper left and drag this down to the lowest price point in the lower right direction.

After drawing, the Fibonacci retracement will divide the chart into five significant parts, including 100%, 61.8%, 50%, 38.2%, and 0%. These will be your strong points of support and resistance.

The Fibonacci lines usually act as a support or resistance zone for the price. By using Fibonacci, traders can have an idea of where the price is heading. For example, the next support can be 38.2% if the price is falling. However, if the price keeps going up, 0% can be this resistant level again (this already hits the 0% and bounces back). According to this information, we can buy if the candle gets close to the 38.2 support level. Otherwise, be ready to sell some of your holdings if the candle keeps going up to the 0% level. Of course, we need to combine Fibonacci with other indicators to come up with the most reliable decision.

In conclusion, Fibonacci can be a great tool to aid your trading if it is used right. Therefore, draw your Fibonacci retracement accurately, and you will know your next support or resistance point.

Trend Lines and Trend Channel

The trend line is a straight line drawn to connect pivot points (minimum of 2–3 or more points) and goes from left to right. This is usually drawn under swing pivot lows or over swing pivot highs to predict the movement of price trends. Trend lines are also visual representations of support and resistance to the price.

Trendline.1

Looking at trendline.1, we see that when we are connecting pivot lows of the chart, the trend line will give us a preference for the future supporting zone. In an uptrend, we use trend lines to look for supporting points so we can buy and be in an extended position. With the same idea in mind, connecting pivot highs will give us a sense of where the resistance zone will be in the future. Therefore, use the trend line in a downtrend to identify resistance so we can sell to be in a short position. The more points the trend line connects, the more accurate and reliable it will be. A line that goes through 2 points can also be called a trend line, but it will not be the most effective one to use. A trend line can also be more reliable if the angle is less than 45 degrees. Those with aspects greater than 45 degrees would not be the best ones to count on. Moreover, if the price breaks through the trend line in either direction, traders need to be careful and keep their eyes on the market. The trend is now broken and might change this course. As demonstrated in the trendline.2

Trendline.2

A trend channel is created when we decide to use two trend lines at once, one on top connecting the pivot highs and another at the bottom supporting the pivot lows. The trend channel will only be valid when the price is bouncing up and down within the channel, not outside the channel.

With the trend channel, we will have more information about the market all at once: the support, the resistance, and the general trend.

In conclusion, you use the trend line and trend channel to look for supporting and resistance zones as well as to identify the overall trend. Connect pivot lows in an uptrend to look for support or draw this through pivot highs in a downtrend to look for resistance.

Chart patterns refer to the design of the price line on the chart. This helps to identify trading signals or shows signs of future movements. These patterns reflect human psychology when the price line moves a certain way. And yes, social psychology hasn't changed much since the beginning. That's why specific chart patterns keep reappearing and consistently give the same outcomes.

Chapter 7
Trade in Crypto

Trading in cryptocurrency: Cryptocurrency is receiving a considerable amount of publicity. This has arisen mainly from the fantastic rise in the dollar value of Bitcoins, Ether, and other altcoins.

In 2017, the value of one Bitcoin (BTC) has risen from around $1,000 in early January to over $8,000 in November. Ether has also done well throughout 2017. In November 2017, one Ether was worth around $450 per coin. In Jan 2017 one ETH had a dollar value of around $8; this exceeds a 5000% rise!! If only we had invested then!

Unfortunately, investments in altcoin are not always so rosy. In June 2017, at one exchange at least, the value of 1 ETH fell to less than $0.10(US)! Fortunately for those who had a lot of ETH, the dollar value of 1 ETH, by late August 2017, rose again to greater than $350.

This brings us to you. Should you invest in cryptocurrency? There are a lot of commentators on the Internet that think you should make such an investment. As far as they can see cryptocurrency will always have an increasing value. Cryptocurrency is compared to the situation of desktop and laptop computers. In the 1980s it was thought by some discredited experts (?) that personal computers had no future.

History has shown they were utterly wrong. Anyone who was wise enough to invest in what are now technology giants, such as Apple, Hewlett-Packard, Microsoft, and Dell, who were all starting then will have laughed all the way to the bank.

Some words of advice before investing in any cryptocurrency, learn as much as you possibly can. There are many who failed to realize that you cannot assume the value of an asset will always increase just because its value is rising at present. History is full of examples of substantial increases that are followed by even higher falls. This foolish belief caused the recent economic crisis of 2007–2008 that there could be no collapse in property values after an extended period of growth. The reasons that values seem to rise forever may be deliberate lies, complete incompetence, and massive exaggeration.

Please heed this warning, before rushing into the purchasing and trading of cryptocurrency. If you are determined to start then start with exchanges specializing in cryptocurrencies. These exchanges make it possible to buy cryptocurrency with fiat money. You will need to do this initially unless some kind person has given you some BTC, ETH, or another altcoin.

Good exchanges will help you begin and should be delighted to assist you with the advice you might need, before taking the plunge and starting to trade in cryptocurrency. Thoroughly investigate an exchange before doing business with them. When an exchange has the personnel, who are unable or unwilling to answer questions, and display arrogance, ignorance, or both, then take your business elsewhere.

Fortunately, there are some terrific exchanges for those who are beginners at trade in cryptocurrency. Among those in the USA are Coinbase, Kraken, and Cex.io. Sometimes in another country, you could find the country is only just beginning or hasn't even started in cryptocurrency. Despite this, there are usually one or more local exchanges that will help you. Always be sure to check them out carefully though.

Some exchanges only deal with significant cryptocurrencies such as Bitcoin, Ether, and Litecoin. Generally, after selecting an exchange, you have to fill in some forms. This is a legal requirement before they can accept you. They are required to do this to ensure you are legitimate and not some money launderer or another criminal. You have to do this before you begin trading.

You should get experience with the big coins, such as Bitcoin and Ether, before trying some of the more mysterious ones. Once you have this experience and want to try something more exotic, then Bittrex and Poloniex are exchanges that can assist with smaller coins. In some countries, there may be difficulties in getting smaller coins.

When you start, finding some trustworthy person to assist you to begin is a great blessing. There are many resources on the Internet, such as articles, blogs, forums, and Youtube videos, on every feature of the trading in cryptocurrency. You must take great care as it is so easy to make mistakes. Never forget that if you lose your cryptocurrency, it is gone forever.

There is a final point that should be made about cryptocurrency, and that is the use of bots for trading.

Bots are automated systems for sharing information, answering queries, and performing actions, such as trading altcoin for money and vice versa. A good example is Haasbot, a trading bot that is popular among some cryptocurrency traders, which does the majority of the required tasks for its users. Haasbot watches prices and exchange rates. It trades and even does more.

Bots are used in many other fields besides cryptocurrency. As they are very efficient, you may have interacted with a bot without knowing this was happening. Many bots require a subscription to use them. In some cases, it is possible to subscribe in this way with Bitcoin.

Bots are based on AI or artificial intelligence. Bots improve their performance by using machine learning. The more people interact with bots and use them for more and more tasks, the more the bots learn. The creation of such bots is at the cutting edge of modern technology.

To generate income in cryptocurrency, you need to pay attention to what is happening on the market. Shifts in the market can occur very quickly, and you can lose money, by not acting soon enough, or not having the time to trade at the right time. For this reason, what is called trading bots have become popular.

Usually, in the past, you needed time, knowledge, or skills for really successful trading. It is possible to dabble and earn some money, but not a substantial amount, without you being a very active participant on a full-time basis. As a result of bots, you can be involved in the trade of cryptocurrency, while focusing elsewhere.

At the very least, there are bots available that can answer your queries. These bots will make it easier to trade. They can provide cryptocurrency updates. The abilities of bots go up from there. You can use them to look up recent trends and inform you what others are trading and the amounts traded. It is possible for bots to provide all the resources necessary to be successful and active traders.

But what effect is the having on the cryptocurrency industry and market? Trading has become more competitive as a result of the widespread usage of bots, which is one of the causes for the bitcoin rise. Arbitrage trading, which means the buying of commodities in one market and selling them for higher in another is a possibility with bots. Bots can also be used in market making, which means making profits that arise from long-term sales and orders.

There are many such bots available. Among them are Haasbot, Tradeware, Zenbot, Cryptotrader, and Gecko; to name a few.

Although there are numerous possible benefits, there are also risks, and these must be borne in mind. Always remember that bots are a tool, NOT a complete solution. It is up to you to have the final say; to select the trade. A bot can only focus on a trade you pick. Pick wrong and lose money!

Chapter 8
Identifying Top Performing

Our top cryptocurrencies to invest in 2020 and beyond:

Ethereum

- Ticker symbol: ETH
- Market cap: $0.3 trillion
- Performance percentage in 2017: +5,700%
- Who created it? Vitalik Buterin

Ethereum, as an open-source blockchain, allows developers to design and build decentralized applications by executing SMART contracts. Ether, Ethereum's token cryptocurrency has grown over the years to become one of the most valuable coins.

Ethereum's ICO (initial coin offering) launched July 21st, 2014, eventually managing to sell 50 million ether in tokens. Ether sold at $0.311 to raise $15,571,000, which the developers used to build what we now know as Ethereum.

In early 2018, ether commanded a rising trading price at $1,400.38, to make this second only to Bitcoin.

Why Should We Invest in Ethereum?

Ethereum, which officially is the second most significant crypto coin when measured by market cap, rose in value to trade at an all-time high on various exchanges on 10th January 2018.

According to figures provided by the reputable Coindesk, a cryptocurrency data site, Ethereum managed to hit a record $1,417.38, before again paring those gains.

An analysis shows that Ethereum had just in a week surged in value to roughly stand at 50% more than at the start of January.

Comparing this rise to figures and charts from a year ago shows that Ethereum has gained value at a mega 13,000%.

So, why do we see strong buying support for Ethereum? This can undoubtedly be linked to several factors in the market.

- First, there was a bullish blog post by Ethereum that transactions had doubled in volume to stand at over ten times every second. What this update did was excite traders and make them view Ethereum as the safest cryptocurrency to invest in. The upgrade and the subsequent increase in Ethereum interest saw the simultaneous drop in the price and volume of other cryptocurrencies.

- The other factor could be the ever-growing number of ICOs that are built on the formidable and versatile Ethereum blockchain technology. The high numbers are drawing investors towards Ethereum, which is seen as the future of cryptocurrency.

- When the public sees such trusted and established companies join the Ethereum network, this is just as well that they leverage that endorsement to invest. Should these partnerships work well in the future, Ethereum has the potential to be a perfect investment vehicle.

- Energy and electricity companies are exploring ways to tap into Ethereum's technology to develop applications that would run the smart contracts and enable households to buy or sell power within their neighborhoods.

- Eris, a consulting company, wants to use a forked Ethereum platform to offer privacy for firms by helping the institutions involved develop specialized private networks.

One scenario that could play thyself out soon is the fact that more investors might be encouraged by Ethereum's performance and hence invest in other coins. Though not entirely good news for Ethereum, this would be an avenue for them to compete with and eventually overtake Bitcoin.

Where Can You Buy Ethereum?

Ethereum's massive growth in value and an increasing understanding of blockchain technology is helping the ordinary investor realize that this cryptocurrency could be worth buying.

Though not as lucrative as in 2016 or 2017, Ethereum's still valuable with potential for further growth. So here is how you can buy Ethereum and tap into this potential.

The simplest and easiest way to purchase ether is through an online exchange site. There is a multitude of places out there that do legitimate business when it comes to buying and selling Ethereum.

All cryptocurrency trading and exchange sites have similar operations that aim at providing a platform for buying and selling of crypto, Ethereum included. You can buy ether using:

- Fiat Currency
- Debit/Credit Cards
- Swift (Bank Transfers)
- Bitcoin

Buying Ethereum will follow the following steps that are more or else similar at many exchange sites:

- Identify the exchange site that you wish to buy Ethereum from after research to establish its reliability and reputation.
- Proceed to sign up with the site for an account from which you will buy ether.
- Complete the required verification procedure where applicable and secure your account with a passcode/encryption.
- Add payment method—this will depend on the available payment options at the site. Some use fiat currency,

while others allow the use of cryptocurrency and bank transfers.

- Proceed to buy Ethereum on the site using the site's interface.

Buy Ethereum at Coinbase

Coinbase started allowing the trading of Ethereum on its website in 2016 and provides the majority of the services it offers for Bitcoin exchange.

Coinbase is easy to use and one of the trusted sites in cryptocurrency exchange platforms. The US-based company complies with all the legal requirements.

Coinbase is supported in over 30 countries around the world.

I recommend Coinbase because this is supported in several countries around the world. It is also effortless to access and use for those engaging in cryptocurrency buying and selling for the first time.

My experience with Coinbase is that doing transactions on it does not require a lot of prior cryptocurrency knowledge.

Why is Coinbase better?

- Coinbase displays the price and fees for each transaction. This will ensure that you know exactly how much you are going to spend. It also makes it less complicated to navigate marketplaces looking for prices and fees.
- Coinbase provides you with a price-lock on every order you place. The price lock enables you to buy Ethereum at the price you first encountered as you placed the order. This may protect you against sudden upsurges in price.
- Coinbase allows you to buy using credit/debit cards. However, limitations may considerably lower the amount of ether you can buy at a time.

To buy on Coinbase:

- Get an account with Coinbase
- Complete your account registration process

- Verify the account
- Deposit funds
- Choose the appropriate payment method
- Place an order
- Buy Ethereum
- Transfer your ether to your wallet.

Buy Ethereum on CEX.IO

CEX.IO started in 2013 to offer both crypto exchange services to investors and to provide cloud mining opportunities to interested users. Initially, it specialized in Bitcoin but added Ethereum to its trade exchange in 2016. Later on, Dash and cash were added before the company decided to abandon cloud mining.

You can access the full exchange for the available cryptocurrencies or use a simplified UI for instant buy/sell. This is one of the sites that offer their verified account holders opportunities to trade at a higher limit when transacting with credit cards.

However, CEX.IO charges higher transaction fees compared to other established sites. For instance, Coinbase and Panda have lower costs but do not accept credit cards.

It is user-friendly and straightforward, therefore suitable for beginners who want to buy Ethereum for the first time.

Payment methods include BTC, euro, and USD.

How to buy ether on CEX.IO:

- Open an account at CEX.IO
- Log in to your account using your new password
- Scroll down to buy
- Select Ethereum
- Choose the payment method and key in your amount (BTC, USD, or Eur)
- Click on buy

One good thing about CEX.IO is that it gives you the exact details concerning the Ethereum market value. It also recalculates every 120 seconds.

How Should You Store Your Ethereum (Ether)?

One standard piece of advice we give to investors is that they should not leave vast amounts of their cryptocurrency at an exchange for long. The reasons for this are as follows:

If you expose your wallet online for an extended time, you run the risk of having it hacked. To prevent this, you should leave the least amount of coins in your online account or wallet.

- You should also enable additional security features like 2fa and create a robust password.
- You can also add beauty and google authenticator.

Another reason you should transfer your crypto to your offline wallet is the issue of control. If the exchange controls your wallet/account and you happen to leave your Ethereum there for long, this is possible malicious and untrustworthy companies may rip you off.

Litecoin

- Ticker symbol: LTC
- Market cap: $13.95 billion
- Performance percentage: +6,025%
- Who developed it? Charlie Lee, formerly of Google

Litecoin prices surged recently to suggest that the cryptocurrency has the potential to become a stable investment opportunity, an alternative to Bitcoin, and even more so, other altcoins like Ethereum and Ripple.

The surge also indicates that more and more investors are beginning to put their money in Litecoin.

Litecoin is fast becoming the alternative to Bitcoin that founder Lee envisioned when he launched it in 2011. Catching up on the dominant Bitcoin is not a short-term possibility, given that Bitcoin is by far the most significant crypto by market capitalization.

Nevertheless, Litecoin's efficiency in mining and because this is not expensive to mine, make it have an appeal as an investment project.

Litecoin is also not as expensive as its predecessor.

Why Should You Invest in Litecoin?

Litecoin's supply will taper at 84 million coins, an aspect that will see its price soar as demand rises. This makes it a lucrative venture for anyone looking for a long-term prospect.

Litecoin has improved the speed of generating blocks in the chain, substantially reducing the time it takes to secure and verify/complete a transaction.

This means that the cryptocurrency can be adopted by any institution whose core business is about delivering services faster. It takes only 2.5 minutes to complete a transaction, compared to Bitcoin, which takes 10 minutes.

If more institutions and corporations take up the Litecoin blockchain, then the coin could eventually be very profitable.

Litecoin is soon going to be the medium of small-scale transactions due to relatively low fees per transaction. This then means that you will spend very little when buying Litecoin for investment.

Although it uses the slightly slower proof-of-work, Litecoin uses an algorithm that is very simple to adopt, and therefore, less power is needed to complete the mining process.

Another critical factor going forward for Litecoin is the equipment needed for mining. Since Litecoin can be mined on computers using less power, users of Litecoin can then adopt graphics cards that aren't so expensive. A faster network and quicker transactions are suitable for Litecoin.

Bitcoin Cash

- Ticker symbol: BCH
- Market cap: $45.61 billion
- Performance percentage in 2017: +623%
- Who created it? Bitcoin fork

Bitcoin Cash (BCH) successfully splintered from Bitcoin on Aug 1, 2017, after the original Bitcoin (BTC) experienced a hard fork.

Bitcoin Cash is currently ranked an impressive 4th on the cryptocurrency lists as per market capitalization. Only Bitcoin Classic, Ethereum, and Ripple (XRP) are more significant.

What Makes This Attractive to Investors?

- One major factor that is likely behind its soaring prices is Bitcoin Cash's transaction speeds that have been improved by Bitcoin Cash developers.
- Bitcoin cash has a market capitalization of $42,112,661,421 and a 24 hour trading volume of $980,732,000. Its circulating supply stands at 16,911,425 BCH at the time of this writing.
- Like the Bitcoin Classic, BCH has a set max supply of 21,000,000 BCH.
- This cryptocurrency is doing well enough in daily trading volumes to warrant a look like a possible investment, especially as Bitcoin continues to stall.

Iota

- Ticker symbol: MIOTA
- Market cap: $11.10 billion
- Performance percentage in 2017: +525%
- Who created it? David Sonstebo, Dr. Sergey Popov and Dominik Scheiner

Iota is a new cryptocurrency that works to enable what we call machine-to-machine transactions. Iota aims at powering the internet of things economy.

However, Iota is significantly different from the other cryptocurrencies because, whereas many run on blockchain technology, Iota uses a radically new concept technologically known as "directed acyclic graph" (DAG). This is a DAG that is referred to as "the tangle."

Iota is driven by the need for the internet of things to have or to be:

- Scalable
- Decentralized
- Modular
- No transactions fees

What Is the Tangle?

The tangle is the leading innovative idea that runs on a distributed ledger that is said to be completely scalable, lightweight, and as the first in the crypto-era, a system that allows transactions to take place without the need for fees.

How Does Tangle Work?

Tangle is instrumental in helping to solve issues related to scalability and transaction fees that plague many blockchain cryptocurrencies. When a sender wants a transaction carried out, the knot will require them to participate in the securing and verification of the operation. This system leads to a scenario where there are no unique miners, leaving only those making the transactions as participants. The network then becomes fully decentralized.

Scalability is solved because network speed multiplies as the number of transactions increases. Therefore, it won't get slower, like what happens with blockchains cryptocurrencies.

And because Iota charges no fees, and with issues of scalability tackled, this cryptocurrency promises to be the technology that will be used by many applications. Already there are partnerships in place to explore how to adopt Iota's technology and make it practical and achievable in the real world.

Why Iota?

The reason Iota is increasingly looking for a significant investment is a result of the possibility of this scaling.

Primarily, it is the reason many new investors are putting their money on Iota (MIOTA).

My thoughts on this are that iota has the technology to change the IoT in the world. That alone makes the cryptocurrency get the much-needed interest to make Iota a worthy investment.

Chapter 9
Crypto Mining

B y now you probably already know a decent amount about cryptocurrencies. They are digital assets that function as a medium of exchange and use cryptography to secure transactions and to create additional units. Cryptocurrencies are mined into existence through a process known as mining.

This process of mining new cryptocurrencies involves two functions. These are adding transactions to the blockchain and releasing new currency to the system.

Mining Cryptocurrencies

In order to mine cryptocurrencies, you need access to a powerful computer and special software. There are new, sophisticated computers in the market that have been developed specifically for cryptocurrency mining.

A miner is basically anyone who invests their time confirming cryptocurrency transactions and adding new currencies to its network. Mining cryptocurrency requires plenty of resources. The computers needed for this process are costly and operating costs are very high. This is because the mining process consumes a lot of electricity.

Miners generally spend most of their time trying to confirm a block containing data using hash functions. To understand better how the mining process works, it is important to first understand the basic aspects of blockchain technology.

Mining and the Blockchain

Cryptocurrencies use publicly distributed and decentralized ledgers known as the blockchain. Blockchains are secure networks and this is in part due to the mining process. Mining is, therefore, an essential component of the blockchain and is integral to its stability. It provides an additional level of security because the process validates each transaction that takes place on the blockchain.

In fact, the validity of each cryptocurrency coin is secured by the blockchain. Each block contains what is known as a hash pointer. The blockchain is decentralized with no central server to log in all transactions. However, without sufficient computing power, the blockchain ledger cannot operate. Cryptocurrencies rely on the combined power of numerous mining computers spread out across the world.

These computers are operated by miners who lend their computers for a common cause. In return for their input, they receive an incentive or reward. Miners receive payment when they solve a challenging mathematical puzzle and validate transactions before others do.

Each block in the blockchain contains transaction data, a timestamp, and a hash pointer.

Hash Function

The hash function in cryptocurrency is an algorithm that maps data of varying or arbitrary size to a hash and is by design a one-way function. A hash pointer is present in all blocks and always points to the previous block. It acts as a pointer, making it easy to track transactions.

Proof of Work

Most of the blockchains in use today use a concept known as Proof of Work. Proof of Work protocol or system is simply an economic measure that requires some work from the requesters to be done. This work is often processing time by a computer. This helps prevent service abuse.

Proof of Work scheme is the first timestamping scheme that was invented for the blockchain. The most popular proof-of-work schemes are based on scrypt and SHA-256. Scrypt is the most widely used among cryptocurrencies. Others include SHA-3, Crypto-Night, and Blake.

CPU vs. GPU Mining

There are several options available when it comes to cryptocurrency mining. At the onset of cryptocurrencies, you could effectively run the mining algorithms on your computer as an individual miner. The regular computer at your home or office operates on a CPU or central processing unit which was powerful enough to handle mining functions.

Mining at the onset simply meant downloading or compiling the correct mining software and the wallet for a preferred coin. A miner would then configure the mining software to join their preferred cryptocurrency network then dedicate your computer to the task of mining cryptocurrencies.

In recent months and years, miners turned from CPU computers to GPU-based PCs. The GPU is the graphics processing unit that processes video systems on your computer. Basically, a GPU is like a CPU but a lot more powerful and designed to execute specific tasks. It is this specialization that makes the GPU suited for tasks such as cryptocurrency mining.

Compare CPU vs. GPU Capacity

A CPU core can execute only 4 or 32-bit instructions per clock while a GPU can execute 32—32-bit instructions in the same period of time. This simply means a GPU processor executes 800 times more instructions per clock.

Even though the latest, most modern CPUs have even 12 cores and much higher frequency clocks, still one GPU, like the HD5970, is more than 5 times faster than 4 modern CPUs combined. Therefore, GPU mining can result in faster transaction times and you can gain more coins in the same time frame.

Functions of the GPU vs. the CPU

The CPU is the executive arm of the computer. The central processing unit is essentially a decision-maker that is directed by the software in use. CPUs do all sorts of mathematical computations. On the other hand, a GPU is more of a laborer than an executive. GPUs contain large numbers of ALUs, or arithmetic and logic units. This makes them capable of executing large quantities of bulky mathematical labor in a greater quantity than CPUs.

What you need to be concerned with is the fact that the advent of GPU mining has made CPU mining almost obsolete. This is because the hash rate of most cryptocurrency networks increased exponentially. CPU mining is hardly profitable on some cryptocurrency networks but is thriving on others. It has largely been affected by the increased hash rate.

GPU mining is significantly faster in comparison and hence profitable on all cryptocurrency systems. Today, cryptocurrency mining heavily relies on GPU-based mining rigs. A mining rig is a computer system or arrangement that is used for mining coins. Most rigs are dedicated to accomplishing only one task, which in this case, is crypto mining.

Chapter 10
Crypto Futures and Options

While cryptocurrencies have been around for a little over a decade, they are still very new. Over time their value and popularity are likely to continue to increase, due to the fact that many people see them as a better alternative to fiat currency.

In addition, since Bitcoins and other cryptocurrencies are not regulated by a central authority, they are not subject to the same kind of manipulation that regular currencies experience. For example, when the US government raises interest rates of exchange rates, it has a direct impact on the value of the US dollar. However, when the government raises interest rates of exchange rates there is no such effect on cryptocurrency because they are not directly affected by any changes.

Let's find out, shall we?

The Future of Cryptocurrency

Ever since the initial boom of bitcoin back in 2013, there has been no shortage of people claiming that cryptocurrencies are the future. Some go so far as to say they will be bigger than the internet, while others believe that they will replace fiat currency as we know it. However, there is one thing we can all agree on and that is: cryptocurrencies will not go away anytime soon.

In fact, there are several reasons why cryptocurrencies will continue to thrive in the coming years:

The Rise of Mobile Payments

While cryptocurrencies may not be the most popular form of payment by any means, they are becoming more popular by the day. This is due in large part to the rise in mobile payments. After all, when people can pay for things with their smartphones and leave their wallets at home it makes a lot more sense for them to use cryptocurrencies because they don't need to worry about carrying around large amounts of cash. Of course, as this technology becomes more widely used, there will be an increased demand for cryptocurrencies in general. As people become more comfortable with using cryptocurrencies it could help push them into mainstream adoption and this would open up new avenues of growth for the industry.

Technical Improvement

Just like any other technology that has been around as long as cryptocurrencies have, there is always room to improve and make them better. For example, one of the biggest issues that many people have dealt with when using cryptocurrencies is transaction speed. While fiat currency transactions are processed and completed in seconds, many cryptocurrencies can take hours or even days to be processed. Fortunately, there are a number of companies working to improve transaction speeds and bring them more in line with traditional methods of payment by using blockchain technology. Ultimately, this will make cryptocurrencies more appealing to the general public and help push them into mainstream adoption.

The Rise of Smart Contracts

One area where cryptocurrencies have proven to be a bit lacking is in their ability to facilitate smart contracts. However, the sheer number of new applications that have been developed for blockchain technology make it clear that smart contracts are going to be one of the key areas where cryptocurrencies can grow and thrive. In fact, many people believe that the use of smart contracts will help push cryptocurrencies into mainstream adoption because it will allow them to be used in ways that were never thought possible. In other words, if a company develops a game where people can pay with cryptocurrencies then people will start using it simply because they want to play the game. This could lead to mass adoption through demand alone and could push cryptocurrencies into mainstream use with little effort.

Increased Regulation

When cryptocurrencies first came onto the scene the general public was very skeptical and it was difficult to use them in any capacity. However, as time went on there has been a push for increased regulation and this has done wonders for the growth of cryptocurrencies. When people know that their money is safe and there are regulations in place to protect them then they are more willing to use cryptocurrencies. As more people begin to trust cryptocurrencies more they will begin using them more frequently and this could lead to a massive increase in growth when compared with the early days of cryptocurrency.

The Rise of Cryptocurrency Exchanges and Trading Platforms

While most people who have heard of cryptocurrencies have heard of exchanges like Coinbase, many others have not. However, these exchanges play a key role in the bitcoin ecosystem because they allow people to buy, sell/trade, and invest in various cryptocurrencies daily. In fact, some exchanges like Binance have grown so rapidly over the past year that they have become the biggest cryptocurrency exchanges in the world.

In addition to exchanges, there are many trading platforms that have also developed over the past few years. While there is plenty of competition in this space, companies like eToro have shown that it is possible to bring cryptocurrencies to a wider audience and provide them with a way to invest without having any technical knowledge.

Of course, this has helped make investing in cryptocurrencies much easier and it has also made them more appealing to casual investors.

The Outlook for Cryptocurrency

Cryptocurrencies are still a very recent development and as such, they face their fair share of risks and criticisms. However, cryptocurrencies have survived every one of these controversies and setbacks, so there is no doubt that they will continue to grow in popularity and use. As a result, we can be sure that cryptocurrencies will remain relevant well into the future.

In 2021, cryptocurrencies will be more widely used than ever before. As time goes on, more and more people will start to adopt cryptocurrencies and they will become an everyday part of our personal and professional lives. The only question is: how far will they go?

While there is no way to predict the future with any certainty, there are a few possible scenarios that could have a significant impact on cryptocurrency. These scenarios include:

Scenario 1: Cryptocurrency Becomes a Mainstream Currency

The first and most obvious scenario is that cryptocurrencies will become the dominant form of currency used in all aspects of life. Imagine being able to buy goods and services with bitcoin just as easily as you can with cash. In fact, they would be just as easy to use as cash because you wouldn't have to worry about exchanging them for fiat currencies or dealing with any transaction fees. This means that your entire day-to-day life would be completely cashless.

However, this scenario is highly unlikely because it involves people giving up their fiat currencies altogether and adopting cryptocurrencies. Many people will never see the appeal of giving up cash altogether because there are many benefits to using fiat currency over cryptocurrency. This includes the ability to physically hold your money and exchange it easily for goods and services. Even so, there are some who are willing to give up their fiat currencies and make the switch to cryptocurrency; this is especially true for those who are already familiar with digital currency.

Another reason why this scenario is unlikely is that cryptocurrencies are currently not backed by any government or central bank. This can be very unsettling for some people who only trust their government to ensure that their currency is safe and secure. However, it would be a mistake to think that cryptocurrencies are not secure; in fact, they will never be affected by inflation or devaluation.

Scenario 2: Cryptocurrency Becomes a Mainstream Investment

A second scenario would be if cryptocurrencies become the dominant form of investment. This would be similar to the first scenario in that you would be able to buy, sell and trade cryptocurrencies just as easily as you do stocks and bonds. However, the big difference here is that you could easily buy and sell these investments 24/7, 365 days a year.

Since cryptocurrency is not tied to any country or currency, you no longer have to worry about taxes or internationalization issues. This means that you can trade 24/7, 365 days a year without having to worry about tax laws or rules limiting your ability to invest in foreign markets. And while this may seem like a great way to make money, it also means that there is always going to be someone ready and willing to take your money away at any time of day or night.

Scenario 3: Governments Regulate Cryptocurrency

A third scenario would be if governments regulated cryptocurrency. This would mean that cryptocurrencies are not used as a form of currency or investment, but rather, they are regulated and monitored by governments.

This is not the same as cryptocurrencies being backed by their respective governments. Instead, it means that cryptocurrencies would be regulated in a similar way to other forms of currencies; only this time, they would be digital rather than fiat currency. As such, you could still invest in them just as easily as you do with other currencies and assets, but you wouldn't have to worry about any sort of volatility or fluctuation because they would have a fixed value just like fiat currency.

Scenario 4: All Cryptocurrencies Are Regulated by One Particular Government

A fourth and final scenario is that all cryptocurrencies are regulated by one government. This would mean that digital money would no longer exist as separate forms of currency; instead, they would all be tied together under a single government regulatory agency. This agency would ensure that cryptocurrencies were used safely and securely.

However, this scenario is highly unlikely because cryptocurrencies are designed to be entirely decentralized and not tied to any government or currency. In fact, the very nature of cryptocurrencies is that they are supposed to be separated from all governments and currencies. So while it may be possible for one country to regulate all of the cryptocurrencies, it wouldn't last for long because other countries would likely follow suit.

The Future of Cryptocurrency and Fiat Currency

Many people believe that cryptocurrencies will eventually replace fiat currency and become the only form of digital money. However, this is highly unlikely to occur because there will always be some sort of need for fiat currency. For example, when large purchases are made it is important to have cash in hand. Also, certain places don't accept cryptocurrencies and unless there are crypto-friendly solutions available, people will still need to use physical money.

However, the future of cryptocurrency does not depend on whether or not it replaces fiat currency. Instead, it depends on how well cryptocurrencies integrate with other forms of digital money such as fiat currency and points. For example, if cryptocurrencies can be used as a form of payment at multiple different retailers, they will probably survive over the long term in some capacity.

This is where things get really interesting. In the future, it is likely that all forms of money will be digital and cryptocurrencies will play an important role in this new financial ecosystem. This means that cryptocurrencies may not replace other forms of money, but they may become a crucial part of our financial system.

Cryptocurrency Around the World

As cryptocurrencies continue to grow in popularity so too will their use around the world. There are currently just over a thousand cryptocurrencies, but many more will come onto the scene in the next few years. Even today, some cryptocurrencies are only used within certain countries; these types of currencies will become even more common as time goes on.

There is also a possibility that many of today's coins will be phased out and replaced by new ones. It is entirely possible that some of today's most popular coins won't last another decade, which means that investors need to carefully select their investments if they want them to be profitable in the future.

Another factor to consider is how different countries around the world will deal with cryptocurrencies. While some countries may embrace them, others might decide to ban them, which could lead to significant changes in how they are used around the world. Some countries might even decide to create their own version of a cryptocurrency, which could lead to some interesting debates and conflicts between countries.

Today, one of the biggest problems that cryptocurrencies face is their popularity in certain parts of the world while being completely ignored by others.

For example, in countries like Venezuela and Zimbabwe, cryptocurrencies are extremely popular because of strict government regulations that have caused people to lose faith in their fiat currencies. However, countries like the US and Japan have been reluctant to adopt cryptocurrencies because they see them as a risky investment.

This conflict between countries has the potential to cause major problems in the future, especially if cryptocurrencies become even more common.

Furthermore, you should also consider the impact that cryptocurrencies could have on businesses. In the next few years, there will be a growing number of businesses that accept cryptocurrencies for payments and transactions. This will make it easier than ever before for people to buy things with their cryptocurrency investments.

There is also a possibility that some businesses will create their own digital currencies, which could lead to them becoming just as popular as some of the current cryptocurrencies. This could help cryptocurrencies become more mainstream and prove to be a lucrative investment opportunity.

Regulations and Cryptocurrency

In the past, cryptocurrencies were largely ignored by governments, and they were not required to follow any particular regulations. However, as they become more popular, governments around the world are starting to realize their potential impact on society.

For example, Switzerland has created a cryptocurrency regulatory body that is supposed to help establish clear guidelines for all crypto-related businesses. South Korea has also announced plans for a new regulatory agency that will be responsible for overseeing the cryptocurrency market. Many other countries around the world will likely follow suit in the next few years because of how quickly cryptocurrencies are growing in popularity.

In the United States, the Securities and Exchange Commission (SEC) has been the most active when it comes to dealing with cryptocurrencies. So far, they have been fairly strict about how cryptocurrencies are regulated.

The regulations of cryptocurrency in the US have led to some major problems, including the recent collapse of the popular cryptocurrency exchange, Bitconnect.

The company was accused of operating as an illegal pyramid scheme by the SEC and other regulatory bodies around the world. As a result, they lost their license in Texas and were forced to shut down their exchange platform. The fact that they were able to operate in the US for so long is a testament to how difficult it can be for regulators to keep track of cryptocurrencies.

Regardless of how strict or lax regulations are around the world cryptocurrencies will need to be regulated in some way for them to become accepted on a global scale. For example, if no regulations are put in place then cryptocurrencies could become targets for hackers and criminals looking to make quick cash from illegal activity. Whatever regulations are put into place will have an enormous impact on how cryptocurrencies are used around the world.

Regulations are a major concern for many people who want to invest in cryptos. While these regulations may seem like a bad thing at first, many experts believe that they will actually be good for the industry as a whole because they will help create a more stable ecosystem for investors and traders.

As the regulatory environment continues to evolve, many people will keep a close eye on which countries will embrace cryptocurrencies and which ones will ban them. This could play a major role in how much money is invested into cryptocurrencies in the future because some investors may choose to simply avoid countries that are specifically anti-cryptocurrency.

Institutional Investors and Cryptocurrency

In the past, institutional investors have stayed away from cryptocurrencies because they wanted to avoid the high-risk, high-reward nature that this type of market presents. However, as cryptocurrencies become a more legitimate option for investing, institutional investors are starting to take notice. The reason that these institutional investors are starting to get involved in cryptocurrencies is that they are starting to see that the value of cryptocurrencies could increase significantly over time. This means that having a portion of their investments in cryptocurrencies could end up being one of the best investments they ever made.

For example, in 2017 Goldman Sachs announced plans to open a cryptocurrency trading desk. A few months later BlackRock, the largest money manager in the world with over USD 6 trillion under management, announced that they were considering investing in cryptocurrencies as well. These are just a couple of examples of how institutional investors are slowly becoming interested in cryptocurrencies as an investment vehicle.

The SEC has also been very adamant that traditional financial institutions are not allowed to invest in cryptocurrencies until they are properly regulated. However, many institutional investors don't seem to be respecting these rules, and they are finding ways to invest in the cryptocurrency market anyway.

For example, some of the largest hedge funds are investing large sums of money as part of their digital currency strategies. At some point, the SEC will likely have no choice but to allow institutional investors into the cryptocurrency market since it is starting to become too large for them to ignore.

Chapter 11
Using Technical Analysis

T raders in the crypto market rely on a wide range of tools to assess the strengths and weaknesses of a crypto asset. One of the most commonly used tools in trading is technical analysis. Technical analysis of charts helps traders understand the market sentiments, price trends, and data analysis to predict future trends on Bitcoin assets. With the information provided through technical analysis, crypto traders can make the right decision on when to invest in Bitcoin.

Technical analysis (sometimes abbreviated as TA) forecasts future cryptocurrency prices and market trends based on historical data. It anticipates whether the price trends will be up (bulls) or down (bears). This is done through the use of technical indicators, which calculate the historic and current market price of an asset and analyze price trends.

Analyzing historical price charts and collected volume data determines whether the coin is undervalued or overvalued.

Technical analysis is based on the following assumptions:

1. **The price movement follows certain trends.** Bitcoin prices do not change randomly but tend to follow particular trends that last for either short or long periods. It uses past performance to predict future prices.

2. **Bitcoin prices are determined by multiple variables.** The price movement of the coin is due to past and future demand of the coin, current market prices, and regulations governing the cryptocurrency market.

3. **History tends to repeat itself.** What happened in the past is used to predict what will happen in the future. Past changes can easily predict future market changes. Traders tend to behave the same way when presented with a similar market condition.

Types of Technical Analysis

There are three components used in technical analysis:

- **Chart lines:** Chart lines are used to indicate the points where price changes. Using historical price data, current prices, and volume data, analysts can draw charting lines to show the exact points where the prices tend to change.
- **Patterns:** Chart patterns predict price movement. They show the price direction and extrapolate to show where prices are headed to.
- **Indicator oscillators**: This analysis tool uses statistical methods to determine the buy and sell signals.

Analysts and crypto investors rely on the charts to get visual data on price trends and market momentum.

Technical Indicators

Technical indicators are investment analysis tools used to calculate and interpret market trends. Traders rely on these tools to determine the right time to invest in cryptocurrencies (crypto). Investors can receive alerts on any new investment opportunities and price changes.

Traders can know the price movement of crypto assets whether they move up, down, or sideways. The price movement is calculated using historical price data, current prices, and trading volume data.

Technical indicators are very important in analyzing cryptocurrency investments. They help investors to:

- Predict price movement and future price direction.

- Confirm market trends in the price movement of cryptocurrency assets such as Bitcoin.
- Alert investors to whether prices are going up, down, or sideways to make arrangements necessary for trade.

Cryptocurrency investors rely on these indicators to determine the short-term price movement. They also evaluate the asset's long-term price changes to determine when to enter or exit the market.

Some of the common technical indicators used include calculating Moving Averages (MA) and the Relative Strength Index (RSI). For example, you can plot a chart to show the Bitcoin price direction for 12 and 26 days, respectively.

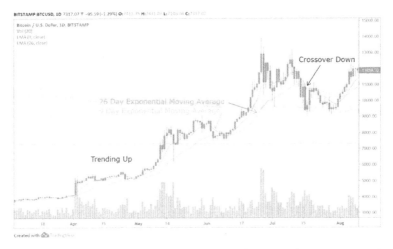

There are several indicators to observe when analyzing a particular cryptocurrency asset. To choose the right indicator, you need to first understand how each indicator works and how each indicator will affect your investment strategy.

Because of the volatile nature of crypto assets, monitoring the price direction or Bitcoin price chart will help the investor evaluate both high and low trading patterns. If the chart assumes an upward trend, that will indicate higher trend lines whereas a downward trend indicates a series of low trend lines.

Sometimes the cryptocurrency will move sideways. In such a case, it does not move in any particular vertical direction at all. Investors should be very careful when using only one indicator such as trend lines to predict future prices since the trends can move in any form. It is much better to use 2 or more indicators as confirmation of a move up or down.

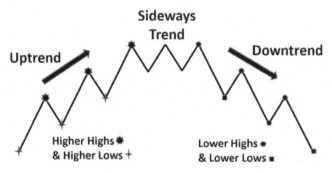

A technical analysis chart drawn based on historical prices and trading volume data represents the past decisions made by investors on the buying and selling of crypto assets. As investors, we use past data to predict future investments.

For example, a typical investor who bought Bitcoin cryptocurrency assets will monitor the price of Bitcoin assets. If the price falls in comparison to the initial buying price, the investor may wait until the price reaches the break-even point to sell the crypto asset. As savvy investors, we recognize this as Support/Resistance explained later in this book and can use this to our advantage.

Price movement is influenced by both internal and external constraints. Multiple forces including human emotions like fear, panic, greed, anxiety, hope, and hysteria affect the prices of cryptocurrency. These emotions lead to dramatic shifts in the prices of the crypto asset. Therefore, price movement is not only based on facts but also on expectations.

Trend Analysis

Trend analysis uses technical analysis tools to determine price movements and help traders know when to buy, sell, or hold a cryptocurrency asset.

This technique analyzes past cryptocurrency prices to predict future price movements. It determines an upward trend when asset prices continue to rise and detects a downward trend when prices keep decreasing over several consecutive days.

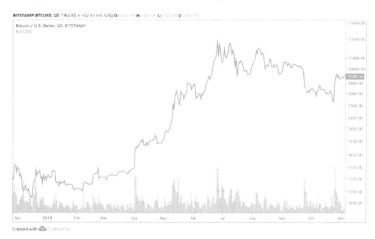

Trend lines, moving averages, and polarity analysis are the major tools used to determine price trends.

Using trend lines is one of the most popular techniques used in technical analysis, and they are used to show the consistent movement of prices either up, down, or sideways. Price movement trends vary based on the time frame and whether the investor is observing a daily, weekly, monthly, or quarterly basis.

Drawing Trend Lines

Trend lines indicate the general direction of the price. Straight lines are drawn above and below the price line. Trend lines also show support and resistance areas that can determine when to enter or exit a trade. Trend lines can show increased supply or demand.

Downward trend lines are drawn above the price of the plotted chart, while upward trend lines are drawn below the price. The upward trend line is used to estimate support while the downward trend line is used to estimate resistance.

Rules of Thumb for Trend Lines

1. There must be at least two highs or lows to have a valid trend line (3 points is preferred). The trend line is further validated if it intersects the price line a 3rd time. Bitcoin is so volatile that it may be hard to find the 3rd point validation.

2. Larger time frames result in better trend lines. Start with weekly or daily charts and then check the smaller time frames to confirm.

3. Sometimes trend lines cut through the low or high portion of a candle. Try not to cut through the body of the candle. If the trend line doesn't fit without being forced, it probably isn't a valid trend.

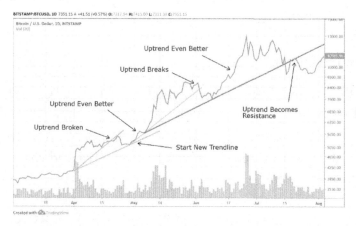

In the above chart, the prices touched the trend line at least 2 times in the given time frame. The line represents the area of support, and it indicates when traders should be looking for buying opportunities. Sometimes the upward trend line can become a resistance line as shown on the right side.

We will discuss support and resistance in more detail below.

The downtrend touched the trend line 3 times in the given time frame. The trend line in the graph represents resistance and indicates where the buyers are expected to slow down their buying. Traders use this to sell their crypto assets near the top.

How to Draw Trend Lines

Open the Trading View website, and then choose BTC/USD charts. This displays the real-time trending price for Bitcoin in US Dollars.

You can customize the chart and draw trend lines on it. To do so, click on the Full-featured chart icon to open advanced chart tools to customize your chart.

You can change the chart trend to be daily, weekly, or monthly, and then draw trend lines from the available tools. Select the Trend Line Tool on the left side of the chart.

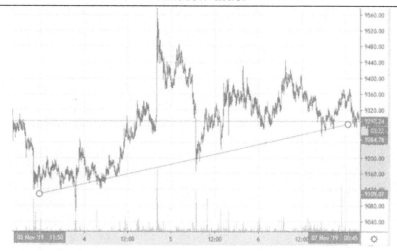

Trading Channels

A channel consists of a pair of straight lines, with one line drawn at the top of the uptrend trend line and the other line drawn in parallel but at the bottom linking the troughs of a price series chart.

Channels are used in visualizing data to determine when to buy and sell crypto assets. The top and bottom lines are drawn to show both the support and resistance levels in the trade chart.

Trading channels show where prices will likely reverse direction. If an asset trades between the boundaries of two trend lines for a certain period, then it is trading within the channel.

If the trading price is on an uptrend, then it is an ascending channel. If the price moves downward between the trend lines, it is referred to as a descending channel. When the price moves in a range, then a horizontal channel is created.

The channel can be drawn by either using the trend lines to draw two lines or using channel tools available in the software.

Let's walk through what happened above.

When Bitcoin was at $274 (the bottom left corner of the channel), many people bought it. As a result, the price increased to $400. Investors who bought at $274 want to sell their Bitcoin at the increased price and take their profits. This leads to increased supply and less demand, which drops the Bitcoin price to $320.

At that point, investors may start buying Bitcoin expecting that the price will increase back to $400. The rise was not as rapid this time but it eventually hits $452 before the sellers take control and push the price back down to $360.

The buyers and sellers trade back and forth without much rise or fall until late May 2016 when Bitcoin becomes more attractive and rises quite fast from $450 to $750 in mid-June.

Using Channels to Make Trading Decisions

Traders rely on the channel for trading with the assumption that the price will typically remain enclosed within the channel.

If confirmed by other signals, a trader sells their Bitcoin when the price touches the upper boundary of the trend line or buys Bitcoin when the price touches the lower boundary.

Note how selling wasn't a good decision when the price touched the upper right channel because Bitcoin continued to rise. This is another example of where a good trader would realize the mistake and buy back in.

Sometimes, you may have a false breakout, which occurs when the price breaks outside the channel. In such a case, some investors may immediately buy in thinking the crypto is rocketing upwards. It is best to wait until it closes outside the channel before you trade. Many times, the price will immediately return inside the channel and the extra caution is worth the confirmation.

Volume Analysis and Price Action

Volume analysis is a very powerful tool in trading. Volume analysis determines the number of times a crypto asset has been traded for a certain period. It measures how many units are sold or bought within a specific time frame. Traders use this tool as the key metric in determining the asset liquidity level.

The tool also enables traders to know how easy it is to enter and exit the market. If well utilized, traders and investors can maximize profits as well as reduce the risks involved.

If the assets have a higher volume, then it will be easy to trade both a large number or a smaller quantity of assets since there are several traders available.

False Volume on Exchanges

Unfortunately, the volume can be falsely indicated inside a cryptocurrency exchange. Since the exchange is its own ecosystem, some exchanges report more volume than is actually occurring. They do this for publicity since an exchange with a lot of volumes would be better at matching buyers and sellers and attract more traders.

You could look at the cryptocurrency blockchain to determine the number of actual transactions. This still does not capture the actual interest because the people buying and selling are doing so on the exchanges. The exchange only needs to "settle" the transactions with the blockchain if it needs more liquidity. It is helpful to look at the charts for several exchanges and compare the volume.

Buying and Selling Volume

Volume determines the strength of price trends and warns investors about the weakness of price movements. Buyers need increased asset volume to push the prices higher.

If there is an increase in the price but a reduced number of units, then there is a lack of market interest that is likely to lead to a price reversal.

On the other hand, if the price doesn't change but large volumes that don't affect price are have occurred, this is called churn. At some point, the buyers and sellers will be exhausted and the price will likely remain steady.

Large volumes of assets traded may result in price declines or gains if the buyers and sellers are not evenly matched. This indicates a major fundamental change in the market.

Let's go back to the Supply and Demand graph. When prices rise, this is because buyers are controlling the price movement. More buyers in the market push the prices higher resulting in increased buyer volume.

The volume of each crypto asset is shown at the bottom of the price chart. The real-time charts show the trading volume in the form of vertical bar graphs at the bottom, with each bar representing the number of units exchanged for a specific period.

Volume bars are either red or green. A red bar indicates that the prices of the asset decreased for a specific time frame. It also indicates a selling volume in the market.

If the volume bars are green, it is an indication that prices increased during that time frame, resulting in increased buying volume.

Chapter Summary

Trend analysis is a powerful tool that provides a visual chart to help analyze cryptocurrencies and get real-time data about asset performance in the world market.

Trend lines are used to show the support and resistance levels in the price trends. Traders use trading channels to determine the entry and exit points in the market.

Volume information is useful for determining how excited the market is.

Chapter 12
Minimizing Losses and Maximizing Gains

T rading in crypto with an understanding of the market is either a very lucrative or very expensive venture. Most common crypto traders will probably lose money, but experienced investors are able to profit and, more importantly, protect themselves against huge losses.

To understand how a loss is inevitable, let us consider that the price of a currency can change in two ways: up or down.

If we buy coins when the market is up, we will most probably benefit from this increase. But if we buy coins when the market is down, we will most probably lose money.

There are some trading techniques that can help us to trade effectively, minimizing losses and maximizing gains. But there is no way to turn a loss into a gain or vice-versa.

Losses Are Inevitable in Crypto Trading

To begin with, let us consider that it is not a good idea to trade on margin; margin trading provides unlimited leverage and therefore more potential profits, but also bigger losses.

If you trade on margin, you will have to pay interest daily. And there is the risk of being liquidated if your trading balance falls below a certain percentage of your total deposit (25%). This means that your broker will start selling parts of your portfolio in order to reduce the amount you owe.

For this reason, we can say that losses are inevitable in crypto trading.

Our goal should be to minimize losses and maximize gains by employing various strategies. Here are some guidelines:

As we know it, buy low and sell high is a good rule to follow for any trading strategy, but it is especially important when the market is moving up or down very fast. The market may be going up or down very fast but, in a short period of time, the price usually crosses the important resistance/support levels and that can make a strong upward movement (bull move) or a strong downward movement (bear move). To maximize gains, we should always buy low and sell high. For a bullish move, we should buy when the price is below the important support level and sell when it is above significant resistance. For a bearish move, we should sell when the price is above significant support and buy when it is below this level. All the time doing this, we are maximizing our gains. The same strategy can be used in a sideways market and it will always give us a big positive return.

Never stick to one trading system.

Being too optimistic or too pessimistic about the market can destroy any trading strategy. In case of an upward trend, traders will usually buy high and sell low; in case of a downward trend, they will usually buy low and sell high. Both strategies are wrong and should be avoided. So we must keep in mind that it is better to buy low and sell high, but we must also protect ourselves against huge losses. The best way to do this is to keep our trading system as simple as possible. For example, when the market is going up, it may be a good idea to buy low and sell high, but this strategy alone will not always make our profit. There are many other factors that must be taken into consideration such as support and resistance levels, MACD momentum indicators, Fibonacci retracements, and potential trend reversals. So, we must add indicators to our trading strategy in order not to stick to one trading system too much or ignore some of these important indicators.

Always have a stop loss and a take profit—in simple terms, having a stop loss means defining at what price we will automatically sell our coins. Having a take profit means defining at what price we will automatically buy coins. Having these two levels defined, we will always know the exact amount of coins that we can lose. There is no way to avoid losses, but this strategy helps us to understand how much of our investment capital is really at risk and how much money we can earn or lose. Stop loss and take profit should be placed carefully when the market is moving very fast upwards or downwards in order to prevent any unnecessary losses or too big profits.

Do not panic.

We have our stop loss and take profit levels, so what should we do when the price goes below our level? Many people would sell at a very low price and book the loss. That's a bad idea. We should stick to our trading system and never sell automatically below our stop loss or take profit levels without analyzing the situation first. If we do that, we will eventually lose all our investment capital. We must be patient and wait patiently for the right time to sell.

Chapter 13
Using Ichimoku and Fibonacci Techniques

There are tons of techniques for crypto trading out there but not many people talk about the Ichimoku and Fibonacci techniques. A lot of analysts use these complicated and more difficult-to-understand methods, but I'm going to break them down for you guys in a much more simple version because, hey, you deserve it!

Ichimoku is a Japanese technique that is basically a charting tool that lets you see patterns over time. It tells you how the market has been moving and where it might go next. Fibonacci is also another charting technique that was developed by Leonardo Fibonacci, an Italian mathematician around 1200AD. This technique is very similar to Ichimoku.

Ok, so let's first explain what you need to know about the Fibonacci and Ichimoku techniques: Fibonacci studies the relationship between the changes in a price and how far it has moved along its path. It uses a mathematical formula that counts the number of terms in any sequence of numbers. The sequence also usually starts with two terms, 0 and 1. The first is called zero and the second one is one. For example, if you are looking at the Bitcoins chart, I can see that at the beginning of 2017, its range was between 500$–750$. After this period, Bitcoin dropped to 400$ where it would run until April 2018 when it reached 200$ and then after this drop, we could see its next move was a correction of 80$. This is just one example of how Fibonacci sequences can be used in trading as they follow the pattern of a golden ratio. The one above shows you how the price did exactly what I said it would do.

Now that we know who invented the Ichimoku and Fibonacci techniques you'll want to know what they actually look like on a chart. If you're familiar with the Fibonacci sequence that Fibonacci studies, you will already be familiar with the Ichimoku cloud. The cloud is basically a line that forms a trendline and it is used to confirm your buy and sell points. It helps sell your pairs when there are signs of an uptrend in price while buying pairs when there is a downtrend in price.

Ichimoku Cloud and Fibonacci

The Ichimoku cloud is a visual way of helping you see if the market is going to continue to move up or down.

The Ichimoku cloud is based on 4 simple lines that are all used to draw a trendline. These lines are: ichi cloud, senkou span A, senkou span B, kijun sen.

Ichimoku Cloud: this line is the most important one, it represents the average price over a period of time. It measures whether the market is overbought or oversold. The Ichimoku cloud uses two main components to determine if a currency is trending up or down, the current price and the average of recent prices (26 periods). This is why you'll often see Ichimoku charts with 26 price bars on them.

The average cloud (blue line) is your friend, it will help you find the perfect exit points and entries.

Add Mass Back to the Trade: We've recommended adding a lot of margin to your trades; however, as market conditions change we can quickly get too bullish or bearish. The Ichimoku Cloud helps reduce this risk and shows us where we are trending before we create too much risk. It is important to note that in an uptrend, the cloud shows support areas, and in a downtrend, it shows resistance levels. This will allow you to gauge if you need more or less leverage depending on the current momentum of the pair and that will help you mitigate some of this risk.

Fibonacci Retracement: you want to stay away from trades that are 20–40% in a retracement. The reason for this is that the support and resistance lines of the chart have a tendency to act as kill zones and can often play out at this level and exit results in losses. So, if you're looking to take trades towards the end of a retracement, it is wise to wait until you hit your exit point. A Fibonacci retracement is a dotted line that marks off times where prices underwent extreme volatility. As for Fibonacci retracement levels, these are used as guidelines when trading any pair in which we want to achieve maximum profit or minimize risk. For instance, if you want to predict when Bitcoin has reached its bottom or top, you will need to use Fibonacci retracement levels. In this case, the whole thing is quite straightforward. The difference lies in how we actually test it. We will not concern ourselves with the final outcome and changes in price that have already happened. We will only be focusing on the trend since we believe this to be a key indicator that can help us visualize price fluctuations in a clear manner. The neat thing about Fibonacci retracement levels is that they offer a wide range of trading opportunities. They are also relatively easy to understand and easy to use.

This is what an Ichimoku chart looks like:

The green lines on this chart represent support & resistance, while the red line represents the "cross-over" or cloud. The more the lines converge, the more bearish or bullish the market. The best strategy to follow in this case is to either go long (buy) if there is a break above the cloud or go short (sell) if there's a break below it.

Chapter 14
n.15 Considerations Before Getting Started with Crypto

ryptocurrencies have become one of the most innovative and rapidly developing systems that are set to revolutionize the world as we know it. There is a lot to be said about their rapid growth, but there are also some disadvantages. Crypto exchanges often provide a platform for manipulation and scams with investors losing their money or getting scammed in the process. Cryptocurrencies themselves are also very volatile, making it hard for newcomers not keen on investing in them before becoming invested in Bitcoin or Ethereum. In order to avoid these issues and get started with cryptocurrencies, such considerations should be considered first before getting started with such innovative technology.

1. The Difference Between ICOs and Cryptocurrencies

One of the most important distinctions that have to be made is the difference between ICOs and cryptocurrencies. ICO is an acronym for Initial Coin Offering. This generally refers to a crowdfunding event in which new cryptocurrencies, tokens, or coins are sold and when investors purchase these through exchange platforms, they are known as tokens. Cryptocurrencies are intangible assets that have value and can be used to conduct transactions outside of the exchange platforms. There are some similarities between the two, but it's essential to know when one is being raised over another within the context of ICOs and cryptocurrencies.

2. Understand the Source of Funds

One of the first things that have to be understood is what supplies are being used to invest in the ICOs. Assess whether they are being raised through equity or debt and how much these funds will be able to generate after the sale. There are many ways for funds to be used, such as market capitalization tokens, revenue tokens, or fundraiser tokens. For those who intend to invest in cryptocurrencies, it's imperative that they have an understanding themselves of what kind of a token is being raised, as well as the proceeds after the sale.

3. Know the Product

It's important to know and understand what the product is that's being offered with an ICO. The development of this product or service is crucial for the growth and development of an ICO. It will also be expounded on by the founders whose goal is to launch the ICO within a period of time that's appropriate for their business plan. The number of people who can benefit from it is another important thing to look into as it impacts whether an ICO gets marketed properly prior to its launch date.

4. Know the Team Behind the Product

One of the most important things that an ICO can start off with is a well-organized and balanced team. This team should also possess the knowledge, experience, and expertise in providing their product. The overall vision of the project should be understood and there should be a real-time understanding of what goals are to be accomplished. Those who have vast experience in developing their product will need to make sure that they're well aware of how technical expertise differs from various other kinds of expertise. This includes what kind of software development language needs to be used for implementing their product. These kinds of issues are important since it affects both its quality and its cost.

5. Know the Competition

It's important to know what the competitors are in terms of quality, features, and price of the product or service being offered. This will also include what plans of action they're going to use for their business development and whether they'll actually meet them. Crowdfunding platforms offer platforms for various ICOs to present their ideas and get feedback from investors. It's crucial that due diligence is done first as it helps investors have a better understanding of the project behind an ICO before purchasing any tokens or coins to invest in. The road ahead should be thought out, as well as the role that each team member will play in creating a quality product that's desired by all stakeholders involved with it.

6. The Token's Value

It's necessary to know the extent that the value of a token will increase after the sale. The value can be either fixed or calculated as a percentage. It can also range from a percentage of the overall project to an amount that's established by the developer. The value could also be based on how many sales are generated or how much interest there is for one of its services. However, it's important to keep in mind that not all tokens will perform in such a manner, considering their market value, especially if it's set below $1 at the time of sale and is deemed undervalued after the launch date.

7. Know the Type of Tokens

There are a few kinds of tokens, and the most common ones are the native token, revenue token, and equity tokens. Native tokens are created to be used on a specific platform that will only be compatible with it. Revenue tokens represent resources that can be used by its holders for services provided by the ICO's development team. Equity tokens are similar to revenue tokens, but these represent shares into the body which will help determine how effectively it works in developing their product or service.

8. Know Your Customer (KYC) Laws and Regulations for ICOs

Know Your Customer (KYC) laws can differ from one country to another for various financial products, including cryptocurrencies and ICOs. Some countries have strict laws and regulations on some forms of cryptocurrencies, and others don't. An ICO will need to be launched in an appropriate region where the token can be purchased legally and without fail. Before you buy an ICO token, it is important to understand what type of requirements are being met in your country before buying it. This includes KYC laws for cryptocurrency that's being used by investors. Investors should also make sure that their country has a good legal framework for ICOs before investing in them.

9. Know How the Token Will Be Used

There are various tokens that can be used for different products and services that are being offered by ICOs. These tokens can be exchanged for products and/or services. Utility tokens are used to pay for services, while asset-centric coins are used to own assets in companies or cryptocurrency exchanges. Equity-based ICOs represent ownership of a company, while debt-based ICOs represent a debt owed to the company's equity holders. There are many other kinds of tokens that ICOs can issue as well as properties, but investors should know them all; especially if they're planning on investing in an ICO that has several types of tokens.

10. Know the Company's Business Development Plan Before Investing

The business development plan is an essential part of what an ICO will implement once it becomes a successful venture. There should be a concise business plan with several deadlines as well as milestones that need to be met by the development team of an ICO prior to its launch date. These goals should also reflect what kind of distribution and exit strategies are available for investors, as well as the basic structure of how different tokens will perform after they're purchased by investors. The business development plans can vary depending on the size and scale of the project, but these plans should be laid out for investors before investing in their product or service.

11. Know Project Code and Roadmap Prior to Investment

The code that is being used for the development of a product or service will need to be checked out before investing in an ICO. This is essential because it helps investors have a better understanding of how the product or service is going to work. Investors should also make sure that everything they've seen, heard, or read about the project is accurate. For example, if the developers are planning on raising funds through an ICO, they should make sure that their code has been published in a manner that's easily understandable to investors.

12. Know the Team Behind an ICO

Investors should make sure that each team member is added to the whitelist prior to any investment being made. This can be done by either sending an email to the official address that's available on their website or contact them through social media such as LinkedIn, Twitter, Facebook, or other networking sites. It's vital that investors check out and research each team member before they invest in them because this will help them understand what kind of potential their business can have and how it will affect its quality and effectiveness. This is especially important for those who are investing in ICOs that have only one team member behind their project.

13. Know Where to Buy ICOs

The best place to buy ICOs is on an ICO's official website. There are other places that sell coins or tokens, but the individuals or organizations that offer them aren't linked with the actual development team behind the ICO. You can also purchase your tokens at cryptocurrency exchanges, including Cryptopia, Bittrex, Poloniex, and many others. However, there have been numerous fraud cases in which some of these exchanges were hacked and investors were scammed; sometimes even resulting in the theft of their money and/or cryptocurrency. Before you invest in an ICO or cryptocurrency exchange, research them first and understand what kind of security features they have in place, if any at all.

14. Know Where to Store Your ICOs

There are several forms of wallets where you can store your tokens, including hardware wallets, desktop wallets, and mobile wallets. However, investors need to know that there are many different types of wallets such as hot and cold storage. Before investing in an ICO or cryptocurrency exchange, you should make sure that you have the proper cryptocurrency wallet where your funds are being stored. This will allow you to view your transactions at all times; as well as having total access to them without worrying about any third parties taking them away from you.

15. Know How to Protect Yourself From Scams

Cryptocurrency and ICOs are extremely volatile. Due to their nature, there will be a lot of risks that surround them. Investors should do whatever they can to protect themselves from scams, including researching the legitimacy of a project before investing in it. There are many websites on the internet that provide up-to-date information on ICOs and cryptocurrency, such as CoinDesk's ICO Tracker website. They also have a lot of useful information about upcoming and ongoing tokens as well as links to their whitepapers and official websites. Other useful websites include CryptoCoinNews and CoinMarketCap, which offer daily updates on the state of the cryptocurrency market and news stories related to it. There are many other websites available that offer valuable information about ICOs and cryptocurrency, so make sure to research them thoroughly before investing in either one.

Chapter 15

n.15 Possible Moves When Your Portfolio Is Down

D ay trading cryptocurrencies is difficult. It's not just because their volatile nature sets them apart from traditional markets. It's also because they're unique, and time-intensive projects for the most part. Day traders must become experts in a number of topics, from economics to blockchain technology to technical analysis. Fortunately, there are some tools that can help you trade successfully without as much work involved, and these tools are called "heuristics." In the following blog post we've compiled 15 common heuristic moves traders make when their portfolio is down in crypto trading. These moves will help you stay afloat while looking for better trading opportunities in other currencies or assets!

1. Stop and Reassess the State of Your Portfolio

This first rule is pretty straightforward. It's important to take a look at your portfolio and ask yourself some questions. What was your original strategy? Did you stick to it? Are there any assets that you may want to sell or abandon in favor of? Was your strategy too risky for your liking, or are you just facing a rough patch that will eventually pass? Have you been spending more money than you've been making? If so, this may be the time to cut your losses while they're still not too great. This is especially true if your portfolio has lost value over the last few weeks. You don't have to keep losing money on bad crypto trades. Resigning yourself to losing money in the short term may be necessary.

2. Don't Trade When Your Portfolio Is Down

This is a very important rule for crypto traders. It's also one that many people tend to break. It's easy to see your portfolio become lower than ever before and make the decision that "this is just not my day" or "this can't possibly get worse." However, it's not a good idea to start trading before you've taken time out of your day to review your portfolio and consider your trade strategy. The result will likely be another day of losses, and you will be no closer to turning things around.

3. Stop Trading for a While if You're Scared

Many people watch the markets frequently, and not just because they're day traders. Many cryptocurrency traders are on the lookout for exciting new opportunities rather than waiting for things to happen in the markets themselves. When you see big price spikes, it's easy to get tempted into buying or selling regardless of what your strategy is or what your funds may allow for. If you feel this temptation when your portfolio is down, consider switching off of trading platforms until you've had time to take stock of where your money is going and how it's been doing recently.

4. Don't Trade When Your Portfolio Is Low

You know what it's like to fall in love with a coin and see its value spiral upwards, only to have your emotions take over when your portfolio looks weak. Obsessing over tiny gains or losses could also lead you to make bad decisions about selling assets when they're down. Luckily, there are other times when you don't need to be worried about your portfolio being low on funds or falling into a dip because of this market opportunity.

5. Don't Trade Often or Frequently if You're Broke

This is another move more typically made by day traders than long-term ones. Day trading is an industry that requires a lot of liquidity. If your portfolio is broken, you're not going to have much money to put into trading or withdrawals. Because of this, it's not a good idea to keep trading with no money in reserve if your portfolio is down. That way you'll end up trading more than you can afford and will end up losing your entire account. It's also important to avoid frequent trading if you're working off of a low bankroll. This means that if you have $100 in an account and you want to make one trade, consider doing nothing until that $100 grows back up or until the trade opportunity presents itself again later on.

6. Sell Into a Dip if You're Upside Down

If you're already down in crypto trading, it's not going to be long before you see the value of your portfolio go right back up. This is fine as long as there's still a chance that this happens. If you sell close to the top or bottom of a bear, you could lose money because of this reversal. However, if there are signs that the market has turned around and is beginning to go up again, then you should probably be looking for buying opportunities elsewhere.

7. Diversify Your Holdings

This rule would also apply if your portfolio becomes too bearish. If you had some cryptocurrency that was doing just fine while everything else was going down, then it might be a good idea to sell off your weaker assets for stronger ones. This way you will end up with a more balanced portfolio when things start picking back up again. If you don't, then you could end up losing your entire account when your long-term crypto investment strategy was going as expected.

8. Stay Invested

Despite the temptation of selling off hastily after your portfolio loses value, it's important to remember that all of your assets have performed well for a reason at one point or another. Crypto is a market that tends to rebound quickly, so it's best to just hang on for the ride.

9. Take Longer-Term Positions

Selling crypto assets when your portfolio is down can be tempting because you may want quick money while you wait on the markets to recover. However, if you're interested in long-term investing, then it's a better idea to hold onto your assets for the time being and keep your eye out for some promising new opportunities. You may even want to switch over to an entirely new strategy if this bear run has affected most of your holdings poorly!

10. Don't Expect Much

If you're having a really rough time with short-term crypto trading, then it's okay to be pessimistic about the rest of the world. You don't need to convince yourself that everything will turn around within a few days or even weeks. This will give you no room for error when trading your way out of a dip, and the goal is to try to build some positive momentum in your investment portfolio as soon as possible.

11. Set Your Margin for Success

There may be times when you look at your long-term investment strategy and get discouraged that whatever you invested in looks so weak compared to what the market is doing right now. However, this isn't always the case. If the ones that you've been relying on are still doing okay, then the market could be overreacting to their poor performance. In this case, it's a good idea to look into buying more of them as they go higher because there's a chance that you're missing out on some great opportunities within your portfolio.

12. Keep an Eye on Coins You're Not Trading

If you are looking to take advantage of dips in the cryptocurrency market while holding onto your funds for day trading and short-term price speculation, then you can't just ignore any solid investments that aren't in an obvious dip right now. These will remain relevant to your long-term strategy so you should give them a little bit more attention.

13. Don't Be Afraid to Change Your Strategy

If you're not sure about how your portfolio is doing, maybe it's time for a change. Maybe it's time to transfer some of your assets from one wallet or exchange to another because of this market dip or because they have better opportunities today that you're missing out on? This is when switching over is very helpful because you have the opportunity of finding something new and exciting that fits into your long-term investment strategy.

14. Be Patient and Realistic

In this type of market, patience is a crucial idea. If you're impatient about the cryptocurrency market after all of these dips, you could be annoying yourself before things even begin to turn around again. It's very important to keep your head and remember that you only have a few options when dealing with this market opportunity. You can either sell everything off and start over as if it never happened or you can put your faith in your long-term strategy and stay the course regardless of what happens right now.

15. Don't Give Up

If you're doing everything right and your portfolio is down, and then one day it's suddenly up a lot then you have no idea what hit you. That often happens in the market, so don't be surprised. It's important to remember that this is just the market trying to balance out all of the new opportunities that it has seen lately. If you hang around long enough, they'll eventually turn around.

Chapter 16
n.15 Challenges and Opportunities for Crypto Investors

C rypto investing might sound like a new and difficult investment style, but it can be a lot more manageable with some knowledge of what you're going up against. Here are 15 challenges and opportunities for crypto investors to keep in mind. This will make navigating the world of crypto much easier!

1. **With the rise of cryptocurrency, most banks and governments have little control over their citizens' money.** That means they have less control over how people spend their money than they ever had before. This is a big challenge for those who are used to intervening in the private spending habits of citizens, and it might change the face of our economic systems. How to deal with this is anyone's guess, but for the time being, it could cause problems such as the balance of payments issues and tax collection issues.

2. **The more people use crypto to pay for goods and services, the more value that cryptocurrency will have.** This essentially means that as crypto becomes widely used, its value will go up. If you choose to invest in cryptocurrency, you have an inside view as to how likely you think this is going to happen.

3. **Just like the human body needs food to survive, so do cryptocurrencies.** Mining is essentially how the body gets

fed. This means that every time a cryptocurrency transaction happens, it will need mining for the transaction to be confirmed and for one crypto 'body cell' to give some of its power to support another cell. The more transactions that happen within a cryptocurrency ecosystem, the more mining there will be.

4. **If you have invested in a cryptocurrency that has a high value, then you might notice a significant increase in your bank account each time you go to sell it back into fiat currency.** This is a great opportunity to have some fun with your cryptocurrency. You can use it to pay for things you wouldn't ordinarily pay for, or you can treat yourself to something nice.

5. **During periods of high crypto usage, there will be a higher demand for graphics cards that run on electricity.** This works in the favor of miners who will make a lot of money as they sell their graphics cards on the open market. However, it is also an investment opportunity for those who can react quickly enough to buy the graphics cards at a discount and then sell them for profit when demand falls once again.

6. **There is no limit to how much money you can make on the markets.** You could become incredibly rich overnight. However, you may also lose a lot of money just as quickly without warning. You should always be prepared for the worst, but always be positive about your chances of making a profit. If you're feeling positive about your investment and it still looks like it will go up in value, then you might want to consider holding on to it for as long as possible before selling it and rebuying it if necessary.

7. **You should only invest what you are willing to lose if there are any signs that the price is going down.** That is a great attitude to have! However, you must remember that the market can see foreseeable changes in trends before they happen. This means that if anybody can see a sign that something is going to significantly change in price, then it

might already be too late for you to do anything about it. You should never be investing more than what is necessary.

8. If there is a sell-off of cryptocurrency due to some sort of natural disaster or man-made calamity, you will probably have less time than usual to take your investments out on time and into fiat currency. During such times, the market demands a lot of attention from all investors.

9. You should be able to recognize a trend in the market, whether it is going up or down. Those who can't see trends are likely not going to be successful in their finances. This means that you should have a clear understanding of what is going on with your investments throughout the day, and you should also have control over when you take your profits or make your purchases based on market trends.

10. If you want to speculate on which coins will do well in the future, then you may want to think about investing in them now before other people get excited about them and start buying them up like crazy. If you wait until the hype is at its highest, then there are so many investors that it could be difficult to buy in before all of the hype has passed.

11. No one can predict the future. This means that even if you do everything according to plan and fully expect a profit, you might find that your investment goes down in value instead. You should always be prepared for the worst-case scenario. This means that you shouldn't just simply assume that any investment is going to make a profit, or even survive at all. Instead, every time any new opportunity comes up, you should use logic and common sense to figure out whether it is worth investing in or not. If you do that, then you will be able to make good decisions with your money.

12. You should only invest in a cryptocurrency if you have the time and the patience to keep up with it. This means that if you are investing money in crypto that you are not too familiar with, or one you don't have any experience with, then it is probably best to avoid it. If something looks too good to be true, it usually is!

13. You should always use multiple investment choices when making investments. This means that every time you make an investment decision, you should compare between different options by looking at the pros and cons of each coin as well as the market trends themselves. As long as you stay one step ahead of the trends, you will be able to make the most money from your investments.

14. If you want to maximize your profits, then you should find a coin that has a great team that is dedicated to making sure that they can support it in the future and that people start using it right away. You should also find a coin where there is a lot of demand for it. There is nothing wrong with investing in a coin that has no real use or one which has not been tested yet by the general public. However, this does not mean that other people are going to continue spending their funds on such things once they know better and stop buying them up while they still have value.

15. You should only invest in a cryptocurrency that is ready to be used as soon as it comes out in the open market. The best way to do this is to buy some before it comes out and holds its value all on its own. If you are not ready to use it, then you should consider selling the coin and putting your money into one that has a better chance of being adopted by people in the real world. During different stages of market growth, you will find different points at which it could be beneficial for you to hold or sell your investments.

Chapter 17
n.24 Signals That Every Trader Should Know

E very day, there are always going to be new developments that can affect your portfolio in one way or another.

Today I'll give you insights into how to identify these signals without having to do any research on your own. Keep track of these 24 signals so when they start popping up, you'll already know what's happening and be able to make the correct choices for yourself.

When Trading too Much

This signal is usually associated with major events taking place in the economy and markets—such as a change in monetary policy—which can lead traders to believe that prices will increase over time because investors feel more confident about investments as a result of these changes.

When Trading too Little

This signal is usually associated with global economic slowdowns, which cause investors to perceive a decrease in market confidence.

These signals are very important to keep in mind because when you don't do so, you'll be trading too much or too little. When you trade too much, it's easy to miss opportunities because you're not paying attention to the right information and reacting accordingly. But when you trade too little, it's an even bigger problem because you will be trading based on incorrect information and not reacting appropriately.

When trading less, you'll inevitably lose money because you're not making any decisions in the market. And when you trade too much, being on the go all the time can hurt your trading performance and lead to emotional trading. Plus, when you're not being disciplined enough to stick to what you know is right, it will ultimately lead to bigger problems down the road—such as overtrading, excessive losses, and so on. So make sure that you keep these signals in mind at all times, so that you can stay out of any trouble in the future.

Momentum Selling

This is a signal that occurs when investors get nervous about the markets and sell their holdings in an attempt to cut their losses.

Sell signals are usually accompanied by panic selling that sets off alarm bells among investors and traders alike. When this happens, you should consider selling your assets as well in order to protect yourself from further market losses.

Momentum Buying

It's the opposite of momentum selling, which is when investors and traders buy stocks, bonds, or other investments at a high price because they believe that prices will continue to move up in the future.

For example, if you received a signal that the markets were about to rise and you purchased an asset that was already at a high price, then you would be buying without momentum. If this was the case, your trade might be successful if prices continue to move up or it could lead to losses if prices go down. Either way, it's crucial that you focus on buying assets when momentum is moving them upward.

Beware

These warning signals are something that every trader should be aware of because they can tell you whether or not something is going wrong in the market. I've seen many new traders lose money because they never noticed these signals in the first place and then tried to make up for their losses by taking risky trades.

People don't realize that risky trades are usually the reason why they're losing money in the market in the first place. But if you take these signals into account, at least you'll be able to tell when and how to avoid high-risk trades altogether.

Excessive Shorting

This is a signal that occurs when traders start taking out short positions on securities that have an unfavorable outlook.

For example, if there's a lack of interest for an asset, such as a commodity or security, this is usually associated with lower prices because nobody wants it. Traders who believe that the price will fall are then encouraged to take out short positions.

The problem is, shorting security when the price has dropped significantly is usually the result of an unfavorable outlook. When this occurs, it's a signal that you shouldn't get involved with the security in question because it doesn't look like it will continue on its current path.

Before you take out any trades, make sure that you understand what's happening in the markets at all times so that you can avoid getting involved with any securities or commodities if they don't look like they'll be moving any higher in the future.

Spike Trading

This is a signal that occurs when the price of an asset moves up or down quickly due to a major event that has just taken place.

For example, one day you wake up and notice that the price of gold has increased by 15% overnight. You then start to panic because you don't know what's happening, so you immediately get out of the market because you're afraid that more losses are going to be taking place. The problem is, even though prices spiked higher than they did before, it's still in your best interest to hold onto your assets rather than take any risks at this point (such as shorting or attempting to sell high).

Spike Selling

It's the opposite of spike trading, which is when traders take out short positions on assets that have spiked higher in price. They believe that the asset's price will eventually come down and lead to a loss for their position.

It's important to understand that this is one of the biggest mistakes a trader can make because it leads to losing money. Spike selling will only be successful if the downward spike occurs immediately after your trade. However, if it doesn't occur right away, then you're likely going to lose your money on these trades quickly.

Always remember that price spikes are just a warning signal to indicate that something may cause the price of an asset to change in the future. And if an asset has spiked higher in price without any specific event taking place, then it's likely going to be associated with a major correction—which is why you shouldn't get involved with it at all.

Dollar Trend

This is a signal that occurs when investors and traders start buying or selling dollars in order to increase profits and cut losses. When this happens, you should follow suit and do the same thing as well.

Price Trends

This is a signal that occurs when investors and traders start buying or selling assets in order to increase profits and cut losses. When this happens, you should follow suit and do the same thing as well.

Trends can occur right away, but they're usually associated with market corrections that take place over time. And when this occurs, you don't want to be involved in the market because it will be too difficult to predict which way prices will move next.

For example, let's say that there's a trend in the markets and gold is increasing in price at an exponential rate. If you decide to buy assets at this point, then there are two possible outcomes: one good and one bad. If prices continue to move higher, then you'll make money. However, if prices go down significantly, then you'll be losing a lot of money on these trades.

Therefore, it's important to know when a trend is taking place so that you know how to avoid getting involved with assets that are moving in the wrong direction.

Dollar Selling

It's the same as buying dollars in terms of losing money on these trades. When this happens, you should definitely sell your dollars and get out of this position right away because there could be additional losses coming your way soon (since dollar trends are a signal that confirms that something bad could be taking place).

Price Selling

It's the same as selling an asset when the price spikes higher without any specific event taking place. When this occurs, you should definitely sell your asset and get out of this position right away because there could be additional losses coming your way soon (since price spikes are a signal that confirms that something bad could be taking place).

False Earnings Reports

This is one of the most common warning signals that I've seen when it comes to investing in penny stocks. And unfortunately, many people don't even know about these false reports because they haven't done any research on the history of certain companies before trading them.

For example, I heard about one company several years ago that was doing extremely well because it had received a $100 million contract to build fighter jets for the government. This was an extremely positive development that showed that the company would be able to maintain its current production levels for the next few years, which meant that its income levels were going to increase significantly.

However, one day I received a phone call from one of my brokers and he asked me if I could explain why the stock price was dropping. The next day, I opened up Forbes magazine and read about how this company misrepresented its financial statements by taking out loans in order to generate more revenue during its last fiscal year.

It turned out that the CEO of this company had the financial backing of one of his friends, who in return got a substantial amount of shares in this company in exchange for financing it. He then used these assets as collateral to put more money into the company, which ended up giving it false earnings reports during its last fiscal year. However, these financial statements didn't show that the CEO was responsible for repaying about $50 million for these loans (which made him lose control over 100% of his shares held at this company).

In this situation, analysts were looking at the wrong financial statements (which were showing inflated profits) when determining how much to pay for the stocks. This was an extremely rare scenario that only a few investors knew about, and they were able to profit from it as well. However, if you're not careful and research the history of a penny stock before buying it, then you could be making a huge mistake because something like this could occur again in the future.

Closed Trade

These are trades that haven't been completed yet due to a significant price movement in either direction within a 24 hour period. In situations where these trades are still open, it's best to simply leave them alone unless you want the opportunity to take on even more risk than usual.

For example, let's say that a trade is going to be closed and the price has moved to the right. In this case, you should wait at least 24 hours and then make a decision as to whether you want to take the position or not. If you decide that it's too late to take this position, then you should say goodbye to that penny stock without taking any additional risks.

Flooding

This is one of the most common warning signals when it comes to investing in penny stocks because there could be a series of these events taking place in the near future.

For example, let's say that a penny stock has been receiving positive news from the business media and this is causing it to increase in value. If you choose to hold onto this stock at this point, then there will probably be more floods in the future because the company is going to experience financial difficulties if it doesn't receive additional funding in a short period of time.

If you see that a company is flooding the market with shares, then you should make sure that you're not involved with its stock until it stabilizes. Otherwise, there's a good chance that you'll lose money on these trades.

Quick Changes in Price

Even though most of these changes tend to be negative, there have been instances where a company's value has gone up significantly due to the news being released. However, these situations are only temporary because the stock will come back down to earth over time. When this occurs, it's important to move quickly so that you can lock in some gains before everything returns to normal.

Insider Buying

If an insider is purchasing large amounts of shares within their company at a current price level, then it's a strong indicator that this asset could be on the rise (although it's still best to take into account all of the other warning signals before making any investment decisions).

For example, let's say that a large insider purchases 500,000 shares of a certain penny stock within the last 90 days. After looking at all of this data, you should recognize that the price movement could be an indication that it's about to advance because there was just a lot of news being released in this company. In this case, it may be best to buy more shares of this penny stock and hold your position for the next several months because this is one of the best signals that you can receive when it comes to penny stocks.

Earnings Surprises

These are actually rare occurrences in my experience with these types of investments. However, if you did receive one, then you should consider buying more shares because the company's earnings report will probably be seen as a positive development.

For example, let's say that a penny stock has been doing extremely well for the past three years and it's going to announce its final earnings report. In this case, it could surprise analysts by increasing its EPS by 60% in the 3rd quarter of this year. This is going to cause the stock to spike up in price because investors are going to realize that there's a lot of potential for growth within this company. However, there's also the chance that this company will miss its earnings for the quarter. If this happens, then you may be able to get in on this stock at a very low price because of all of the negative attention it will receive.

However, everything depends on the situation because even if an insider is purchasing shares or there is good news being released about a penny stock within a short time, it doesn't mean that the price will go up immediately.

Talk to the Management Team

Even though this sounds like a very basic task, it's not uncommon for CEOs and other executive-level employees to put on a big show in order to convince you that their company is worth investing in.

Information Overload

This is a serious problem that plagues many penny stock investors because there's so much data being released on these stocks on a daily basis that it can be difficult to make a decision as to whether or not they're undervalued. To make matters worse, you have all of these information sources (including the business media) giving you conflicting tips about your trades so it can be tough to find what is useful and what isn't when it comes to trading information.

If you're dealing with all of this information overload, then you're going to need an expert who can break down the data for you so that you can make a better-informed decision.

Analyst Issuance

Even though analyst comments are usually positive, there could be some red flags that cause them to downgrade a stock within a short period of time. For example, let's say that a bank is starting to become concerned about the company's balance sheet because it has excessive debt and liabilities on its books. If this is the case, it could cause the stock to experience downward pressure. If you see that there a lot of downgrades are being issued in a short period of time, then you should make sure that you're not involved with this penny stock.

In addition, most analysts are well aware that they have a significant amount of influence on the share prices for these investments so it's important for them to refrain from making any comments about the potential for up-ticks or down-ticks within these stocks. For example, let's say that an analyst is going to give his comments about a stock at 5:00 pm. If there are a lot of negative things being said about the stock, then it probably won't be able to maintain its price during the day. Therefore, he may choose to not comment on it if it looks like the share price is going to fall significantly within a short time.

Upward Pressure

Many penny stocks will rise in value because there is a lot of upward pressure on them from various sources (such as the business media and other investors). For example, let's say that there are 10 million shares of a certain penny stock being held by insiders and they decide to sell them all at once. In this case, there will be a massive amount of downward pressure on this stock because all of the shares are being sold at once.

If you're going to invest in penny stocks, then you should always keep in mind that there is upward pressure on these investments and that they could be pushed up to extreme price levels depending on the fundamentals (or lack thereof) being released.

Earnings Reports

It's not uncommon for penny stocks to report earnings in a less-than-ideal situation. For example, let's say that a company has been doing well for the past two years but it is going to be releasing its earnings report in the middle of its biggest quarter of the year. In this case, the company could be forced to show its true colors and investors may realize that it has been overvalued prior to this point. If this happens, then there will probably be a lot of downward pressure on the stock as it goes into freefall.

This is going to be the big risk that you'll have to take when investing in penny stocks because it's a terrible investment if there's going to be something like this going on.

Stock Splits

A stock split occurs when a company wants to make it seem like its finances are in good shape after the price of the stock has fallen too low. In reality, nothing has really changed about the company's performance and it was just another way for management to boost their share prices. Because of this, you shouldn't get involved with these penny stocks unless you're willing to double your money in a short period.

This is one of the most complicated aspects of penny stocks because it's possible for you to double your money in a very short period of time after you take advantage of a stock split. For example, let's say that there's a stock that has fallen to $5, and then it announces a 2-for-1 stock split. This means that each investor will be given two shares for every share they currently have so now they have 20 shares. Now, let's say that this stock goes up to $10 again; if you sell all of your shares then you would make $100 per share, even though the company hasn't really changed anything about itself.

You'll also notice that there was no distribution of any cash to the existing shareholders. Even though you just doubled your money, you're still working with the same underlying company (albeit with a much higher share price).

Chapter 18
Resources for Personal Portfolio Management

What Is a Portfolio in Cryptocurrency?

A cryptocurrency portfolio is a collection of cryptocurrencies that an individual holds. It may be a diversified investment vehicle, or it may be used to track the holdings' values to determine profit and loss.

What Are the Different Types of Cryptocurrency Portfolios?

There are two types of portfolios: Technical Analysis Portfolios and Fundamental Analysis Portfolios.

1. Technical Analysis Portfolio

A Technical Analysis Portfolio is created by buying a certain number of coins based on price charts. Typically, technical analysis involves price patterns that indicate whether the coin will be increasing or decreasing. Technical charts are popular among people who use bots to conduct arbitrage trading. An arbitrage trader simultaneously buys and sells an asset to profit from the mismatch in the price across exchanges.

2. Fundamental Analysis Portfolio

A Fundamental Analysis Portfolio is created by buying certain coins because you believe in their fundamentals. Fundamental analysis involves looking at the history of a coin or an investment and determining the reason for its price.

For example, you might buy Bitcoin because you believe it will be accepted as a form of payment or own Litecoin because you think it will be used as a payment form.

How to Build a Portfolio?

There are 3 steps to building your portfolio in cryptocurrency:

1. Create an account on an exchange
2. Purchase your first coins
3. Start investing your coins

Where to Create an Account on an Exchange?

Each exchange has a different process for creating a new account. If you are using Luno, then click here. On Coinbase, click here. On Poloniex, click here. If you are using Binance, click here. Our recommendation is to use Coinbase or Poloniex—these two exchanges process thousands of transactions per minute and have a simple user interface with similar functionality across each platform. They also have the most trading pairs for Bitcoin.

How to Use an Exchange?

Exchanges can seem daunting with so many features and functions, but there are essentially only four things you can do on an exchange:

1. **Deposit.** Deposit Bitcoin into your account by going to the "Balances" page, searching for and clicking the bitcoin icon, then clicking "Deposit." This will bring up a wallet

address to send bitcoins from your wallet or exchange account.

Note that you can deposit bitcoins from an exchange account or your wallet.

2. Buy. To buy BTC you need to go to "Exchange" and enter the BTC amount you want to buy and click "Buy." Also, suppose your country doesn't support Bitcoin. In that case, you can always purchase it on a different exchange with a different currency by clicking the currency symbol (the yellow one) for Bitcoin, then clicking "Buy."

3. Sell. If you want to sell your coins, then simply go back to the "Balances" page, find the bitcoin icon, and then click "Sell."

4. Withdraw. If you want to withdraw your cryptocurrencies to a personal wallet, click "Withdraw."

At this point, you're ready to start investing in cryptocurrencies!

Keeping Track of Your Portfolio Value and Profit/Loss

Since crypto coins are volatile, it is important to track your portfolio's value as time passes. You could track the fiat currency value (for example, USD) or cryptocurrency (BTC or ETH). We will look at both tracking methods here and give our recommendation for which one you should use.

Chapter 19
Tips for Getting Started with Cryptocurrency

A s a beginner, it is important that you understand the concept well and plan your portfolio in such a way that you strike gold soon. Here are a handful of tips that can help you get there!

Ignore Sources that Are Biased

When you decide to trade with Cryptocurrency, it is extremely important that you don't rely on biased sources for investing ideas. The minute you start browsing online for trading options, you will come across multiple sites promising good returns. As a beginner, you must stay away from phony sites, which offer surprisingly high returns. Seek advice only from reliable sources before you begin investing. Rely on your judgment and risk appetite and choose your portfolio accordingly. Do not get swayed by fake success stories posted on certain websites and make a hasty decision.

Start Small

As a beginner, until you get a good grasp of how the market works, it is important that you do not exhaust your life savings at once. Start small. Keep aside a small portion of your income every month, for trading purposes. Invest small amounts at first and understand the nuances of the trading process. As you start making a profit, slowly increase your investments. Do not make the mistake of investing huge sums, as soon as you experience a profit for the first time. Take your time to decide the optimal portfolio for your risk appetite. Once that is figured, you can gradually increase your investments.

Have Realistic Goals

Do not look at Cryptocurrency trading as an easy and quick way to become rich. As you already know, the Cryptocurrency market is highly dynamic and volatile. It will take you some time to get a grasp of the trading process. Hence, it is important that you have realistic goals before you commence trading. Do not aspire to achieve a 25% growth on your portfolio immediately and then get disappointed if that does not happen. Have a realistic goal of starting with no loss, no profit scenario, when you begin trading. From there, move on to setting your growth rate at 5%, 10%, etc. Have minimal expectations when you begin trading. This way, you will be able to study the market in a keen fashion and design your portfolio accordingly.

Don't Try to Guess and Trade

Trading is not about making the right guesses. When it comes to an extremely volatile market, such as that of cryptocurrencies, it is not possible to sustain your returns, purely by making guesses. You might get lucky once or twice, but your guesses can only help you to a certain extent. You need to do your homework before you make an investing decision. Even if you are not a beginner, you cannot predict exactly how the market will react tomorrow. Make sure you keep an eye on the trends and watch out for market reports before you invest. Despite all the homework, there is still a possibility of you not making a profit. However, one failure should not deter you from doing your homework.

Be Patient and Don't Panic

When it comes to trading with cryptocurrencies, it is extremely important that you learn to be patient. As a beginner, you might make some trading mistakes. Or it might take you more time to understand the nuances of the market. Do not immediately give up on trading with cryptocurrencies, because of few mistakes. In fact, you will learn more from the mistakes, which will help you make informed decisions in the future. You must embrace the uncertainty element of the future and be prepared for the worst-case scenario too. This way, you will not panic if you make a mistake or incur a loss. You will be able to regard it as a short-term phenomenon and try to come up with a strategy to overcome this.

When you learn to be patient, you will also cultivate the habit of reading the market carefully. When you read the market carefully, you will be able to make an informed decision. When that happens, the chances of you committing mistakes are minimal and the reasons to panic are also minimal. Hence, it all comes down to how patient and calm you are.

Learn From Your Mistakes

As I mentioned before, it is absolutely normal to make mistakes. These mistakes should not dissuade you from trading with cryptocurrencies. Given that the market for these cryptocurrencies is booming, it is only a matter of time and effort from your end before you make a tidy profit. Hence, you must learn from your mistakes and correct your investing strategy accordingly. Your mistakes should be an opportunity for you to learn and better understand the market. Understand the root cause behind your mistake. Is it because you didn't do your research properly? Or is it because the market is currently a little unstable? If the mistake was within your control, you will be able to avoid it the next time. If the mistake/loss is because of market conditions and out of your control, you should stay low and wait until the market conditions improve. This applies to you, whether you are a beginner or an experienced trader.

Plan Ahead

If you want to sustain your profits from trading, in the long run, you will have to come up with an investing plan. You can't aspire to make huge profits by just focusing on trading for the day, without keeping the future implications in mind. As I mentioned before, it is extremely important that you come up with an appropriate investing portfolio. This selection of the portfolio should be based on your goals, both short-term and long-term. For instance, if your desire is to make a return of 20% on your portfolio in the next 2 years, you need to plan out your investment strategies for the next few months. Of course, there is no assurance that your plan will work 100% at all times. But, at the same time, having a plan will provide you a sense of direction and help you invest wisely.

Now, if you are new to trading, it might be difficult for you to come up with an investing plan for the future, on your own. This is where you need to take that extra step and learn from others. Seek the advice of other experienced traders, study the market, watch out for trends and come up with your tentative plan. When you see that your plan is working, see how you can further improve it to optimize your returns. If your plan is not working, well, it is a lesson learned! Remember, you can't just rely on others' counsel before investing. You need to do your bit of research as well to validate their counsel.

Don't Trust Others Completely

When it comes to trading with cryptocurrencies, you are out there, on your own. You can't rely on the success stories of others alone and make your investing decisions. While it is extremely important that you seek the inputs of others, who are regular traders, you can't blindly rely on their trading advice. This is because a certain investing strategy or choice of investments might have worked for a certain individual at that point in time, due to various reasons. There is no reason for it to work that way for everyone. Hence, you should not be basing your investment decisions based on what worked for others.

In trading, you must realize that there is no single solution to make profits. There is no one optimal portfolio combination, which can help everybody make profits. What is optimal for another individual depends on their risk appetite, goals, long-term strategy, the amount at disposal for investing, etc. These aspects need not and will not be the same for each individual. Hence, it is important that you don't plan your investments only based on what others did.

As a beginner, you can seek the inputs of other traders to understand the market better and how it works. You should go ahead and do your research to understand it for yourself. This is because the Cryptocurrency markets are highly evolving by the day. Since it is extremely dynamic, the modalities and market environment undergo a lot of changes. You have to constantly update yourself and adjust your plan and strategy accordingly. You have to rely on your judgment before you make a choice. While a little distrust is good, it becomes a problem when you completely eliminate the idea of learning from others. Other traders may not be able to give you foolproof advice. But, you can most certainly learn from their mistakes and market conditions and tweak your portfolio accordingly.

Pick Currencies that Have Huge Communities

With over 800 cryptocurrencies to date, you can be confused about which Cryptocurrency you should pick. If you want to invest in something new, do not go into a currency that no one has ever heard of.

Instead, choose a currency that has a good and established platform. The currency that you choose should have the support of a lot of community members. People should know about the currency. Having a community dedicated to a particular currency would mean that the currency is popular with the people, is stable, and going to last.

Don't Get Bored

As a beginner, it is totally possible for you to get bored with the market. Unfortunately, the Cryptocurrency market is a little dry and difficult to understand at first. When you grasp the intricacies of the trade, you will learn to appreciate it better. You will be able to figure out matters of interest and come to love trading in due course. Until such time, it is important that you exercise patience and keep an open mind about trading. I know people who have given up too soon because they got bored with the market. If only had they stuck around, they would have made a good profit. Remember that the cryptocurrencies market is tested and proven. If you employ the right strategy, you will definitely be able to make good returns in the long run. Hence, when the boredom sets in, look at the big picture. That should dissuade you from giving up at the moment.

As I mentioned before, trading with cryptocurrencies is not an easy way to get rich fast. Hence, if you see that your returns are not doubling or tripling immediately, don't get bored with the market and underestimate its potential. Just trust your research and judgment and invest. You will reap good returns eventually.

Don't Forget to Have Fun!

Do not look at trading as a mundane job or activity. At the same time, do not spend too much time overanalyzing the market. This will just ruin all the fun. You will forget to enjoy trading when you are submerged under market information. Learn to draw a line between being prudent and paranoid. When you are prudent, you will be willing to play around, have some fun and make money on the go. On the other hand, if you are paranoid, you will be thinking so much before making any investment decision. Time is of the essence when it comes to trading. When the market is quickly changing, you can't forever question your decisions and lose out on the opportunity to make money. Enjoy trading. That way, you will learn more than you expected! With time, you will be able to develop a passion for trading. When that passion sets in, it is going to be an interesting journey for you!

These are just a few illustrative tips to get you started. You will learn more, as each day goes, and this will help you customize your investment strategy accordingly. As I have already said, the keys to making good profits in the cryptocurrencies market are patience and knowledge. Build your knowledge base, bit by bit, and get rewarded in due course. Do not give up easily. This market is a gold mine, where only people who are patient and persistent strike gold. Hence, stick around, invest wisely and grow in the process. I hope you found these tips useful.

Chapter 20
n.5 Cryptocurrencies to Invest in 2021

T he best cryptocurrencies. It's enough just to think about such a list to make many of the best investors snicker.

Warren Buffett, the trading rock star, named Bitcoin rat poison, a mirage and useless. He also noted that since "they do not produce anything," cryptos are practically worthless.

Carl Icahn went on record labeling cryptocurrencies as "ridiculous." But at least he also noted that to appreciate them, he may just be too old.

The owner of the Dallas Mavericks, Mark Cuban, has said he'd rather have bananas than Bitcoin... At least you can eat bananas, after all. But for more than 150,000 bananas, you could also sell a single Bitcoin. That may not be the funny advice provided by Mr. Shark Tank.

Then there's CEO Jamie Dimon of JPMorgan Chase. He is referred to as a "fraud" in digital currency. He also said that in the future, people foolish enough to buy it will pay the price for it. It turns out, he was close. Bitcoin investors were paying a price. And a sizeable one at that.

And "the fools" who jumped in on Bitcoin have seen a return on their investment during their 2017 highs. And though it's been a few years. And it was even luckier for those who waited until the 2017 crypto frenzy died down.

If something has been proved in the past year, it is that cryptocurrencies have far more staying power than the naysayers assumed. And that it is most definitely a worthwhile effort to list the best cryptocurrencies.

Close to 6,000 separate cryptocurrencies are out there. And the space they take on your hard drive isn't worth a whole bunch of them. For instance, take internet darling Dogecoin. This altcoin was developed in 2013 and cracked into uncharted territories only recently when it was worth an entire cent.

But this also helps to clarify part of the cryptocurrency draw. There are plenty of people out there who threw a few hundred bucks at it when it was worth a fraction of a cent a while ago. A single Dogecoin was worth $0.001774 in March of 2020.

Less than a year, fast forward and a buy-and-hold strategy (or hodl, if you will) would have brought returns of upwards of 460%. No matter what kind of investment it is, that's a solid return. That takes us to the best cryptocurrencies for the near future to pick up and hodl.

The highest investment in 2021 cryptocurrencies:

Bitcoin (BTC)

Sure, it's one of the most obvious. But for good reason, that is. There's something to tell, after all, about the cryptocurrency that started it all. With a market cap of over $600 billion, it's the biggest cryptocurrency out there, without a question.

But it keeps many potential investors on the sideline with its steep price. But the situation doesn't need to be that. I just happened to have $17 worth of Bitcoin picked up in my Robinhood account.

Sure, that just scored me a Bitcoin number of 0.00046577. But I am introduced to the most popular and one of the best cryptocurrencies out there by the tiny holding stills.

Ethereum (ETH)

There's a Robin for every Batman. And while Bitcoin rules the crypto roost, with lots of upside potential, Ethereum is a strong second fiddle. Like Bitcoin, Ethereum is regarded as an alternative to fiat money by enthusiasts. But the blockchain technology (AKA database) is more oriented than digital currency on decentralized applications. But that did not slow the rapid increase in value of this AltCoin.

It allows decentralized applications to be designed and run without fraud or third-party intervention when running as a software platform (take that Apple and Google). With its own cryptographic token, the applications run on its platform operate. That makes this crypto a sought-after one within this network by developers looking to build and run apps.

Ethereum is also one of the few cryptos that can be used to buy other cryptocurrencies on exchanges. Though its market cap pales next to Bitcoin's, it has been making headway steadily. And with momentum on its hand, Ethereum is a simple option for one of the finest available cryptocurrencies.

Litecoin (LTC)

This crypto, which was created by former Google employee Charlie Lee, has several similarities with its big brother, Bitcoin. It was created to increase transaction times (approximately 2.5 minutes) and lower transaction fees. It has a block generation rate considerably faster than Bitcoin. And the number of merchants accepting Litecoin is increasing rapidly, unlike most cryptos.

As the use of Litecoin becomes more popular, it is fair that its value will only increase. Whether you want to keep it and watch it grow or use it as a form of payment that makes this one of the best cryptocurrencies out there.

Bitcoin Cash (BCH)

Bitcoin Cash will hold a special position in cryptocurrency history forever. It's one of the earliest rough Bitcoin forks. And the most effective, up to now.

Since cryptos are decentralized in nature, no changes can be made without a consensus when there is controversy about potential problems to its underlying code. If miners and developers do not reach an agreement, it is possible to break the digital currency or fork it.

There was a heated discussion about Bitcoin's scalability in this situation. The same Bitcoin remained. And with changes to its code, Bitcoin cash was developed. The size of blocks was increased from one megabyte to eight by this code shift. This caused transaction times to be much faster.

While it still has some catching up to do with some of its rivals, the scalability of Bitcoin Cash could cause the value to accrue much faster than most of the competition.

Binance Coin (BNB)

Binance is the world's biggest volume-based crypto-currency exchange. And it's not near either. The official token of the Binance trade, of course, is Binance Coin. It enables users with smooth efficiency to trade in other cryptos. Transaction payments may also be simplified by Binance Coin and also pay for products and services. The Binance Card is also available now. It encourages people to pay for stuff just as they would with their standard credit card. The only difference is that with Bitcoin or Binance Coin, they load up the card and pay for groceries or a new hard crypto wallet.

Binance Coin is undoubtedly one of the best available cryptocurrencies on the basis of usability alone. And it is also the most accessible, as of right now.

To Date the Not-So-Great Cryptocurrencies

For two major reasons, two of the biggest cryptos out there that didn't make this list skipped it. One is under inquiry. The other still doesn't exist.

For years, Ripple (XRP) has become one of the most commonly recognized cryptos. Much like the others, it has had similar ups and downs in value. But while many are growing upwards, in a major way, Ripple is floundering. Ripple scored a big hit at the end of 2020 and it's unclear how long the harm will last. But it'll be for a while, in all probability.

At the end of 2020, the Securities and Exchange Commission (SEC) filed suit against Ripple Labs Inc and two of its managers. The claims are that, through an unregistered digital asset protection offering, $1.3 billion was raised. It is a big no-no. And Ripple's price has been falling significantly. Is it going to rise to its former heights? To be seen, that remains. But investors should steer clear for now. Or be exceedingly weary at the very least.

There's Diem, then (formerly known as Libra). Perhaps it's the most hyped-up crypto ever. Heck, Congress is responsible for attempting to wrap its collective brain around precisely what cryptocurrency is. While it is no shock that our politicians are still largely in the dark, the opportunity allowed the future cryptocurrency of Facebook to be in the spotlight for a lot of time. And it wouldn't be too surprising if name recognition rewards early adopters when it's published later this year.

Chapter 21
Why the Interest in
Cryptocurrency Is Growing?

To put it simply, cryptocurrencies are digital money that is produced by computer code. Consider how Bitcoin, the most well-known cryptocurrency, is used to transmit money over the internet.

To utilize cryptocurrencies, users must either purchase them from one of the numerous current exchanges or mine them using a computer.

Simply defined, mining is the process of utilizing a computer to solve a complicated mathematical problem in order to "mine" a block, which results in the release of a certain quantity of cryptocurrency into a person's account. This makes it possible to create additional cryptocurrencies, which can then be exchanged.

How Much Bitcoin Is There?

As of Tuesday 27 April, the Bitcoin value has increased from $9,759.46 to $11,720.01.

The price of bitcoin peaked in December 2017, when one coin was valued at $19,783.70. Bitcoin values, on the other hand, have been on the fall since then, with a few swings.

The worth of a Bitcoin is determined by the amount of effort necessary to create it. They are produced when someone conducts a time-consuming and energy-intensive mathematical calculation known as mining.

Bitcoin mining, on the other hand, isn't cheap. According to Coindesk, mining fees may cost more than $150,000 (£109,859.75) per coin, or roughly $961,564.66 (£697,284.36) each year.

What about the United Kingdom? Bitcoin is genuine money, and the Royal Mint is planning to launch its own.

Where Can I Buy Bitcoin?

Bitcoins may be purchased through Kraken, Coinbase, Cryptomate, Bitstamp, and CEX, among other exchanges.

However, there is one drawback: bitcoin exchanges are notoriously volatile. If you buy Bitcoin or another cryptocurrency at a low price, you risk losing a lot of money if its value declines.

How Much Money Is in Bitcoin?

According to the BBC, there are roughly 15 million Bitcoins in circulation, valued at approximately $170 billion. Since its inception in 2009, Bitcoin's value has gradually grown, but it still has a long way to go before it surpasses the value of the world's most precious currency, the US dollar.

What Are the Benefits of Cryptocurrency?

Because cryptocurrencies are meant to be nearly difficult to forge or tamper with, they have the potential to greatly improve the efficiency of the global financial system.

They may also be used to buy and sell items on sites like eBay, Worldpay, and Overstock.

Although cryptocurrency cannot replace the US dollar or the Euro, it can provide customers with more protection and privacy. It implies you won't be able to be tracked while sending or receiving money.

In terms of its real-world use, a number of companies are currently selling goods and services that include technology.

It's now quite straightforward to utilize cryptocurrencies for a variety of activities, such as booking flights and vacations, paying your dentist, finding a place to stay while on vacation, purchasing music, and even arranging your tax returns.

Is Bitcoin a Scam?

In certain ways, a buyer's ability to protect oneself against losing money is limited.

You are basically transferring money out of the economy when you swap cryptocurrencies for fiat currency.

Because cryptocurrencies are essentially digital assets with no physical reality, this is the case.

The software that runs Bitcoin has the ability to "bank" bitcoins. However, being "banked" by a financial institution such as the Royal Bank of Scotland or Barclays is not the same thing.

"Because Bitcoin and other virtual currencies are not backed by any type of assets, such as a government, the US dollar, or gold, they have no inherent value," argues Joshua Lawrence Chamberlain, MD of Credply, a financial services technology business.

"In fact, the possibility of making a profit even if prices decrease is one of the reasons individuals may want to acquire a cryptocurrency and put it on an online wallet."

How Do I Get Hold of Bitcoin?

If you want to acquire Bitcoin, you'll need to create an account on the internet.

You may use a site like Coinbase to purchase and sell cryptocurrencies using regular fiat currency, or you can use one of the other popular platforms like Blockchain or Localbitcoins to trade Bitcoin for cash.

Depending on the service you choose, you will be asked to enter a bank account or credit card number, and monies will be sent from your bank or credit card to your account.

After you've created an account, you'll be able to download the relevant app.

Will This Affect Me When I Retire?

The immediate concern for many older people will be what impact, if any, this will have on their pensions.

The notion that retirees may suddenly have that much more money on their hands may seem far-fetched, but some pension providers are enabling crypto asset holders to invest up to 25% of their pension fund in cryptocurrency, subject to the permission of their financial adviser.

Some providers may let you buy cryptocurrencies with funds from your defined contribution or drawdown pension plan.

Others, on the other hand, will only let you buy crypto assets using the money you've already put into your pension.

This implies that, while your contributions may have been used to purchase Bitcoin or other cryptocurrencies, you will not get them in your pension fund, which may come as a shock to savers.

New participants in the market are also generating new cryptocurrencies called coins for ordinary investors to trade in.

In September, for example, the debut of Bitcoin Cash triggered a spike in Bitcoin prices.

As a result, it's possible that the value of Bitcoin may rise in the next years.

You will almost surely make a fortune if you buy Bitcoin today and it suddenly skyrockets in price.

If it falls, though, you might lose a lot of money, and no one can guarantee that.

Are All Cryptocurrencies the Same?

Not all cryptocurrencies are created equal, and not all cryptocurrencies are made equal.

To make money with Bitcoin, you'll need a computer capable of running its smart contracts or blockchain-based apps.

Bitcoin is unusual among cryptocurrencies in that its blockchain—the mechanism that records all network transactions—can be used to conduct transactions in a variety of virtual currencies.

Litecoin, Ethereum, Ripple, and Dash are examples of these.

Virtual currencies with comparable blockchain-based features are also available, however, they differ in terms of the number of coins in circulation, technological features, and popularity.

Some are used to pay for online purchases, while others are simply toys that cybercriminals employ.

Digital currencies are new and have only been around for a short time.

In 2010, for example, at least 600 distinct virtual currencies were accessible. There are more than 3,000 now, although many have vanished completely.

Could the Value of Bitcoin Crash Again?

While the blockchain-based currencies described above are built on the same technology as Bitcoin, their market values are vastly different, making them incomparable.

Bitcoin commands a high level of investor trust as the first widespread, internationally acknowledged virtual currency, and this has backed its excellent performance over the previous ten years.

Bitcoin's price plummeted by more than $1,000 in a single day on Sunday, wiping away a fifth of its market worth.

Investors should not anticipate the price to continue to rise in the long run, even if it remains high.

Although, as a minority, there is no way to quantify the market precisely, the cryptocurrency industry is presently believed to be worth $700 billion—the same amount as New Zealand's yearly gross domestic product.

For analysts seeking to gain a handle on the market, there is also a huge margin of error.

It is difficult to estimate how many digital currencies will be available in the future since the supply is fixed.

Even Bitcoin, which is already projected to be 'decentralized,' meaning that it will be controlled by no single person or group, is not immune to failure.

If the bulk of the market loses trust in it, or if a big incident disrupts its network, individuals may find it more difficult and expensive to move cash.

Why Is the Government Getting Involved?

The money is currently unregulated, which is why the government is attempting to control digital currencies and the criminals that utilize them.

The government can only control tangible money—the cash in our wallets and bank accounts—under existing rules.

Digital currencies are unregulated and are occasionally used for illicit activities such as money laundering.

The government is drafting regulations to combat the usage of digital currencies in order to guarantee that they are not utilized for unlawful purposes.

The law would specifically prohibit virtual currencies from being used to facilitate illegal activities such as drug trafficking, money laundering, and tax evasion.

These legislations are presently in the works, with the Bill anticipated to be completed by the end of the year.

New Zealand might be the first government to outright prohibit digital currencies, making it more difficult for cybercriminals to utilize them.

What Do Consumers Think?

Consumer watchdog ACC has advised customers to conduct their homework before handing over their money.

"While Bitcoins appear to be a different way to make payments, you can only acquire Bitcoins with actual money," ACC's senior investigator Matthew Culkin-Smith explained.

Mr. Culkin-Smith believes that the law must safeguard consumers.

"Regulatory problems will surely arise as the usage of Bitcoin and other virtual currencies grows. As more people become involved in virtual currency trading, there is a larger possibility that they may lose money," he stated.

"When it comes to investing, people should be aware that there is a genuine danger of losing money." If someone invests money in Bitcoin, they risk losing all or a portion of their investment. Virtual currency may also be exchanged for real money, but there is no way of knowing how much the actual money is worth without any protections in place."

More than 80% of Bitcoin transactions are anonymous, which implies that no one knows who is behind the transaction.

Bitcoin's anonymous character has made it enticing to certain investors while also making it popular among criminals.

Bitcoin's value plummeted earlier this year when allegations surfaced that Chinese investors were betting on the currency's depreciation.

There have even been reports of Bitcoin hoarders attempting to offset their losses by selling their holdings at a loss.

As a result, it may be difficult to tell if your Bitcoin investment has increased or decreased.

Bitcoins, according to some analysts, are unlikely to last much longer as additional digital currencies emerge.

Chapter 22
Trading on Breakouts of Local Tops and Important Levels

Many traders consider breakout trading to be a separate trading strategy. No matter what you call it, it will work when you master its specifics. Although this topic is simple (compared to the Elliott Wave Theory), it still has many peculiarities worth grasping at the early stage. So let's get started.

You already understand that financial markets move in a focused manner. If we observe that the price chart moves towards the upward trend, where each next low is higher than the previous one, and market participants buy more than sell, we get good trading signals in this case. That is, we are confident that the market participants will continue to buy.

If we observe a downward trend, where each new low is lower than the previous one, then we understand that traders will continue to focus on lowering the price.

To determine the willingness of the price to move in a certain direction, many traders use the highs and lows of the chart.

Let's look at an example of how you can get an additional entry point just on breakouts of local tops.

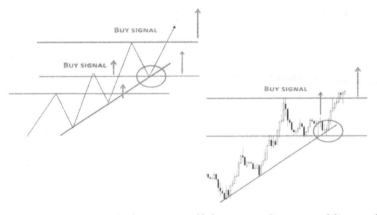

If the price chart not only bounces off the ascending trend line, where we have identified local tops but also crosses them, we receive an additional signal. In the picture on the left, the bottommost arrows indicate that we receive a buy signal even after bouncing off the support level. But if you need a more reliable signal, you should wait for a new local top.

Those traders who trade quickly after the first signal are the aggressive traders, who tend to take risks. You may ask: Why is it risky if the price bounced off the support level? Remember those false breakouts can occur in the market. Besides, the news background can break your uptrend in one minute. That is why such traders take risks. However, those who wait for the second signal are proponents of a more moderate trading style. They prefer waiting until the price chart reaches a new high and then making their purchase.

Below I will give another example of when the price chart not only bounces off the ascending trend line but also continues to go up, forming a local top.

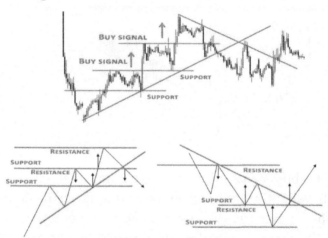

And now let's take a closer look at the ascending and descending tops.

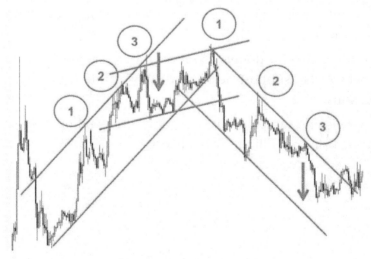

Consider how you can use a pending buy order during the breakout of the local top.

We get a buy signal even when we notice that, although the price chart has slightly retraced after the next peak, it still did not go below the moving average. We place a pending order above the resistance level. As soon as the local top is breached, the price chart will reach your pending order.

As a rule, the breakout of a local top is followed by an acceleration of the upward trend, so I recommend using a pending order in order to take your profit.

If you still have some doubts about your forecast, you can put a stop loss below the support level and thus protect yourself from unnecessary losses.

And here is an example of how you can use pending orders when you trade using the Elliott Wave Theory.

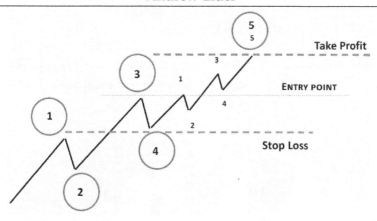

If the price chart has already formed impulse wave 1 and corrective wave 2, then impulse wave 3 and corrective wave 4, it is easy to guess that the market can go further upwards since the price chart is in the upward movement phase. We place a pending buy order slightly above the impulse wave 3 and expect the completion of a five-wave movement within the framework of wave 5. Place Take Profit depending on your patience (or greed :-). As for Stop Loss, put it a little below the corrective wave 4.

Here is an example of how you can make money during the corrective phase of the price chart.

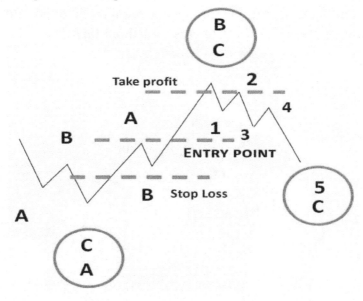

Triple Taps Strategy

Now we proceed to an interesting strategy called "Triple Taps." It reveals the topic of trading on the breakout of local tops.

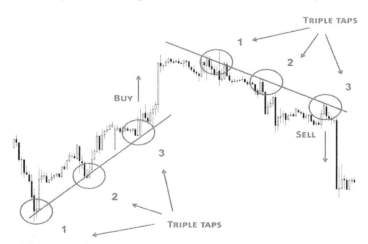

The most important thing in this strategy is to determine the level correctly. If you see that your level is tested repeatedly (three price taps are obvious), the uptrend is often accelerated then after the third tap.

The same things, but in an inverse manner, happen during a downtrend: the price chart lowers and three taps of the level are formed, followed by downtrend acceleration.

This chart shows that we receive an accurate signal for making a transaction after the last third price tap. In this situation, it is also possible to enter both after breaking a line and after forming a local top or even after breaking this top.

To get a more reliable forecast, the Triple Taps strategy can be combined with the Fibonacci tools.

After the third tap, we extend the Fibonacci lines from the second tap to a local top further to the third tap. Thus we will see where the price chart can reach in case of its further growth.

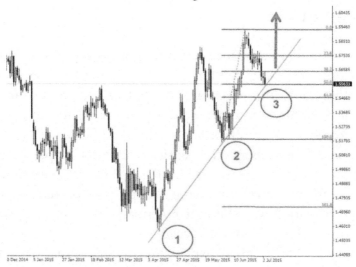

And the last example. Here the third tap took place in the golden section area according to the Fibonacci Retracement tool. The price reached the area of 38.2%, fixed in the area of 50%, and even has a pullback to the area of 61.8%. This signal shows that the corrective movement may end.

Now let's summarize. The principle of trading on breakouts of local tops and important levels is simple and clear. If you want to trade in the market, expect the breakout of a local top. If you are willing to wait a bit because you do not want to trade aggressively, use pending order on the breakout of this local top. If you want to trade from the top to the top, choose the Triple Taps trading strategy. If you fear the price will not break the level of the third tap, place a pending order to buy after the breakout of this level. When the chart breaks the level, you will be calm as you are already in a higher price range.

Remember that this trading strategy seems to be very simple and easy at first glance. In fact, its main hitch is hidden in a large number of false breakouts when the price breaks the level but then comes back. This makes a large number of traders, especially beginners, lose their capital.

You should combine several tools.

Homework

1. Find reference points for placing take profit and stop-loss orders after the third tap of defining level on H1 or H4 timeframe (this practical task will teach you to determine the nearest highs and lows so that you will be able to place stop loss and take profit orders)

2. Use Fibonacci extension within the Triple Taps from the low of wave 2 (second tap) to the low of wave 4 (third tap) on the H1 or H4 timeframe. The purpose of this assignment is to learn how to find the potential of movement during the break of the important level

3. Make a small explanation of your observations below each chart.

Chapter 23
Cryptocurrency Trading
Mistakes to Avoid

C ryptocurrency trading is not just for anyone. It can only be done by individuals who have the knowledge, skills, and attitude for it. It is also impossible to be mastered overnight. It takes practice and perseverance to be able to succeed in this venture.

Even though cryptocurrency trading can earn you a lot of money, it can also overexpose you of digital assets. If you are not careful with your trading, you may also end up lacking balance in your portfolio. This is why you should not only focus on winning strategies. You also have to plan for failures.

The cryptocurrency market has very low entry barriers. This means that anyone who has a computer or a smartphone, as well as access to the Internet, can start cryptocurrency trading. Then again, as mentioned previously, cryptocurrency trading is more than just having an electronic device, an Internet connection, and starting capital.

If you want to do well with this venture, see to it that you do your research well. Learn about the successful traders who came before you, and find out what made them successful. Likewise, you have to find out about the mistakes they made and how you can avoid making them yourself.

To help you out, here are some of the cryptocurrency trading mistakes that you have to avoid:

Mistake #1: Using Real Money to Trade Instead of Practicing Paper Trading as a Beginner

Beginner traders should practice before they go out into the financial markets and trade using real money. It is not a good idea to use real money right away if you are just beginning to trade, especially when there are a lot of platforms and resources available for paper trading.

Those who want to become professional traders have to create a system that is based on simple guidelines for risk management, entries, and exits. At first, you have to do paper trading until you are ready to get out into the real financial markets and risk losing real money.

Mistake #2: Trading Without Any Stop Loss

Because beginner traders are not used to trading, they are not yet exposed to the ups and downs of the financial markets. Hence, they tend to be emotional when it comes to their trading. They tend to have a hard time accepting losses.

You have to understand that traders have to possess the ability to move on and accept losses as quickly as possible. This way, they can go on to the next trade without any heaving feelings. Those who are not able to do this become more prone to losing more money. Yes, that's right. If you are not able to get over your feelings and let go of a loss quickly, you will tend to lose more money in the long run.

Thus, if you want to become a successful trader, you have to know how to regulate your emotions. You need to set a stop loss and refrain from moving it if the trade does not go in your favor. Otherwise, your behavior will become destructive and it will end up blowing your account.

Mistake #3: Not Maintaining Balance Properly

Expert traders know how to maintain their balance properly. In fact, they have balanced portfolios that prevent them from going broke. It is actually up to you how much money you would allot for your trading.

For example, you can allot 10% of your money in cryptocurrency trading. Within your cryptocurrency portfolio, 70% can be your long-term holds, 15% can be for trading, and another 15% can be in cash. You can choose to just trade with 15% of your portfolio, with this portfolio being 10% of your total net worth.

Always consider your investment plan. See if you have outlined your target asset allocation. Rebalancing is actually the process of returning a portfolio to the target asset allocation.

A lot of traders find it difficult due to its tendency to force traders to sell their asset classes that are performing well while also forcing them to purchase more of their asset classes that are performing the worst. Such contrarian action proves to be difficult to comprehend for many beginner investors.

Mistake #4: Adding to Losing Trades

Do not be confused between trading and investing because they are two different things. Investors generally average down their positions in sound assets that have long-time horizons.

Traders, on the other hand, have defined risk levels as well as invalidation for trades. Once their stop loss hits, such trades become invalidated and they have to move on to other assets. If you choose to become a trader, you should never average down.

Mistake #5: Not Keeping a Journal Specifically for Trading

Journaling may seem elementary, but it is actually necessary for trading. Expert traders have plans, and they write down these plans in their journals. As a trader, you have to hold yourself accountable for all your actions.

You can only do this by recording the details of your trade in a journal. You can keep a paper journal or a digital journal, although many traders prefer to write down their trades on paper because doing so allows them to understand everything much better.

Keeping a trading journal is actually the best way to avoid making the same mistakes that you have done in the past. It also allows you to learn new things by recalling your past trading styles. Make it a point to always record your emotional state, trade results, and thought process. This will greatly help you succeed at trading.

Mistake #6: Risking More Than You Can Afford to Lose

In cryptocurrency trading, people are generally drawn to the idea of making a lot of money if they are at the right place and time. Because of this belief, they tend to go all in and risk everything they have.

Well, it is a good thing if they end up having great trades. However, this is not always the case. If you are not careful, you can end up losing a lot of money, and you cannot just blame it on luck. You have to be accountable for your actions, so you need to make calculated risks when it comes to trading.

Mistake #7: Not Having Enough Capital

You do not have to have a huge capital, but you should not be undercapitalized either. Remember the old saying that you need money in order to make more money. So, before you start cryptocurrency trading, see to it that you have enough funding in your account.

A lot of beginner traders think that they can make tons of money even without getting out of the couch. While cryptocurrency trading can be done at home and on your couch, this sole belief is false, unless of course, you have a lot of capital to begin with. You still have to get out there and make a living so that you can support your cryptocurrency trading.

If you want to be a professional trader, you have to aim to support your whole life through trading. This means that your profits have to cover your living expenses, without putting a dent in your trading capital. Usually, this means that you have to have $50,000 to $100,000 for trading as well as a regular profit of ten % every month.

Now, this may be quite hard to achieve if you are just a regular person. So, you really have to prepare yourself before you get into cryptocurrency trading. Beginner traders who look into rose-colored glasses often find themselves getting stressed whenever they fail to have their expectations align with their actual results.

Mistake #8: Using Leverage

In cryptocurrency trading, leverage can be a double-edged sword. Hence, you should refrain from using it. Remember that it may increase your returns from a profitable trade and exacerbate your loss on a losing trade.

You should only use leverage if you are confident enough about your skills in trading. Only expert traders who have been trading cryptocurrency for years may use leverage successfully. If you are not yet experienced, using leverage might just compound your losses rapidly and leave you without any money.

Mistake #9: Acting on Trading Indicators and Patterns That Are Not Very Clear to You

When you first started with cryptocurrency trading, it is understandable that you are not yet good with technical analysis. You might identify chart patterns that are not existing or are wrong based on chart placement and context.

So, you have to develop a simple system for your trading as well as refrain from making decisions on indicators or patterns that you do not completely understand. You have to begin with simple resistance and support. You can also begin with clear indicators such as exponential moving averages.

Mistake #10: Going With the Herd

Do not be a sheep because you are not one. You are a human being who is capable of thinking on your own. Thus, you have to refrain from merely following the herd. Otherwise, you might end up spending more money than necessary.

Expert traders are used to exiting trades once it gets too crowded. Beginner traders, on the other hand, might stay in a trade longer than necessary, even after the smart money has exited. They may also not be confident enough to be contrarian whenever necessary.

Do not be like the cryptocurrency traders who blindly follow so-called trading gurus. You should also be wary of individuals who might be manipulating you to their own advantage. Always use your common sense and rely on your own abilities.

Mistake #11: Bottom Trading

Beginner traders often make the mistake of bottom trading. They monitor a cryptocurrency asset's downturn and aim to purchase at the lowest possible price. If this sounds appealing to you, you have to learn that it is not a good way to trade. If you bottom trade, you can lose all your investments.

Mistake #12: Hodling

Just like bottom trading, you can lose your investments from hodling. Hodling is basically hoarding. It refers to keeping digital assets instead of actively trading them. If you hold onto your cryptocurrencies for far longer than necessary, you can lose money.

Mistake #13: Relying on Gut Instinct Alone

It is not bad to trust your instincts. However, you should not rely on your instincts alone, especially when trading cryptocurrencies. As you know, the price of cryptocurrencies is highly volatile. One minute it can be low, the next minute it can be high. You just can never be too sure about its price.

This is why you have to be careful when making trades. Take note that trades can collapse and yield major losses all of a sudden. You need to master your emotions just like fiat brokers. Use logic rather than feeling.

Mistake #14: Trading Worthless Cryptocurrencies

Bitcoin is the most popular of all cryptocurrencies. Many years ago, it was actually the only cryptocurrency. Today, however, there are more than three thousand known cryptocurrencies.

Then again, a lot of these alternative cryptocurrencies or altcoins, as they are more commonly known, do not have much worth. So, you have to do your research well and avoid investing in cryptocurrencies that are not valuable.

Mistake #15: Not Having Security

Since cryptocurrencies are digital, they are prone to get hacked. Virtual money, unlike fiat money, cannot be locked up in vaults. So, you should be careful with the exchanges that you use. You should never allow your cryptocurrencies to stay on an exchange if you are not trading actively.

Keep in mind that a lot of exchanges are prone to hacking. In fact, more than one and a half billion cryptocurrencies have been lost due to hacking. This left a lot of traders devastated.

Mistake #16: Anthropomorphizing the Market

Keep in mind that the financial markets do not have an agency. You have to understand them well so that you can trade cryptocurrencies effectively. The market is actually the sum of every economic transaction. It is not a monolithic entity that competes with you. Thus, you have to refrain from anthropomorphizing or personifying it.

Mistake #17: Not Diversifying

There is a saying that you should never put all your eggs in a single basket. This saying can be applied to cryptocurrency trading. The concept of diversification has actually been around for centuries. It is true that if you bet everything, you may also lose everything.

So, you have to diversify even if you think you have found a sure thing. It will not hurt you to diversify and have more variety. With diversification, you will be able to keep some money instead of losing it all on a trade.

Mistake #18: Relying on Chance Instead of Skill

Trading is not like playing the lottery. With trading, you can actually increase your odds of winning if you have a good plan and you stick to it. With the lottery, there is nothing you can do except choose a combination of numbers and wait for the results to be released.

If you want to be successful at trading, you have to be knowledgeable and well-read. You should also be updated with the latest trends and news on cryptocurrencies. You should never rely on good luck alone. Expert traders may seem to be lucky, but they actually spent tons of hours researching and practicing.

Mistake #19: Believing Other People Easily

Simply put, you should not believe just about anyone and anything. This is especially true with cryptocurrency trading. Throughout your trading career, you will encounter people who will claim to be experts or gurus.

These people will try to make you watch their webinars or buy something they are selling. They will try to force their beliefs on you. You should not give in to the pressure. Instead, you have to believe in your own self. After all, you are the cryptocurrency trader.

Mistake #20: Panic Selling

Traders are a special kind of people because they have iron stomachs. They are able to deal with the financial markets, which are hard to predict. As a beginner trader, you have to refrain from making the mistake of panic selling. You should resist the urge to sell even when things seem to be rough. You need to develop an iron stomach so that you can be like expert traders.

At times, it would be more sensible to cut losses. Then again, remember that they are not losses until you sell. Your investment may go up again if you merely hold onto it. As a trader, you should not merely aim to sell low and buy high. Doing so will just make you lose money. You have to be wise enough to avoid making mistakes. Do not panic easily. Use your logic and reasoning skills.

Mistake #21: Not Knowing How to Keep the Money and Then Make Some More

If you do not know what you have to do after making some money, you will have a tendency to lose what you have. This is why you have to practice staggered selling. You should not hold on too long that you begin to lose money. You should not sell everything at once either. It will only make you miss out on the largest boom. Practicing staggered selling will allow you to make money while possibly making even more.

Mistake #22: Committing the Sunk Cost Fallacy

The sunk cost fallacy is about staying involved in something just because there are a lot of resources invested in it. It does not really matter how major these resources are. You should not risk losing money just because you care too much about the labor, time, emotions, or money that you have already invested.

Mistake #23: Being Envious

As you know, being emotional while trading is not a good thing. Even worse, being envious of other people's success will only prevent you from being successful yourself. You have to learn how to appreciate what you have and to always see the bright side. Keep in mind that whenever someone else wins, you win as well. You become a winner when you are able to learn something from such a win.

Chapter 24
Innovative Cryptocurrencies

F ollowing our examination of the Alternative Coin landscape, we now turn our attention to creative cryptocurrencies or those that operate in a way that is significantly different from Bitcoin. Two of the most important cryptocurrencies may be recognized among them; the first is Ripple, and the second is IOTA.

Both are atypical cryptocurrencies, meaning that their fundamental characteristics are unusual and profoundly different from those of normal cryptocurrencies. Ripple stands out for being a centralized cryptocurrency, in the sense that the operation, security, and authentication of transactions are managed by a company. IOTA, on the other hand, is profoundly innovative because it does not use the blockchain, but functions through the "Tangle."

Ripple

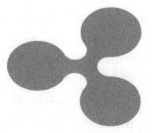

Ripple is a company, founded in 2012 by Ryan Fugger, based in California, that deals with the transfer of assets (understood as fiat currency, gold, and other commodities), through its platform. The creation and development of the Ripple platform is the corporate purpose of the company in question and is pursued by the so-called "Ripple Lab" in San Francisco.

The Ripple Company was created with the aim of developing a technology that was designed so it could allow a new real-time payment system, and whose main function was to allow the transfer of funds between banks or financial companies. The company collaborates with a large number of banks, in particular European ones, and has developed a platform that was conceived as a competitor to SWIFT (Society for Worldwide Interbank Financial Telecommunication) from which the term "SWIFT bank transfer" is used in technical jargon to mean an interbank and interstate payment.

Although it is only in the initial phase, the collaborations with financial intermediaries are numerous and are leading to a feasibility study regarding the use of Ripple as a new platform for carrying out interbank transactions.

Another thing is the XRP cryptocurrency, commonly known as Ripple is an atypical digital currency, which many experts in the crypto world do not even consider a cryptocurrency. This foreclosure against XRP is mainly linked to the fact that the digital currency is not decentralized. Although it is based on the blockchain structure, it is controlled by the Ripple Company, which develops and guarantees the transactions that take place within its platform.

Another peculiarity of Ripple, which distances it from the world of cryptocurrencies, is precisely the same goal with which it was created. Unlike most cryptocurrencies, XRP was not conceived as a commonly used "coin"; in fact, its function is that "money" that can be used between financial intermediaries, to allow the overcoming and efficiency of old technologies such as SWIFT.

This last feature of Ripple is perhaps the one that moves digital currency the farthest from the "crypto" world and the closest to the world of conventional finance. From this point of view, it can be said that XRP is the first point of conjunction between finance and the world of cryptocurrencies. In a context in which banks and financial institutions very often look to cryptocurrencies as a threat, and as a dangerous source of speculative bubbles, Ripple is the first among cryptocurrencies, that has managed to find concrete interest from financial intermediaries.

XRP has been released since 2012 by the same Ripple Company. One of the fundamental characteristics of the cryptocurrency is that all the XRP units envisaged by the system were issued immediately; the expected amount of 100 billion units of XRP was "mined" at the time of the cryptocurrency's birth. A large amount of Ripple mined (if you relate for example to the Bitcoin maximum limit of 21 million), was chosen precisely for reasons of functionality.

The value of Ripple cannot be as high as that of Bitcoin, because the creators did not want XRP to become a virtual store of value (virtual gold) as Bitcoin has become. But they envisioned it could be used in a practical way by Banks for the execution of interbank transactions. If the company's goal of replacing SWIFT technology was met, all banks would like to hold substantial amounts of XRP to sufficiently be able to secure the operations they want to carry out.

IOTA

IOTA is an open-source, non-mineable cryptocurrency project, developed and launched between 2015 and 2016 by a group of German developers. In support of the project, the "IOTA Foundation" was founded with the contribution of funds donated by users.

IOTA is an innovative cryptocurrency born with a specific goal; to overcome the burden and heaviness of blockchain technology. As also stated on the official IOTA website, the developers wanted to operate in the direction of a "lightweight" cryptocurrency.

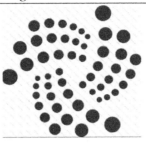

The inventors of the IOTA started from a very important assumption, namely that in the next decade it is estimated that there will be more than 50 billion devices connected to the Internet. These devices will be connected all over the world, even in countries where banking structures and financial services, in general, are almost absent.

In addition to the problem of the poor development of the financial economy, these new countries that are facing the interconnected world, are characterized by inadequate state institutions, which fail to forcefully impose the state currency and which often subject it to strong devaluations. Such weak and highly depreciated coins prevent those who use them from making everyday payments. IOTA has the objective of allowing the management of "micropayments," guaranteeing their safety and having almost zero costs.

Interconnected devices will need to be able to exchange tiny amounts of money with each other, instantly. Precisely for this purpose, IOTA was conceived, which remains suitable for any other scenario in which there is the need to manage any type of transaction, even large ones.

To achieve this ambitious goal, at the time of designing IOTA, it was decided that it must distance itself from blockchain-based cryptocurrencies. While maintaining the vision linked to distributed consensus, a different approach was needed to make the network scalable within the IOTA ecosystem, where there will be tens of billions of connected devices. In fact, from the point of view of IOTA, we want to encourage the use of cryptocurrencies for everyday operations; doing so would have to validate thousands of transactions every second. As previously stated for other cryptocurrencies, including the expansion of blockchain blocks and the reduction of validation times, no cryptocurrency has so far been able to validate more than 200 transactions per second.

IOTA uses the Tangle, which is a software protocol based on direct acyclic graphs that are profoundly different from the blockchain protocol. Before proceeding with the explanation of the substantial innovation of the "Tangle," it is necessary to dwell on the concept of "direct acyclic graph." In computer science, and sometimes in mathematics, we mean by the direct acyclic graph, also called "acyclic graph-oriented" (from the English Directed Acyclic Graph, DAG), a particular category of graph direct or digraph.

The digraph is the more general structure of a simple tree chart. In a tree chart, there is a common source and a set of nodes, positioned in multiple levels. The digraph, unlike the tree chart, does not have such an organized structure, but to each "source," nodes are not ordered in a regular manner. Inside the digraph, there are "nodes," or "boxes" of the graph, and "arcs" or the path necessary to get from one node to another.

Features of Iota

- **No transaction costs:** To send an IOTA transaction, the sender's device must verify two previous transactions in the Tangle, performing a "Proof of Work" operation. IOTA lacks the differentiation between "user" and "miner." All the subjects participating in the network are nodes of the IOTA network and must necessarily "work" to be able to participate.

- **Infinitely scalable:** To send a transaction, two more must first be confirmed, and as the number of users increases, the efficiency of the network also increases. This way, the problem of other cryptocurrencies that allow a limited number of operations per second is overcome. The more the network grows, the more IOTA speeds up its transactions. The system adjusts to its size.

- **Quick transactions:** The transaction execution times are inversely proportional to the number of transactions in the Tangle. When IOTA reaches mass adoption, transactions will be virtually instantaneous.

- **Fixed money supply:** All existing units were created in the "genesis block," and that amount will never vary. The total amount corresponds to 2.779.530.283.277.761 iota.

Chapter 25
Principles of Crypto Trading

I f you are new to cryptocurrency, there are guiding principles you need to imbibe just like any other thing. You need to have them at your fingertips to help you fly higher in the crypto world. Next are some outstanding principles:

1. **Learn risk management:** You will need this a lot for your sanity.

2. **Trade less often:** This is the best advice for newbies rather hodl more.

3. **Learn the difference between fundamental and technical analysis:** You need to know this.

4. **Don't trade on emotion:** You need to be objective discipline.

5. **Create and develop your system:** You can watch others but dare to be different. You can adapt your approach on your terms.

6. **Take profits on winning positions:** So this simply means buy low and sell high.

Understanding the Ideas and Processes of Trading

You need to understand the different processes of trading cryptocurrencies before indulging. So here are the different processes you need to undergo if you want to trade cryptocurrency smoothly.

Step 1: You Need a Cryptocurrency Brokerage Account

So, go create an account either with eToro, Coinbase, or Gemini. Provide details like your date of birth, email, social security number, etc.

Step 2: You Will Need to Fund Your Account

You start by connecting your bank to the crypto brokerage. It can do the funding via wire transfers or debit cards.

Step 3: You Would Then Choose Crypto to Invest In

Though many people allocate their bitcoin and eth, you can choose yours or go with the popular two. This is so because these two cryptos move more predictably than the smaller coins. And again, trading with technical indicators with them is a lot easier.

You can still invest a bit in the small altcoins too.

Step 4: Pick a Strategy to Use

You need to have your strategy to help you scale through. There are a lot of trading indicators to pick from. So you look at them and go for any that you are comfortable with. You can even go for a cryptocurrency trading course. All these will add up to give you a good insight to do better with your investment.

Step 5: Have Storage for Your Cryptocurrency

You would need good storage for your coins. If you are actively trading, leaving your coins in an exchange will be your best bet. You would have access to your coin very fast. But if you are buying then what to hold for a mid-term or long term, then a wallet will be preferable.

Trading Rules that Guide You Through Creating Disciplines

With cryptocurrency making a profit requires effort, so if you need your financial investments to always yield return, you must be disciplined. This simply means acting like a grown-up and setting some rules for yourself. So I will be listed below the important rules you need to follow to create discipline.

Start Your Day Trading

- You need to discipline yourself to make trading part of your daily routine.
- Decide on your future action plan before leaving an exchange.
- You will have a clear direction in mind. This way, you wouldn't be trading blindly.

Discipline will be created this way.

Create Your Daily Direction

You know that planning has never harmed anyone, so you need to have your daily plan. You need to disciple yourself this way.

Check Your Open Positions and Orders

You need to always be aware of what is going on inside the crypto world. You need to do this to show you are working by your disciplines.

Always Update Your Prices

You need to always check with exchanges regularly to be abreast with the current prices.

Trading Strategies

When it comes to trading cryptocurrencies, you need to employ strategies to maximize profits. The truth is that you would encounter a lot of strategies that promise to turn you rich overnight, but you need to be careful and pick the ones that are reasonable and would give you the needed push to excel. Trading cryptocurrency for a profit is one of the universal trading strategies you would need to adopt. Of course, this is the most reason why you are in the system already. Below are the crypto trading strategies you can adopt to make the best from your trading of cryptocurrency:

Grow Your Profits

You need to first grow your profit from all angles. This is focusing on all to make a profit no matter how small it is. You can start by diversifying your trades; you need to combine a lot more cryptos. You can trade Ripple, Ethereum, Bitcoin, Litecoin, etc. this will help reduce the daily risk associated with a coin. You would need to follow the news to always stay ahead of the market. These will help in growing your profit for you to minimize loss.

Cut Your Losses

In cryptocurrency trading, you need to cut off as many losses as possible as you can. This strategy with help you fight losses. You can use stop losses by setting stop-loss orders on all trades. Starting with a profit loss ratio of about 2:1 wouldn't be a bad idea. And not forget to apply technical analysis as well. It will help you justify each of your trades. All of these will help you point to the positive to cut out losses.

Trade the Trend

This is an investment strategy you would need to adopt. You would need to base your investment decisions on the analysis of a certain asset's momentum. This has to do with the value of the asset moving up and own. So you should always try to capture gains through the analysis of an asset momentum. You can achieve this by following the leaders in the market. You need to keep up with the current market conditions, get to know the factors influencing pricing, and always prepare yourself for volatility.

Crypto Trading Tools

Almost all investment areas need one using some tools to succeed. The same applies to the crypto world. You need to have some trading tools in your arsenal to make the best of it. Trading tools are products that can help you boost your trades. These tools will help you have a clear picture of the markets, you would easily identify the asset's trending direction, you would be able to create your entry and exit points for trade with them, and of course, you can generate and confirm buy and sell signals. So you need these trading tools in your arsenal. The below tools are the outstanding ones you need:

Open Ocean

You would need this tool to help you have a single entry point to access a deep liquidity pool across centralized and decentralized exchanges. Open Ocean can be used to uncover the best prices out there via their smart algorithm and show you the price comparison.

Charting Tools

This is one tool that you would need to visualize different market practices. You can use this tool to grow your very important technical analysis skill. The charting tools you would need are Tradingview and Cryptowatch.

New Aggregator Tools

You would need to always view thousands of articles about cryptocurrency in one place. This will help you in getting a quick pulse on the market and seeing updates immediately. So you can go for tools like Crytopanic and FAWs.

Research Reports Tools

With trading crypto, you would always need to do some research. This research will help you provide technical analysis, fundamental analysis, and even opinions on the current, future, and past market. So you can go for a tool like a crypto research report that will give you an in-depth quarterly report.

Trading Bots

You would need to have these pieces of software so that you would be able to set particular parameters. You would be able to define when the bot should start trading on your behalf. So the bots will help execute trades on your behalf. The two trading bots you should consider are HaasOnline and Gekko.

Portfolio Trackers

You would need the portfolio trackers tools; they will help you keep a pulse on your portfolio. You can easily check at a glance your total value of an investment, check the performance of each coin, and view the 24 hours change in the value of your portfolio. So, you can use any of these, and you would get the best tracking—Coin Tracking, Coinstats, or Block Folio.

Understanding Fundamental and Technical Analysis

As you venture into trading cryptocurrencies, you must master the fundamental and technical analysis that analyzes the crypto world. You need to first know about the basics so the technical and fundamental analysis in the crypto world will be explained below.

Technical analysis is the use of real-world data to predict the future of the market. All you need to do here is look at the past statistics of the cryptocurrencies. You are maybe looking at the cryptocurrency movement and its volume. Technical analysis dwells more on the principle that history will repeat itself when it comes to crypto trends and pricing.

So, this simply means that technical analysts make predictions concerning cryptocurrency. So the bottom line here is that technical analysis offers crypto traders insight into the past of crypto, which helps to facilitate future predictions. It is never advisable to use only technical analysis, though. The best bet will be combining it with other methods to get an accurate result.

Crypto fundamental analysis, then, is about taking a deep dive into the available information about a financial asset. Investors use this to establish the intrinsic value of an asset. With fundamental analysis, an investor can conclude whether such an asset was either undervalued or overvalued. The essence is to leverage the information gathered to strategically exit positions or enter them. The indicators in the fundamental analysis include earning per share, price-to-earnings ratio, price–to–book ratio, and price/ earnings-to-growth ratio.

Chapter 26
Creating a Personalized Trading Plan

N o single investing strategy is going to be right for everyone because every investor is going to have different reasons for wanting to invest, different levels of comfort when it comes to risk, different timeframes for doing so, and different metrics for success. As such, in order to create a truly personalized trading plan, it is important to consider several different factors about your own life first.

Consider Trading Goals

First, it is important to determine the goals you have when it comes to investing which can be done by first asking yourself what your objectives are when it comes to investing. For some people, safely maintaining their principal investment will be enough, while others will be trying to accumulate money for a long-term goal.

Depending on your goals for the investment you may even want to go ahead and create different investments for different goals. Regardless, before you go ahead and invest it is important to have a clear idea of the reasons you are doing so to make it easier to determine the best way to go about reaching the goal you are seeking. Finally, it is important to keep in mind that goals should not be completed in a vacuum; you will also need to keep in mind your desired timeframe and level of risk tolerance in order to make goals that are realistically achievable.

Consider Your Risk Tolerance

Before you can accurately determine your goals, it is important to consider your overall tolerance for risk, specifically the risk of losing money. The basics of determining the amount of risk you are comfortable with involve considering how much money you would be willing to risk and still be okay with not receiving any profit and even possibly having that amount be reduced to zero.

It is important to keep in mind that all investment involves risk and without some level of risk, there can be no profit. The amount of risk that you are going to be able to deal with is likely going to be, in part, about how soon you need to see a return on your investment. If you are saving for retirement and have 20 or more years to go before the day arrives then you will be able to make riskier investments than someone who is already in their sixties who will naturally have a much lower level of risk as a result.

Consider Trading Limits

Once you are aware of your relationship to risk, you will then need to establish trading limits, both for trades that have soured as well as those that are going along as planned. This upper limit is what is known as a price target which can be thought of as the best-case scenario for the investment you are currently tracking. This is the number that you will be happy with taking the profits from, even if the price continues to move past that point in a positive direction.

A price target can be thought of as your expectation for how the cryptocurrency in question is going to move in the short term which means it might have numerous different price targets depending on who is doing the trading and their personal feelings about the cryptocurrency in question. There is no one right price target it is purely based on what is right for you.

Consider Your Ideal Level of Involvement

Once you know how adverse to risk you are, you will also need to consider how active you are going to want to be in your investments. If you are comfortable holding onto the specific investment for a prolonged period of time while only checking in on it occasionally then you are most likely going to want to pursue a buy-and-hold strategy, where relatively reliable investments are going to return reliable, if unimpressive, returns. If you are more interested in micromanaging your investments, then you can pursue riskier investments that have a greater potential for large payouts, but you might need to bounce between several different investments as needed. In general, you should not pursue a daily trading strategy unless you are a professional.

Consider Your Familiarity With Trading

When it comes to creating a trading plan that is sure to lead to success, the first thing that you will want to consider is your overall familiarity with the ins and outs of trading in general and higher-risk trading in particular. The greater your overall experience level, the more ambitious your plan and your trades can be, but there is no shame in sticking with the basics if you are just getting started overall. When it comes to determining your personal skill level, it is important to be honest with yourself as overestimating your abilities is only going to come back to haunt you later on when you end up in over your head with more than you can realistically afford to lose on the line.

Consider Your Strengths and Weaknesses

Next, you will need to determine how knowledgeable you are in the arena you are investing in as well as your overall level of comfort when it comes to monitoring your investments and making decisions based on their future. Your investment decision should be based on your comfort level and your willingness to devote time to researching your choices. Finally, it is also important to be frank with yourself when it comes to knowing what you don't know. Never let yourself be talked into investing in something that you aren't comfortable with or don't understand and never invest more than you can afford to lose no matter how good the deal might seem on the surface.

Consider the Other Challenges in Your Life at the Moment

Once you know what personal hurdles you are going to have to overcome, the next thing that you will need to do is to consider the other facets of your life and make note of things that might make it more difficult than it otherwise might be day trade successfully. External challenges are often things like a weak starting fund, other time commitments, or anything else that will prove difficult when it comes to planning out the perfect trade strategy. The exact issues are going to be different for everyone, but knowing what they are is half of the battle. The market is inconsistent enough, don't try and come at it without having all of the other possible variables on lock.

Stick With It

In order to determine if your plan is successful, the first thing you are going to need to do is to give it some time to generate real results. Based on the time frame for profit you determined previously, you are going to want to wait and gather enough data to ensure that you are likely to turn a profit using your plan in the long term. During this time, you are going to want to take detailed notes including when trades were made, what factors went into your consideration for the trades, the costs, and if the trade ended in success. Keep in mind that anything above 50% will eventually turn a profit given a long enough timeframe.

Most importantly, if you find a trading plan that works for you, you are going to want to stick with it as diligently as possible, even if your emotions are telling you to go a different way. When trading, your goal should always be to minimize the effect that emotions have on your actions as completely as you can. Trading successfully is all about the numbers, which means that emotions are only going to get in the way and almost always end up doing you more harm than good. The more robotically you can execute the trades you are looking for, the greater your profits are going to be across the board. If you find yourself considering making a trade based on emotion, take a moment to ask yourself if you would make the trade if your emotions weren't a factor and then make a choice depending on the answer.

Don't Be too Anxious to Get Started

In order to trade successfully, it is important that you start off on the right foot which means having enough trading capital to push through the early days when you are more likely to make a poor decision. If every trade, you make represents the difference between continuing to trade and having to go back to a traditional 9-to-5 then you are likely to be more focused on this fact as opposed to making the best trades possible and sticking with your trading plan. This, in turn, will make it more likely for you to trade based on fear rather than anything truly rational such as what the market is currently telling you is the right thing to do.

It is important to always be aware of your personal limits when it comes to trading both mentally and in regard to trading capital, but it is equally important to not have to deal with such strict limits that you chafe under them and fail to trade properly as a result. Remember, no trader is ever going to be 100% successful which means that if you hope to play the long game you need to be able to survive long enough for your plan to work out in the long run.

Conclusion

C ryptocurrency trading is a 24/7 job—sometimes you'll see a huge sell-off in an asset class, and for the next few hours it could seem like everything is crashing. Knowing the difference can take years of practice, but here are some basic essentials that will help you along the way in any situation.

Crypto Trading Guide

- Cryptocurrencies are volatile assets that can make people rich or leave them broke. So it's important to know where to put your money when this stuff happens.

- The best way to prepare yourself for a volatile market is to practice risk management. Be sure you keep your money in different types of cryptocurrency so that if one dumps, you still have others.

- Using a top exchange for all your cryptocurrency trading is risky since they all have different financial situations and performances. This often results in a dip in the trade value for one or even all assets on that exchange, so it's important to diversify your portfolio into several exchanges (sometimes up to 5) and trade across them.

- Know the coins you'll be trading well before you invest, or at least the basics of what they do. For example, if you're looking to buy a few coins, make sure you research them so that when the price drops, you can see which one is still worth holding on to.

- Don't be too greedy. Find an entry point that's reasonable for all your coins and see how that entry point will affect your profit.

- Plan ahead. One of the best ways to get the right price for an asset is to predict it and buy it at a low price. This way even if the market pump, your entry point will have been low enough that it won't hurt as much when the markets recover later on.

- Following trends can be good or bad depending on how well you understand them. Study up on the popular assets and how they perform and you'll be able to catch the huge profits that those trends can bring.
- Never trade with money you can't afford to lose.
- There is no such thing as an absolute assurance of future returns, especially with the vulnerable fluctuations of cryptocurrencies.
- Don't invest more than you can lose if your investments begin to fail or slow down. Having said that, it's better to risk a little more for a chance at winning a lot more than not risking anything and come up empty-handed.
- If your investments don't follow this rule, then stop trading them until you have regained some of your losses.
- The best way to avoid losing money on an asset is to know how to identify when it's about to fall. Cryptocurrencies are very volatile assets, so they can go from being a profitable investment in a few hours and turn into a disaster in the same amount of time. So your goal should be to identify these trends and trade around them before they happen.

Glossary

Algorithm: A set of calculations used by a computer to solve problems.

Altcoin: A term used to describe all other cryptocurrency units launched after the creation of bitcoin.

Bitcoin: A cryptocurrency invented in 2008 by pseudonymous Satoshi Nakamoto.

Bitcoin address: The digital address that a bitcoin gets registered to, created by picking a random private key.

Bitcoin faucet: A website or software that rewards users in the form of satoshis for completing a task.

Bitcoin network: A network specific to the exchange of bitcoins from user to user.

BitPay: A payment processor used specifically for the cryptocurrency known as bitcoin.

Block number 0: The first Bitcoin block.

Blockchain: A public ledger that records bitcoin transactions.

Bonds: A government or company-issued contract when borrowing large sums of money.

Broker: A person who buys or sells goods for others.

BTC: Abbreviation for "Bitcoin."

Capital gain: Money gained from the sale of an asset that has increased in value over the holding period.

Captcha: A spam protection system used to differentiate computers from humans when entering data.

Central bank: A bank that provides money services regulated by the government.

Cipher: A tool used to decode an encrypted message or algorithm.

Coinbase: A platform for buying, selling, transferring, and storing digital currency.

Common stocks: A form of ownership in a company, also known as company shares.

Cryptanalysis: The process of studying encrypted codes in hopes to decrypt them.

Cryptocurrency: A digital asset designed to work as a medium of exchange, usually has a value that can be equated to physical currency.

Cryptocurrency exchange: A site where users can buy, sell, or trade cryptocurrency units.

Cryptography: Also known as cryptology, it is the practice of storing and exchanging information in a private and secure way.

Crypto-yield: Also known as yield farming, the practice of lending crypto assets to create a high return in the form of more cryptocurrency.

Decryption: The process of returning an encrypted message back to its original form.

Digital currency: A currency that exists solely online but can carry an equivalent value to a fiat currency, can be spent like fiat money through the use of special payment processors, the value increases or decreases based on transactions as well as the value of the digital currency unit at the time.

Diversification: To have a range of stocks and investments in order to minimize risk.

Dividends: A sum of money that a company pays to shareholders regularly.

Economy: The production and distribution of goods dictated by its participants.

Electronic money: The electronic equivalent to fiat money whose value increases or decreases based on transactions.

Encryption: The process of taking an intelligible message and turning it into an unintelligible form.

Exchange: A public market where financial instruments such as stocks, bonds, etc. are traded.

Exchange-traded funds: Securities that trade on an exchange and can be bought and sold throughout the day.

Expense ratio: Fees paid to the mutual fund company for managing and operating a mutual fund.

Fiat money: Government-issued currency, such as the US dollar, that does not need to be backed by a commodity; banks can control how much money is printed, which gives them more control of the economy.

Financial market: A marketplace where participants trade financial securities.

FinCEN: Financial Crimes Enforcement Network, part of the United States Department of Treasury, whose purpose is to prevent financial crimes.

Fork: This refers to when a blockchain splits due to a block that is found by multiple miners at the same time, usually involves a shift in the protocol, resolved by the longer chain absorbing the shorter chain.

Fractional-reverse banking: Only a portion of deposits at a bank is backed by physical currency available for withdrawal.

Hash: A sixty-four-digit hexadecimal number used to solve part of the bitcoin mining process equation.

Hexadecimal: A numeral system using a base of sixteen rather than the common decimal system that uses a base of ten digits.

Holding period: The amount of time an asset is held by the investor.

Investing: Putting money into something in the hopes of achieving a greater profit.

Junk bonds: Bonds issued through a company with financial instability and other underlying risk factors.

Load: A fee associated with purchasing and investing in mutual funds.

Ledger: A book where account transactions are recorded.

Liquidity: The amount of cash an asset is worth.

Miner: A person actively trying to uncover new bitcoin units through computer programming and software.

Mining: Refers to the process of gaining more bitcoins by using computer processing software to uncover new bitcoins with no money necessary to start.

Money markets: Refers to a component of the financial market where financial instruments are traded.

Money services business: Any business involving money such as currency exchanger, check casher, money transmitter, or issuer/seller of traveler's checks and money orders.

Mutual funds: A group of investors managed by a professional who invests in multiple stocks that are bought and sold at the day's end.

Payment processor: A software designed to accept payments and transactions using digital currencies.

Peer-to-peer: Refers to a bitcoin network that is reliant on user-to-user exchanges without the use of go-betweens.

Preferred stocks: A form of ownership in a company also known as company shares, preferred stockholders are entitled to a fixed dividend as payment.

Private key: Used in the exchange of bitcoins and paired with a public key, the bitcoins under this key become unusable if the private key is lost.

Public key: Used to publicly sign for the exchange of bitcoins, generated using the bitcoin algorithm and paired with a private key.

Recession: Two or more consecutive quarters of an economic decline.

Satoshi: A fraction of a bitcoin worth one-hundredth of a millionth of a bitcoin, named after the pseudonymous creator of bitcoin.

Stocks: Represents ownership of a fraction of a corporation.

Transaction: Designated input and output of bitcoins between users.

Wallet: A storage device, digital or physical that holds cryptocurrency and can sometimes offer to encrypt and sign capabilities.

Create Automatic Income for Life Immediately!

Forex Signals.

High Conversions Verified Forex Results.

https://1e503-r5sjod5kcm4z3ggybs8j.hop.clickbank.net

OR

BOTS Live Trading Room

https://db240ys-r9r60z39q8rgnkuklg.hop.clickbank.net

Book 3
Day Trading Options:

The first investors guide to know the secrets of options for beginners. Learn trading basics to increase your earnings AND ACQUIRE the right mindset for investing.

Andrew Elder

Introduction

Introduction to Day Trading

Understanding the basics of day trading is crucial before you embark on this journey. Unlike investing, where you purchase an asset and hope for long-term gains over years or decades, day trading is about capitalizing on short-term market movements. Let's take a closer look:

Comparing Investing and Day Trading:

Investing involves buying an asset and holding onto it for an extended period, banking on its value appreciation. Investors analyze companies' backgrounds, ensuring they steer clear of potential pitfalls and promising sound profitability. On the other hand, day traders buy and sell stocks within a day. Their aim is to make profits from minute price fluctuations of highly liquid stocks, with the age-old wisdom of "buy low, sell high." However, their transactions are swift.

For instance, a day trader might buy 1,000 shares at 10 AM and sell them at 10:15 AM if the price rises. Profits are made from such small price changes, and after subtracting commissions and considering tax implications, the net gain might seem modest. But remember, day traders execute numerous trades daily, potentially amplifying their profits. They also avoid holding stocks overnight to minimize risks, responding rapidly to market changes.

Other Trading Styles:

Between day trading and long-term investing, there are other methods like swing trading (holding stocks for days) and position trading (holding for weeks or months). Each carries its own risks, with day trading being among the most volatile.

Day Trading's Historical Context:

- **1867:** Introduction of the first ticker tape, enhancing transactional communication.
- **1928:** Despite the booming bull market, traders lacked direct market access, relying on brokers and ticker tape info.
- **1971:** The establishment of NASDAQ.
- **1975:** SEC eliminated fixed commissions, marking the onset of the discount brokerage era.
- **1987:** Most trades were conducted via phone, leading to the SEC's introduction of the SOES, giving priority to 1,000 share orders.
- **Late 1990s:** The dot-com era saw a surge in tech stocks and the rise of online trading platforms, democratizing market access.
- **1999-2000:** Day trading gained immense popularity, but also faced scrutiny due to unfortunate incidents and potential risks. Post the dot-com bubble burst, many traders retreated.
- **2008 onwards:** Day trading transformed into a more professional and careful endeavor.

Becoming a Day Trader:

To excel in day trading, one must possess:

- **Market Knowledge:** Understand market fundamentals and continuously research.
- **Capital:** While some traders use borrowed funds (leverage), others prefer using their savings.
- **Business Acumen:** A business plan is vital, detailing goals, strategies, and operational details.
- **Discipline:** Avoiding emotional decisions, adhering to set strategies, and managing risks.
- **Technology:** A reliable tech setup is essential for swift decision-making and execution.

Essential Day Trading Tips:

1. **Trade Responsibly:** Only use funds you can afford to lose.
2. **Diversify Risks:** Don't allocate a large portion of your capital to a single trade.
3. **Explore Other Assets:** Stocks aren't the only option. Consider futures, options, and Forex.
4. **Learn and Move On:** Mistakes happen. Learn from them and avoid dwelling.
5. **Supply-Demand Dynamics:** Watch for these as they heavily influence prices.
6. **Set Targets:** Know your desired profit and maximum acceptable loss beforehand.
7. **Maintain a Favorable Risk-Reward Ratio:** Ideally, aim for a 3:1 ratio for potential profit to potential loss.

In conclusion, day trading is not for everyone. It requires a specific skill set, knowledge, and temperament. But with dedication, understanding, and a solid strategy, it can become a profitable venture.

CHAPTER 1:

What Is Options Trading?

Understanding Options Trading: A Beginner's Guide

Options trading offers two primary methods for traders. The first involves buying options and speculating on their premium prices. These premiums fluctuate based on the movements of the underlying stock, offering profit potential. For instance, if you believe a stock will rise, you can purchase an "in-the-money call" option. As the stock's value increases, so does the option's intrinsic value, leading to an overall premium increase. In the case of "puts," as the stock falls, the put option's intrinsic value and premium rise. Remember, buying a put aims to profit from price declines, not selling the put.

The second approach to options trading shifts focus from premiums to the underlying asset. This strategy is less concerned with price changes and prioritizes exercising the option. While this method involves an extra step, it may be preferable if your goal is to own the stock. Many options traders often avoid exercising the contract, as premiums typically reflect intrinsic value changes sufficiently.

So far, so good, right? You can trade options for swings or day trading similar to regular stocks, but it requires forming a directional view of the market, which increases risk and is akin to typical trading. The key is that you don't need options to trade this way. How, then, can you intelligently trade options?

The most effective approach is to leverage the structure of option contracts to shield yourself from major market risks, especially volatility. In traditional swing or day trading, traders use stop-loss orders to limit potential losses, but these can be unreliable during high market volatility. As a result, traders may face unexpected losses, which could even wipe out their entire account. Options, on the other hand, avoid such complications. You only pay the premium upfront, significantly limiting your initial investment. Then, you use solid contracts to safeguard against unexpected price jumps. Even if prices fluctuate, your contract specifies a fixed price, ensuring you receive it as stated.

The Risks of Options Trading

Up to this point, we've mainly discussed options trading concerning movements in the underlying stock. You can buy calls when you expect the stock to rise or puts when you anticipate a fall. Can you also sell calls or puts? Yes, you can, but this is where the risks in options trading come into play.

When you buy an options contract, your risk is confined to the contract's terms. The person who sells you the contract earns the premium, irrespective of what transpires. This seller is usually called the writer. Writing options has its benefits, as most options tend to expire out of the money, allowing the writer to retain the premium without worrying about contract exercise. However, if the option is exercised, it presents substantial risks.

Consider this scenario: if you've written a call (i.e., sold it) and it becomes in-the-money due to a stock's unexpected rise, your potential loss is theoretically unlimited. Remember, when you write a call, you're essentially betting that the underlying stock won't rise. If it does rise, it can theoretically reach any level. For example, if your call's strike price is $10 and the stock reaches $10,000 before the expiry date (unlikely but possible), your losses can exceed your account equity.

While writing puts doesn't entail unlimited downside, it still involves significant risks. If the put you've written has a strike price of $50, your maximum potential loss is $50 per share since stocks cannot fall below $0. This underscores the importance of cautious options writing.

Given the substantial risks, why do people write options? Aside from the fact that option writing often results in a profit by earning the premium, most option writers hedge their downside by covering their option positions. For instance, if someone writes a call, they might buy the underlying stock first. Alternatively, they could buy a put at a lower strike price, effectively covering potential losses.

It's essential to differentiate between writing options without protection (naked writing) and writing them with safeguards (covered writing). Naked option writing is highly risky and is typically prohibited by brokers. Covered writing, however, is perfectly acceptable and doesn't face broker restrictions.

If you're wondering, after writing an option, you can buy it back at a lower price before the expiry date, effectively shorting an option, similar to shorting a stock. Generally, this isn't necessary unless you need to adjust your trades.

Options inherently have leverage, where each contract controls 100 shares of the underlying stock, magnifying the impact of market movements. This underscores the importance of executing strategies with precision.

Beyond these risks, options can help mitigate trading risks associated with market volatility. While volatility can be profitable for directional traders, it can also lead to significant losses when market swings go against them.

Options Trading Accounts

To start trading options, you'll need to open a brokerage account. You have a choice between full-service and discount brokers. Full-service brokers offer various financial services, including retirement planning and tax advice, but typically charge higher commissions. While they might provide a sense of security, it's important to understand that U.S. markets are well-regulated, regardless of what some may claim.

Your broker has no obligation to provide trading advice; their primary duty is to execute your trades. Beware of conflicts of interest when brokers offer in-house products, often with higher fees. Don't blindly trust your broker, especially if they employ CFAs. They typically can't offer unbiased investment advice, let alone trading advice.

Discount brokers focus on execution, charging lower commissions. Transaction costs are a crucial factor in trading, and it's essential to consider them in profit and loss calculations. For instance, if your broker charges 0.1% per trade, you'll pay that fee when buying and selling, regardless of whether you win or lose. This cost can accumulate, impacting your profitability, especially if you place numerous trades.

Options traders face a reduced impact from commission costs compared to directional traders. Fees from discount brokers vary depending on the type of trader they cater to. Beginners should consider fees per leg or fixed fees per share, along with any additional charges for options transactions. Choose the most cost-effective platform that aligns with your needs. In many cases, Interactive Brokers is a popular choice, although advanced options traders might consider Lightspeed, which may not be suitable for beginners.

CHAPTER 2:

Understanding and Managing Risk in Options Trading

Effective risk management is paramount in options trading. While risk is inherent to any investment, your exposure to it can be controlled. The key is to prudently manage your risk capital and ensure that you are comfortable with the level of risk being taken, avoiding irrational losses.

The same principles apply to managing your capital. Trade with funds you can afford to lose, avoiding overextending yourself. As effective money and risk management are essential for successful options trading, we will explore methods to control your budget and risk exposure.

Managing Risk with Options Spreads

Options spreads are powerful tools in options trading. A spread combines multiple positions in options contracts based on the same underlying asset to create a unified trading position. For example, creating a bull call spread involves buying in-the-money calls on a specific stock while simultaneously writing less expensive out-of-the-money calls on the same stock. This strategy limits potential losses while retaining the opportunity for gains if the stock's value rises. Spreads can be used to manage risks effectively by reducing potential profits but minimizing overall risk.

Spreads are also valuable when entering short positions. For instance, by writing cash-secured puts on a stock and simultaneously purchasing cheaper out-of-the-money puts, you can cap potential losses. This strategy is known as a bull put spread. Spreads are instrumental in risk management and are widely used in options trading.

Managing Risk through Diversification

While diversification is a common risk management technique for stock investors, its application to options trading differs. In options, diversification does not work in the same way, but it remains useful. You can diversify in several ways, such as employing a variety of strategies, trading options on different underlying assets, and using a mix of option types. Diversification ensures that you have multiple avenues for making profits. This way, you are not solely reliant on a single outcome for all your trades to be successful.

Managing Risk Using Options Orders

One of the simplest ways to manage risk is by using various order types. While basic market orders execute trades at the prevailing market price, other order types can assist with risk management. Limit orders allow you to specify the highest price you're willing to pay when buying or the lowest price you're willing to accept when selling. This helps avoid unfavorable executions, especially in volatile markets.

Stop orders, including trailing stops and market stops, can help you automate exits, securing profits or limiting losses. Properly using orders can effectively control the risk of each trade you make.

Money Management and Position Sizing

Managing your money is intrinsically linked with risk management. You have a finite amount of capital, so it's essential to carefully control your capital allocation to ensure you don't deplete your funds and can continue trading.

One of the most fundamental approaches to money management is position sizing. This involves determining how much of your capital you want to allocate to a particular trade. By diversifying and only committing a small portion of your capital to each trade, you avoid becoming overly dependent on a single outcome. This approach mitigates the impact of losses, ensuring that a series of losing trades won't deplete your resources.

For example, if you allocate 50% of your capital to a single trade and it results in a loss, you risk a substantial portion of your funds. On the other hand, allocating only 5% to 10% of your capital to each trade can withstand several consecutive losses while preserving your overall capital. If you are confident in the effectiveness of your trading plan over the long term, this approach will allow you to endure difficult periods and still have sufficient capital to continue trading.

CHAPTER 3:

Software Required Before

Getting Started

Before delving into the world of day trading, it's crucial to have the necessary software tools. One of the most widely used platforms for this purpose is MetaTrader 4 (MT4).

What is MetaTrader 4 (MT4)?

MetaTrader 4, or MT4 for short, is a software product that enables traders to participate in various financial markets, including foreign exchange, stocks, commodities, indices, cryptocurrencies, and more.

Developed by MetaQuotes Software in Russia, MT4 made its debut in 2005. While other trading platforms have been developed since then, including MT4's successor, MT5, MT4 has remained the preferred choice for many forex brokers to offer services to their clients.

How to Use MetaTrader 4

The essential features of MetaTrader 4 are conveniently located in the top three bars. The primary bar contains all the features, the second bar consists of the most frequently used features, and the third bar focuses on tools for technical analysis, such as drawing trendlines and period charts.

To access these features, click "Views," which will reveal a table of essential elements. The most significant item in this list is "Market Watch" (if not displayed, press Ctrl + M to activate it).

Market Watch

In Market Watch, you'll find a list of all the currency pairs you want to trade, including Symbol, Bid, and Ask. By right-clicking on a Symbol, you can access various options, including "New order," "Show all," "Hide," "Hide all," and "Chart window."

- **New order**: This allows you to enter a new trade. You can also use the F9 shortcut to open the order execution window.
- **Chart window**: Opens a chart screen for the selected currency pair or asset when you right-click on it.

Account Information

The "Account" section displays details about your trading account, including balance, equity, and margin. It also provides information on your current open or pending orders.

Charts

Under the "Charts" section, you should be aware of various elements:

- **Candlesticks (shortcut Alt + 2)**: Candlesticks are the preferred chart type in MT4 and are used to analyze price movements.
- **Time Frame**: You can select different timeframes for chart analysis, such as M1 (1 minute), M5 (5 minutes), M15 (15 minutes), M30 (30 minutes), H1 (1 hour), H4 (4 hours), D1 (1 day), W1 (1 week), and MN (1 month).
- **Grid**: You can choose to display a grid on the chart for better visualization.
- **Properties**: Use this button to customize the MT4 interface according to your preferences.
- **Template**: Save chart layouts and settings as templates for easy access in the future.

Analyzing Stocks for Trading

Before embarking on day trading, it's essential to conduct thorough research. Select the stocks you plan to work with. Initially, familiarize yourself with a few stocks that you can study extensively. You can switch between them based on market conditions and your strategy.

If you have specific trading strategies in mind, this is a great place to start. Focus on stocks that align with your strategies to achieve the best results.

It's important to understand that market conditions change daily, making it necessary to adapt to different trading approaches. Analyze charts, patterns, and trends to determine the right time to enter a trade.

By selecting the most suitable stocks, conducting detailed analysis, and adjusting your trading strategy as needed, you'll be well-prepared to begin your day trading journey.

CHAPTER 4:

Platform and Tools for option Trading

Before you dive into options trading, it's crucial to familiarize yourself with some key terms and concepts that will be essential for your trading journey. Understanding these terms is fundamental to navigate the world of options trading effectively and to make informed decisions across various markets. We will take some time to explore these terms and concepts in this guide, helping you lay the foundation for your options trading knowledge.

Annual Report:

An annual report is a comprehensive document that a company prepares to provide crucial financial information to its shareholders and potential investors. It includes details such as the company's debt, income, cash flow, and management strategy. Reading an annual report can provide valuable insights into a company's financial health before you consider investing, whether it's in stocks, long-term investments, or options trading.

Arbitrage:

Arbitrage involves buying and selling the same security on different markets, often at different price points. This strategy aims to profit from price disparities. For instance, if you find an option trading for $10 on one exchange and $12 on another, you can buy it on the first exchange and sell it on the second to make a profit.

Averaging Down:

Averaging down is a strategy where an investor purchase more of a stock as its price decreases. This strategy aims to reduce the average purchase price. It's employed when you believe the current market sentiment about a particular company is incorrect and that the stock's price will rebound in the future. You can buy options at a lower price while waiting for a market upturn.

Bear Market:

A bear market occurs when prices in a financial market experience a prolonged period of decline. It signifies a pessimistic market trend, where stock prices are falling. Being aware of bear markets is crucial for options traders as it can impact their strategies and positions.

Blue-Chip Stocks:

Blue-chip stocks represent shares in large, well-established companies that are considered financially stable and reliable. These stocks often offer stable returns and dividend payments. They are called "blue-chip" because of their association with the highest-value poker chips in casinos.

Bull Market:

In contrast to a bear market, a bull market indicates a sustained period of rising stock prices across the entire market or for a specific stock. It's essential to recognize bull markets as they can significantly influence trading decisions.

Bid and Ask:

The "bid" represents the highest price that a buyer is willing to pay for a security, while the "ask" is the lowest price a seller is willing to accept for that security. The difference between the bid and ask prices is called the spread.

Leverage:

Leverage is a technique used in trading where you can borrow funds from your broker to invest in securities, typically increasing your potential profits. However, it also amplifies your potential losses, making it a risky strategy, especially for beginners.

Margin:

Margin accounts allow you to borrow money from your broker to purchase securities. The margin is the difference between the total borrowed amount and the cost of the securities. Margin trading can be high-risk, and it requires a minimum account balance.

Portfolio:

Your portfolio represents your entire collection of investments. Many successful traders diversify their portfolios, holding various securities to reduce risk and increase profit potential.

Short Selling:

Short selling involves selling a security that you do not own, with the intention of buying it back at a lower price in the future. This strategy can be profitable when you expect the security's price to decrease.

Spread:

The spread is the difference between the bid and ask prices, indicating the cost of entering or exiting a trade. It's crucial to consider spreads when trading options, as they affect your overall profit.

Call and Put Options:

- **Call Option:** A call option gives you the right, but not the obligation, to buy a specific security at a predetermined price within a set time frame.
- **Put Option:** A put option provides the right, but not the obligation, to sell a particular security at a predetermined price within a set time frame.

Time Decay:

Time decay, or theta, is the reduction in the value of options as they approach their expiration date. Options are considered wasting assets, as their value decreases with time.

As a beginner in options trading, it's essential to grasp these terms and concepts to build a strong foundation for your trading endeavors. Learning and understanding these fundamentals will help you make informed decisions, manage risks, and develop effective trading strategies.

CHAPTER 5:

Understanding the Basic Techniques

Understanding Basic Techniques in Technical Analysis

In the world of trading, the ability to make informed decisions is paramount. Success in the market is not merely a game of chance; it requires calculated and methodical approaches. This is where technical analysis comes into play. Before entering any trade, be it in stocks, options, or other financial instruments, you must conduct technical analysis to enhance your chances of profitability and reduce risks.

Technical Analysis - The Bedrock of Trading

Many traders understand that the foundation of any trade is a thorough technical analysis. It is the cornerstone of every purposeful and educated decision, helping to minimize risks and maximize profits. Although the stock market may appear to some as a gamble, trading is a discipline that demands precision and strategy, not blind luck.

Successful trading hinges on the harmonious blend of research, facts, confidence, and intuition. The former is your safety net, while the latter ensures the quality of your decision-making and your mental state during the trade. A well-researched trade minimizes risk, while confidence instills a calm, focused mindset in the often turbulent world of trading.

Key Technical Indicators for Trading Options

In options trading, three key technical indicators play a crucial role in identifying trends and patterns:

1. Relative Strength Index (RSI):

The RSI is a momentum indicator represented as a scale from 0 to 100, situated alongside candlestick charts. It identifies overbought and oversold conditions, giving insight into potential market reversals.

- When the RSI rises above 70, the market is considered overbought, indicating a potential upcoming sell-off.
- Conversely, when the RSI falls below 30, it signals an oversold market, suggesting a potential buying opportunity.
- Most stocks will not oscillate consistently between overbought and oversold; they usually lean towards one of these extremes before making significant moves. Therefore, tracking these trends is essential to confirm their occurrence.

2. Moving Average Convergence Divergence (MACD):

The MACD indicator comprises a fast line, a slow line, and a histogram. It provides valuable insights into market behavior, albeit it can be somewhat complex.

- The fast line and slow line display moving averages, offering a glimpse into market volatility.
- A significant gap between these lines suggests higher market volatility, while their crossover indicates a change in market direction.
- The histogram shows historical volatility patterns, helping you determine if current volatility is standard or exceptional. Higher volatility stocks tend to have greater potential rewards, albeit with increased risks.

3. Stochastic Indicator:

The stochastic indicator, another momentum indicator, helps identify potential trend reversals. It provides information similar to the RSI, confirming your trade positions.

- The stochastic indicator is represented by two lines, typically beneath the market chart. When both lines cross above 80, it may indicate a downtrend and a possible bearish market. At this point, selling call options or buying put options may be favorable.
- When the indicator drops below 20, the market is considered oversold and may indicate an uptrend or bullish market. This is a good time to buy call options, sell put options, or position yourself strategically for profit.

Both lines crossing above or below these key levels reinforces the likelihood of a market direction change. It's important to remain attentive to stocks hovering near these levels as they may soon provide favorable trading opportunities.

The Importance of Technical Analysis in Options Trading

Options trading necessitates less technical analysis compared to other trading styles. However, it is still vital to perform a technical analysis to ensure your market entry point is well-informed. The failure to conduct proper technical analysis may result in increased risks and the potential for losses.

Technical analysis for options trading should become routine practice. By rigorously adhering to a defined system for position validation and entry-point selection, you can maximize profit potential while minimizing risk. Ultimately, your level of education and understanding is directly proportional to your trading success.

Always remember that informed and methodical trading is the path to success. Technical analysis is your ally in navigating the intricate world of trading, ensuring that every decision you make is purposeful, well-informed, and calculated.

CHAPTER 6:

Learn to Become a Day Trader

Becoming a Proficient Day Trader

Day trading gained prominence during the late 1990s, particularly with the Dot-com bubble. In those times, when stock markets experienced significant fluctuations, day traders could easily capitalize on these fluctuations and make substantial profits without an extensive skill set. However, the day trading landscape has since evolved, and success now demands expertise, knowledge, and refined strategies.

Understanding Day Trading

Day trading entails buying and selling financial instruments within a single trading day. It requires various skills and tools, a fundamental understanding of stock markets, and the ability to identify opportune moments to enter or exit positions.

Key Skills to Master

If you aspire to become a successful day trader, you must acquire specific skills:

1. **Knowledge of Stock Markets:**
   o A fundamental understanding of stock markets is essential. Identify popular stocks with high trading volumes as these play a crucial role in day trading.
2. **Basic Technical Analysis:**

o Unlike fundamental analysis, technical analysis is critical for day traders. You must interpret price movements over shorter timeframes accurately. Consider enrolling in online courses or offline workshops to learn about technical analysis and chart reading.

3. **Money Management:**
   o Effective money management is crucial. Define a budget for your trading activities and manage your capital prudently. Regularly assess your gains and losses to gauge the success of your trading endeavors.

4. **Trading Psychology:**
   o Emotions can be detrimental in day trading. Explore resources on trading psychology to learn how to control emotions and make rational decisions.

Distinguishing Characteristics of Day Traders

Day traders primarily rely on technical analysis, focusing on chart patterns to execute trades. They pay less attention to fundamental factors such as a company's financial health, P/E ratios, or debt-to-equity ratios.

Day traders typically complete all their trades within a single trading session, closing positions by the day's end. Traders who hold positions overnight are referred to as swing traders.

Chart Timeframes for Day Trading

Day traders employ various timeframes on technical charts, ranging from one minute to hours. While some may dedicate hours each day to trading, others, with time constraints, opt for longer timeframes, such as weekly or monthly charts. Regardless of the chosen timeframe, it is vital to select timeframes that align with your trading style.

Scalping - A Riskier Approach

Scalping is a highly skilled and riskier form of day trading, focusing on small timeframes, such as one minute or even seconds. Scalpers aim to accumulate tiny profits by trading more frequently with larger lot sizes. Precision and quick decision-making are essential, as scalping can result in significant losses if not executed skillfully.

Intraday vs. Swing Trading

While day traders complete their trades within a single trading day, swing traders, a subset of day traders, extend their holding period to multiple days. Their trading style permits more flexibility and is better suited to those who cannot dedicate hours to trading every day.

Day trading in the stock market typically yields higher volatility during the opening and closing hours. Traders often focus on these specific hours to capitalize on the increased price movements.

Part-Time or Full-Time Day Trading

Day trading can be pursued both full-time and part-time. The choice depends on your level of commitment and available resources:

1. **Full-Time Trading:**
    - Joining a financial institution as a day trader offers a stable income. The institution may provide trading recommendations and insights that you can incorporate into your strategies.
2. **Individual Full-Time Trading:**
    - As an independent trader, you are responsible for your setup, investment, and decision-making. This path demands a significant amount of knowledge, discipline, and dedication.
3. **Part-Time Trading:**
    - Part-time day trading can be accomplished by focusing on the most active trading periods, usually during market opening and closing hours. This approach is suitable for individuals with other commitments.

Exploring Forex Markets

Forex markets provide the flexibility of 24-hour trading sessions, making them popular among day traders. Forex trading is highly technical, and understanding technical analysis is paramount. Major currency pairs are commonly traded in this arena.

Conclusion

Day trading offers potential for substantial financial rewards, but it demands discipline, knowledge, and risk management. It can be pursued as a full-time or part-time endeavor, depending on individual circumstances and trading preferences. Success as a day trader hinges on well-honed skills, the ability to control emotions, and a deep understanding of the markets. While the promise of quick riches may be enticing, day trading should be approached with a focus on strategy, risk management, and personal discipline.

CHAPTER 7:

Fundamental Analysis

Fundamental Analysis in Trading

Fundamental analysis in trading provides a more comprehensive, long-term perspective. It involves evaluating a country's economy and its trading system to determine trade viability. By focusing on economic factors, this approach helps traders understand the reasons behind the rise or fall of a currency.

Understanding Currency Movement

A key aspect of options trading is understanding the underlying reasons for currency fluctuations. Fundamental analysis empowers traders to interpret economic indicators, such as employment and unemployment rates, and assess the overall economic health of a country.

Fundamental Analysis vs. Technical Analysis

While technical analysis is based on trends and patterns, fundamental analysis delves into the root causes behind market movements. Successful traders often prioritize fundamental analysis due to its fact-based nature. Technical analysis, while accurate, does not guarantee results like fundamental analysis does.

Market Response to Economic Health

Fundamental analysis involves assessing a country's economic performance. Robust economies attract foreign investors, leading to increased demand for that currency. Therefore, when the economy is flourishing, the country's currency tends to strengthen. For instance, the U.S. dollar depreciated during the 2007-2008 financial crisis, while the Canadian dollar appreciated significantly due to the relative health of the Canadian economy.

Fundamental Analysis Methodology

To effectively employ fundamental analysis:

1. **Create a Baseline:**
   o   Gather data about the company, industry, and the wider market. This broader perspective ensures a comprehensive analysis that considers the far-reaching effects of market shifts.
2. **Recognize Market Phases:**
   o   Markets experience different phases, influencing the value of penny stocks. High market popularity in a sector results in lower volatility and higher liquidity.
3. **Consider Global Influences:**
   o   Examine worldwide factors, especially in technology, which can drive substantial paradigm shifts, impacting penny stock values. Remaining oblivious to these shifts is a risk to be avoided.
4. **Synthesize Information:**
   o   Combine your insights to compare past market conditions, potential upcoming developments, and the current market status. This holistic view aids in predicting investor behavior under different circumstances and identifying assets on the brink of desired movement for binary options trading.

Selecting Underlying Assets for Binary Options Trading

When choosing an underlying asset for binary options trading, opt for one that is near the end of a post-boom or post-bust phase, depending on your call or put position. These periods present greater market flexibility and higher risk tolerance, making them favorable for your trades.

Remembering Risk Management

The amount of risk you can handle without increasing your likelihood of failure decreases as the market moves further into the boom or bust phase. Hence, acting quickly is essential to maximize your potential profits.

Relative Strength of Trades

Incorporate the concept of relative strength when evaluating a trade. This enables you to determine how well a specific asset is positioned relative to other options, guiding you to make well-informed trading decisions.

In summary, fundamental analysis plays a crucial role in trading by helping you understand the broader economic factors influencing the market. It complements technical analysis, and together they can significantly enhance your trading strategy. Starting with technical analysis for short-term trades, building confidence, and then incorporating fundamental analysis for more extended positions provides a comprehensive approach to options trading.

CHAPTER 8:

Technical Analysis for Training Options

Technical Analysis for Options Trading

When delving into technical analysis for options trading, it's important to understand that it operates based on the belief that the historical price movements of a trade can provide reliable insights into its future behavior. Regardless of the market you choose to focus on, there is a wealth of technical data available. Luckily, you won't have to analyze it all on your own, as there are various tools at your disposal, including charts, trends, and indicators.

Understanding Key Assumptions

Technical analysis relies on three fundamental assumptions:

1. The market factors in everything.
2. Trends can be reliable predictors of price.
3. Historical patterns tend to repeat over time.

This approach asserts that the current price of an underlying asset reflects all available information. Thus, all you need to make informed decisions is the current price and an understanding of the broader economic climate.

Interpreting Market Sentiment

Technical analysis allows traders to gauge market sentiment and predict future price movements based on price patterns. These patterns, whether short or long-term, offer insights into possible future trends, enabling traders to use historical charts to anticipate future price movements.

Price Charts in Technical Analysis

Price charts are the cornerstone of technical analysis. Different types of price charts are available, including:

- **Line Chart:** Presents closing prices over time. It's straightforward but doesn't display opening, high, or low prices.
- **Bar Chart:** Displays a range of data points, including open, high, low, and close prices. It provides more information than a line chart.
- **Candlestick Chart:** Similar to a bar chart but provides more detailed information, such as daily price range.
- **Point and Figure Chart:** Depicts price movements as Xs and Os, offering a pure indicator of price without market noise.

Determining Trend or Range

In technical analysis, it's crucial to decide whether you want to focus on trading based on trends or within a price range. Your emphasis on one of these aspects depends on your trading strategy.

Chart Patterns to Watch For

Several chart patterns are essential for technical analysis, including:

- **Flags and Pennants:** These patterns signify short-term retracements against the primary trend.
- **Head and Shoulders Formation:** A grouping of three peaks, where the head signals a bearish pattern and a potential trend reversal.
- **Gann Angles:** Used to determine the future direction of a currency by analyzing price, time, and pattern data. They are diagonal lines that can predict future price levels based on current trends.

In conclusion, technical analysis is a valuable tool for options trading. It's based on the idea that past price movements can help predict future ones. Understanding chart patterns and trends can empower you to make informed trading decisions.

CHAPTER 9:

How to Find the Best Options to Get Started

Achieving the Right Mindset for Successful Options Trading

For a trader aspiring to excel, cultivating the appropriate mindset is paramount. Options, as versatile financial instruments, offer substantial potential, provided you understand how to harness them effectively. Part of this journey involves acquiring the mindset of a proficient options trader.

Strategies for Adopting an Options Trader's Mindset

It's not just about formulating winning strategies; it's equally about cultivating a mindset that breeds success. Extensive analysis can guide your decisions, but your psychological outlook plays a pivotal role in your trading journey. In fact, trading isn't solely about strategies, numbers, or intellect; rather, it hinges significantly on your psychological mindset.

The Predicament of Beginner Traders

Many beginners grapple with the notion that finding the perfect strategy will usher in a stream of profits. However, trading proves to be more complex in practice. There's a multitude of traders, equipped with sound strategies, vying for their piece of the financial pie. Yet, losses still occur, underscoring the importance of understanding the psychological facet of trading.

The Crucial Role of Trading Psychology

Trading psychology is a well-studied and indispensable aspect of trading. Psychological attributes, beliefs, attitudes, and mindsets all bear a substantial influence on a trader's performance. Some common misconceptions, such as viewing the market as rigged against them, can detrimentally affect one's trading outcomes. It's imperative to shed such fallacious beliefs and recognize the market's neutrality. The market isn't biased; it doesn't favor either gains or losses.

The Power of Self-Doubt and Self-Fulfilling Prophecies

Self-doubt, deeply ingrained in one's subconscious, can trigger a self-fulfilling prophecy. If you perceive yourself as unlucky or incapable of winning, it can hinder your ability to act decisively in trades. This, in turn, leads to missed opportunities, reduced profits, and negative financial results.

The Confidence Factor

Successful traders exhibit a high degree of self-confidence. They appreciate market conditions, acknowledging that even the best strategies may falter. They don't plunge into cycles of self-blame when circumstances go awry. This self-assuredness sets them apart from their less successful counterparts, enabling them to seize genuine opportunities.

Differentiating Between Losing and Bad Trades

Understanding the difference between a losing trade and a bad trade is essential. A losing trade is one where you lose money, whereas a bad trade is determined by whether the potential reward outweighs the risk. Winning isn't the sole criterion for a trade's quality; it hinges on whether the odds favor your position, regardless of the eventual outcome.

Mastering Trading Psychology

Trading is demanding and evokes intense emotions, whether a trade succeeds or fails. Managing these emotions is crucial. Adopting a mindset that embraces probability can help mitigate the emotional rollercoaster. Recognizing that not every trade will yield profits, and that losses are an intrinsic part of trading, fosters discipline and resilience.

Essential Traits for Success

Several traits distinguish successful options traders:

1. **Risk Management Skills:** Accurate risk assessment and effective risk mitigation strategies are indispensable. Understanding position implications, assessing potential downsides, and employing diversification are key.
2. **Money Management:** Prudent capital management is vital. A trader who wisely allocates and manages their funds is better equipped to withstand market fluctuations.
3. **Effective Risk Mitigation:** Controlling and minimizing risks is paramount. Regardless of market conditions, a sound risk management strategy should prevail.
4. **Diversification:** Spreading risk across multiple trades rather than concentrating it in one is a common risk reduction strategy.
5. **Position Sizing:** Aligning the trade size with the account capital, ensuring it doesn't jeopardize the entire account, is fundamental.

6. **Discipline:** Consistency in adhering to your trading plan, even in the face of emotional turbulence, is vital.

In conclusion, a trader's mindset is as pivotal as their trading strategies. Embracing the psychological aspects of trading, along with these essential traits, can pave the way for success in the complex world of options trading.

CHAPTER 10:

Theoretical and practical training of operational techniques

Theoretical and Practical Training of Operational Techniques in Options Trading

To commence your journey in options trading, it's crucial to grasp the fundamental operational techniques. Options trading can sometimes appear daunting, with complex entry and exit strategies. However, this apparent complexity can be attributed to a lack of comprehensive knowledge about the core strategies involved.

Once you've acquired an understanding of how options function, including market trends, moods, and behaviors, it's imperative to hone your strategies. For novice traders, commencing with foundational techniques is advisable. A solid grasp of these basic strategies is a prerequisite before venturing into more intricate and advanced trading methodologies.

While you may have attained a foundational understanding of options, it's essential to continuously reinforce and refine your knowledge. Options trading operates within a two-party framework: one party selling and the other buying. The traded assets, however, are not stocks or conventional financial instruments. Instead, options facilitate the right to buy or sell an asset at a predetermined price within a specified timeframe.

Options trading encompasses a broader spectrum than just stocks. Various financial instruments can be traded through options in the financial markets, such as bonds, indexes, EFTs, commodities, currencies, futures, and derivatives. Although these securities or derivatives may vary, the fundamental trading principles remain consistent.

Bearish, Bullish, and Neutral Trading Strategies

Success in the stock market hinges on the analysis of market trends and stock behavior. It's imperative to predict market movements, whether upward or downward, and select appropriate options strategies. Effective options trading requires the ability to generate profits while managing risk and trading capital.

Bullish Trading Strategies

When you anticipate an upward movement in the price of an underlying security based on fundamental and technical analysis, adopting a bullish trading strategy is recommended. The underlying security can be a stock, an index, or any other asset. Profiting from bullish trading strategies entails using options to predict that the underlying security's price will increase. An effective approach is to buy a call option.

Buying a call option allows you to profit when the underlying security's price surpasses the option's strike price during the specified contract period. Your options trade becomes profitable if the call option is "in the money" at the contract's expiration, signifying that the security's price has risen beyond the strike price.

Another strategy is buying a protective put, which allows you to hedge against potential price declines in the market. A put option enables the holder to safeguard their capital from losses due to downward price movements in a security.

Bearish Trading Strategies

If you anticipate a decrease in the price of an underlying security, bearish options trading strategies are suitable. In bearish strategies, you aim to profit when the price of the underlying security falls below the strike price of the options contract. Various strategies, such as Long Put, Put Back Spread, Bear Put Spread, Covered Put, and Naked Calls, can be employed to capitalize on a bearish outlook.

Understanding that market conditions may deviate from predictions is critical. When the market moves against your expectations, there is a risk of incurring losses in options trading. It's essential to consider all relevant factors before making trading decisions.

Neutral Option Strategies

Neutral trading strategies are utilized when no significant changes in the market are anticipated. In situations characterized by reduced market volatility and stability in security prices, neutral strategies, such as Ratio Spreads, Strangles, Straddles, and Condors, can be deployed.

Before embarking on your options trading journey, it's essential to understand the basics of the chosen options strategy and conduct a thorough analysis to identify the optimal entry points. Options trading offers a variety of strategies, including long calls, short calls, naked calls, covered calls, long puts, short puts, and naked or covered puts, to cater to different market conditions. Once the fundamentals are comprehended, you can begin crafting your trading plans and strategies.

Risk/Reward Analysis for Long Call Options Strategy

The long call option strategy offers several advantages:

- It requires less capital, making it appealing to novice traders.
- Losses are limited, providing a safety net in case the underlying asset's price decreases.
- It involves straightforward execution without complex calculations.
- Margin debt is not a concern, and commissions are typically lower than for more intricate option strategies.

However, it's important to exercise caution and not overcommit to long call options. Allocating substantial funds to numerous out-of-the-money call options may result in significant losses. Additionally, bear in mind that call options are subject to time decay, which diminishes their value as the expiration date approaches.

In summary, options trading offers a diverse array of strategies tailored to specific market conditions. A solid grasp of the fundamentals is the foundation for success, and as you gain experience, you can explore more advanced options trading strategies to achieve your financial goals.

CHAPTER 11:

Psychology of An Option Trader

The Psychology of an Option Trader

In the world of trading, the psychology of traders plays a pivotal role in decision-making. Two fundamental emotions that influence these decisions are fear and greed.

Fear

Fear, at its core, is one of the most paralyzing emotions for a trader. It often leads to impulsive decisions driven by panic rather than a rational strategy. When faced with a significant market selloff, the trader is often inundated with an overwhelming urge to take action, even if that action may not be the right one.

Fear tends to emerge when traders believe they have a deep understanding of the market's near-term direction. This misplaced confidence can lead to impulsive entry or exit points, resulting in emotional reactions rather than calculated decisions.

As fear becomes more dominant, traders tend to become hesitant and cautious. Fear encompasses various facets, and let's explore some of them:

1. **The Fear of Losing:** The dread of losing capital often paralyzes traders, hindering their ability to execute a well-

thought-out strategy or enter and exit positions at the right moments. The fear of loss erodes confidence and can lead to analysis paralysis, making decision-making a daunting task.

2. **The Fear of a Positive Trend Reversal:** Many traders are lured by the prospect of quick profits and prematurely exit trades to lock in gains, driven by a fear of losing their accrued profits. Instead, traders should adhere to the trend until they receive a signal indicating a reversal.

3. **The Fear of Missing Out:** Traders often grapple with the apprehension that they might miss out on a potentially lucrative trade. This fear is often compounded by greed, which can cloud judgment and lead to impulsive trades based on the notion that others are profiting from a particular market move.

4. **The Fear of Being Wrong:** Some traders fixate on always being right rather than focusing on the sound execution of their strategies. This quest for perfectionism can lead to a fear of failure, as losses are not accepted gracefully.

To overcome the fear associated with trading, traders should embrace the inevitability of losses and accept the fact that the probability of winning or losing is approximately 50/50. Adopting this perspective can alleviate the fear of trading and enable traders to take positions with confidence.

Greed

Greed, an overpowering desire to extract excessive profits from trades, can be even more detrimental than fear. While fear may lead to losing a trade but preserving capital, greed drives traders to act recklessly and risk their entire capital.

The perils of greed manifest as irrational behaviors, including overtrading, excessive leverage, holding positions for too long, or chasing various markets. As greed takes over, rational decision-making recedes into the background.

Overly greedy traders expose themselves to heightened risks, often acting without a sound understanding of market dynamics and fueled by unrealistic profit expectations. When overcome by greed, judgment becomes clouded, and the negative consequences of certain decisions are often ignored.

Traders driven by greed may face significant losses and are prone to disillusionment, potentially leading them to abandon trading.

Overcoming Fear and Greed in Trading

To combat these emotional obstacles in trading, several strategies can be employed:

- **Education:** Expand your knowledge of the financial markets to make informed decisions. Understanding the assets and strategies at your disposal enhances your capacity to make rational choices.
- **Set Goals:** Establish clear short-term and long-term goals to guide your trading. Having a predefined set of objectives and rules helps navigate periods of fear or greed.
- **Big Picture Perspective:** Continually evaluate your trading performance to acknowledge both your successes and failures. Learning from your mistakes is key to making more informed choices in the future.
- **Start Small:** Begin with modest investments to mitigate fear and minimize financial risk. As confidence grows, gradually scale up your trading activity.
- **Effective Strategy:** Implement a well-defined trading strategy that matches your skills and risk tolerance. Simple and straightforward strategies are easier to execute and monitor.
- **Taking Action:** Overcome the fear of taking action. Although initially uncomfortable, it's essential to become proactive in your trading endeavors. Preparedness and a clear plan of action are key components of success.
- **Persistence:** Accept that losses are part of the trading journey. Learn from your mistakes, adjust your strategy, and continue forward.

In summary, understanding the psychological factors of fear and greed is vital for traders. Through education, goal setting, perspective, starting with small investments, adopting effective strategies, and taking action, traders can conquer these emotions and pave the way for more rational and profitable trading decisions.

CHAPTER 12:

What Kind of Trader Are You?

Determining Your Trading Style

In the realm of trading, it's essential to identify the trading style that resonates with your personality and objectives. Selecting your trading style is a pivotal decision, as it significantly influences your profitability. Therefore, it is imperative to choose your path thoughtfully before embarking on your trading journey. Hesitation and experimenting with various styles can lead to a lack of focus, ultimately jeopardizing your success. Remember, trading is not a game or a hobby but a legitimate business with real financial stakes. You wouldn't start and run multiple unrelated businesses simultaneously; similarly, it's crucial to determine whether you want to be a day trader, a swing trader, a position trader, or an options trader. Once you've made your choice, dedicate yourself to mastering that specific style, as attempting to juggle multiple approaches may result in suboptimal results at best or significant losses at worst.

Day Trading

Day trading is a high-intensity trading style suited for individuals who can commit 100% of their focus to the task. It demands 2-4 hours of active trading during market hours, making it a full-time commitment. Day traders rely extensively on technical analysis, dedicating hours to stock research and the precise timing of trade entries and exits. As a day trader, you must remain vigilant during the trading session, as you'll be dealing with highly volatile stocks, necessitating same-day profit generation. The stress level is high, and substantial capital is required, with a minimum of $25,000 in your account (in the United States) to adhere to regulatory requirements.

Swing Trading

For those who appreciate the idea of profiting from price movements and enjoy technical analysis but are not inclined towards the intensity of day trading, swing trading is a suitable choice. Swing traders employ the tools of technical analysis but hold positions for days or weeks, offering a more relaxed trading lifestyle. It can be done on a part-time basis, and trading large-cap stocks and index funds is common, unlike day trading. Swing trading does not impose specific capital requirements.

Position Trading

Position trading extends the timeframe of swing trading, focusing on longer-term price trends, often spanning months to even 1-2 years. Position traders aim for long-term price swings or appreciation. This style can be integrated into a swing trading business or used alongside traditional buy-and-hold investment strategies. It demands more fundamental analysis but does not require specialized knowledge beyond what is used in swing trading.

Options Trading

Options trading offers a more affordable entry point with the potential to start with a few hundred dollars. However, it demands specialized knowledge, and traders should consider focusing solely on this style. Combining options trading with other styles is generally discouraged. If you are inclined towards options trading, it's advisable to dedicate your full attention to it, with the exception of any concurrent long-term stock investments.

Risk Mitigation

Regardless of your chosen trading style, managing risk is a crucial aspect of successful trading. This entails never risking more capital than you can afford to lose and having well-defined profit-taking and exit strategies. It's recommended to risk 1-2% of your account on a single trade, though not exceeding 3% as a novice trader. The risk amount per trade is calculated as a percentage of your total account value. Establishing stop-loss orders for each trade helps enforce this risk management strategy, ensuring that losses are controlled.

Trader Mindset

To cultivate a successful trader's mindset, it is imperative to disassociate from unrealistic expectations. Trading is not a get-rich-quick scheme. Instead, it's a serious business endeavor where consistent profits are built up over time. Adopt a patient and methodical approach to your trading activities. Remember, trading is a journey that demands discipline, focus, and an unwavering commitment to your chosen style.

CHAPTER 13:

Common Mistakes to Avoid in Day Trading

Common Mistakes to Avoid in Day Trading

Errors Committed by Day Traders

Many aspiring stock traders enter the financial markets with hopes of achieving significant profits. However, they soon realize that consistent, profitable trading is not as straightforward as they initially believed. Some become disheartened by this reality and ultimately abandon their trading endeavors. The allure of financial gain draws people into the world of trading, but it's a harsh wake-up call when they face losses.

The foreign exchange market offers a low entry barrier, making it one of the most accessible day trading markets. It's relatively easy to get started—all you need is a computer, an internet connection, and a few hundred dollars. However, there are no guarantees of making a profit. If you are undeterred by the risks and costs associated with day trading, it's essential to familiarize yourself with common mistakes to avoid for successful day trading. Before you embark on this journey, please consider some of the frequent errors you should steer clear of, as they are often the causes of failure among new traders:

1. **Insufficient Preparation and Planning**: Entering the world of trading demands thorough preparation. Many traders neglect the essential step of educating themselves before venturing into the market. It's crucial to learn from experienced traders if you intend to swim with the sharks. Numerous books are available that offer valuable information about stock trading. It is advisable to study as many of these books as possible. Success in trading requires time, commitment, and dedication. Remember that this is trading, not gambling.

2. **Emotional Decision-Making**: New traders often incur losses due to their fixation on monetary gains. Maintain a long-term focus on your trading endeavors. Regularly monitoring your account on a monthly or yearly basis is more prudent than daily tracking. This approach can reduce emotional attachment to money and help minimize stress.

3. **Inadequate Recordkeeping**: Many traders become emotional when dealing with stocks. It is vital to maintain control over your emotions. Keeping an organized trading journal can help you analyze each trade. Record every trade, create charts, and jot down your reasons for trading—whether technical, fundamental, or based on tips. This practice can facilitate learning, profit generation, and your growth as a trader.

4. **Lack of Proper Trading Tools**: Trading is an art that requires the right tools and resources. Before you begin trading, ensure you have the necessary tools, including educational resources, a reputable broker, and trading software.

5. **Overcommitting**: New traders are often drawn to trading as a way to turn a small investment into substantial profits. Proper budgeting is the first step to success in the markets. A well-defined trading strategy is essential for protecting your capital and avoiding excessive risks. Do not risk your entire capital in one trade; effective money management is crucial.

6. **Learning but Not Blindly Following**: Seek to learn from experienced traders, but avoid blindly following their strategies. Aim for self-sufficiency and make informed decisions based on your own research.

7. **Profit Expectations**: New traders often underestimate the possibility of losses in their trades. Entering the market with a

guaranteed expectation of substantial profits can be perilous. Adopt a neutral mindset and be prepared for both gains and losses.

8. **Lack of Specialization**: Focus on a specific market segment to become a successful trader. Trying to master all types of securities, including stocks, commodities, options, futures, and currencies, can be overwhelming. Specialization in a specific category can give you an edge.

9. **Incorrect Timing**: Mistiming your trades, such as purchasing stocks at inconvenient price levels, can lead to losses. Wisdom dictates securing profits and losses at favorable times.

10. **Overreliance on Automated Systems**: Relying too heavily on trading software without understanding the mechanics can lead to errors. Learn how trading systems work and avoid complete dependence on them.

11. **Ignorance of Short Trading**: Ignorance of short trading methods may limit your profit potential, especially in declining markets. Mastering shorting is an essential skill in trading.

12. **Improper Stop Placement**: Incorrectly placed stop orders can lead to early trade exits and larger losses. Base your stop placement on market dynamics, like support and resistance levels, rather than solely on profit goals.

13. **Neglecting Risk-Reward Ratios**: Failing to calculate the risk-reward ratio before entering a position can expose you to unnecessary risks. Evaluate potential gains versus potential losses before making a trade.

14. **Crowded Trades**: Avoid getting caught up in crowded trades, where various traders possess different information. Always consider your time frame and maintain a cautious approach.

15. **Failure to Cut Losses**: Refusing to cut losses can hinder your trading progress. Accept losses as part of the process and avoid holding onto losing positions.

In the world of trading, understanding and avoiding these common mistakes is critical for long-term success. These pitfalls often cause the downfall of new traders, but with discipline and learning, they can be overcome.

CHAPTER 14:

Advanced Trading Strategies

Advanced Trading Strategies

In this section, we will delve into some advanced trading strategies.

Long Straddle

In a long straddle, you simultaneously purchase a call option and a put option for the same underlying stock. These options also share the same strike price and expiration date. This strategy is typically employed when dealing with highly volatile stocks, as it allows you to profit regardless of which direction the stock price moves. To understand how this works, let's first consider how we determine if a trade will be profitable, looking at it from the buyer's perspective.

In a call option, you profit when the stock price exceeds the strike price, taking into account the premium you paid. For instance, if you expect a stock to rise above $54 and you paid a $1 premium per share, you should consider purchasing a call option with a strike price of at least $55.

For a put option, the premise is similar, but you anticipate the stock's price to fall below the strike price. In our case, buying both a call and a put at the same strike price and expiration date entails purchasing a put option with a $55 strike price. For simplicity, let's stick with a $1 premium.

Now, you need to calculate the net premium, which is the total premium from both the call and put options. In this case, it amounts to $2. A profit in this strategy occurs when one of the following conditions is met:

1. Price of the underlying stock > (Call strike price + Net Premium). In our example, you'll make a profit if the stock price surpasses $55 + $2 = $57.
2. Price of the underlying stock < (Put strike price - Net Premium). In our model, you'll realize a profit when the stock price falls below $55 - $2 = $53.

The maximum loss for a straddle is incurred if both contracts expire with the underlying security trading at the strike price. In such a case, both options expire worthless, and you lose the premiums paid for each.

A long straddle has two breakeven points, which are:

- Lower breakeven point: Strike price - Net premium
- Upper breakeven point: Strike price + Net premium

Remember that you are buying call and put options with the same strike price and expiration date.

Let's illustrate this with a simple example. Suppose a stock is trading at $100 per share in May. An investor purchases a call option with a $200 strike price that expires on the third Friday in June for $100. Additionally, the investor buys a put option with a $200 strike price expiring on the same date for $100. The net premium is $100 + $100 = $200.

Now, let's assume that on the expiration date, the stock is trading at $300. In this case, the put option expires worthless as the stock price is significantly above the put's strike price. However, the investor's call option expires in the money with an intrinsic value of 100 x ($300 - $200) = $10,000. After deducting the premium paid, the investor has realized a profit of $9,800.

Conversely, if the stock's value drops, and on expiration, it's trading at $50, the call option expires worthless. The investor can then purchase 100 shares at $50 each for a total cost of $5,000. Subsequently, the investor can exercise the put option to sell the shares at $200 each, resulting in a net gain of $20,000 - $5,000 - $200 = $14,800.

This is a simplified example, and the numbers may not be realistic, but the point is that the investor can profit regardless of the stock's price movement.

Strangle

A strangle is a variation of the straddle. In this case, you also simultaneously purchase a call option and a put option, but they have different strike prices. This strategy involves buying slightly out-of-the-money options and is used when expecting significant short-term volatility in the underlying stock. You can profit from a strangle when either of the following conditions is met:

1. Price of the underlying stock > (call strike price + Net Premium Paid)
2. Price of the underlying stock < (put strike price - Net premium paid)

Typically, the put's strike price is set at a lower value. Profit is calculated based on either:

- Profit = Price of underlying stock - call strike price - net premium
- Profit = put strike price - Price of underlying stock - net premium

These are some of the advanced trading strategies that experienced traders use to maximize their opportunities and manage risk effectively. Understanding these strategies can help traders make more informed decisions in the market.

CHAPTER 15:

Covered Call Strategy (or Protected Puts)

Covered Call Strategy (or Protected Puts)

Understanding Covered Calls

A covered call, also known as a buy-write, entails selling the right to purchase a specific asset you already own at a predetermined price within a specified time frame, typically less than 12 months. It's a two-part strategy where you first acquire the stock and then sell it on a per-share basis.

The seller of a covered call benefits immediately by receiving a premium payment from the option holder. Risk is mitigated because the seller already owns the underlying stock. Hence, your costs are covered if the stock price rises above the strike price. If the option holder chooses to exercise their right to purchase before the expiration date, you merely fulfill the agreement and collect any additional gains.

The most commonly used asset in this type of option is stock.

When considering covered calls, you must be prepared to own the stock at your purchase price, even if its value decreases. Remember that there is no guarantee of substantial profit due to the volatility of financial markets. It's essential to focus on acquiring high-quality stocks that you'd be content to own, even during market downturns.

As the seller of a covered call option, you must be willing to relinquish the stock if the price rises. Once you've entered into an option with a willing buyer, you cannot change your mind if the stock price increases. If the option holder decides to exercise the option, you must fulfill that obligation.

The maximum potential profit from covered calls is attained when the stock price equals or exceeds the call's strike price by the expiration date. The formula for calculating this is:

(Sum of Call Premium) + (Strike Price - Stock Price) = Maximum Potential Profit

The seller should also consider the break-even point at the expiration date. The formula for this is:

(Purchase Price of the Stock) - (Call Premium) = Break-Even Analysis

Determining the maximum risk potential is essential, as it is equal to the stock's purchase price at the break-even point.

The seller should also assess the static return rate and the if-called return rate on the stocks. The static return represents the approximate annual net profit of a covered call, assuming the stock price remains unchanged until expiration. To calculate this value, the seller needs to know:

- The purchase price of the stock
- The strike price of the option
- The price of the call
- The number of days until the option expires
- If there are any dividends and the amount of these dividends

The formula for calculating the static rate of return is:

(Call + Dividend) / Stock Price × Time Factor = Static Rate of Return

The if-called return is an approximation of the annual net profit on a covered call, assuming the stock price is above the strike price at or by the option's expiration and the stock is sold at expiration. To calculate this percentage, the same factors need to be determined. The formula for calculating the if-called rate of return is:

(Call + Dividend) + (Strike - Stock Price) / Stock Price × Time Factor = If-Called Rate of Return

Benefits of Covered Call Options

The first benefit of covered call options is that the seller receives a premium payment, providing income whether or not the option is exercised. Serious investors can establish a consistent income stream by regularly selling covered calls in relatively neutral or bullish markets, potentially generating monthly or quarterly income.

The second benefit is the ability to target a selling price for a particular stock above its current price. Covered calls allow investors to set a specific exit point.

Lastly, covered calls limit risks, as the asset shields the seller from potential losses.

Risks Associated with Covered Call Options

The primary risk with covered calls is that the seller can lose money if the stock price falls below the break-even point, which is a risk inherent in stock ownership.

Another risk is the inability to anticipate a significant rise in the stock price. While stocks offer unlimited profit potential, if the option holder exercises their right, the seller must surrender the stock, potentially missing out on substantial gains.

How to Create a Covered Call Option

The initial step in creating a covered call is to purchase the stock in lots of 100 shares, allowing the sale of one option contract for every 100 shares of stock. Buyers have the flexibility to choose the number of options they wish to sell, even if they hold 1000 shares, as an example. This strategy enables the seller to retain a portion of the stock.

The final step involves waiting for the covered call to either be exercised or expire. If the covered calls are not exercised, the seller retains the premium. While there is an option to buy back the call before expiration, sellers rarely choose to do so. It is crucial to remember that the seller must be willing to part with the stock upon exercise.

How Covered Calls Work

Covered calls operate in three primary scenarios:

1. **The Stock Price Goes Down**: In this case, the covered call becomes worthless upon expiration. While the stock price may decline, the seller retains the premium from selling the call, offsetting the decrease in stock value. The option can be repurchased at a lower cost, should the stock price fall before expiration.
2. **The Stock Price Does Not Change or Goes Up Slightly**: If the stock price remains steady or experiences a minor increase, the covered call expires worthless. However, the seller retains the premium, resulting in a profit.
3. **The Stock Goes Above the Strike Price**: Should the stock's price surpass the strike price by the expiration date, the option holder will exercise their right, and the seller must sell the 100 shares of stock. While this may seem like a missed opportunity, the seller realizes maximum profit from the transaction.

These scenarios exemplify how covered calls function and the outcomes they produce for the seller.

CHAPTER 16:

Brokers

Brokers: A Comprehensive Overview

Introduction

When it comes to selecting a brokerage firm, you are faced with a multitude of choices. Full-service brokers, discount brokers, online platforms, and more are at your disposal. Understanding the distinctions between these types of brokers and choosing the one that aligns best with your goals is essential for your success in trading. Many beginners tend to overlook the importance of brokerage regulations, which can have substantial implications for your capital and risk management strategies.

Choosing the Right Broker

Brokers fall into two major categories: full-service and discount. It's worth noting that many full-service brokers now have discount branches, creating some overlap between the two. A full-service broker operates as part of a larger financial institution, offering a wide range of financial services, such as investment solutions and estate planning strategies. They often provide in-house research reports to aid your trading decisions and offer telephone support for inquiries or order placements.

Building a strong relationship with a full-service broker can be advantageous, as it can facilitate networking and open doors to industry connections. However, it comes at a price, usually in the form of higher commissions. In today's electronic trading environment, there's no significant advantage in execution quality when using a full-service broker. Order matching is done electronically, leveling the playing field.

Discount brokers, on the other hand, focus solely on facilitating trades. They do not provide personalized advice or telephone ordering services. However, they typically maintain excellent customer service. The key benefit of discount brokers is their lower commission rates compared to full-service counterparts. They may not offer additional financial services or investment recommendations outside the realm of trading. Some traders prefer to consolidate their accounts with a single broker, and for this, discount brokers are ideal.

So, the choice between a full-service or discount broker hinges on your preferences and needs. If cost-effectiveness is your priority, a discount broker is likely the better choice. Opt for a full-service broker only if you require comprehensive financial services. In most cases, there's little difference between the two in terms of trade execution.

Understanding Margin

Margin refers to the assets held in your trading account, including both cash and positions. As the market values of your positions fluctuate, so does the amount of margin available in your account. Understanding margin is essential as it forms the foundation of your risk management strategy.

When you open a trading account, you must decide between a cash account and a margin account. To trade options, you are required to have a margin account. In essence, a cash account lacks leverage and restricts you to trading only stocks. These accounts typically have low or no minimum balance requirements.

In contrast, margin accounts are subject to different rules. Most brokers set a minimum balance requirement for margin accounts, typically starting at \$10,000, or even higher, depending on your trading style. This minimum balance does not serve any specific purpose but acts as a commission for the broker. It indicates a level of seriousness on the part of the trader.

Another rule associated with margin accounts is the Pattern Day Trader (PDT) designation, enforced by the SEC. A PDT is defined as an individual who executes four or more day trades within five business days. If labeled as a PDT, your broker will ask you to maintain a minimum balance of \$25,000 in your margin account. This balance acts as a buffer to absorb any potential trading losses.

The strategies outlined in this book could lead to PDT classification, depending on your trading behavior. Each strategy has a duration of a month or more, allowing you to monitor and adjust positions as needed. PDT status is primarily determined by the number of positions you enter, which is limited to three per trading week to avoid PDT classification.

It's advisable to start with a cautious approach. Begin by trading a single instrument to gain confidence before expanding your trading activities. This approach will help you determine the capital requirements for your trading endeavors. Keep in mind that even closing a position is considered a trade and falls under PDT regulations.

Margin Calls

An essential aspect of margin is the margin call, a term that often strikes fear into the hearts of traders, both novice and institutional alike. Effective risk management is aimed at preventing margin calls. A margin call occurs when the funds in your account are insufficient to meet its requirements.

It's crucial to understand that your margin consists of the cash you hold and the market value of your positions. If you hold \$1,000 in cash but your positions are in a loss of -\$900, a margin call will be triggered to cover the potential losses you might incur. These calls are usually issued well in advance to provide traders with an opportunity to deposit additional funds into their accounts.

The point at which a margin call is triggered is referred to as the maintenance margin. Typically, you need to maintain 25% of the initial position value in cash when you enter a position. Most brokers offer indicators that show how close you are to the maintenance margin limit.

Leverage is a common cause of margin calls. Margin accounts allow traders to borrow funds from their brokers to amplify their returns. However, leverage is a double-edged sword. For instance, if you trade with $10,000 of your own capital but borrow an additional $20,000 to enter a position, your total control over the position amounts to $30,000. A $10,000 gain translates to a 100% return on your $10,000 investment, while the position's overall return is only 33%.

It's essential to differentiate between leverage inherent in an instrument's structure and borrowing money to trade. Leverage should be approached cautiously by beginners, and borrowing to trade is generally discouraged. Leverage within options trading differs from borrowing money for trading and is more cost-effective.

Execution

Traders often find themselves blaming their brokers for poor execution. It's a common complaint among unsuccessful traders, but it's important to understand that the price displayed on your screen does not always match the exact price traded on the exchange.

The current era of high-frequency trading has reduced the smallest unit of time in the market from seconds to microseconds. With an influx of trades in real-time, pinpointing the precise price of an instrument is nearly impossible for humans.

Blaming your broker for execution discrepancies is unlikely to yield favorable outcomes. Broker choice should be based on factors such as customer service and the quality of the trading platform. Brokers aim to facilitate trading rather than act against traders. The price quoted on your screen is not identical to what is executed on the exchange, given the high-speed market dynamics.

Understanding Price Quotes

When viewing trading screens, you may notice two different prices for every security. While financial channels typically display only one price, trading platforms show two different prices within the same price box. This is a fundamental concept to comprehend.

The lower price you see is the bid, which represents the price you receive when selling an instrument. The higher price is the ask, and it reflects the price you pay when buying the instrument. It's important to note that the single price displayed on your screen, known as the "Last Traded Price" (LTP), is not the actual price since market prices are in constant flux.

Understanding the bid and ask prices, as well as the concept of LTP, is crucial for trading effectively. The market is characterized by constant price movements, and traders must adapt to these fluctuations.

CHAPTER 17:

Options Day Trading Styles

Options Day Trading Styles: A Comprehensive Overview

Introduction

Options day traders employ a variety of styles and strategies, but three key components must be considered consistently. These critical elements encompass:

1. **Liquidity**: Liquidity measures the speed at which options or other assets can be bought and sold without significantly impacting the current market price. For options day traders, highly liquid options are preferred, as they allow for smoother trading. In contrast, illiquid options create friction in opening and closing positions, prolonging transaction times and potentially leading to losses.
2. **Volatility**: Volatility reflects how susceptible the assets linked to options are to price fluctuations triggered by external factors.
3. **Volume**: Volume represents the number of options traded within a specific time frame. It serves as an indicator of the asset's market interest and can influence its price movement. Higher trading volume indicates greater trader interest in an option. Volume contributes to open interest, which encompasses all active options that have not been liquidated, exercised, or assigned. Neglecting timely actions on options

can lead to unfavorable outcomes and avoidable losses. Thus, options traders must be vigilant in appropriately closing their positions.

To effectively employ the options day trading styles outlined below, traders should have a solid understanding of these factors and how to leverage them to their advantage.

Resistance Trading Strategy with Options

The Resistance Trading Strategy involves capitalizing on price breakouts, which occur when prices depart from their typical price range. For this trading style to succeed, it must be accompanied by an increase in trading volume. One of the most common types of breakouts is based on support and resistance levels.

Support and Resistance Breakouts:

Support and resistance levels indicate points where an asset's price either stops declining (support) or halts its upward movement (resistance). In this strategy, the day trader takes specific actions based on these levels. If the asset price surpasses the resistance level, the trader enters a long (buy) position. Conversely, if the asset price drops below the support level, the options day trader initiates a short (sell) position. The trader's decision depends on whether the asset encounters support or resistance at the new price level.

Notably, as the asset breaches its typical price boundaries, volatility tends to increase. This heightened volatility often results in the asset's price moving in the direction of the breakout. By identifying and reacting to support and resistance breakouts with the right timing, options day traders aim to capitalize on market movements and maximize their trading performance.

In conclusion, understanding these essential elements – liquidity, volatility, and volume – is fundamental to success in options day trading. The Resistance Trading Strategy is just one example of how traders can utilize these factors to their advantage and develop a winning trading style. By remaining attentive to market conditions and employing sound strategies, options day traders can navigate the complex world of options trading effectively.

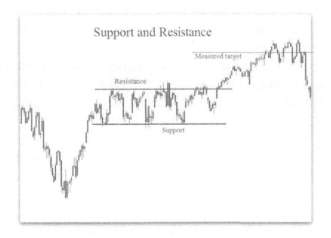

Resistance Trading Style Continued

When considering the Resistance Trading Style, meticulous planning of entry and exit strategies is crucial for options day traders. The entry strategy hinges on the relative position of prices concerning the resistance and support levels:

- **Bearish Position**: If the price is poised to close above the resistance level, an options day trader may choose a bearish approach. This suggests a belief that the asset's price will decline.
- **Bullish Approach**: Conversely, if prices are anticipated to close below the support level, a bullish strategy is typically adopted, indicating a positive outlook on the asset's price trajectory.

Exit strategies, in comparison, necessitate a more sophisticated approach. Here, options day traders should assess past performance and employ chart patterns to identify an optimal price target for closing their position. Once this target is attained, the day trader can execute the exit, securing the associated profit.

Momentum Options Day Trading

Momentum Options Day Trading revolves around the exploitation of price volatility and the rapid change in trading volume. This style derives its name from the central concept that the momentum of an asset's price movement is sufficiently robust to maintain its direction. As an asset's price ascends, it tends to attract more investors, further propelling the price upward. Day traders employing this strategy harness this momentum, aiming to capitalize on the anticipated price movement.

Technical analysis forms the foundation of this style, offering insight into the asset's price behavior. Several key momentum indicators are utilized:

- **Momentum Indicator**: This metric evaluates the strength of price movement as a trend by examining the most recent closing price of the associated asset.
- **Relative Strength Index (RSI)**: RSI compares gains and losses over a defined period, providing valuable insights into the asset's market dynamics.
- **Moving Averages**: These indicators help day traders uncover historical fluctuations and analyze market trends.
- **Stochastic Oscillator**: The stochastic oscillator compares the most recent closing prices of the associated asset over a specified period, facilitating trend analysis.

Momentum options day trading, while effective and straightforward when executed correctly, demands that day traders stay well-informed. Monitoring news updates and earnings reports is essential to make informed decisions within this trading style. By using these momentum indicators and staying apprised of market developments, options day traders can confidently navigate the intricate landscape of options day trading.

In conclusion, a thorough understanding of these distinct options day trading styles empowers traders to select and employ the most suitable strategy for their financial goals, taking into account market conditions, risk tolerance, and available resources. Mastery of entry and exit strategies is vital, as it can make a significant difference in the success of an options day trading venture.

Reversal Trading and Scalping Options Day Trading Styles

Reversal Trading: Trading Against the Trend

Reversal trading, often referred to as trend trading or pull-back trading, is a style that involves trading against the prevailing market trend. In contrast to momentum options day trading, reversal trading seeks to identify price pullbacks against the current trend. While it can be a lucrative strategy when executed successfully, it is also considered high-risk. This style demands a deep understanding of market dynamics and substantial trading experience, making it less suitable for beginners.

In reversal trading, the approach is typically bullish, involving the purchase of an out-of-the-money call option and the sale of an out-of-the-money put option. Notably, both profits and losses can be potentially unlimited, emphasizing the high-risk nature of this strategy.

Scalping Options Day Trading

Scalping in options day trading entails the rapid buying and selling of the same associated asset multiple times within a single trading day. This style is particularly profitable when market conditions exhibit extreme volatility. The options day trader capitalizes on price differentials by buying an options position at a lower price and selling it at a higher price, or vice versa, depending on whether the chosen option is a call or a put.

The effectiveness of scalping is heavily reliant on liquidity. Illiquid options are unsuitable for this style because options day traders executing scalping must open and close positions frequently throughout the trading day. Utilizing liquid options enables day traders to maximize profitability when entering and exiting trades.

A typical strategy in scalping is to trade numerous small options positions, aiming to accumulate profits incrementally rather than engaging in infrequent, large trades. Trading substantial positions in this style can lead to substantial losses in a short time frame, making it a style recommended for disciplined options day traders who are content with seeking modest but consistent profits.

Scalping represents the shortest form of options day trading, often spanning just a few hours within the trading day. Day traders who adopt this style are commonly known as scalpers. Effective scalping necessitates the use of technical analysis to identify optimal opportunities based on the price movements of associated assets.

Scalping comprises various approaches, including "time and sales" scalping, which involves analyzing historical records of executed, sold, and canceled transactions to determine the best options to trade and the ideal timing for these trades. Additional scalping methods encompass using charts and bars to analyze price movements and predict future trends.

In conclusion, understanding the distinctive options day trading styles of reversal trading and scalping equips traders with versatile tools to adapt to varying market conditions and trading objectives. While reversal trading involves trading against the current trend and can yield substantial returns, it is considered high-risk and more suitable for experienced traders. Scalping, on the other hand, focuses on rapid, small trades within a single day, capitalizing on price differentials during moments of extreme market volatility. Scalping is most effective with liquid options and is well-suited for disciplined traders seeking consistent, albeit modest, profits.

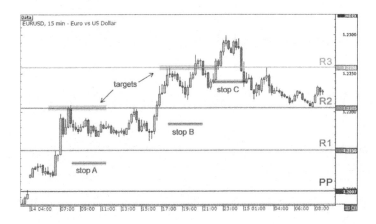

Using Pivot Points for Options Day Trading

Options day trading, particularly in the forex market, often involves utilizing pivot points to make strategic trading decisions. Pivot points signify key price levels at which assets tend to reverse or pivot after reaching a support or resistance level, similar to support and resistance breakouts.

In this style of options day trading, traders typically implement two primary strategies:

1. **Buy the Position**: Traders consider buying the position as the asset approaches a support level, placing a stop order just below that level to manage risk.

2. **Sell the Position**: When the asset approaches a resistance level, traders may choose to sell the position, again setting a stop order just below the resistance level to mitigate potential losses.

To calculate the pivot point, options day traders analyze the previous day's trading activity, specifically focusing on the highs, lows, and closing prices. The pivot point is determined using the following formula:

```
(High + Low + Close) / 3 = Pivot Point
```

Once the pivot point is calculated, the support and resistance levels can be determined using the following formulas:

First Support Level: `(2 x Pivot Point) - High = First Support Level`

First Resistance Level: `(2 x Pivot Point) - Low = First Resistance Level`

For the second set of support and resistance levels, the following formulas are used:

Second Support Level: `Pivot Point - (First Resistance Level - First Support Level) = Second Support Level`

Second Resistance Level: `Pivot Point + (First Resistance Level - First Support Level) = Second Resistance Level`

The most profitable options trading opportunities often arise when the pivot point falls between the first support and resistance levels.

However, it's essential to acknowledge that this style of options day trading can expose traders to sudden price fluctuations, potentially leading to significant losses if not managed effectively. To limit losses, options day traders can implement stop orders, strategically placed based on recent price activity.

For short positions, a stop order is typically positioned just above the most recent high price close. Conversely, for long positions, the stop order is placed just below the most recent low. To add an extra layer of safety, day traders may opt to set two stop orders, including a "hard" stop representing the maximum tolerable capital loss and another that aligns with a predefined exit strategy.

The placement of these stop orders should take into account the asset's current volatility. Higher volatility may warrant wider stop orders to accommodate price fluctuations, while lower volatility may allow for tighter stop placements.

In conclusion, options day trading using pivot points involves capitalizing on price reversals at critical support and resistance levels. By calculating pivot points and determining support and resistance levels, day traders can identify optimal entry and exit points. Nevertheless, it's essential to implement effective risk management strategies, including stop orders, to mitigate potential losses, especially in the face of volatile market conditions.

CHAPTER 18:

Historical Events in the FX Markets

The world of foreign exchange (Forex) trading, which involves the exchange of currencies, has a rich history dating back centuries, all the way to the time of the Babylonians. Today, the Forex market stands as one of the largest, most competitive, and most accessible financial markets globally. It has been significantly influenced by key global developments, such as the Bretton Woods Agreement and the Gold Standard. For Forex traders, understanding the historical context of Forex trading and the pivotal events that have shaped the industry is crucial. This understanding allows traders to anticipate similar events that may reoccur, impacting market dynamics, as history has a tendency to repeat itself.

History of Forex Trading: Origins

The roots of trading can be traced back to around 6000 BC, when the Mesopotamian civilizations introduced the barter system. It started with the exchange of commodities for other goods, evolving over time to include items like salt and spices as common mediums of trade. As the concept developed, traders would venture out to distant lands to exchange these goods, marking the earliest form of foreign exchange. The introduction of gold coins in the 6th century BC marked a significant milestone, as gold coins met essential criteria such as portability, durability, divisibility, consistency, limited supply, and acceptability, making them ideal as currency.

Gold coins gradually became widely accepted as a means of exchange. However, their size and weight were impractical for day-to-day transactions. The Gold Standard emerged in the 19th century, where governments pledged to redeem paper money for a specific amount of gold, providing monetary stability. The Gold Standard was effective until the outbreak of World War I, which necessitated the printing of more money by Western countries, leading to the suspension of the Gold Standard.

It was during this period, in the early 1900s, that the Forex market was initially influenced by the Gold Standard. Countries exchanged their currencies, effectively turning over their currencies for gold. However, as the amount of US dollars in circulation increased due to mounting government debt and spending, the Gold Standard's integrity was compromised. In 1971, President Richard M. Nixon ended the Bretton Woods Agreement, which led to the US dollar floating freely against other foreign currencies.

The Free-Floating System Begins

Post the Bretton Woods Agreement, the Smithsonian Agreement emerged in December 1971. This agreement was similar but allowed a broader range of currency fluctuations. The US dollar was pegged to gold at $38 per ounce, effectively devaluing the currency. In 1972, Europe sought to reduce its reliance on the US dollar, leading to the formation of the European Joint Float by several European nations. All of these agreements, including Bretton Woods, eventually failed, leading to the official adoption of the free-floating system.

The Plaza Accord

By the early 1980s, the US dollar had appreciated significantly relative to other major currencies. This presented challenges for exporters and resulted in a 3.5% GDP deficit for the US. In response to this issue, a group of major nations, including the US, Great Britain, France, West Germany, and Japan, met at the Plaza Hotel in New

York in 1985. They reached an agreement known as the "Plaza Accord," aimed at strengthening non-dollar currencies. This accord led to a significant depreciation of the US dollar.

The European Union and the Euro

The early 1990s saw significant changes in the currency markets. Europe, once divided, worked on reuniting countries through various agreements. One of the most influential agreements was the Maastricht Treaty in 1992. This treaty led to the establishment of the European Union (EU), the creation of the euro currency, and a closer integration that included foreign policy and security initiatives. The development of the euro has enabled European banks and businesses to reduce transaction costs and operate effectively in a globalized economy.

Web Trading

During the 1990s, significant advancements occurred in the currency markets. Communication and technology improvements allowed individuals to access real-time pricing data and execute trades from the comfort of their homes. These changes marked a pivotal shift in how currency trading was conducted. It was during this time that foreign currencies historically constrained by totalitarian financial systems became more accessible and liquid.

Asian Financial Crisis (1997–1998)

The Asian Financial Crisis of 1997-1998, which impacted Asian tiger economies, serves as a vivid example of the interconnectedness of global financial markets and their influence on foreign currency platforms. The crisis, triggered by various underlying issues such as overextended lending practices, growing trade deficits, and fragile financial markets, led to significant currency devaluations. The crisis not only affected equity markets but also had a pronounced impact on currency exchange rate volatility.

The Bubble

Until 1997, many investors were drawn to opportunities in Asia, focusing on property and local equities. The incoming tide of foreign capital significantly affected economies as growth rates surged. However, this increased external capital led countries like Thailand to peg their currency to the US dollar. This move aimed to ensure financial stability in these economies and maintain steady exchange rates with the world's largest economy. Ultimately, the national currencies in the region appreciated significantly, and the underlying factors that had driven currency speculation were altered.

Increasing Current Account Deficits and Nonperforming Loans

By the mid-1990s, mounting current account deficits became challenging for governments to manage, and lending practices were proven detrimental to the financial system. For example, Thailand's current account deficit had grown to $14.7 billion by 1996, with an increasing trend since 1992. These circumstances set the stage for the Asian Financial Crisis, with the appreciation of national currencies and growing financial imbalances, leading to the eventual unraveling of economic stability.

The history of Forex markets after the pivotal year 1944 serves as a remarkable example of a free market in action. Competitive forces have cultivated an environment with unparalleled liquidity, significantly lowering spreads and increasing accessibility through online platforms. The currency trading landscape has witnessed remarkable changes, contributing to the diverse and dynamic Forex market we know today.

These historical events have molded the currency markets as we know them, significantly influencing trading strategies and market dynamics. Understanding this historical context is essential for Forex traders as it provides valuable insights into the evolving landscape of foreign exchange trading. As history unfolds, traders must adapt and learn from the past to navigate the future of Forex trading successfully.

CHAPTER 19:

Introduction to Candlestick

Introduction to Candlestick Patterns

Candlestick patterns represent a specialized tool that condenses information for various time periods into single value bars. This feature makes them more valuable than conventional open-high, low-close bars (OHLC) or simple lines that only imply closing prices. Candlesticks encapsulate patterns that predict price direction upon completion.

Price Action

Price action delineates the dynamics of a security's price movements. This progress is continually assessed with regard to price changes in the recent past. In basic terms, price action is a trading strategy that empowers a trader to analyze the market and make informed trading decisions based on recent and real price movements, rather than relying solely on technical indicators. As it disregards fundamental analysis and leans more towards recent and past price events, the price action trading method is open to specific analysis tools.

A candle comprises a body and upper or lower shadows.

Tools Used for Price Action Trading

Since price action trading relies on recent historical data and past price movements, all technical analysis tools like charts, trend lines, price clusters, high and low swings, technical levels are evaluated based on the trader's preference and strategy fit. The instruments and patterns observed by the trader can range from simple price bars, price clusters, breakouts, trend lines, or complex combinations involving candles, volatility, channels, and more.

Depending on the trader's discretion, psychological and behavioral interpretations and subsequent actions constitute a significant part of price action trades. For example, if a stock currently trading at 580 crosses the psychologically significant level of 600, a trader may anticipate a further upward move and take a long position. Another trader might have an opposing view, predicting a price reversal and taking a short position when 600 is reached. Price action is inherently subjective, as each trader interprets it uniquely, based on individual rules and social context. In contrast, a specific technical scenario (such as a 15-day moving average crossing a 50-day moving average) would elicit similar behavior (going long) from different traders.

Price action trading is, at its core, a discretionary trading practice. It combines technical analysis tools with recent price history, allowing traders to make individual decisions within a given context to take trading positions based on their speculative, behavioral, and psychological state.

Who Uses Price Action Trading?

Price action trading is an approach to price prediction and speculation used by retail traders, investors, arbitrageurs, and trading firms employing traders. It is applicable to various asset classes, including stocks, bonds, forex, commodities, derivatives, and more.

Price Action Trading Steps

Experienced traders practicing price action trading employ a variety of methods for identifying trading patterns, entry and exit points, stop-loss levels, and other insights. Relying on a single strategy for one stock (or multiple stocks) may not yield enough trading opportunities. Most situations require a two-step approach:

1. Identifying a situation: For example, a stock price entering a bull or bear phase, a breakout, a trend line, or other trends.
2. Within the situation, identifying trading opportunities: For instance, once a stock is in a bull market, traders may speculate on an extension of the uptrend or a retracement. This is a subjective decision and may vary from one trader to another, even within the same context.

The Popularity of Price Action Trading

Price action trading is particularly suited for short- to medium-term, limited-profit trading rather than long-term investments. Most traders believe that the market follows a random pattern, and there is no one-size-fits-all strategy that always works. By integrating technical analysis tools with recent price history to identify trading opportunities according to their unique understanding, price action trading holds a significant place in the trading world. Its advantages include self-determined approaches, applicability to various asset classes, compatibility with trading software and applications, and the potential for straightforward backtesting of identified strategies using historical data. Above all, traders feel in control as they are empowered to make their decisions rather than blindly following a set of rules. Numerous theories and strategies in the field of price action trading promise high success rates. However, traders must be aware of survivorship bias, as only success stories make headlines. Trading can be lucrative, but it depends on the individual trader to test, choose, decide, and act in a manner that serves their needs for the best profit opportunities.

Candle Patterns

Chart patterns are a crucial aspect of day trading. Candlestick and other charts provide a visual roadmap that cuts through the noise of price action. The most effective patterns form the basis for a profitable day trading strategy for trading stocks, cryptocurrencies, or forex pairs.

Every day, you face numerous trading opportunities due to a wide range of factors influencing the market. Day trading patterns allow you to decipher these choices and motivations, from the desire for profit to the fear of loss, short covering, stop-loss triggers, hedging, tax implications, and more.

Use in Day Trading

Used judiciously, trading patterns can be a valuable asset. History often repeats itself, and financial markets are no exception. This repetition helps you identify opportunities and anticipate potential pitfalls. Additionally, the combination of technical analysis tools and recent price history for identifying trading opportunities based on personal insights makes price action trading highly adaptable to the trader's context and strategy.

Breakouts and Reversals are two recurring themes in these patterns.

Breakout: A breakout occurs when the price clears a predetermined key level on your chart, which could be a Fibonacci level, support or resistance, consolidation pattern, or a trendline.

Reversal: A reversal is a change in price direction within an existing trend, which could be either positive or negative, against the prevailing trend. Reversals are often referred to as 'rallies,' 'retracements,' or 'trend reversals.'

The models featured in this analysis include the Bull Flag.

Bull Flag: Bullish flag patterns are found in stocks with strong upward movements. They are named "bull flags" because they resemble a flag on a pole. The "pole" results from a steep upward climb in the stock, while the "flag" emerges from a period of consolidation. Bull flags can also be a horizontal rectangle. The flag typically forms downward against the preceding strong trend. Regardless of a powerful upward rally, the stock tends to move upward from the flag, often achieving a significant surge, which could be similar to the length of the preceding flagpole. Similar to bull flags, there are bear flags and pennants. Bull flags have become prominent in the recent years, especially during the market sector rally.

Each pattern has specific characteristics, providing insights into potential future price movements. These patterns are essential tools in the arsenal of day traders seeking an edge in the volatile world of financial markets. By mastering the art of interpreting these patterns, traders can make more informed and strategic trading decisions to maximize their profits.

CHAPTER 20:

How to Trade Options on

Robinhood

Introduction to Robinhood

Robinhood is a user-friendly, online stock brokerage application designed for smartphones. It sets itself apart from other stock trading apps like E*TRADE or TDAmeritrade through a significant distinction: it offers commission-free trading. Unlike platforms that charge fees ranging from 5 to 10 dollars per trade, Robinhood allows you to execute trades without incurring any commission or fees. This fundamental divergence democratizes trading, making it accessible to a broader audience. As an added incentive, Robinhood even provides complimentary shares of companies such as Apple, Microsoft, Ford, and Sirius XM Radio to users who download their app.

When and Why to Use Robinhood

While Robinhood offers an accessible entry point into the stock market, it does not provide the benefits of tax-advantaged accounts like Individual Retirement Accounts (IRAs) or Roth IRAs. Therefore, it may not be the ideal platform for safeguarding your life savings. Instead, Robinhood is most beneficial for initiating a stock portfolio from scratch and expanding it cost-effectively until it reaches a substantial size. At that point, you can consider transferring your holdings into an IRA or Roth IRA to enjoy long-term benefits. In this series, we'll focus on leveraging Robinhood for shorter-term trades, aiming to maximize growth within a span of fewer than five years.

Downloading the App and Acquiring Your First Stock

Robinhood generously offers a free share of stock as a sign-up incentive when you download the app and create an account. The process of opening an account is free, so there are no costs associated with this initial step. To claim your free stock, you should use a referral link such as the one provided. Upon downloading the app and providing your personal information to create an account, navigate to the menu and select "Free Stocks." There, you'll find a link in the top right corner labeled "PAST INVITES." Click on this link to claim your free stock. Furthermore, you can review the list of all the free stocks you've received. Notably, Robinhood awards you a free share of stock from its inventory for every individual you refer to the app.

Watchlist and Search Functions

Robinhood offers a watchlist feature, similar to other stock trading platforms. This tool allows you to monitor the price movements of your preferred stocks. The watchlist comes pre-populated with popular stocks such as Facebook, Apple, Google, and Amazon. Although you can trade these stocks on Robinhood, they are typically expensive, with prices ranging from $100 to $1000. As beginners, our strategy focuses on using the search function to identify more affordable stocks and add them to our watchlist. It's important to note that Robinhood doesn't offer stock recommendations or a comprehensive list of all available stocks. As a result, you are largely responsible for finding the stocks you wish to trade. You can search for stock recommendations online and identify companies with the potential for price increases, obtaining their symbols, such as "FB" for Facebook and "AAPL" for Apple. Once you have the stock symbol, proceed to the Robinhood app, click on the magnifying glass icon in the top right corner, and enter the symbol. This action will bring up information about the company, and you can click on the company's name for more details, including its price, trading volume, average volume, market capitalization, dividend ratios, and other relevant information.

Purchasing Your First Stock

With the groundwork laid out, it's time to dive into buying and selling stocks for profit. We recommend starting with small investments and gradually increasing your exposure. Find a stock that fits your budget and add it to your watchlist. Once it's on your watchlist, click on the stock you want to purchase, and this will open the details page. At the bottom of the page, you'll find a button labeled "Trade" or "Buy." Click on this button to initiate the purchase order. Robinhood typically defaults to a market order, which means it will execute the trade at the current market price. Enter the number of shares you want to buy and confirm your order. It's crucial to understand that when using a market order, Robinhood may execute the trade at a price up to 5% higher than the current market price. If you want to buy stocks at a specific price, it's advisable to use a limit order. You can change the order type by clicking on the link in the top right corner of the trading screen.

Market and Limit Orders - Their Functions

Market orders signal to Robinhood that you wish to buy or sell a stock at the prevailing market price, regardless of whether it goes up or down. For buying, Robinhood will automatically purchase available shares up to 5% over the current market price. Any price increase beyond 5% will not complete the order. For selling, it means the stock will be sold at the prevailing market price, even if it drops rapidly. On the other hand, a limit order conveys to Robinhood that you want to buy or sell a stock but only at a specific price. To switch the order type to a limit order, click on the link in the top right corner of the trading screen. With a limit order, you'll need to specify the exact price at which you want to execute the trade. The order will only be fulfilled if the stock reaches or trades at that price or lower. Similarly, if you're selling, you'll set a minimum price at which you're willing to sell, and the order will be completed only when the price reaches that level or goes higher.

Stop-Loss and Stop-Limit Orders - Their Functions

A stop-loss order is designed to automatically sell a stock when it reaches a specific price point, acting as a safety net to limit losses. We'll explore the utility of this order extensively later in the series for risk management. When setting a stop-loss order, you need to define the price at which you want it to be activated. For buying, you specify the price you'd like to buy at, and when the stock reaches or surpasses that price, your order converts to a market order. For selling, you establish a price below which your order will transform into a market order, enabling you to sell the stock to avoid further losses. Stop-loss orders are valuable as they reduce the need for constant monitoring of your stocks to prevent significant losses. For example, if you buy a stock at $5.00, you can set a stop-loss order at $4.95. If the stock price rises, you continue to hold the stock and profit. However, if the price falls below $4.95, your stop-loss order will trigger, selling the stock to limit additional losses. In contrast, a stop-limit order enables you to sell a stock at a specific price point, but it converts into a limit order when the stock reaches that price. To create a stop-limit order, you need to define two price points: one at which the order activates and another at which it turns into a limit order. This order type allows you to prepare for potential price surges and capitalize on them. For instance, if you anticipate a stock breaking its 52-week high, you can set a stop-limit order with the activation price at $10 per share and the limit at $15 per share. If a large hedge fund buys the stock, causing it to skyrocket to $20 in after-hours trading, your order won't execute since free accounts can't trade

CHAPTER 21:

Binary Trading Options

Binary options trading presents various trading options with distinctive characteristics. Among these, binary options are a prominent choice. Binary options are a derivative that yields a predefined payout at a specific time within a set range. This range can vary from short to long in terms of the expiration period.

60-Second Binary Options

A particularly popular variant of binary options is the 60-second binary option. This trading option revolves around predicting the price direction of an asset in a very brief period, typically one minute. Traders executing 60-second binary options must analyze a price chart with real-time asset data. Subsequently, they make a prediction whether the asset's price will increase or decrease by the end of the one-minute interval.

Trading in this fast-paced binary option variant demands swift decision-making as the timeframes are incredibly condensed. As such, proper preparation and education are paramount. It is advisable to employ a demo account for familiarization and practice. A demo account simulates real trading scenarios, enabling users to hone their skills and develop effective strategies.

Engaging in actual trading with real capital is inadvisable until a trader has mastered the process through a demo account. The duration required for this mastery varies from person to person. Some individuals adapt to a demo account quickly, while others may take longer.

Trading Futures Options for High Returns

Binary options trading, an online trading activity, centers on predicting the direction of various assets, such as commodities, stocks, futures, indices, and currencies. It resembles forex trading but involves speculating on the rise or fall of commodities. This type of trading provides a simple yet potent way to generate substantial returns within hours or weeks, contingent on your chosen trading timeframe.

Investors profit from futures trading by anticipating price changes in commodities. Commodities traded on stock exchanges retain uniformity, regardless of their origin. Option futures, in essence, are financial instruments that grant their holders the right to purchase commodity futures, like gold, paper, or foreign currency, at a predetermined price.

Two primary types of futures options exist: calls and puts. Calls are bought when one expects the underlying asset's price to rise. For instance, if you anticipate an increase in corn futures, you purchase a call option for corn. Conversely, puts are acquired if one anticipates a decrease in the underlying asset's price. For example, if you believe soybean futures will decline, you purchase a soybean put option.

When acquiring options, you pay a price known as the premium. Think of options as wagers: longer odds equate to cheaper premiums, while higher odds demand a higher price. The strike price refers to the price at which you can buy or sell the underlying futures contract. It is crucial to differentiate between options on futures and the actual futures contract. An option on futures represents a financial instrument that provides the buyer with the right to buy a futures contract for a specific item, while a futures contract is a binding agreement to purchase the actual commodity in a specified quantity at an agreed-upon price and time.

Unlike other financial tools, binary options trading does not require intricate financial expertise. You only need to predict whether an asset's price will rise or fall. Risk levels in binary options trading are lower compared to other types of trading. Once you have a contract, you are aware of the precise capital you are risking and the potential profits you can earn. When trading options, there's no need for a complex exit strategy. The contract's duration is predetermined before entering the trade.

While binary options are among the most widely used financial instruments, they are not complicated and involve limited risk. Binary options provide flexibility in trading, allowing traders to employ various tools to manage risks and enhance profits.

Investor Alert on Binary Options Trading

Investing seems to be in the headlines everywhere you turn. You may have heard about it on television, read about it on the internet, as the talk of option trading sweeps across many individuals. People who believe that they are prepared to invest in ventures that could yield a higher return should prepare thoroughly. While trading can be exhilarating, it is crucial to gather essential knowledge beforehand, especially if option trading is unfamiliar territory.

Assessing Your Goals

Binary options trading exists in multiple formats, and it is essential to understand which one to focus on. Conventional options may be a viable choice, and this is what many traders opt for. All payout agreements expire on the third Friday or Saturday, depending on the market in question. Binary options allow you to purchase and predict hourly expiration times.

Both types of trading are valid formats, and it falls on your shoulders to determine which one aligns with your objectives. Those who are eager and seeking faster outcomes may lean toward binary options as they can lead to more immediate payouts.

In theory, a trade can be initiated, and payouts obtained within a matter of hours. For those who prefer a longer time frame, conventional options may offer a more suitable option.

Understanding Trading Styles

Binary options trading can be approached from multiple trading styles, so it's crucial to grasp the styles available and how they fit into your strategy. For instance, binary options trading has two primary styles: American and European. European-style trading relies on whether the price on the designated day ends above or below the agreed-upon level. In American trading, payment can be made if the price surpasses the agreed-upon level at any point by the specified date. Once you understand these trading styles, you can determine which one best suits your trading approach.

Finding a Broker

Numerous investment companies regularly facilitate options trading, making it relatively simple for individuals to find them. Binary options, on the other hand, can be more complex to access as they are often traded online. Those considering binary options should explore online brokers.

To locate binary options brokers, utilize internet searches or business directories. Simply input "binary options broker firms" into the search bar, and a list of websites will be displayed.

Before taking any action, verify the broker's credibility through consumer advocacy groups and government agencies. This is a critical step to ensure the legality and legitimacy of your online options trading.

The goal is to discover a trading company that fits your objectives and suits your chosen style of trading. Timing is essential in trading, as the sooner you trade, the more rapidly payouts can be obtained.

Is Binary Options Right for You?

Trading binary options, also known as digital options, presents traders with more flexibility and choices than traditional option types. This type of trading offers an opportunity to achieve returns of 60-80% on trades in a relatively short time, often as quick as one hour.

The key advantage of this trading format is its simplicity. It involves predicting the price movement of an asset, whether it will rise or fall, making it less complex than other forms of trading. Additionally, binary options trading carries lower risks compared to conventional options trading. Traders must predict the direction the asset will move to profit. Binary options are available around the clock, and traders can choose different durations for each trade.

Risk in binary options trading is pre-determined, allowing traders to know the exact potential profit or loss in each trade. Binary options are safer than other trading forms, such as Forex, as they do not require leverage or a stop-loss mechanism. There is no need to worry about positions going against you. The duration of each contract is determined before entering a trade.

Binary options trading is an excellent way to venture into the financial markets without the need for extensive financial expertise. It is a user-friendly option, with less risk, a predetermined risk and return, and minimal need for complex

CHAPTER 22:

Options Day Trading Rules for Success

Options day trading goes beyond just having a style or strategy. While these are essential, your success as an options day trader is primarily determined by your own skills and discipline. Developing your expertise, seeking guidance when needed, and maintaining dedication are crucial in transitioning from a novice to a proficient options day trader. Disciplined trading is vital for success, and there are specific rules that can aid in building this discipline.

Rule for Success #1 – Have Realistic Expectations

Options trading isn't a get-rich-quick scheme; it's a legitimate career path that requires dedication and effort. Recognize that losses are part of the trading game, and no strategy guarantees consistent gains. The best options traders maintain an 80% winning percentage and acknowledge a 20% losing average. Effective money management and risk control are crucial in managing losses.

Rule for Success #2 – Start Small to Grow a Big Portfolio

In the early stages of options trading, exercise caution and avoid rushing into large positions. Begin with smaller options contracts and gradually increase your exposure as you gain experience and understanding of the market. This approach minimizes losses and helps develop a systematic entry strategy.

Rule for Success #3 – Know Your Limits

Avoid overtrading, as it can lead to significant losses and tie up your investment capital. Each options trade requires careful consideration and planning. Be conscious of the size and frequency of your trades, and never exceed your established risk limits.

Rule for Success #4 – Be Mentally, Physically, and Emotionally Prepared Every Day

Options day trading is mentally, physically, and emotionally demanding. To excel in this career, maintain your overall well-being. Prioritize self-care through proper sleep, balanced nutrition, regular exercise, and stress reduction. Your physical and mental health directly impact your trading performance.

Rule for Success #5 – Do Your Homework Daily

Conduct pre-market preparation every day by studying the financial environment and reviewing news before the market opens. This allows you to create a daily trading plan and adapt to short-term market conditions. A pre-market checklist is a helpful tool for analyzing markets, assessing news events, monitoring competitors, identifying exit strategies, and considering market seasonality.

Rule for Success #6 – Analyze Your Daily Performance

Track your daily options trading performance to identify patterns in your profits and losses. Understanding the reasons behind these outcomes is essential for refining your strategy. Daily performance analysis also informs your long-term trading approach.

Rule for Success #7 – Do Not Be Greedy

Avoid excessive greed and recognize when to take profits. If you achieve a substantial return on an investment, consider selling to secure your gains. Overextending your positions can lead to adverse outcomes.

Rule for Success #8 – Pay Attention to Volatility

Volatility, indicating the likelihood of price changes in a specific timeframe, plays a crucial role in options trading. Be aware of how market volatility can impact your trading strategy. Adjust your approach accordingly, and consider strategies like strangles and straddles in volatile markets.

Rule for Success #9 – Use the Greeks

Greeks are essential measures that assess an option's sensitivity to various factors. Delta gauges the price relationship between an option and its underlying asset, Vega measures sensitivity to implied volatility, Theta reflects the time decay of an option's value, Gamma assesses changes in delta, and Rho evaluates the impact of interest rate changes.

By adhering to these rules and understanding the fundamentals of options trading, you can progress from a novice to a successful options day trader. Remember that success in this field is an ongoing journey, requiring continuous learning and adaptation.

CHAPTER 23:

Creating Your Own Day Trading

Strategy

As you delve deeper into day trading, you may find the need to develop a personalized trading strategy. While many effective trading strategies exist, there may be specific market conditions or personal preferences that drive the creation of your unique approach. It often takes experimentation and practice to discover a strategy, or a combination of strategies, that best suits your trading goals and style.

As you progress in your trading journey, you'll come to realize that you may lean more towards swing trading than day trading, depending on your chosen methods. The beauty of trading is that it accommodates diverse trading preferences, and there are numerous strategies available for customization based on your individual needs.

Before you venture into the market with your own strategy, especially if you're a beginner, it's essential to start by selecting a well-established strategy outlined in this guidebook or from your research. Allocate time to acquaint yourself with the strategy and gain some experience trading within the market environment. Keep in mind that day trading differs significantly from other trading methods, and hastily adopting a strategy that may have succeeded in other contexts could lead to unfavorable outcomes.

It's crucial to spend time within the market, getting acclimated to its nuances, identifying promising stocks, and acquiring insights before crafting your strategy. By engaging with one or more strategies, you will begin to discern patterns that resonate with your trading style and learn what to look for in the market, ultimately simplifying the process of creating a successful strategy.

For traders at every level, having a structured strategy is paramount. Beginners often make the mistake of selecting stocks and trading without a clear plan, a risky approach that hinges on emotional decision-making. Emotions can lead to staying in a trade for too long or exiting prematurely, both of which may result in losses. Thus, it is crucial to select a specific strategy, whether from this guidebook or self-designed, and adhere to it unwaveringly.

It is advisable to become well-versed in the rules and parameters of your chosen strategy. Understand how to adapt your approach based on market conditions and master the behaviors that lead to success at different times within the market. While it's acceptable to switch strategies between trades, it is inadvisable to change your strategy after entering the market, as such shifts can result in unanticipated losses.

The reality of trading is that all traders, irrespective of their level, will encounter losses at some point. Novice traders may fail due to inadequate training or succumbing to emotional decisions, while even seasoned traders will have losing trades. Market conditions are not always predictable, and strategies may not consistently yield positive results. Therefore, it's essential to evaluate your risk tolerance before entering the market and allocate a budget you can afford to lose, should the need arise.

If you are apprehensive about starting your trading journey or wish to explore different strategies to observe their effectiveness, especially if you have devised a unique strategy, consider employing a trading simulator. Brokers often offer these tools, and they can provide a safe environment for testing various approaches without risking real capital. It's a valuable resource for beginners, allowing them to gain practical experience and assess the feasibility of their strategies.

Selecting Your Trades Based on the Time of Day

Understanding the best strategies for different times of the trading day is a crucial aspect of successful day trading. Recognize that each trading period offers unique characteristics, and some strategies work more effectively during specific times. The key is to align your chosen strategy with the market's prevailing conditions to optimize your trading results.

1. **The Open (9:30 AM - 11:00 AM):** The market's opening is a high-activity period when traders react to overnight developments. This phase is conducive to strategies like VWAP trades and Bull Flag Momentum. During this time, you can consider increasing your trade size due to higher liquidity.

2. **Mid-Day (11:00 AM - 3:00 PM):** The mid-day phase is characterized by lower liquidity and increased market volatility. It can be a riskier time for trading, especially for beginners. It is recommended to exercise caution, maintain tight stop losses, and trade with smaller share sizes. Strategies like support or resistance trades, moving averages, VWAP, and reversals can be suitable during this period.

3. **The Close (3:00 PM - 4:00 PM):** The closing hour is marked by directional movements in stocks. Traders often take profits and make position adjustments, contributing to more predictable trading patterns. You can consider raising your trade size compared to the mid-day phase but avoid going as high as during the opening. Focus on stocks with clear upward or downward trends.

Understanding the distinct characteristics of each time period and selecting your strategy accordingly can enhance your trading effectiveness. Tailor your approach to the specific opportunities and challenges posed by the time of day to maximize your chances of success in the dynamic world of day trading.

CHAPTER 24:

How Options Prices are Determined

Options prices are determined by several key factors, including the price of the underlying stock, the time remaining until expiration, and various other influences. A comprehensive understanding of these factors is essential for anyone venturing into options trading, especially novice traders.

The Influence of Underlying Stock Prices

The predominant factor influencing an option's price is the market price of the underlying stock it is associated with. However, it's important to note that this relationship isn't always one-to-one. The degree to which the underlying stock price affects the option's price depends on factors such as whether the option is in the money, at the money, or out of the money.

Intrinsic Value and Option Pricing

Intrinsic value is the portion of an option's price attributable to the difference between the underlying stock's price and the option's strike price. Options that are out of the money have zero intrinsic value, while options in the money have intrinsic value.

- For call options: An option has no intrinsic value if the market price is equal to or lower than the strike price. In contrast, when the market price exceeds the strike price, the call option gains intrinsic value.
- For put options: An option has no intrinsic value if the market price is equal to or higher than the strike price. Conversely, when the market price falls below the strike price, the put option acquires intrinsic value.

Even when an option is at or out of the money, the underlying stock's price exerts an influence on the option's value. This influence is quantified by the delta, a value ranging from 0 to 1 for call options and represented as a negative value for put options. The delta indicates how much an option's price is likely to change in response to a $1 movement in the underlying stock's price.

For instance, if the underlying stock is priced at $105, and the call option's delta is 0.77, a $1 increase in the stock's price would lead to a roughly $0.77 increase in the option's value per share. Given that an option typically represents 100 shares, a $1 stock price rise would result in a $77 increase in the option's total value.

Delta and Its Significance

Delta plays a crucial role in understanding the sensitivity of an option's value to stock price movements. It indicates the likelihood of the option expiring in the money and is a vital factor when deciding to buy or sell options.

Delta is dynamic and changes as the underlying stock price fluctuates. If the stock price increases, the delta increases for call options and decreases in magnitude for put options. Conversely, a declining stock price has the opposite effect.

Gamma - The Rate of Change in Delta

Gamma measures how the delta of an option changes concerning stock price movements. While it may not be the primary concern for novice traders, it provides insight into how an option's delta responds to shifts in stock price. For example, a gamma of 0.03 implies that a $1 increase in the stock price will increase the delta by 0.03 for a call option and decrease it for a put option.

Options' Probability of Expiring In the Money

Delta also provides an estimate of the probability of an option expiring in the money. When selling options, one generally prefers a lower delta to reduce the likelihood of the option expiring in the money. Conversely, when buying options, a higher delta is preferred to increase the chances of the option becoming profitable.

For example, if a call option has a delta of 0.66, there's a 66% probability that it will expire profitably, or in the money.

Implied Volatility and Its Significance

In addition to delta and time decay, implied volatility is a crucial factor to consider. Implied volatility gauges the expected price fluctuations of the underlying stock over the option's lifetime until its expiration.

Understanding how the stock price volatility changes over time is essential. A stock that frequently experiences substantial price swings has high volatility. To evaluate a stock's volatility, it's compared to the overall market's volatility, typically represented as beta.

- Beta: A stock with a positive beta generally moves in sync with the broader market. A beta of 1.0 indicates average market-level volatility, while a beta below 1.0 suggests lower volatility relative to the market. Conversely, a beta above 1.0 implies higher volatility than the market.
- Implied Volatility: Implied volatility measures how much the market expects a stock's price to fluctuate. It plays a crucial role in determining option prices, as increased volatility can substantially impact option values.

Keep in mind that implied volatility is dynamic and can change, influencing the pricing of options. An understanding of how implied volatility affects option values is vital for successful options trading.

CHAPTER 25:

Pro Tips for Day Trading Options

For those delving into the world of options trading, it's essential to grasp some fundamental principles. Here are invaluable tips and insights to guide you in your online options trading journey.

1. Understanding the Three Directions of Stock Prices

Stock prices can move in three fundamental directions: up, down, or remain unchanged. Your approach to call options hinges on your understanding of these movements. It's a common misconception among novice traders that stocks will always rise or fall, but stocks can also remain stagnant. This realization is pivotal in options trading.

Consider a real-life example where a stock, like KOL, traded within a $4 range for 23 consecutive days. If you had invested in call or put options on such a stock, you would likely incur losses. Experienced traders often recognize that achieving profit with call or put options isn't a 50% probability, but closer to 33% due to the random nature of stock price movements. Stocks rise, fall, or remain stable approximately one-third of the time.

If you hold a long call or put option, time can be your adversary, especially in the case of out-of-the-money options. On the contrary, in-the-money options can partially recover your investment in a stable market. Be aware that stock prices may surge soon after your options expire, signaling the importance of patience.

To mitigate risks, consider long-term call options over shorter-term ones. In general, about 70% of traders holding long call or put options experience losses, while 70% of options sellers profit. This explains why conservative traders often opt to write or sell options.

2. Analyzing the Underlying Stock's Chart

Before investing in call or put options, diligently study the performance and history of the underlying stock. Examining stock charts provides insights into the stock's recent performance over various timeframes, including the past 30, 90 days, and one year. Chart analysis can help you identify trends, ranging from a narrow trading range to upward or downward movements.

For identifying trends, draw a central line within the stock's price range, and add upper and lower lines to represent the general flow channel. These chart patterns guide your decisions in options trading.

- **Chart Readings for Buying Call Options:** Consider buying call options if you anticipate the stock's price to rise based on strong support levels at lower prices. However, exercise caution and avoid excessive greed; when you see a profit, seize the opportunity.
- **Chart Readings for Buying Put Options:** If there is substantial resistance at higher stock prices on the chart, purchase put options when the stock nears these levels. Be ready to profit from the ensuing price movement, while avoiding greed.
- **Chart Readings for Call and Put Options:** When the chart indicates the stock is at lower levels within its range, anticipate price movements towards the middle range. Capitalize on price increases for profitable gains, even if they are modest.

3. Calculate Your Breakeven Point

Always determine the breakeven point before investing in options. Consider factors such as commissions and bid spreads when calculating the breakeven point, as it is essential to ensure your underlying stock's movement will surpass this point for a profitable outcome.

As an options trader, you must understand how to calculate the breakeven point, which varies between short-term and long-term options. Factor in commission rates and bid spreads when holding options until expiration. For short-term trading, calculate the difference between the asking and bid prices, known as the spread.

4. Embrace the Stock's Trend

Respect the prevailing trend of the underlying stock as your ally. It's often more profitable to align your strategy with the stock's direction than to fight it. If the stock is trending upwards, seek strategies that complement this movement. Similarly, when the stock is in a downtrend, adapt your strategy accordingly. While this "trend is your friend" adage is a guideline, it's important to consider external factors like news events that can impact stock trends.

5. Stay Alert to Earnings Release Dates

Options tend to become more expensive when earnings release announcements are imminent. This anticipation reflects expectations of significant price movements following the announcement. Be cautious, as options prices can substantially decline after earnings releases. Keep a watchful eye on earnings announcements as well as the stock's reaction to them, as it may not always align with expectations.

Additional Tips for Advanced Options Traders

Advanced options trading requires a solid foundation in financial education. Key aspects include evaluating stocks, conducting fundamental and technical analyses, and making informed decisions about the future direction of individual stocks and market trends.

Options can be complex and time-sensitive, so predicting stock and market movements accurately is paramount. Additionally, recognize that options trading involves contracts tied to underlying securities, which requires a nuanced understanding to navigate effectively. This knowledge is indispensable for advanced traders and a good refresher for all.

CHAPTER 26:

Risk Management Strategies

Risk Management Strategies: Protecting Your Capital

In this pivotal chapter, we will extensively explore the art and science of risk management, a fundamental aspect of successful options trading. Aspiring traders, from novices to seasoned market participants, will benefit from the comprehensive knowledge and techniques presented here. Effective risk management is the bedrock upon which profitable trading strategies are built. Let's delve deeper into the strategies and practices that safeguard your precious trading capital.

1. Understanding Risk in Trading

Before we dive into specific risk management techniques, it's crucial to grasp the inherent risks in the world of options trading. Options provide ample opportunities for profit, but they also carry the risk of capital depletion. You'll learn about the risks associated with leverage, market volatility, and potential loss, setting the stage for effective risk mitigation.

2. The Role of Stop-Loss Orders

Stop-loss orders are indispensable tools in risk management. We'll dissect their purpose and implementation in great detail. You'll discover how stop-loss orders protect your positions by triggering an automatic exit when prices move against you. Additionally, we'll explore setting stop-loss levels based on various criteria, including technical indicators and volatility.

3. Position Sizing Strategies

Position sizing is a core element of risk management. It governs the amount of capital allocated to each trade, preventing overexposure and potential catastrophic losses. We'll delve into different position sizing techniques, such as fixed-dollar risk, percentage risk, and the Kelly Criterion. You'll gain insights into how to select the optimal position size for each trade, aligning with your risk tolerance and portfolio objectives.

4. Portfolio Diversification

The age-old adage "Don't put all your eggs in one basket" holds significant weight in options trading. Portfolio diversification is a risk mitigation strategy that spreads your capital across various assets, reducing vulnerability to single-trade disasters. We will explore the principles of diversification, asset correlation, and the construction of a diversified options portfolio. Understanding how to balance different options positions effectively is a crucial component of this strategy.

5. Risk-Reward Ratio Assessment

Effective risk management extends to assessing the risk-reward ratios of your trades. We will guide you through the process of evaluating the potential reward in relation to the risk you assume. Learn how to set risk-reward parameters for your trades, ensuring that your potential gains justify the risk taken. We'll explore how these ratios align with your overall trading strategy and financial goals.

6. Historical Analysis and Backtesting

To further strengthen your risk management practices, we will delve into the importance of historical analysis and backtesting. You'll discover how analyzing past trades and strategies can uncover valuable insights for optimizing risk management. Backtesting your trading systems allows you to refine your approach based on historical performance data.

7. Contingency Planning

Unforeseen events can disrupt even the most meticulously planned trades. In this section, we discuss the importance of contingency planning and risk mitigation for exceptional circumstances. Understanding how to react when market shocks occur and having predefined exit strategies can prevent catastrophic losses.

By the end of this chapter, you will possess a comprehensive understanding of risk management in options trading. Armed with these advanced techniques, you will be better equipped to protect your capital, enhance your trading discipline, and ultimately improve your prospects for sustainable success in the dynamic world of options trading. Remember, it's not just about making profits; it's about preserving and growing your trading capital over time.

CHAPTER 27:

Advanced Technical Analysis

Advanced Technical Analysis: Elevating Your Trading Acumen

Building upon the foundation of technical analysis laid out in Chapter 8, we now embark on a journey into advanced technical analysis tools and strategies. This chapter is designed to empower traders with the knowledge and skills needed to make highly informed trading decisions, based on comprehensive analyses of price charts and market patterns. Let's delve into the intricacies of advanced technical analysis, exploring concepts such as Fibonacci retracement, Elliott Wave theory, and advanced chart patterns.

1. Fibonacci Retracement: The Golden Ratio in Trading

Fibonacci retracement is a powerful tool that allows traders to identify potential price reversal levels. We'll unravel the mysteries behind the Fibonacci sequence and explain how these mathematical ratios are applied to price charts. You'll learn to pinpoint key support and resistance levels using Fibonacci retracement, enhancing your ability to time market entries and exits with precision.

2. Elliott Wave Theory: Predicting Market Cycles

Elliott Wave theory provides a framework for understanding market cycles and the psychology of crowd behavior. This advanced tool enables you to identify trends, corrections, and reversals with a high degree of accuracy. We'll guide you through the principles of Elliott Wave analysis and teach you how to count waves, apply wave rules, and make probabilistic price forecasts.

3. Harmonic Patterns: Mastering the Art of Pattern Recognition

Advanced chart patterns go beyond basic trendlines and channels. We'll introduce you to harmonic patterns, which encompass a variety of formations like Gartley, Butterfly, and Bat patterns. Recognizing these patterns will allow you to predict potential price reversals and exploit trading opportunities. You'll gain insights into identifying harmonic patterns, interpreting their significance, and using them to formulate effective trading strategies.

4. Pitchfork Analysis: A Unique Perspective on Price Channels

Andrews' Pitchfork, a lesser-known yet valuable tool, provides an innovative approach to drawing trendlines. You'll discover how to apply the Pitchfork concept to identify hidden support and resistance levels and forecast future price movements. This tool excels in different market conditions and can be a valuable addition to your trading toolkit.

5. Multi-Timeframe Analysis: Enhancing Perspective

Trading decisions are often improved when considering multiple timeframes. In this section, we'll discuss the benefits of multi-timeframe analysis. You'll learn how to synthesize information from various timeframes to make well-rounded trading choices, increasing your probability of success.

6. Automated Technical Analysis: Utilizing Indicators and Algorithms

As trading technology evolves, automated technical analysis tools become increasingly relevant. We'll explore the world of technical indicators, oscillators, and algorithmic trading. You'll discover how to leverage these tools to streamline your analysis, generate trading signals, and enhance efficiency.

7. Integrating Advanced Technical Analysis into Your Strategy

A vital component of this chapter is learning how to integrate advanced technical analysis into your overall trading strategy. You'll understand the importance of combining different technical tools and methodologies to make holistic trading decisions. We'll provide real-world examples of how traders utilize these advanced techniques in their everyday trading activities.

By the conclusion of this chapter, you will have unlocked the potential of advanced technical analysis, enabling you to elevate your trading skills to a new level. These tools and strategies offer a deeper understanding of market dynamics and will provide you with a competitive advantage in the ever-evolving world of trading. Whether you are a short-term day trader or a long-term investor, advanced technical analysis will prove invaluable in making informed and profitable trading decisions.

CHAPTER 28:

Options Trading Strategies

Options Trading Strategies: Maximizing Opportunities

In this dedicated chapter, we will delve into the fascinating realm of options trading strategies, each carefully designed to cater to different market conditions and trader objectives. By the end of this chapter, you will have a comprehensive understanding of options strategies, including straddles, strangles, iron condors, and butterflies. You'll learn when and how to deploy these strategies effectively to maximize your trading opportunities.

1. The Versatility of Options Strategies

Options are highly versatile financial instruments, offering a wide array of strategies for traders to choose from. We'll begin by emphasizing the importance of selecting the right strategy based on your market outlook and risk tolerance. Understanding the versatility of options is key to unlocking your trading potential.

2. The Straddle Strategy: Capturing Volatility

The straddle is a powerful strategy used to profit from significant price fluctuations, regardless of the direction in which an asset's price moves. We will dissect the straddle strategy, explain how it works, and provide practical examples of when to use it effectively. This strategy is particularly valuable during earnings reports, major news releases, and other high-impact events.

3. The Strangle Strategy: Embracing Market Uncertainty

Similar to the straddle, the strangle is designed to profit from market volatility. However, it is a more cost-effective alternative that requires a smaller initial investment. We will discuss how to implement the strangle strategy, outlining scenarios where it can be the preferred choice for traders.

4. Iron Condors: Profiting from Range-Bound Markets

Iron condors are tailored for range-bound markets, providing traders with a way to capitalize on a lack of significant price movement. We'll explain how to structure and manage iron condor positions effectively. This strategy's risk-reward profile and the importance of strike selection will be thoroughly discussed.

5. Butterflies: Balancing Risk and Reward

Butterfly spreads are versatile strategies used for various market conditions. We will cover both long and short butterfly spreads, elucidating how they work and when to use them. Butterfly spreads allow traders to balance risk and reward while benefiting from anticipated price ranges.

6. Real-Life Application of Options Strategies

To solidify your understanding of these strategies, we will provide real-life trading examples and case studies. By examining actual trades and the thought processes behind them, you'll gain insights into how professional traders use these strategies in practice.

7. Adjustments and Risk Management

The success of any trading strategy is contingent on proper adjustments and risk management. We will guide you on how to monitor and adjust options positions to mitigate potential losses and maximize profits. The chapter will emphasize the importance of having a well-defined exit strategy in place.

8. Choosing the Right Options Strategy for You

To conclude, we'll help you determine which options strategy aligns best with your trading goals, personality, and market outlook. Making an informed strategy selection is a critical step towards long-term trading success.

Armed with the knowledge from this chapter, you will be prepared to navigate diverse market conditions and make informed decisions using an array of options trading strategies. Whether you seek to capitalize on price volatility, exploit range-bound markets, or manage risk, understanding and implementing these strategies will provide you with a competitive edge in the world of options trading.

CHAPTER 29:

Options Greeks and Volatility

Options Greeks and Volatility: The Art of Pricing and Risk Assessment

In this chapter, we will explore the fascinating world of options Greeks and delve into the crucial role they play in options pricing and risk management. We'll introduce you to five key Greeks: delta, gamma, theta, vega, and rho, and shed light on how they influence the value of options. Additionally, we'll discuss the impact of implied and historical volatility on options, revealing the intricate relationship between these factors and pricing dynamics.

1. Delta: The Price Sensitivity Metric

Delta is a fundamental Greek that measures the sensitivity of an option's price to changes in the underlying asset's price. We will provide an in-depth explanation of delta, its significance in risk assessment, and how traders utilize it to gauge potential profit and loss. You'll learn why delta can vary between 0 and 1 for call options and -1 and 0 for put options and how to interpret these values.

2. Gamma: The Rate of Change Indicator

Gamma is a dynamic Greek, representing the rate of change in an option's delta concerning fluctuations in the underlying asset's price. We will discuss gamma's critical role in options trading, particularly for those employing complex strategies. Traders use gamma to assess how delta may evolve as market conditions shift.

3. Theta: The Time Decay Factor

Theta, also known as time decay, gauges how an option's value erodes as time passes. We will explain why theta is a constant concern for options buyers and sellers and how it impacts the pricing of both. Moreover, you'll discover how traders use theta to their advantage, especially in strategies like covered calls and calendar spreads.

4. Vega: The Volatility Gauge

Vega measures an option's sensitivity to changes in implied volatility. We will clarify the concept of implied volatility and its connection to market sentiment. You'll learn how to interpret vega values and comprehend the significance of managing volatility risk, especially when trading options around earnings reports or significant news events.

5. Rho: The Interest Rate Factor

Rho evaluates an option's sensitivity to changes in interest rates. We'll explore the relationship between interest rates and options pricing and how traders factor this into their decision-making processes. While rho may not be as prominent as other Greeks, it remains essential to certain trading strategies, particularly those involving longer time horizons.

6. Implied and Historical Volatility

Implied volatility reflects market expectations for future price fluctuations. Historical volatility, on the other hand, quantifies past asset price movements. We will differentiate between these two types of volatility and elucidate their roles in options pricing. Understanding how options traders employ implied and historical volatility will provide you with valuable insights into their strategies.

7. Harnessing the Power of Greeks and Volatility

To solidify your understanding, we will walk you through practical examples and case studies that showcase how traders incorporate

Greeks and volatility analysis into their decision-making processes. You'll see how these concepts are applied in real-life trading situations.

8. Risk Management and Greeks

Lastly, we'll emphasize the importance of risk management in options trading and demonstrate how Greeks play a central role in evaluating and mitigating risk. You'll learn to use these metrics to construct strategies that align with your risk tolerance and market outlook.

By the end of this chapter, you will be equipped with a comprehensive understanding of options Greeks and their profound impact on pricing and risk management. Moreover, you'll be well-versed in the nuances of implied and historical volatility, providing you with the knowledge to navigate the complex world of options trading with confidence and competence.

CHAPTER 30:

Risk Assessment and Trade Selection

Risk Assessment and Trade Selection: Mastering the Art of Smart Trading

In this chapter, we will embark on a journey into the realm of risk assessment and trade selection, essential components of successful options trading. We'll provide readers with valuable insights on how to evaluate potential trades, calculate risk-to-reward ratios, identify high-probability setups, and make informed decisions when choosing the right options contracts.

1. Assessing Risk-to-Reward Ratios

Understanding the risk-to-reward ratio is the cornerstone of making prudent trading decisions. We will clarify how to calculate and interpret this ratio and why it's pivotal for assessing the potential profitability of a trade relative to the risk involved. We'll explore scenarios where a favorable risk-to-reward ratio can significantly enhance your trading strategy.

2. Identifying High-Probability Setups

Distinguishing high-probability setups from lower-probability ones is an art that successful traders have mastered. We'll introduce you to various technical and fundamental indicators that can help you identify situations with a higher likelihood of success. You'll learn about candlestick patterns, support and resistance levels, moving averages, and other tools that can guide you in making well-informed choices.

3. Choosing the Right Options Contracts

The universe of options contracts is vast, and selecting the right one is critical to your trading success. We will guide you through the process of choosing options contracts that align with your trading goals and market outlook. You'll understand the factors to consider, such as expiration dates, strike prices, and types of options (calls or puts), to optimize your trade selection.

4. Diversification and Position Sizing

Diversification is a risk management strategy that can mitigate losses. We'll elaborate on the concept of diversifying your options portfolio to spread risk across different assets or industries. Additionally, position sizing, which determines how much capital to allocate to a specific trade, is another crucial aspect. We will offer strategies for effective position sizing based on your risk tolerance.

5. Trading Psychology and Emotions

Trading is not just about numbers and charts; it's also about managing your emotions. We will explore the psychological aspects of trading, including the impact of fear, greed, and overconfidence on decision-making. You'll gain insights into how to maintain discipline, manage stress, and stick to your trading plan.

6. Case Studies and Real-Life Examples

To reinforce the concepts discussed, we will provide real-life case studies and examples of trade assessments. By examining these scenarios, you'll see how risk assessment and trade selection are applied in practice. We'll also delve into both winning and losing trades to illustrate the importance of prudent risk management.

7. Continuous Learning and Adaptation

The trading landscape is ever-evolving, and traders must continuously adapt. We'll emphasize the importance of staying informed, adapting your strategies as market conditions change, and learning from your experiences. You'll discover valuable resources for ongoing education and skill development.

8. Trading Journals and Record-Keeping

To ensure accountability and track your progress, we'll discuss the significance of maintaining a trading journal. You'll learn how to record your trades, emotions, and thought processes. A trading journal can be a valuable tool for self-improvement and learning from both successful and unsuccessful trades.

By the end of this chapter, you'll possess the knowledge and skills required to assess risk effectively, identify high-probability trade setups, and make informed decisions when selecting options contracts. You'll also appreciate the importance of diversification, position sizing, and the psychological aspects of trading. This chapter serves as a critical building block for your journey towards becoming a successful and disciplined options trader.

CHAPTER 31:

Trading Psychology and Discipline

Trading Psychology and Discipline: Mastering the Mental Game of Trading

In the world of trading, where fortunes can be made and lost in the blink of an eye, understanding and managing your trading psychology is as critical as any technical or analytical skill. This chapter is dedicated to unraveling the intricate web of trading psychology, focusing on handling emotions, maintaining discipline, and adhering to a trading plan. A trader's mindset can often be the deciding factor between success and failure, and this chapter aims to equip you with the mental tools necessary to thrive in the dynamic world of trading.

1. Emotions and Trading

The emotional roller coaster of trading is well-documented. Emotions like fear, greed, and anxiety can lead to impulsive decisions that erode profits. We will delve into these emotions, exploring why they occur and how they can impact your trading. Recognizing and managing these emotions is a crucial step towards becoming a disciplined trader.

2. Discipline in Trading

Discipline in trading is synonymous with consistency and adherence to a structured approach. We will guide you through creating a trading plan that outlines your strategies, risk management rules, and goals.

A well-structured trading plan acts as a blueprint for your trading decisions and serves as a compass during turbulent market conditions.

3. Overcoming Impulsivity

Impulsivity can be a trader's worst enemy. We will discuss strategies to overcome impulsive behaviors and focus on the importance of pre-defined entry and exit points. We'll provide techniques to help you stick to your plan, even when the market becomes erratic.

4. Risk Management and Capital Preservation

Risk management is the backbone of any successful trading endeavor. We will emphasize the significance of protecting your trading capital. You'll learn about stop-loss orders, position sizing, and portfolio diversification to minimize the impact of losses. Capital preservation is the first step towards achieving consistent profitability.

5. The Trading Plan

A well-structured trading plan is your roadmap to success. We'll break down the components of a comprehensive trading plan, including setting realistic goals, defining trading strategies, and outlining risk management principles. With a solid trading plan in place, you'll be better prepared to navigate the markets.

6. Staying Calm Under Pressure

Maintaining a clear and focused mind during stressful trading situations is a valuable skill. We'll provide techniques to help you stay calm under pressure, make rational decisions, and avoid knee-jerk reactions. Traders who can keep their cool during market turbulence often come out ahead.

7. The Role of Patience

Patience is not only a virtue but also a necessity in trading. We'll explore how being patient can help you avoid overtrading, wait for high-probability setups, and stick to your trading plan. Impulsive actions born out of impatience can lead to significant losses.

8. Learning from Losses

Losses are an inevitable part of trading, but they can also be valuable learning experiences. We'll discuss how to analyze and learn from your losses, using them to refine your strategies and avoid repeating the same mistakes. In trading, every setback can be a stepping stone to success.

9. Self-Reflection and Improvement

Finally, we'll highlight the importance of self-reflection and continuous improvement. Self-awareness is a key component of successful trading. Regularly evaluating your trading performance, adapting your strategies, and seeking opportunities for growth will help you evolve as a trader.

By the end of this chapter, you'll have a comprehensive understanding of the psychological aspects of trading. You'll be equipped with the mental resilience and discipline required to navigate the challenging and often unpredictable world of trading. Trading psychology can be your most potent ally, and mastering it is a significant step towards becoming a consistently profitable trader.

CHAPTER 32:

Real-Life Case Studies

Real-Life Case Studies: Learning from Practical Examples

In the dynamic world of options trading, theory and strategies are essential, but real-life case studies provide invaluable insights and practical applications. In this chapter, we will delve into a selection of real-life options trades to illustrate the strategies and concepts discussed throughout the book. These case studies offer a unique opportunity to learn from both successful and unsuccessful trades, gaining a deeper understanding of how to navigate the complexities of options trading.

1. Case Study 1: The Iron Condor that Soared

In this case study, we'll examine an iron condor options strategy that not only achieved the desired outcome but also exceeded expectations. We'll walk through the trade setup, the market conditions at the time, and the decision-making process. Understanding the factors that contributed to this success will provide valuable insights for implementing similar strategies.

2. Case Study 2: When a Bull Put Spread Turns Bearish

Options trading isn't without its pitfalls, and sometimes even the most well-thought-out strategies can go awry. We'll explore a case where a trader initially implemented a bull put spread with optimism but had to adapt when market sentiment shifted. This case study highlights the importance of flexibility and risk management.

3. Case Study 3: Navigating Earnings Season with Straddles

Earnings season presents unique challenges and opportunities for options traders. We'll investigate a case where a trader used a straddle strategy to capitalize on potential price swings following an earnings announcement. We'll discuss the trade setup, considerations during earnings releases, and the outcome, providing insights into trading during earnings season.

4. Case Study 4: Lessons from a Covered Call Strategy

Covered calls are a popular strategy among income-focused options traders. We'll examine a case study where a trader utilized a covered call strategy on a dividend-paying stock. We'll discuss the reasoning behind this strategy, the impact of dividend payments, and the trade's overall performance.

5. Case Study 5: The Perils of Neglecting Risk Management

In the world of options trading, risk management is paramount. We'll explore a case where a trader overlooked risk management principles and faced significant losses. This case study serves as a stark reminder of the importance of stop-loss orders, position sizing, and capital preservation.

6. Case Study 6: Leveraging Technical Analysis for Profit

Technical analysis plays a crucial role in options trading. We'll analyze a case where a trader leveraged technical indicators and chart patterns to identify an optimal entry point. We'll dissect the technical analysis tools used, the trade setup, and the outcomes, highlighting the role of technical analysis in decision-making.

7. Case Study 7: The Impact of Market Volatility

Market volatility can significantly affect options pricing and trading strategies. We'll delve into a case where a trader navigated a highly volatile market, emphasizing how implied and historical volatility can impact options. This case study provides insights into adapting strategies to changing market conditions.

8. Case Study 8: Strategic Hedging with Puts and Calls

Options can serve as effective hedging tools. We'll examine a case where a trader employed a combination of puts and calls to hedge an existing stock position. We'll discuss the rationale behind the hedge, its execution, and the risk mitigation it provided.

These real-life case studies offer a diverse range of scenarios, each with its unique challenges and lessons. By studying these examples, you'll gain practical insights into applying options strategies, managing risk, and adapting to changing market conditions. Whether you're a novice or an experienced trader, these case studies provide valuable real-world experiences to enhance your options trading knowledge.

CHAPTER 33:

Tax Implications and Record-Keeping

Tax Implications and Record-Keeping in Options Trading

While the thrill of options trading lies in the potential for substantial profits, traders must also consider the tax implications associated with their trading activities. In this chapter, we'll explore the critical aspects of tax planning for options traders and emphasize the significance of maintaining meticulous records for accurate tax reporting.

Understanding Capital Gains and Losses

Options trading results in capital gains or losses, which are categorized into short-term and long-term. Short-term gains or losses occur when you hold an option for one year or less, while long-term gains or losses result from holdings of more than one year. The tax rate varies for these two categories, with short-term gains typically subject to higher tax rates.

Strategies for Tax-Efficient Trading

Options traders can employ various strategies to manage their tax liability effectively:

1. **Offsetting Gains and Losses:** Consider matching your capital gains with capital losses to minimize your overall tax liability.

If you have incurred capital losses from previous trades, you can use them to offset gains.

2. **Tax-Advantaged Accounts:** Explore the option of trading within tax-advantaged accounts, such as IRAs or 401(k)s. These accounts offer tax benefits that can help you reduce your tax liability.

3. **Tax-Deferred Trading:** Some strategies allow you to defer taxes until you close a position. For instance, the Section 1256 contract tax treatment permits traders to defer taxes until the position is closed, regardless of the duration it was held.

Reporting Options Trades

Accuracy and completeness are essential when reporting options trades for tax purposes. When preparing your tax return, consider the following:

1. **IRS Forms:** Familiarize yourself with the specific IRS forms used for reporting options trades. Common forms include Form 8949 for reporting capital gains and losses and Form 6781 for Section 1256 contracts.

2. **Transaction Details:** Keep detailed records of each trade, including the trade date, description of the option, strike price, expiration date, trade type (buy to open, sell to close, etc.), and the final outcome (profit or loss).

3. **Cost Basis:** Calculate the cost basis accurately. This includes the original purchase price of the option, any commissions or fees paid, and adjustments for corporate actions or splits.

4. **Holding Period:** Clearly distinguish between short-term and long-term holdings. Ensure that you accurately determine the holding period of each option.

5. **Account Statements:** Retain your account statements, trade confirmations, and any supporting documents. These records serve as evidence and help in the event of an IRS audit.

Tax-Efficient Trading Practices

To minimize your tax liability, consider incorporating the following practices into your options trading:

1. **Strategic Holding Periods:** Plan your trades with the intent to qualify for long-term capital gains, which are typically subject to lower tax rates.
2. **Offsetting Gains and Losses:** Utilize tax loss harvesting to offset capital gains with capital losses, reducing your overall tax liability.
3. **Stay Informed:** Keep abreast of tax law changes and consult with a tax professional who specializes in options trading to ensure compliance.
4. **Documentation:** Maintain organized and comprehensive records of your trades, ensuring you have all the necessary information for tax reporting.
5. **Consult a Tax Advisor:** Given the complexities of tax regulations and the unique nature of options trading, it's advisable to consult with a tax advisor or CPA experienced in options taxation.

Conclusion

Options trading can be lucrative, but understanding and managing the associated tax implications is vital for your financial success. By adopting tax-efficient trading strategies and maintaining meticulous records, you can navigate the tax landscape effectively, minimizing your tax liability while staying compliant with tax regulations. This chapter equips you with the knowledge and practices necessary for tax-smart options trading.

CHAPTER 34:

Regulations and Compliance

Regulations and Compliance in Options Trading

Options trading, like all financial markets, operates under a framework of regulations and compliance standards aimed at ensuring fairness, transparency, and the protection of investors. In this chapter, we'll explore the crucial aspects of trading regulations, compliance requirements, and the roles of regulatory authorities in options trading.

The Role of Regulatory Authorities

Several regulatory authorities oversee options trading in different regions, with the primary goal of maintaining market integrity and safeguarding the interests of market participants. Some of the key regulatory bodies include:

1. **U.S. Securities and Exchange Commission (SEC):** In the United States, the SEC plays a central role in regulating securities, including options. It enforces securities laws and ensures that markets operate fairly and transparently.
2. **Commodity Futures Trading Commission (CFTC):** The CFTC is responsible for overseeing options on futures contracts and ensuring the integrity of the derivatives markets.
3. **Financial Industry Regulatory Authority (FINRA):** FINRA is a self-regulatory organization that oversees broker-dealers and ensures they adhere to industry standards and regulations.
4. **Exchanges:** Options are traded on various exchanges, each of which has its regulatory body. For example, the Chicago

Board Options Exchange (CBOE) regulates options trading on its platform.

5. **International Regulators:** Depending on the region, options trading may be subject to the oversight of international regulators like the Financial Conduct Authority (FCA) in the UK or the Australian Securities and Investments Commission (ASIC) in Australia.

Regulations and Compliance Requirements

Options trading is subject to a set of rules and regulations designed to protect investors and maintain market integrity. Here are some of the key regulations and compliance requirements:

1. **Licensing and Registration:** Brokers and traders may need to obtain specific licenses and register with regulatory authorities. This process helps ensure that market participants are qualified and competent.
2. **Account Approval:** Brokers are required to follow a Know Your Customer (KYC) process to verify the identities and financial backgrounds of their clients. This helps prevent fraud and money laundering.
3. **Margin Requirements:** Regulatory authorities set minimum margin requirements to ensure traders have sufficient funds to cover potential losses. These requirements can vary based on the type of options and market conditions.
4. **Reporting and Transparency:** Traders and brokers must maintain accurate records and report trades to regulatory authorities. This enhances transparency and allows regulators to monitor market activity.
5. **Customer Protection:** Regulations often include provisions for the protection of customer funds. Segregation of client funds from the broker's capital is a common practice to safeguard customer assets.
6. **Trade Execution Rules:** Regulations may dictate how trades are executed, including price-time priority and best execution practices.
7. **Anti-Fraud Measures:** Rules are in place to prevent fraudulent activities, insider trading, and market manipulation.

8. **Options Disclosures:** Traders are provided with options disclosure documents that explain the risks, characteristics, and mechanics of options.

Compliance and Your Responsibilities

As an options trader, understanding and complying with regulations is essential. Your responsibilities include:

1. **Due Diligence:** Research and choose a reputable broker regulated by the appropriate authorities.
2. **Documentation:** Maintain records of your trades, statements, and correspondence with your broker.
3. **Risk Management:** Adhere to margin requirements and employ risk management strategies to protect your capital.
4. **Transparency:** Report your trades accurately and transparently.
5. **Stay Informed:** Keep up-to-date with changes in regulations and compliance requirements.
6. **Consult a Compliance Expert:** If necessary, consult with a compliance expert or legal advisor to ensure your trading activities are in compliance with regulations.

Conclusion

Regulations and compliance are fundamental aspects of options trading, designed to protect both traders and the integrity of the financial markets. Traders must be aware of the rules, regulations, and requirements that govern their activities and take steps to ensure they operate within the bounds of the law. By doing so, you can trade with confidence and trust in the fairness and transparency of the options market.

CHAPTER 35:

Options Trading Tools and Software

Options Trading Tools and Software: Enhancing Your Trading Strategies

In the world of options trading, having the right tools and software at your disposal can be the difference between success and disappointment. This chapter delves into advanced options trading software and tools that can elevate your trading strategies, providing you with a competitive edge in the market.

1. Backtesting Platforms

Backtesting is a critical component of options trading, allowing you to evaluate the effectiveness of your strategies using historical data. Advanced options trading software often includes robust backtesting capabilities, enabling you to:

- **Analyze Strategy Performance:** Backtesting helps you assess how your trading strategies would have performed in the past, revealing their strengths and weaknesses.
- **Refine Your Strategies:** By identifying which strategies worked well historically, you can refine and optimize your trading approaches.
- **Risk Management:** Backtesting helps you understand the potential risk and drawdown associated with specific strategies, assisting you in creating risk management plans.

2. Options Scanners

Options scanners are powerful tools that help traders identify potential trading opportunities by scanning the market for specific criteria. These criteria may include:

- **Volatility:** Scanners can detect options with high implied or historical volatility, which may indicate potential trading opportunities.
- **Price Movements:** Scanners can identify options that have experienced significant price movements, helping traders spot trends or outliers.
- **Volume and Open Interest:** These scanners can highlight options contracts with unusual volume or open interest, suggesting increased market interest.
- **Greeks:** Scanners can filter options based on their Greeks (delta, gamma, theta, vega, and rho), allowing traders to find contracts that align with their desired risk profile.

3. Trade Analyzers

Trade analyzers are invaluable for evaluating the risk and potential outcomes of your options trades. They offer features such as:

- **Risk Assessment:** Analyzers can calculate and display the potential risks of your trades, helping you make informed decisions.
- **Profit and Loss Projections:** These tools provide profit and loss projections based on various market scenarios, allowing you to visualize potential outcomes.
- **"What-If" Analysis:** Trade analyzers allow you to perform "what-if" analyses by adjusting variables like stock price, volatility, or time decay, so you can anticipate different trade scenarios.
- **Performance Tracking:** Analyzers often include features to track the performance of your trades over time, helping you identify which strategies and setups are most successful.

4. Execution Platforms

Execution platforms are the interface through which you place and manage your options trades. Advanced software provides features like:

- **Real-Time Data:** Execution platforms offer real-time market data, enabling you to make timely decisions.
- **Order Types:** These platforms support various order types, including market orders, limit orders, stop orders, and more, to execute your trades with precision.
- **Options Chains:** They typically include options chains, allowing you to view and select options contracts easily.
- **Risk Management Tools:** Advanced platforms provide built-in risk management tools, like setting stop-loss and take-profit orders.

5. Options Analytics

Options analytics tools are designed to help traders gain deeper insights into options pricing and behavior. They provide:

- **Greeks Analysis:** Analyzing how options Greeks (delta, gamma, theta, vega, and rho) impact your positions.
- **Implied Volatility Analysis:** Understanding how changes in implied volatility affect options prices.
- **Probability Calculators:** Estimating the probability of options expiring in or out of the money.
- **Position Simulators:** Simulating the potential outcomes of complex options strategies.

6. Educational Resources

Many advanced options trading platforms offer educational resources, including webinars, tutorials, and articles to help traders better understand how to use their software effectively.

Conclusion

Mastering options trading requires not only a strong understanding of strategies and market dynamics but also access to advanced tools and software. Whether you're looking to backtest your strategies, identify opportunities with scanners, or analyze your trades comprehensively, the right software can make a substantial difference in your trading success. By incorporating these advanced options trading tools into your trading arsenal, you'll be better equipped to navigate the complex world of options and make well-informed decisions that can lead to greater profitability and risk management.

CHAPTER 36:

Options Trading in Different

Market Conditions

Options Trading in Different Market Conditions: Adapting to Bulls, Bears, and Sideways Markets

In options trading, adaptability is key to achieving consistent success. Market conditions are ever-changing, and astute traders must be prepared to tailor their strategies to different scenarios. This chapter explores how options trading strategies can be adjusted to thrive in varying market conditions, including bullish, bearish, and sideways markets.

1. Bull Markets

Bull markets are characterized by rising asset prices and overall optimism among investors. In such market conditions, options traders can employ strategies that capitalize on upward price movements:

- **Call Options:** Buying call options allows traders to profit from the bullish sentiment. A call option gives you the right to buy the underlying asset at a specified price (strike price) before a set expiration date. As the asset's price rises, the call option becomes more valuable.
- **Bull Put Spreads:** This strategy involves selling an out-of-the-money put option while simultaneously buying a lower strike put option on the same asset. It's a limited-risk, limited-reward strategy suitable for moderately bullish markets.

- **Covered Calls:** Traders with a long position in the underlying asset can sell call options against it. This generates income from the call premiums and offers some protection against potential downward moves.

2. Bear Markets

Bear markets are characterized by declining asset prices and pessimism among investors. Traders can adapt by implementing strategies that profit from falling prices:

- **Put Options:** Buying put options grants traders the right to sell the underlying asset at a predetermined strike price. As the asset's price falls, the put option gains value.
- **Bear Call Spreads:** This strategy involves selling a call option with a specific strike price and simultaneously buying a call option with a higher strike price. It's a limited-risk, limited-reward strategy for moderately bearish markets.
- **Protective Puts:** Traders can buy put options to hedge against potential losses in a bear market. These puts increase in value as the asset's price declines.

3. Sideways Markets

In *sideways markets*, prices move within a relatively narrow range. Options traders can use strategies that benefit from price consolidation:

- **Iron Condors:** This strategy combines a bear call spread and a bull put spread. It profits from limited price movement within a defined range.
- **Straddles:** A straddle involves buying both a call and a put option with the same strike price and expiration date. Traders employ this strategy when they anticipate a significant price movement, regardless of direction.
- **Calendar Spreads:** This strategy involves selling a short-term option and simultaneously buying a longer-term option with the same strike price. It's designed to capitalize on the

time decay of the short-term option while maintaining a long position with the longer-term option.

Conclusion

Adaptability is the hallmark of successful options trading. Understanding how to navigate various market conditions is vital for options traders looking to thrive in both bullish and bearish markets, as well as when prices move sideways. By applying the right strategies to match each market scenario, traders can enhance their ability to manage risk and maximize returns. Whether you're leveraging call options in a bull market, employing protective puts in a bear market, or utilizing iron condors in a sideways market, the key is to remain flexible and responsive to the ever-evolving dynamics of the financial markets.

CHAPTER 37:

International Options Markets

Options trading is a financial instrument that provides investors with the opportunity to speculate on the future price movements of various assets, including stocks, commodities, and currencies. These markets are not limited to domestic exchanges; they have expanded globally to cater to the needs of traders and investors across the world. Here, we'll explore international options markets and highlight some of the key differences between them.

1. **Geographic Diversity**:
   - International options markets exist in numerous countries, such as the United States (CBOE and NASDAQ), Europe (Euronext and Eurex), and Asia (Hong Kong Stock Exchange and Singapore Exchange).
   - Each region's options markets often focus on assets and industries relevant to their respective economies. For instance, Asian markets may offer more options tied to Asian stocks and currencies.
2. **Regulatory Variations**:
   - Different countries have their own regulatory bodies overseeing options trading, leading to variations in rules and requirements.
   - Traders must be aware of the specific regulations in each market, such as margin requirements, position limits, and trading hours.
3. **Underlying Assets**:
   - International options markets cover a wide range of underlying assets, including stocks, indexes, commodities, interest rates, and foreign exchange.
   - Investors can access options on unique assets or sectors that may not be available in their home market, expanding their investment opportunities.

4. **Trading Hours**:
   - o Time zone differences mean that international options markets operate on different schedules.
   - o Traders must consider these time variations when planning their strategies and executing trades. Some markets offer extended hours trading, providing opportunities for 24-hour trading.

5. **Contract Specifications**:
   - o The contract specifications, such as contract sizes, expiration dates, and exercise styles, may differ between international options markets.
   - o Traders need to be familiar with these specifics to make informed decisions.

6. **Currency and Language**:
   - o Trading in international markets often involves different currencies and languages.
   - o Traders must consider exchange rate fluctuations and any language barriers when trading in foreign options markets.

7. **Tax Implications**:
   - o Tax rules for options trading can vary significantly between countries.
   - o Investors should understand the tax implications of trading options in international markets, as these can impact profitability.

8. **Liquidity and Volume**:
   - o Liquidity and trading volume can vary widely among international options markets.
   - o Major exchanges like the CBOE in the U.S. tend to have higher liquidity, making it easier to execute trades, while smaller markets may have limited options and lower trading activity.

9. **Risk Management**:
   - o Different markets may offer unique risk management tools, such as different types of options or derivatives for hedging purposes.
   - o Traders need to understand how these tools can be used to manage risk effectively.

10. **Information Access**:
    - o Access to real-time market information, news, and research resources may vary between international options markets.
    - o Traders should assess their information sources to make well-informed decisions.

In conclusion, international options markets provide diversification opportunities, but they come with their own set of complexities and considerations. Traders and investors looking to participate in these markets should conduct thorough research, understand the specific nuances of each market, and carefully manage the risks associated with international options trading. Additionally, consulting with financial professionals or advisors familiar with the international options landscape can be valuable for those looking to expand their trading activities beyond domestic markets.

Legend of Terms

A -

1. **American Option**: An option that can be exercised at any time before or on the expiration date.
2. **At-the-Money (ATM)**: An options contract with a strike price equal to the current market price of the underlying asset.
3. **Assignment**: When the holder of an options contract exercises their right, and the writer (seller) of the option is obligated to fulfill it.
4. **Automatic Exercise**: Some brokerage platforms automatically exercise in-the-money options at expiration.
5. **Arbitrage**: The practice of simultaneously buying and selling similar assets to profit from price discrepancies.

B -

1. **Bear Call Spread**: An options strategy involving the sale of a call option with a lower strike price and the purchase of a call option with a higher strike price.
2. **Bull Put Spread**: An options strategy involving the sale of a put option with a higher strike price and the purchase of a put option with a lower strike price.
3. **Butterfly Spread**: An options strategy using three strike prices to create a limited-risk, limited-reward position.
4. **Backtesting**: Evaluating a trading strategy by applying it to historical data to assess its effectiveness.
5. **Break-Even Point**: The point at which an options trade neither makes nor loses money.

C -

1. **Covered Call**: An options strategy where an investor holds a long position in an asset and sells a call option on the same asset to generate income.

2. **Credit Spread**: An options strategy that involves the simultaneous sale and purchase of options to receive a net premium.
3. **Collateral**: The assets or cash used to secure obligations in options trading.
4. **Cash Settlement**: Settling an options contract by the payment of cash, rather than the actual delivery of the underlying asset.
5. **Collateralized Debt Obligation (CDO)**: A type of structured financial product that may include options and other derivatives.

D -

1. **Double Barrier Option**: An option with two specified price levels, one above and one below the current asset price.
2. **Delta**: A measure of how much the option price will change for a $1 change in the underlying asset's price.
3. **Day Trading**: Buying and selling options within the same trading day to profit from short-term price movements.
4. **Digital Option**: A type of option with a fixed payout if the underlying asset reaches or does not reach a specified price level.
5. **Debit Spread**: An options strategy that requires an upfront payment to establish the position.

E -

1. **European Option**: An option that can only be exercised at expiration, not before.
2. **Expiry Date**: The same as the expiration date, the last day when an options contract can be exercised.
3. **Exotic Options**: Complex options with non-standard features, often tailored to specific trading needs.
4. **Exchange-Traded Fund (ETF)**: Investment funds traded on stock exchanges, often used as underlying assets for options.
5. **Exercise Price**: The same as the strike price, the level at which an option can be exercised.

F -

1. **Futures Options**: Options based on futures contracts, providing exposure to commodities, indexes, or interest rates.
2. **Floating Strike Option**: An option with a strike price that changes based on the current market price of the underlying asset.

3. **Front-Month Option**: An options contract with the nearest expiration date.
4. **Financial Derivative**: An options contract is a financial derivative because its value is derived from an underlying asset.
5. **Fibonacci Retracement**: A technical analysis tool used to identify potential support and resistance levels in the market.

G -

1. **Gamma**: A measure of how much delta changes for a $1 change in the underlying asset's price.
2. **Greenshoe Option**: An over-allotment option allowing the sale of additional shares in an IPO if there's high demand.
3. **Good 'Til Cancelled (GTC)**: An order type that remains active until it is executed or manually canceled.
4. **Greeks**: A collective term for measures like Delta, Gamma, Theta, and Vega used to assess options' sensitivity to various factors.
5. **Granger Causality**: A statistical test used to determine if past information about one variable can predict another, helpful in options pricing models.

H -

1. **Hedge Ratio**: The number of options contracts needed to hedge a specific position or portfolio.
2. **Historical Volatility**: A calculation of an asset's past price fluctuations, used in options pricing models.
3. **Holder**: The person who possesses the right to exercise an options contract.
4. **Horizontal Spread**: An options strategy that involves options with the same expiration date but different strike prices.
5. **High-Frequency Trading (HFT)**: A trading strategy that relies on rapid order execution and high-speed algorithms.

I -

1. **Implied Volatility**: A measure of expected future price volatility derived from options pricing models.
2. **In-the-Money (ITM)**: When an options contract has intrinsic value, meaning it would be profitable if exercised immediately.
3. **Iron Condor**: An options strategy involving the simultaneous sale of a put spread and a call spread.

4. **Intrinsic Value**: The actual value of an options contract, calculated as the difference between the current asset price and the strike price.
5. **Initial Margin**: The amount of funds required to open an options position, as collateral against potential losses.

J -

1. **Joint Account**: A brokerage account owned by more than one individual or entity, used for options trading.
2. **Justification**: Careful consideration and analysis should justify each options trade to align with your investment strategy.
3. **Jump-Diffusion Model**: A financial model used to account for sudden, large price movements in options pricing.
4. **Joint Backtesting**: Evaluating the effectiveness of a trading strategy by considering its historical performance in conjunction with other strategies.
5. **Junk Bond Option**: An options strategy often used to speculate on changes in the yield spread between junk bonds and Treasuries.

K -

1. **Knock-In Option**: Becomes active and tradable only if the underlying asset reaches a specific price level.
2. **Knock-Out Option**: An option that becomes worthless if the underlying asset reaches a certain price level.
3. **Kurtosis**: A statistical measure used in options pricing models to describe the shape of the probability distribution curve.
4. **Kappa**: A measure of how changes in interest rates impact an options contract's price.
5. **Key Rate Duration**: A measure of an options portfolio's sensitivity to shifts in specific parts of the yield curve.

L -

1. **Leverage**: Options provide leverage, allowing investors to control a larger position with a smaller amount of capital.
2. **Long Position**: Owning an options contract, entitling the holder to buy (for call options) or sell (for put options) the underlying asset.
3. **Liquidation Value**: The estimated value of an options position if it were to be closed or exercised.
4. **Limit Order**: An order to buy or sell an options contract at a specified price or better.

5. **Lognormal Distribution**: A probability distribution often used to model the price movements of financial assets in options pricing models.

M -

1. **Margin Requirement**: The amount of capital or collateral required to trade options, to ensure potential obligations can be met.
2. **Market Order**: An order to buy or sell an options contract at the current market price.
3. **Market Maker**: A financial institution or individual that provides liquidity in the options market by buying and selling options.
4. **Moneyness**: A term that describes whether an options contract is in-the-money, at-the-money, or out-of-the-money.
5. **Monte Carlo Simulation**: A numerical technique used to model the impact of various factors on options pricing.

N -

1. **Naked Option**: Writing an options contract without holding a corresponding position in the underlying asset.
2. **Notional Value**: The total value of the underlying asset that an options contract represents.
3. **Neutral Strategy**: An options strategy designed to profit from low or no price movements in the underlying asset.
4. **Naked Call**: Writing a call option without owning the underlying asset.
5. **Net Delta**: The sum of delta values for all options positions in a portfolio.

O -

1. **Out-of-the-Money (OTM)**: When an options contract has no intrinsic value, meaning it would not be profitable if exercised immediately.
2. **Over-the-Counter (OTC) Options**: Options traded directly between parties and not on a centralized exchange.
3. **Option Premium**: The price paid for an options contract, comprising intrinsic value and time value.
4. **Options Clearing Corporation (OCC)**: A centralized clearinghouse responsible for the clearing and settlement of exchange-listed options contracts.

5. **Open Interest**: The total number of options contracts outstanding for a particular strike price and expiration date.

P -

1. **Put Option**: An option that gives the holder the right to sell the underlying asset at a specified price before or on a certain date.
2. **Premium Decay**: The reduction of an options contract's time value as it approaches expiration.
3. **Protective Put**: An options strategy where an investor buys a put option to protect their long position in the underlying asset.
4. **Penny Options**: Options contracts with low premiums, typically trading at a fraction of a dollar.
5. **Portfolio Margin**: A risk-based margin approach that considers the potential risks of an entire options portfolio.

Q -

1. **Quoted Price**: The current market price of an options contract.
2. **Qualified Covered Call**: A covered call strategy that may provide certain tax benefits.
3. **Quantitative Analysis**: The use of mathematical and statistical methods to evaluate and model options strategies.
4. **Quick Ratio (Acid-Test Ratio)**: A financial ratio used to assess a company's liquidity and financial health.
5. **Quantitative Easing (QE)**: A monetary policy used by central banks to stimulate economic growth, impacting financial markets, including options.

R -

1. **Rho**: A measure of how much the options price changes for a 1% change in interest rates.
2. **Risk Premium**: The extra cost of an options contract, over its intrinsic value, to account for market uncertainty.
3. **Rolling**: The practice of closing an existing options position and opening a new one with different terms.
4. **Reversal Strategy**: An options strategy that seeks to profit from changes in the direction of the underlying asset's price.
5. **Relative Strength Index (RSI)**: A technical indicator used to identify overbought or oversold conditions in the market.

S -

1. **Straddle**: An options strategy involving the simultaneous purchase of a call and put option with the same strike price and expiration date.
2. **Synthetic Option Position**: Combining multiple options to replicate the risk and reward profile of another options strategy.
3. **Strangle**: An options strategy involving the simultaneous purchase of an out-of-the-money call and an out-of-the-money put option.
4. **Short Position**: Owning an options contract that obligates the holder to sell (for call options) or buy (for put options) the underlying asset.
5. **Settlement Price**: The final price used to determine the value of an options contract at expiration.

T -

1. **Theta**: A measure of how much an options contract's value decreases as time passes.
2. **Time Value**: The portion of an options premium representing the potential for the option to gain value before expiration.
3. **Trading Volume**: The number of options contracts traded during a specific time period.
4. **Theoretical Value**: The calculated value of an options contract based on various pricing models.
5. **Tax-Loss Harvesting**: A strategy to offset gains by selling underperforming options and realizing losses for tax purposes.

U -

1. **Underlying Security**: The asset (e.g., stock, commodity, or currency) upon which an options contract is based.
2. **Uncovered Call**: Writing a call option without owning the underlying asset.
3. **Uncovered Put**: Writing a put option without having enough funds to buy the underlying asset if assigned.
4. **Uniform Margin Rules**: Standardized margin requirements established by regulatory authorities.
5. **Unrealized Gain or Loss**: The profit or loss on an options position that has not been closed.

V -

1. **Vertical Spread**: An options strategy involving the simultaneous purchase and sale of options with different strike prices but the same expiration date.
2. **Vega**: A measure of how sensitive an options contract's price is to changes in implied volatility.
3. **Volatility Smile**: A pattern where options with different strike prices but the same expiration date have varying implied volatilities.
4. **Volatility Index (VIX)**: A measure of implied volatility, often called the "fear gauge," for the stock market.
5. **Variance Swap**: A financial derivative based on the volatility or variance of an underlying asset.

W -

1. **Writer (Seller)**: The person who creates and sells an options contract.
2. **Warrant**: A long-term options contract issued by a corporation, giving the holder the right to buy the issuer's common stock at a predetermined price.
3. **Wash Sale**: A situation in which an investor sells a security or option at a loss and repurchases it within a short period.
4. **Weekly Options**: Options contracts with shorter expiration periods, typically expiring on Fridays.
5. **Wheel Strategy**: A strategy involving the repeated sale of cash-secured puts and, if assigned, covered call writing.

X -

1. **Exercise and Assignment**: The processes of using or fulfilling the terms of an options contract.
2. **Exchange-Traded Options**: Options contracts that are standardized and traded on organized exchanges.
3. **Exotic Option**: Uncommon types of options with unique features or conditions.
4. **Ex-Dividend Date**: The date at which an options contract no longer includes the right to receive the next dividend.
5. **Extreme Value Theory (EVT)**: A statistical approach used to estimate the tail risk of financial events.

Y -

1. **Yield Curve Options**: Options contracts that derive their value from interest rate yield curves.
2. **Yield**: The potential return on an options investment.
3. **Yield Spread**: The difference in yields between different types of financial instruments.
4. **Yield to Maturity (YTM)**: The total return expected from holding an options investment until it matures.
5. **Yield-Based Option Strategy**: Strategies that aim to capture yield from options positions.

Z -

1. **Zero Cost Collar**: A strategy that uses options to protect against downside risk while not incurring any upfront cost.
2. **Zero Volatility Spread (Z-spread)**: A measure of the yield advantage a bond or other fixed-income security offers over a benchmark yield curve.
3. **Zigzag Correction**: A specific price pattern observed in options trading that reflects market trends.
4. **Zero-Sum Game**: A situation where one trader's profit equals another trader's loss in options trading.
5. **Zone of Resistance**: A price range where an asset often faces selling pressure in options markets.

FAQ

Here is a compilation of frequently asked questions that may address any queries arising after completing the book:

Q: What time frame should I use for my charts?

A: I utilize a three-month daily time frame for all my charts. This time frame aligns well with the expiration cycles chosen for my trades, typically falling within the range of 30 to 60 days.

Q: How do I determine the strike prices for my debit spreads?

A: I aim to construct my debit spreads by purchasing one strike in the money and selling one strike out of the money. If this configuration is not feasible, I may choose to buy one strike at the money and one strike out of the money. I emphasize that I avoid fixating excessively on strike prices, as my entry points are determined primarily through technical analysis.

Q: Do I always aim for 100% profit in my trades, or do I close positions early for smaller profits?

A: The approach to profit-taking depends on the trade's performance. If a trade immediately moves in my favor and my spread is significantly in the money as expiration approaches, I aim for 100% profit. In cases where a trade fluctuates between profits and losses, with market direction less clear, I may choose to exit when I've reached 50% to 70% of the maximum potential profit.

Q: How should I scale my trading system as my account size grows?

A: As your account size expands, the risk and reward in your trades should also increase. This can be achieved by widening the spreads rather than trading more contracts. For instance, with a smaller account, you may trade a $500-$510 Call Debit spread, risking $250 to make $250. As your account grows, the same trade might become a $500-$520 Call Debit spread, where you risk $1,000 to potentially gain $1,000. Experience has shown that broadening the spread and increasing the number of contracts lead to better results and quicker profitable position closures.

Q: Can I use Deep-In-The-Money (DITM) Calls and Puts instead of Debit Spreads with this strategy?

A: Yes, you can use DITM options with my trading signals. However, I encourage you to experiment with paper trading and compare the performance of DITM options against debit spreads. In my opinion, debit spreads consistently yield better results than simply buying calls or puts.

Q: Have you applied these methodologies to futures or indexes?

A: I do not trade futures, so I have not employed these methodologies in the futures market. Nevertheless, I believe they can be adapted to work in various markets. Regarding indexes, I actively trade several of them, including SPY, RUT, TLT, IYR, and others, with my methods generating favorable outcomes. During earnings seasons, when I abstain from trading individual stocks, I exclusively focus on indexes.

Q: Do you manage investments on a profit-sharing basis for others?

A: Unfortunately, I do not offer investment management services on a profit-sharing basis. My objective is to share my knowledge and strategies with you, empowering you to improve your trading skills. I provide ongoing email support and guidance to our paid members throughout my challenges.

Q: Will there be a monthly fee to participate in future $25K options challenges?

A: While I have made the 2019 challenge available for free as I approach its conclusion, there will be an opportunity to follow my live trades in future Options Challenges. The pricing structure for such opportunities is currently under development.

Conclusion

In years past, individuals associated with house banking, financial institutions, and brokerages were primarily engaged in conventional stock market trading. The advent of the internet and the rise of online trading houses, however, simplified matters for the average investor, making trading more accessible.

Day trading is a popular and potentially profitable approach in the Australian market and beyond. It involves buying and selling assets within a single business day, allowing traders to close all positions at the end of the day and continue trading in subsequent sessions. This practice extends beyond stock markets to include forex and other markets. Day traders execute multiple trades each day, capitalizing on even slight price fluctuations. Successful day trading requires quick decision-making and the execution of multiple small-profit trades.

Day trading is not a casual endeavor but a serious business that demands dedicated attention. Monitoring market opportunities throughout the trading day necessitates a substantial time commitment.

Select your market wisely and focus on a specific set of business or financial instruments. Concentrating on these assets over time will enhance your understanding of market conditions and trends.

Effective planning is the key to success. Prior to each trading day, thorough preparation is essential. This includes devising a clear strategy for when, where, and how you will execute your trades. Establishing stop-loss positions is crucial to safeguarding your daily gains. This allows you to focus on profit generation for the majority of the trading day.

Discipline is fundamental for day traders. The ability to manage greed and exercise self-control is vital. Do not attempt to capitalize on every single trading opportunity, and be prepared to cut losses promptly. Small losses are preferable to the potential devastation of a significant loss.

Avoid chasing the market; attempting to enter a trade hastily can result in unfavorable entry points. If you miss a trading opportunity, refrain from hasty action as the market may have already shifted significantly. Patience and prudence are essential; avoid trading simply for excitement's sake.

In summary, avoid overtrading and steer clear of extremes at the market's peaks or troughs. The dynamic nature of markets means that they can deviate from anticipated trends. Protecting your capital should always be your primary focus. Profitability follows prudently safeguarding your resources. Never let greed guide your trading, and stay mindful of the impact of news reports on market movements. Do not hold positions in anticipation of market-moving news without assessing the associated risks, as predicting market reactions is challenging until the news is released.

Create Automatic Income for Life Immediately!

Forex Signals.

High Conversions Verified Forex Results.

https://1e503-r5sjod5kcm4z3ggybs8j.hop.clickbank.net

OR

BOTS Live Trading Room

https://db240ys-r9r60z39q8rgnkuklg.hop.clickbank.net

Book 4
DAY TRADING STRATEGIES

THE COMPLETE GUIDE WITH ALL THE ADVANCED TACTICS FOR STOCK AND OPTIONS TRADING STRATEGIES. FIND HERE THE TOOLS YOU WILL NEED TO INVEST IN THE FOREX MARKET.

Andrew Elder

Introduction

I t is essential that you understand and apply all these three elements in day trading. While some strategies only require technical indicators (like VWAP and Moving Average), it will help you a lot if you understand price action and chart patterns, so you can be a profitable day trader.

This knowledge, especially about price action comes only with regular practice. As a day trader, you must not care about the company and its revenue. You should not be distracted about the mission or vision of the company or how much money they make. Your focus must only be on the chart patterns, technical indicators, and price action.

Successful day traders also don't mix technical analysis with fundamental analysis. Day traders usually focus more on technical analysis.

The catalyst is the reason why a particular stock is running. If you have a stock that is running up to 70%, you need to determine the catalyst behind this change, and never stop until you figure that one out.

So, it's a tech company that just got patent approval or a pharmaceutical company that passed through important clinical trials. These are catalysts that can help you understand what is really going on.

Beyond this, don't bother yourself squinting over revenue papers or listening in conference calls. You should not care about these things unless you are a long-term investor.

Day traders trade fast. There are times that you may find yourself trading in time periods as short as 10 to 30 seconds, and can make thousands of dollars. If the market is moving fast, you need to make certain that you are in the right position to take advantage of the profits, and minimize your exposure to risk.

There are millions of day traders out there with different strategies. Each trader requires its own strategy and edge. You must find your spot in the market whenever you feel comfortable.

You must focus on day trading strategies because these really work for day trading. The following strategies have been proven effective in day trading. These strategies are quite basic in theory, but they can be challenging to master and requires a lot of practice.

Also remember that in the market today, more than 60% of the volume is dominated by algorithmic trading. So you are really competing against computers. There's a big chance that you will lose against an algorithm. You may get lucky a couple of times, but supercomputers will definitely win the game.

Trading stocks against computers means that the majority of the changes in stocks that you see are basically the result of computers moving shares around. On one hand, it also means that there are certain stocks every day that will be traded on such heavy retail volume.

Every day, you have to focus on trading these specific stocks or the Apex Predators - the stocks that are usually gapping down or up on revenue.

You should hunt for stocks that have considerable interest among day traders and considerable retail volume. These are the stocks that you can buy, and together, the retail traders can still win the game against algorithmic traders.

One principle in day trading that you may find useful is that you must only choose the setups that you want to master. Using basic trading methods that are composed of minimal setups are effective in reducing the stress and confusion, and will allow you to focus more on the psychological effect of trading. This will separate the losers from the winners.

Managing Your Day Trades

It is always intriguing when two day traders choose the same stock - the one short and the other long.

More often than not, both traders become profitable, proving that trader management and experience are more important than the stock and the strategy used by the trader.

Remember, your trade size will depend on the price of the stock and on your account and risk management. Beginners in day trading are recommended to limit the size of their shares below 1000.

For example, you can buy 800 shares, then sell half in the first target. You can bring your stop loss to break even. Then you can sell another 200 in the next target. You can keep the last 200 shares until you stop. You can always maintain some shares in case the price will keep on moving in your favor.

IMPORTANT: Professional day traders never risk their shares all at once.

They know how to scale into the trade, which means they buy shares at different points. They may start with 200 shares and then add to their position in different steps. For instance, for an 800-share trader, they could enter either 400/400 or 100/200/500 shares. When done properly, this is an excellent way to manage your trades and risks. But managing the position in the system can be overly difficult. Many newbies who may attempt to do this could end up over trading and may lose their money in slippage, commissions, and averaging down the losing stocks. Rare is the chance that you may scale into a trade. Still, there are times that you can do this, especially in high-volume trades.

However, you should take note that scaling into a trade increases your risk and beginners can use it improperly as a way to average down their losing positions. We have discussed this for the sake of information, and this is not recommended for beginners.

Even though they may appear the same, there's a big difference between averaging down a losing position and scaling into a trade. For newbies, averaging down a losing position can wipe out your account, especially with small accounts that are not strong enough for averaging down.

ABCD Pattern

The ABCD Pattern is the simplest pattern you can trade, and this is an ideal choice for amateur day traders. Even though this is pretty much basic and has been used by day traders for a long time, it still works quite effectively because many day traders are still using it.

This pattern has a self-fulfilling prophecy effect, so you just follow the trend.

The chart above shows an example of an ABCD pattern in the stock market. This one begins with a strong upwards move.

Buyers are quickly buying stocks as represented by point A, and making new highs in point B. In this trend, you may choose to enter the trade, but you must not be overly obsessed with the trade, because at point B, it can be quite extended and at its highest price.

Moreover, you can't ascertain the stop for this pattern. Take note that you should never enter a trade without identifying your stop. At point B, traders who purchased the stock earlier begin gradually selling it for profit and the prices will also come down.

Still, you must not enter the trade because you are not certain where the bottom of this trend will be. But if you see that the price doesn't come down from a specific level such as point C, it means that the stock has discovered possible support.

Thus, you can plan your trade and set up the, stops and a point to take the profits.

For example, OPTT (Ocean Power Technologies Inc) announced in 2016 that they closed a new $50 million deal. This one is a good example of a fundamental catalyst. OPTT stocks surged from $7.70 (Point A) to $9.40 (B) at around 9 am. Day traders who were not aware of the news waited for point B and then an indication that the stock will not go lower than a specific price (C).

If you saw that C holds support and buyers are fighting back to allow the stock price to go any lower than the price at C, you will know that the price will be higher. Buyers jumped on massively.

Remember, the ABCD Pattern is a basic day trading strategy, and many retail traders are looking for it. Near point D, the volume immediately spiked, which means that the traders are now in the trade. When the stock made a new low, it was a clear exit signal.

Here are the specific steps you can follow to use the ABCD strategy:

1. Whenever you see that a stock is surging up from point A and about to reach a new high for the day (point B), then wait to see if the price makes support higher than A. You can mark this as point C, but don't jump right into it.

2. Monitor the stock during its consolidation phase, then choose your share size and plan your stop and exit.

3. If you see that the price is holding support at point C, then you can participate in the trade closer to the price point C to anticipate the move to point D or even higher.

4. Your stop could be at C. When the price goes lower than C, you can sell. Thus, it is crucial to buy the stock closer to C to reduce the loss. (Some day traders have a higher tolerance, so they wait a bit more near D to ensure that the ABCD pattern is complete. However, this is risky as it can reduce your profit).

5. When the price moves higher, you can sell half of your shares near point D, and bring your stop higher to your breakeven point.

6. Sell the rest of your shares as soon as you hit your target or you feel that the price is losing momentum, or that the sellers are getting control of the price action.

Bull Flag Momentum

Expert stock analysts consider the Bull Flag Momentum as a scalping strategy because the flags in the pattern don't usually last long. Plus, day traders should scalp the trade in order to get in quickly, make money, and then exit the market.

Below is an example of a Bull Flag pattern with one notable consolidation.

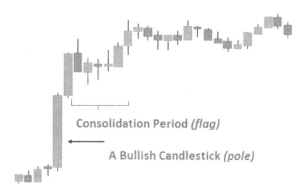

Consolidation Period *(flag)*

A Bullish Candlestick *(pole)*

This chart is called Bull Flag because it is like a flag on a pole. In this pattern, you have different large candles rising (pole) and you also have a sequence of small candles that move sideways (flag) or "consolidating" in day trading jargon.

When there is consolidation in the pattern, it signifies that traders who purchased the stocks at a lower price are now selling. While this is happening, the price doesn't significantly decrease because buyers are still participating in the trades, and sellers are not yet in control of the price. Many retail traders will miss buying the stock before the Bull Flag begins. Buying stocks when the price is increasing could be risky. This is known as "chasing the stock". Successful day traders usually aim to participate in the trade during quiet periods and take their profits during wild periods.

Chapter 1
Know the Market

The first thing to consider when getting started in day trading, is what market you want to use in order to trade. That may sound like an odd question to consider at this point, but depending on how much capital you have, choosing the right market is critical. The important thing to recognize with day trading is that day traders routinely have strings of losses. And we are not talking about amateurs here, experienced day traders will experience losses on a routine basis. Of course, you expect that over time you are going to make profits, but just like flipping a penny can result in 5 tails in a row, making many day trades can result in many losses before a big win hit. So, if you're trading a significant amount of your capital, a string of losses could leave you going broke very quickly. Thousands of dollars can be at stake in an individual trade. For these reasons, there are some rules and recommendations in place to help you avoid getting into super big trouble, but the rules may make day trading seem less appealing especially if you cannot come up with the required capital.

Things to consider before getting started

Day trading isn't a hobby or a game. It's a serious business, and just like any serious business day trading is going to require a serious commitment even before you get started.

- Day trading requires a serious time commitment. You are going to have to study the financial markets, keep up with financial news, and spend time at your computer pouring over financial data. Do you have the time to do all of these things? It's basically a full-time job. You're not going to be a day trader while working your 9-5 and expect to be successful. The day traders who are successful are 100% committed.

- Are you willing to practice before actually beginning day trading? Jumping in and risking tens of thousands of dollars without experience is a bad idea. We have listed links to practice software that lets you simulate stock market trading. Are you willing to spend several months honing your skills using practice methods before actually day trading with real money? You can even open "demo" accounts with many brokers. Consider working on this and practicing now, and then getting into real investing when you've honed your skills.
- Do you have adequate capital to get started? The U.S. government has a $25,000 minimum capital requirement to begin day trading. Do you have the money already? And is this actual money you can lose without getting into serious financial trouble?

Choose a broker

If you are already investing in stocks independently (that is outside an employer or a mutual fund) you may already have a broker that can also act as a broker for day trading purposes. Top brokers that retail investors can use include Ally Bank, TD Ameritrade, Trade Station, Interactive Brokers, ETrade, Charles Schwab, and many others.

Trading on the Stock Market

Of course, you can buy as few or as many shares of stock as you like, but experts advise that you need to have at least $25,000 in the capital that you can risk day trading in order to trade on the stock market. Making four trades in a week will qualify as being a day trader. If you plan to day trade four days per week, it's recommended that you have $30,000, in order to give yourself a bit of a buffer over the minimum. However, this value is quoted on the assumption that you're going to be trading actual shares of stock. It is recommended that your maximum risk on trade be limited to 1% of your total capital.

It's important to know your risk and position risk. Position risk is the number of shares times the risk. If you buy a stock at $20, and the stop-loss is $19, then your risk is $1. If you buy 500 shares, then your position risk is:

500 x ($20-$19) = $500

Stocks with higher volatility will require more risk than stocks with lower volatility. A day trader of stock can access leverage, typically at a rate of 4:1, allowing them to access more shares of stock than they could afford with their own capital.

A good way to get in on day trading on the stock market is --- you guessed it – by trading options. Buying an options contract only requires that you invest in the premium. Trading in options lets you leverage your money.

Futures Markets

You can day trade on futures markets with less capital. This can still let you get involved with stocks, however. For example, you can day trade the S&P 500 on the futures markets with a fraction of the capital required for day trading stocks. You can probably get started on this for between $1,000-$2,500. The daily range of futures can run from 10-40 points depending on volatility.

FOREX Markets

Forex markets are the lowest priced opportunity, with an entry level of capital of about $500. If you are interested in getting into day trading but lack capital, the FOREX markets can be an option to consider in order to get started with day trading. Even though FOREX markets have smaller required minimum accounts, the same rules apply. Traders should not risk more than 1% of their capital on a single trade. If you have a $2,000 account, then the most you'll want to risk on a trade is $20. While FOREX markets might appeal to you because of the smaller minimums, this is an entirely different world, with its own lingo and so forth. That isn't to say that getting some experience in the FOREX markets might be a good idea before risking massive amounts of capital day trading stocks. It very well might be an option to consider in order to use a real testing ground for day trading. This market will require you to study international trade and to spend time analyzing the global economy, rather than focus on individual companies. It's really a different animal, however, it can be complementary, and many traders do both.

Why Day Trade Options

Day trading stocks have a high barrier for entry because of capital requirements. You may or may not already be in a position to do it, but if you're not trading options provide a low barrier to entry alternative. There are several reasons to trade options rather than stocks. To begin with, trading options don't require hardly any money at all (in comparison) and it will allow you to gain experience looking at many of the same underlying fundamentals that day trading stocks require – since they are ultimately based on the same market.

- Options can be cheap. You can trade options at a much lower premium price as compared to the price required to buy stocks.
- Options offer huge upside potential. The percentage gains in options can be orders of magnitude larger than gains in stocks. So, you can invest a smaller amount of money, and reap larger gains on a percentage basis.
- You don't have to exercise the option to profit from it.
- Volatility makes trading stocks risky; it can make trading options profitable.
- The low price required to invest in options contracts means that you can often put together a diverse portfolio, even when making short term trades.
- It may be harder to get competitive spreads with options while day trading.

There are some downsides to day trading options. One important factor is that when day trading options, time value may limit short term changes in price. Options are also less liquid than the underlying stocks, so that can mean wider bid-ask spreads. Trading options will require you to get the same basic knowledge of day trading that we covered when discussing stocks. Ultimately, the value of the option is determined by the value of the underlying asset – the stock price.

Things to watch day trading options

Let's take a look at some indicators specific to options that you'll want to pay close attention to.

- Put/Call Ratio. If this is high, that means more traders are investing in puts for the underlying asset. In other words, the outlook is bearish because more traders are betting against the underlying or shorting it.
- Money Flow Index. This helps identify overbought and oversold assets. It tells you the flow of money that goes into the underlying asset or out of it over a specified period of time. Money flow takes into account both price and volume.
- Open Interest – this is the total number of outstanding options contracts that have not been settled.
- Relative strength and Bollinger bands.

Best Tools to Operate Day Trading

Day traders may have special needs to act fast and get information as quickly as possible in ways that normal stock investors don't require. One of the most important things a day trader needs is access to breaking news related to the markets.

Chapter 2
How to Manage Risk in Day Trading:
Stop Loss and Take Profit

Step Risk Management

All organizations face unexpected risks, be it natural calamities or those caused by people. For instance, loss of finances or a member of an organization getting injured. These events can cost your organization to lose a lot of money which may in return, make the company eternally close. It is therefore important for a company to ensure that one puts strategies that would help in curbing such cases. With risk plan management in your company, you are prepared for a disaster. This is because it will help you to minimize the risk and also the cost you may incur. The risk plan will help you to set aside some amount of money so that it will protect your company in the future if stricken by disaster.

Risk management is a process of finding out the possible risk or disaster before it strikes. These give rooms for the owner of the company to organize his house by setting procedures of avoiding risk and reduce its ineffectiveness. An organization should have a realistic plan of the true level of risk evaluation. A risk management plan should be able to identify and able to deal with the risk. The plans don't need to be costly or should take more time for it to be implemented. Below is a risk management process.

Identifying Risk

You will identify risk by trying to look at it and finding what went wrong. There are many types of risks. They include the environmental risk and authoritarian risk as well as lawful risk and sell and buying risk. If the organization has a risk management tool, it becomes easy. This is because any information will be inserted into the system where it will be available when needed. The information will also be visible to all stakeholders. Being able to identify the risks that may be facing your company gives one a very positive experience.

One can also bring the whole team in the company to take part, which will be of help since they will give useful ideas on ways of managing risks. It will also be able to bring everyone on board and they will give varied experience based on what they have handled. As an employer, you will simply ask everyone to identify the risk they have experienced. The process will promote communication and it will also boost the employee's confidence. They will also be able to learn from each other's experiences. This is because the analysis will be from the management level of the company to the staff members of the company.

Employers can use mind maps that can be used to visualize the possible risk of the plan. They will be useful in inspiring the team members to think outside the box. After that, the management and the group's members will sit down and breakdown the structures to see clearly where risk might emerge. Once you have compiled all the possible issue creates a registered tool that will be used for following and observing all the risk in the plan. When you have all the data it will be easy to manage the upcoming coercion.

Analyzing Risk

What will be the impact of the risk in our organization? Could it make us lose everything we have worked for? Once you have the problem at hand, it becomes very easy to deal with it. In this step, teamwork is also encouraged. Because the team will analyze all the risks and see which one is urgent in dealing with. Prioritizing the risk gives you the idea of how to deal with issues as a whole. You will pinpoint where the team should focus more. They should give workable solutions to each risk. This will speed up the process of dealing with the risk. The determining factors will be time, financial loss and the impact of the risk on the company. If each risk is scrutinized, it will unveil the common topics in the plan and it will simplify the management procedure in the future. When implementing a risk solution is important to map the risk in different credentials, strategies measures, and business progression. It means that the business will have a framework of which it will calculate the risk and make you know the risk they impose.

Controlling and Handling Risk

What can be done to prevent the risk from taking place? If we are already in that mess, how are we going to salvage it? The moment the risk has been identified, it becomes easy to administer medication. You will table your medication plan and dispatch it. You will start with the risk with the highest priority. Assign duties to the team members so that they can help you in dealing with the problem. For mitigation to be effective, you will need help from the team resources. With time you will be having a database of the past plans. It will be easy to deal with others' risks because you will have the risk logs with you. You will not be practical rather than reacting to the advance for more treatment. There are four major groupings.

Transferring a risk means that the whole or part of the risk can be moved to a certain part, but some costs will be incurred. Avoiding a risk means that no activity will be carried out that will have risk. This may be the best way to deal with risks; for instance, not joining a business because you want to avoid losing an also it makes you avoid the possibility of making a profit. Regarding retaining a risk, there are two methods of retention: the self-insurance and captive insurance. Retention risk means the losses from the company or organization will be retained due to the decision from the business company. Controlling risk can be done by either avoiding the risks or by controlling the loss from the organization.

For risk management to be effective, it should ensure that all members of the organization are committed. All the policies and methods should be established. The staff should have clear roles and responsibilities and are very accountable. The teams should also have adequate resources and tools to be able to deal with the risk. If this is done, the benefits could be there will be saving of funds, point in time profits possessions populace and property. Having a safe and conducive environment for the workers, visitors, and also customers. There can also be a reduction in the legal liability and make an increase in the stability of the operations.

Trading Psychology

Trading psychology is referred to as a trader's mental state as well as their emotions which enable them to make sound decisions which in return will dictate their success as well as failure in the trading business. It represents the character and behavior of individuals which affects their actions when trading. For a businessman to succeed in the trading business, they need to ensure that they are good when it comes to trading psychology. This is because trading psychology is helpful in ensuring that a trader makes informed decisions for his company. Their mental, as well as emotional aspects, are helpful in ensuring that they make the right decisions.

Greed and fear, as well as regrets, are emotions that play a vital role in the trading business. In a trading business, greed can be important as well as destructive. This is because when one is greedy, they will always be driven by the desire to make more and more money. A trader should, therefore, utilize it in a good way in order to ensure that they benefit from it. They should learn the situations where they should use greed and when they should not.

Greed is described as an irresistible feeling which makes one want to be in possession of more things than they actually need. Greed is something that is very difficult to overcome. It requires one to have a lot of discipline in order for them to overcome it. Greed makes a trader want to make more money than they already have. Greed is said to have great results when utilized in the bull market. This is because the more a trader stays in the trading business, the more he or she gains experience. The experience enables them to be able to explore all the available opportunities, which helps them to create more wealth. Greed is only destructive when one invests, and then the stock market drops. They may find themselves making losses which are not so good for business.

A trader can, however, overcome greed by ensuring that they come up with a trading plan. The plan will normally be centered on balanced investment decisions. This will help a lot in ensuring that one is not guided by emotions when making business decisions. A trader can even set rules which they cannot go against when it comes to trading. They can also set a specific amount of money that they are ready to win and even to lose daily. They will only have that amount so once they exhaust it, they will just stop and wait to trade another day. This will help them in ensuring that they are disciplined when it comes to investing since they will invest an amount of money that they are ready to lose.

Fear is defined as something that one perceives as a threat to their income and also to their profits. Fear is also beneficial because it encourages the trader to hold back whenever they want to take any step in the trading process. It can also be destructive as well as useful, which will depend on when it is applied. A trader may feel the urge to invest in something, but because of fear of failing, they will stop. For example, whenever a trader receives any bad news about the stock market or even about the market in general, they tend to panic since they do not know whether they are going to make losses or not. There are those whose fear may lead them to liquidate their shares in the market while there are those who will just continue investing. By withholding their shares, it may save them when the prices in the stock market fail but they may lose opportunities to make more money because of the same fear. It is therefore important for a trader to ensure that they find ways of overcoming their fears, especially in situations that they feel like they could make losses. They should take calculated risks in order for them to ensure that they do not make losses after investing their shares in the market. The traders can also study the market which will help them to be able to identify areas that they can invest in without fear. The last emotion to take into consideration when trading is regret. Many businessmen have found themselves engaging themselves in the trading process because of regrets in the other businesses they have engaged in. If not careful, they may find themselves regretting investing in the trade business in a hurry. The regrets will come in when they lose money after investing. It is therefore important to ensure that as a trader, you carry out thorough research before investing your money in any business.

Chapter 3
Quantitative Risk and
Qualitative Risk

When talking of risk, we can divide it into two broad groups: quantitative risk and qualitative. By nature, the quantitative risk is easier to measure and track because a lot of it is just numbers. The most basic is your hit rate and payout ratio.

To get a better idea of your risk, though, you should be tracking the following at a minimum. These numbers will also help clarify the profitability of a strategy, so when you back-test something, make sure to run these numbers as well.

Average Risk Percentage

This is the percentage of your account you are risking per trade. Now, you'll find a lot of sources online saying you should not risk anything over 2% of your account. Personally, I find 2% ridiculously high for beginners.

Think of it this way. If you risk 2% per trade, after taking ten losses in a row, you'll be 20% underwater! Imagine investing your money in something and losing 20%! You might think it's unlikely that ten losses in a row will occur, but this is ignoring the odds.

Based on your hit rate, your strategy will have certain odds of losing streaks based on their size. So the odds of a 10-trade losing streak for a 35% hit rate strategy, theoretically, are 91%. In other words, extremely damn likely.

Your objective should be to protect your capital at all costs. Therefore, risking 2% when you have a 91% chance of experiencing a 20% drawdown (more on this below) is doing the exact opposite. As a beginner, your risk per trade should not be more than 0.25% of your account. This way, if you lose ten in a row, which is very likely, you'll be down just 2.5%, which is easily retrieved.

Drawdown

A drawdown is just the size of the loss you take, so if you lose a trade and are risking 0.25% per trade, your drawdown is 0.25%. More relevant is the max drawdown, which is what most traders refer to when reviewing a strategy's effectiveness. The max drawdown is the difference between the highest and lowest points of your account's equity curve.

So if you lost 10 or 20 trades in a row, your account's equity graph is going to dip. The difference between the start of the dip and the trough or bottom is the total drawdown. The max drawdown is the biggest total drawdown the strategy experiences.

Drawdown size is a function of the hit rate and the per-trade risk. A strategy with a high hit rate can still experience significant drawdown if the per-trade risk is high.

As a reference, if you have a drawdown of over 10%, your account is 99% unlikely to recover. In the professional world, any fund that loses 10% is simply shut down since the managers are unlikely to recover the amount, and it's just more profitable to shut down and open a new fund. For professional traders who can be fund managers or prop shop traders, a monthly drawdown of 2% is the limit for the former and 4% for the latter.

Now, those numbers are for professionals, and as a beginner, you should stick to the 2% goal. In other words, you should structure your per-trade risk in a way that it is remotely possible for you to hit the 2% even with a very probable losing streak. This is how you take care of the downside and let the upside take care of itself.

As you can imagine, risking 0.25% per trade is unlikely to get you rich quick or provide enough income for you to quit your job and give everyone the middle finger. If you're disappointed or feel let down by this, I suggest you read the introduction again to understand what trading is really about. You'll save yourself a lot of time by trying to understand whether it really is for you or not.

Risk Limits

You should have daily, weekly, and monthly drawdown limits. The monthly limit should be around 2% to 3% of your account. The weekly can be set at around 1%. As for the daily, you should set it as a number of losses instead of a percentage. If you're paying attention, you'll see that it will take just four losses to trigger your weekly drawdown limit.

As a beginner, it is essential for you to take as much feedback as possible. This means placing as many trades as you can. Therefore, in order to trade correctly and not hit your risk limits, you need to reduce your per-trade risk to levels far below 0.25%. If you cannot operate in the market with such a low-risk level, you need to gather more capital and demo trade in the meantime.

Why even have risk limits? After all, if the numbers work, doesn't it make sense to keep trading no matter what? Shutting down trading for the week or month if you hit the limits will deprive you of opportunities to make the money back, right?

Well, theoretically, this is correct. However, practically speaking, there is no way you will be able to maintain your composure and simply execute once you've experienced a losing streak. Think of it this way: Olympic athletes who have dedicated their entire lives to training for a specific event also have bad days. These are people whose sole focus is on training and mental conditioning.

Even someone like Michael Jordan had bad games and days when he wasn't at his best. We're all human after all, and unless you can figure out a way to train an algorithm to trade in a discretionary manner, you will need to relax and release the stress of a loss from your mind. Life happens, and you need to account for it in your trading.

The risk limits point to an issue that you're perhaps not aware of but is manifesting itself somehow, causing you to trade poorly. If you're risking 0.1% of your account and you lose 1% in a week, that's ten trades you've lost at a minimum. This is how proper risk management saves you from yourself.

Recovery Period

The recovery period is the time it takes for your account to recover from its max drawdown and form a new equity high. A recovery period that is less than a drawdown period is obviously desirable. So if your account was underwater for two months, a recovery period of one month or three weeks is an excellent metric.

The recovery period measures how robust your strategy is. Every strategy experiences losing streaks. The true measure is not how many times it falls but how far it falls and how soon it can get back up.

Qualitative Risk

We're now leaving the realms of numbers and entering your mind and your habits. Obviously, this is a more difficult thing to measure, and a lot of it ties in with your mindset. Even if you're following a purely mechanical system of trading, you will still need to ensure your mind is prepared for trading in the best way possible.

Consistency and the degree to which you can repeat good habits are key to managing qualitative risk. While the numbers play an important part and your technical strategy takes care of your order entries, you still need to be of sound mind to execute them.

The following habits will calm your mind and prepare it for trading in an optimal way. It is essential for you to see how following these habits will not only make you money but also minimize your chances of losing it in the long run.

Exercise

Get moving and break out into a sweat. Do something to make sure you're exercising—be it walking, playing around with your dog, running, anything at all. Physical activity helps clear the cobwebs in your mind, and it helps you feel fresh and energized. You need to approach trading the same way a professional athlete approaches their game.

This means you must prepare your body for the trading session. While physically trading isn't demanding, you're going to be sitting and staring at a screen for quite some time. This puts stress on your body, and it is not good for your health. Exercise reduces this risk and keeps you fit and fresh.

Try to finish your workout a few hours before you trade. Trading right after a heavy workout isn't ideal for a number of reasons, which I hopefully don't need to go over.

Diet

While you can eat as unhealthy as you want and not have it affect your trading, this is more about just taking care of yourself so as to be as healthy as you can be. Remember, risk management is about managing your downside. If you're sick, you can't possibly trade, so preventing getting sick is far better than treating it.

While this isn't a diet book, make sure you are satiated and try not to eat anything heavy during the session. This causes you to get drowsy, and you might end up executing your strategy wrong.

Sleep

This one is non-negotiable. You cannot function on less than eight or how many ever appropriate hours of sleep you need. Some people think they can tough it out on just five or six hours, but this is simply idiotic. Your brain needs rest in order to function properly, and trading puts serious amounts of stress on your mind.

Therefore, you need to ensure you're well rested and make sleep a priority. Do whatever it takes to sleep well, and if you feel tired or lacking in energy during the trading day, walk away from the screen. The market will always be there, and you don't need to trade every single minute of it.

Lifestyle

If you routinely show up to your trading desk hung-over or, even worse, drunk on alcohol, you cannot possibly expect to make money. Too many people think trading is simply a matter of showing up and placing orders exactly as your technical system indicates, but this is simply not true.

Getting adequate rest and following proper discipline is what ensures success. You're increasing your risk massively by choosing to ignore these principles.

Mental Prep

The trading session is not the time and place for you to analyze anything. Your trade entries should be an automatic go/no-go decision. This boils down to how well you've practiced your strategy and have prepared yourself for the session.

This concludes our look at risk management. However, following and executing these principles will more than ensure your success.

Chapter 4
Day Trading is Really
Possibility to Business

Your Trading Success Plan

Failing to plan is planning to fail. How many of you have heard some version of this saying before? Trading is no exception when it comes to planning. You need to have a long-term plan of success that will serve as your reference guide, as well as a business plan.

Ultimately, trading is a business, and you need to keep meticulous records of performance like you would any business.

Trading Plans

You'll hear a lot of trading gurus tell you to make a plan. Well, what exactly is a trading plan, and why do you need one? To be honest, a trading plan by itself is not going to matter too much. However, when done right, it can help you focus and really nail down your vision when it comes to trading.

Perhaps a more appropriate term for this is to call it a *trading business plan* instead of just a trading plan. Much like how you need to record all key information (both financial and in terms of vision) in your business plan, your trading plan needs to do the same for your trading business. At a minimum, it needs to have the following information.

Instruments to Trade

What instruments will you be trading? List them all out here. You can even take this a step further and list out the individual stocks you will be trading. When starting out, it's best to pick a single instrument and trade just that.

This doesn't mean you go out and try to trade everything under the sun. You build a base with one, then two instruments, and then expand outward. Much like individuals, stocks have natures of their own in terms of liquidity and volatility. Some stocks have certain tendencies, depending on the time of the day.

You need to observe and learn all this in order to trade successfully, and doing so one by one is the way to go about it.

Markets and Timing

Which markets will you be trading? When will you trade them? So it is important for you to note down your session time and stick to it.

Which is the best session for beginners or busy people to trade? Well, there's no such thing as "best" to begin with. In terms of liquidity and best bang for your buck, the open is probably the best. The flip side to this is that the volatility can be pretty extreme. Things pick up toward the end of the day as well, so it's not as if the open is the only worthwhile time to trade.

The afternoon session is usually seen as something of a graveyard with a lot of traders stepping out for lunch. Don't just assume this is so. Observe the market and check its tendencies. While the more active stocks tend to slow down quite a bit, there are some instruments that provide easy pickings.

Capital and Risk per Trade

List out your trading capital and your risk per trade. If this reduced amount is too less for you to buy or sell any stock, then focus on getting more capital to start instead of increasing your risk per trade.

Risk Limits

What is your daily risk limit? Weekly, monthly, etc.? It is also a good idea to execute a gain-protection plan. What this means is that if you have a bunch of winners during the session (say two or more) or if you make a certain percentage of your account during the session (say anything about 0.5%), then you could decide to stop trading during that session if your gains dip below 0.25% or if you lose two more trades.

The idea is that you've made money during the session and you would like to hang on to it. This is to protect a string of winners or a huge gain. Once you've had a great day, it's perfectly fine to set a lower loss limit in order to protect some of it so that no matter what happens, you'll end the day up.

Technical System

Here's where you describe your technical trade entry system along with the exit strategy. I haven't covered a lot with regard to exit strategy because the exit or take-profit level depends on your hit rate. When designing your strategy, evaluate the most common payout it gives you. See if it makes money for you with its hit rate.

More advanced traders will include things like position sizing upon exit and such things. As a beginner, don't bother with partial exits. It'll only complicate your payout ratio calculations. Build and establish a good base, and you'll figure out whether you need partial exits or not.

A general rule of thumb is to aim for a payout ratio of 2. Anything below this requires a high hit rate, which very few systems provide. When exploring your system, remember that you can increase the hit rate by reducing the payout. You can play around with this to see if this makes the system more profitable for you.

Events

The markets have a bunch of external events that affect them, such as earnings announcements, dividends, splits, interest rate announcements, press conferences, and on and on. Generally speaking, you need to pay attention to the following events:

- earnings
- special events pertaining to the individual stock or political events like elections
- interest rate announcements
- nonfarm payrolls (NFP)

That's it. These events are always scheduled in advance, and as a beginner, stop trading an hour prior to the announcement and resume an hour after it has passed. The reason is that volatility jumps like crazy, and your stops will get triggered.

If you have any positions open that are close to profit, take a lower profit just before the announcement, as long as it doesn't affect your risk numbers too much. Similarly, if you have a trade that is in a loss and is near its stop-loss, you have to close the trade out just before the event.

If your trade is in the middle of the road or is even break even, ride the event out and hope for the best. Some stocks are better than others in this regard. Stay away from flashy companies run by Twitter-wielding CEOs who tend to send their products into space instead of building profits. You know who I'm talking about.

Aside from being annoying, you can bet there will be a number of algorithms and bots tracking every character such people type into Twitter, and all it takes for a flash tumble to occur in the stock is a typo or a rash tweet. Stick to boring names no one has heard of, and you'll be much better off, no matter how much you love or hate the company.

Review System

Every successful trader spends a lot of time reviewing their trades and actions over the week. Mention the time you will spend reviewing.

Practice

When will you practice your skills? What skills will you practice? Each strategy has a number of skills you need to execute, not to mention mental skills. Set aside time to practice each of these individually in order to perfect it.

Journals

As important as your trading plan is, the document that is of primary importance for your trading success is your trading journal. This will list all the trades you took over the past week and serve as a record for you to review. In addition to written records, you should also save screenshots of your trades on entry and exit.

Remember to also save screenshots of the market condition on the higher time frame on trade entry. Many times, on review, you will notice how you might have misjudged the higher time frame action. Below are the things your trading journal needs to record at a minimum:

- Date

- Instrument (the ticker or name of the stock)

- Entry price

- Stop-loss level

- Stop distance

- Position size

- Reasons for entry (describe in as much detail why this entry was in line with your strategy and what you saw)

- Reasons or exit

- Exit date

- P/L

- Mental state on entry

- Mental state on exit

You can either have this recorded on a spreadsheet or in a notebook; it doesn't matter where as long as you can review it easily. Save your screenshots in a numbered manner and in appropriate folders. In addition to this, you can also record your screen and yourself during the session and review your demeanor and market action at the time of entry to verify whether you were seeing things correctly.

Remember, the more information you record at the time, the more potential things there are for you to improve and learn.

Aside from the trading journal, you should also keep a *mental journal*. This is simply a record of what your mental state was during the session and if anything was bothering you at the time. It's up to you as to how much information you want to put in here, but you must aim to record whether you followed your preparation routines properly on that particular day.

Your prep routine can include physical exercise, meditation, visualization, affirmations, skill practice, and so on. It's up to you to decide what you want to include. Your aim should be to include things that are as repeatable as possible. Don't include too many things because you like the idea of it but will be stretched for time when it comes to implementing it.

The last journal you need to have is a *review journal*. You can incorporate this within your trade journal itself or as a separate document. When you're starting out, if it is logistically possible, I'd recommend reviewing your session after a 30-minute break once it ends. This way, the action is still fresh in your mind, and you're more relaxed.

Go through all your trades and review the screenshots. Review the video recording as well to confirm and check if what you saw was true. Record what you did incorrectly and, even more importantly, record what you did right. The review is not just about finding things to improve; it's also to celebrate things you did right.

Doing a review after each trading session will increase your rate of improvement as opposed to doing it weekly. Remember, even a session where you place no trades should be reviewed for mental state and whether you were tuned in or zoned out. Did you miss any opportunities? Leave no stone unturned.

Training

Trading is a unique endeavor in that we spend more time in the market (that is, game day) than in practice. Every other high-performance activity requires a minimum of double the amount of time to be spent in practice than in games. So how do you achieve this when it comes to trading?

Chapter 5
Technical Analysis

Technical analysis is a method of looking at stock charts and data in order to spot price trends. It is a method primarily used by traders who are interested in short term profits, but it can be helpful for long-term investors as well. Long-term investors can use technical analysis to determine (estimate) the best entry points into their positions. Note that technical analysis certainly isn't required, and most long-term investors ignore short-term trends and use dollar cost averaging. Nonetheless, it's a good idea to become familiar with technical analysis in case you decide you want to use it in the future.

Technical vs. Fundamental Analysis

Technical analysis is different than fundamental analysis. They could be but aren't necessarily related. Fundamental analysis is focused on the underlying fundamentals of the company. These can include earnings, price to earnings ratio for the stock, and profit margins. The technical analysis ignores all of these things and is simply focused on the trades of the moment. It seeks to discover upcoming trends in buying behavior. So whether or not a company was profitable in the previous quarter – it doesn't necessarily matter. Of course, profitability can drive more stock purchases, and so drive up the price. But many things can drive the price up or down over the short term. Simple emotion can do it, and so traders that use technical analysis study the charts themselves and pay far less attention to external factors or fundamentals.

Trend Seeking

The first thing that technical analysis seeks to discover is the trend. Simply put, a trend is a prevailing price movement in one direction or the other. The time period isn't specific and will depend on the trader's needs and goals. For example, day traders are looking for a trend that might only last two hours. Swing traders may hope to ride a trend that lasts weeks or months. Position traders are looking for longer-term changes, and simply want to enter a position at a low price and exit that position months or between 1-2 years later at a higher price to take a profit.

Trends are easy to estimate, but your estimations have no guarantee of being correct. For an uptrend, traders typically draw straight lines through the low points of the gyrations of the stock on the graph. This will help you estimate where the trend will end up at some future point in time. You can use this to set a selling point when you exit your position.

In the following chart, we see the trend in JNK from April through October.

Support and Resistance

Over relatively short time periods, stocks will stay confined between a range of prices. The low pricing point of this range is called *support.* The upper price point of the range is called *resistance.* The trader seeks to enter their position at a point of support. They can also place a stop loss order slightly below support so that they will exit the position if they bet wrong and share prices drop substantially. Then they can sell their stocks when the share price gets close to resistance levels, on the theory that it's more likely than not to drop back down after reaching resistance. The chart below illustrates this concept. Notice, however, that the stock eventually breaks out of the range. In this case, it's the support on the right side of the chart, and the price drops significantly.

Candlesticks

A *candlestick* is a graphical representation of price and trading that occurred over a specified time period. Candlesticks have a body, and "wicks" sticking out of the ends. On most stock charts candlesticks are in color, with green representing a "bullish" candlestick and red representing a "bearish" candlestick. A bullish candlestick is a time period where buyers were moving into the market buying up shares. The bottom of the body indicates the opening price for the period, and the top of the body indicates the closing price.

A bearish candlestick represents a time period of decline in price. In this case, the top of the candlestick body is the opening price, and the bottom of the body is the closing price.

In either case, the top wick of a candlestick represents the high price throughout the time period. The bottom wick represents the low price for the time period. You can choose what time period you want to be represented, from one-minute out to one year. In the example below, we view the JNK chart but using candlesticks instead of a line. This is with one-day intervals. So the chart tells us whether or not it was a bullish or bearish day, and the sizes of the candlesticks indicate the spread in opening and closing prices for the day.

Traders will look for certain patterns in candlestick charts that indicate changing trends. For example, if the share price has been dropping for a long period, and a large bullish candlestick suddenly appears, that can indicate that buyers are now entering the market, pushing up prices. The trader will confirm the signal by looking up the volume of trading and comparing that to the average. A high-volume trading day is a strong indicator that the price will probably move up.

Alternatively, if the price is at peak value, and there is a bearish candlestick with higher than average volume, that tells us that traders are selling off their shares in droves, and a drop in price is probably coming.

Moving Averages

Another tool used in technical analysis is the moving average. A moving average is defined by the number of periods. So if we were using a chart that is framed in terms of days, a 9-period moving average would be a 9-day moving average. To plot points on the chart, the moving average would take the 9 previous days and average them. This helps eliminate noise from the stock charts and can be useful in spotting trends.

This example shows how a moving average (the purple line) generates a smooth curve for Apple, allowing us to focus more clearly on the trend in price.

The real benefit comes from comparing moving averages with different time periods. That's because it indicates that buyers are moving into the market more recently.

A simple moving average, one that simply calculates the average of the past given number of days, is going to give equal weight to prices days ago and prices more recently. This is an undesirable feature, and so traders prefer to use exponential moving averages to get more accurate data. Exponential moving averages weight the data, giving more weight to recent prices and less weight to more distant prices. Here is the Apple chart with a 9-day exponential moving average and a 20-day exponential moving average. The 20-day moving average is in red. Notice that when the 9-day moving average crosses above the 20-day moving average, the price enters an upward trend. Conversely, when the 9-day moving average passes below the 20-day moving average, the price enters a downward trend.

We also see signals in the candlesticks on the chart as well. Notice that at the low point in June, a larger green candlestick follows the red candlestick. That is a bearish day of selling Apple off was followed by a bullish day of rising prices. When a candlestick of one type is larger than the previous candlestick of the opposite type, we say that it engulfs the other candlestick. Usually, this is a sign of a trend reversal.

Chart Patterns

Traders also look for specific chart patterns that can indicate coming trend reversals. For example, you might be looking for signs that a stick is unable to move any higher in price after having undergone a large and long-lasting uptrend. What happens in these cases, is that the stock price will touch or reach a certain price level that is slightly higher than where it is at the present time, and do so two or more times. But each time it reaches the peak value, it will drop back down in price. That indicates that the stock has been bought up as much as it's going to be bought up at the present time. Traders also look for signals in the chart that a breakout is going to occur. A breakout can happen to the upside, that is, stock prices can increase a great deal, or it can happen to the downside, in which case a strong downward trend in share price will follow. In this case, you will see the price rise (or fall) and then for a short period of time, the trend will reverse. Then it reverts back to the same price rise (or decrease). This is a sign that the stock is "reverting to the mean," where the mean is the overall upward (or downward) trend. If you spot such a pattern early, it's possible to buy shares and be ready to profit from selling them when they reach the peak value.

Bollinger Bands

It's possible to utilize a wide array of more sophisticated tools. Bollinger bands attempt to combine the idea of a moving average with moving zones of support and resistance. The levels of support and resistance for a stock are calculated at any given time using the standard deviation. Bollinger bands will include a simple moving average curve in the center to represent the mean stock price. There will be upper and lower level curves, which show two-standard deviations from the mean. Here we see a chart of Apple using Bollinger bands:

For the time period shown, Bollinger bands provide a great deal of information. The mean share price for the period was $194.38, while the upper line, two standard deviations above the mean, was $206.05. The lower line, which is two standard deviations below the mean, is $182.71.

Knowing these values can be useful to some traders. For example, options traders that sell put options can use the values of the standard deviation to select their prices.

An Overview and Summary of Technical Analysis for the Stock Investor

Technical analysis does have its uses. However, unless you are a speculator, the use of technical analysis is questionable. Over the long term, the price movements shown on charts like these are not very important. If you are investing for the long term, dollar cost averaging is a more useful strategy. Think about the time horizons of your investments. If you are looking at 1-2 years, five years, or ten years, the momentary fluctuations shown here aren't very relevant. So focusing on the exact right moment to buy shares to save a penny is overkill. These charts are really only useful for speculators, that hope to profit for the sake of earning fast money rather than by investing in the companies themselves.

A second concern is a time spent doing this kind of analysis. Any time that you are spending doing technical analysis is the time that you are not spending doing fundamental analysis.

Chapter 6
Consolidation Chart Patterns to Know

Many new traders who are first getting started with technical analysis often have a hard time seeing the less obvious signs that are pointing them towards various positions regarding their desired underlying assets which can lead to them missing out on key trades as the moment comes and goes without their notice. What these types of traders are often failing to take into account is that there is no single right way to trade which means you will want to learn about many different types of chart patterns if you hope to use technical analysis to bring in the profits you have always dreamed of. While there are countless types of technical indicators that you could consider, the following are the ones you should get familiar with first, before expanding your horizons as desired from there.

In order to ensure each effort is as effective as possible, however, you will want to ensure that you have a clear understanding of the benefits of the patterns you choose in addition to being familiar with their strengths and weaknesses. A chart pattern is any one of a variety of different metrics with a value that is directly tied to the current price of an underlying asset. The goal of all chart patterns, then, is to show the direction the price of an underlying asset is going to move as well as what the extent of that movement is likely going to be. This is done through a mixture of analyzing past patterns and determining how and when they are going to repeat themselves in the future.

Instead, they are focused completely on price movement which makes them especially useful in the short-term and ends up losing some of their usefulness in the long-term as they typically lack the breadth of data that is required to be useful in long-term concerns. This then means that long-term investors are more likely to use technical indicators as a means of determining the right entry points to take advantage of, along with the right exit points to have in mind to avoid serious losses that were seriously preventable.

Flags and pennants

Both pennants and flags are signs of retracements or deviations from the existing trend that eventually become visible in the short term if viewed in comparison to the existing trend. Retracements rarely lead to breakouts occurring in either direction, but the underlying asset likely won't be following the dominant trend in the first place so this shouldn't be much of an issue. However, the absence of a breakout will still result in a shorter trend overall. The resistance and support lines of the pennant occur within a much larger overall trend before coming together to a point. A flag is quite similar, with the exception that its support and resistance lines come together in a parallel fashion instead.

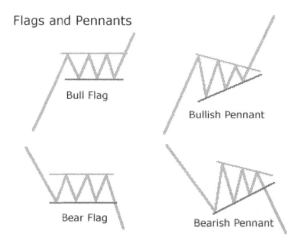

Flags and Pennants

Bull Flag

Bullish Pennant

Bear Flag

Bearish Pennant

Pennants and flags are both more likely to be visible within the middle portion of the primary trend. They also tend to last around two weeks on average before merging once again with the primary trend line. They are frequently associated with falling volume, which means that if you see a flag or pennant with volume that isn't dropping, then what you are likely really seeing is a reversal.

Head and shoulders

If you are looking for indicators of the length of a particular trend, then the head and shoulders formation of three peaks within the price chart tends to indicate an overall bearish pattern moving forward. The peaks to either side of the main peak should generally be a little small than the main peak which makes up the head. The price is the neckline in this scenario and when it reaches the right shoulder you can generally expect the price to drop off steeply.

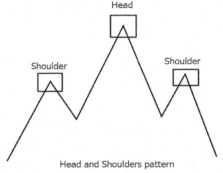

Head and Shoulders pattern

This formation most frequently occurs when a large group of traders ends up holding out for a final price increase after a long run of gains has already dropped most traders out of the running. If this occurs and the trend changes, then the price will fall and the head and shoulders will become visible. It is also possible for the opposite to appear in the form of a reverse head and shoulders. If you see this pattern then you can expect the price to soon be on the rise.

Cup with handle formation

This formation typically appears if a specific security reaches its peak price prior to dropping hard and fast for a prolonged period of time. Eventually, it is bound to rebound, however, which is when you want to go ahead and buy. This is an indicator of a rapidly rising trend which means you are going to want to make an effort to take advantage of it as soon as possible if you want to avoid missing out.

The handle forms on the cup after those who initially purchased the security when it was at its previous high decide they can't wait any longer and begin to sell off their holdings. This, in turn, causes new investors to become interested and then start to buy in. This formation rarely forms quickly, which means you should have plenty of time to act on it once it has started to form.

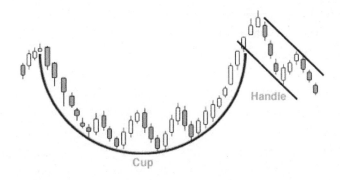

The best-case scenario here would be to take advantage of the details as soon as the handle starts to form to ensure that you have the greatest length of time possible to benefit from the change. If you see the cup and handle forming, you will still want to consider any other day to day patterns that may end up derailing the trend as they will go a long way towards determining its true effectiveness when it comes to buying at a given point.

Gann

While not universally trusted, Gann indicators have been used by traders for decades and remain a useful way of determining the direction a specific currency is likely to move next. Gann angles are used to determine certain elements of the chart include price, time and pattern which makes it easier to determine the future, past and even present of the market as well as how that information will determine the future of the price.

While you could be forgiven for thinking they are similar to trend lines, Gann angles are actually a different beast entirely. They are, in fact, a series of diagonal lines that move at a fixed rate and can likely be generated by your trading program. When they are compared to a trend line you will notice the Gann angle makes it possible for users to determine a true price at a specific point in the future assuming the current trend continues at its current strength.

If you compare a Gann angle to a trend line, then you will see that it makes it much easier to predict the likely movement of the price at a fixed point in the future. This is not to say that it will always be accurate, but it can be useful when it comes to determining the location and relevant strength of a particular trend. As all times exist on the same line, the Gann angle can then also be used to predict resistance, direction strength and support as well as the timing on tops and bottoms.

Gann angles are most commonly used to determine the likely resistance and support as it only requires the trade to determine the right scale of the chart and then draw in the 1x2, 1x1 and 2x1 Gann angles from the primary bottoms to the tops. This makes it less complicated for the trader to frame the market, thus making it easier to determine the way the market is moving based on this predetermined framework. Positive trend angles indicate support in the market while negative trend angles indicate resistance. By understanding the angle on the chart, traders can more easily determine the most profitable times to buy and sell.

Additionally, it is important to always keep in mind the many ways that the market can move between various angles. If the market breaks from a single angle then it will likely move on towards the next, making your job to determine where it is likely headed next. Support and resistance can also be found by combining the angles along with the horizontal lines. If you find that lots of angles appear to be clustering together near a specific price point, especially on a long-term chart, then you should be able to assume the resistance and support in that area is worth a closer look.

The 1x2 angle indicates that one unit of price moves for every two units of time, the 1x1 indicates that price and time move at the same rate and 2x1 indicates that two price units move for every single unit of time. Additional angles can be extrapolated following the same formula including 8x1, 4x1, 1x4 and 1x8. When it comes to performing this type of analysis it is important to always use the proper scale which is a square chart whereby the 1x1 angle moves at an angle of 45 degrees. This is a test then as only when the chart is scaled properly will the angle appear appropriately.

Ascending triangle

This pattern typically forms during an upward trend and indicates that the current pattern is going to continue. It is a bullish pattern that says greater growth and volume are on the way. It can also be formed during a reversal, signaling the end to a downward trend.

Ascending Triangle Formation

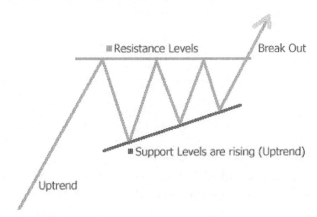

Triple bottom

The triple bottom, named for the 3 bottoming out points of a given stock, tends to indicate that a reversal is on the way. You can tell a triple bottom by the fact that the price rebounds to the same point after each period of bottoming out. After the third period, it is likely to reverse the trend by breaking out.

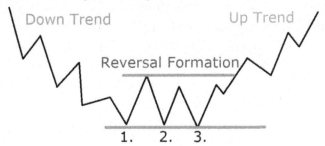

Descending triangle

This is similar to the ascending triangle but is bearish rather than bullish. It indicates that the current downward trend is likely to continue. It can occasionally be seen during a reversal but is much more likely to be a continuation.

Descending Triangle Formation

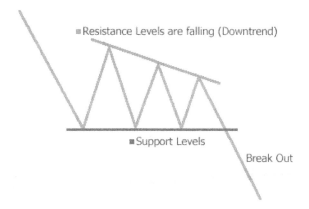

Inverse head and shoulders

The inverse head and shoulders consists of 3 low points always returning to the same higher price. The lowest point is considered the head while the shoulders are a pair of low points that are equal to one another. After the second shoulder, a breakout is likely to occur that will pick up volume as it goes.

Bullish triangle

This is a symmetrical triangle pattern that can be easily determined by a pair of trend lines that converge at a point. The lower trend line tracks support while the upper tracks resistance. Once the price breaks through the upper line then you know that a breakout has occurred that will rapidly pick up both steam and volume.

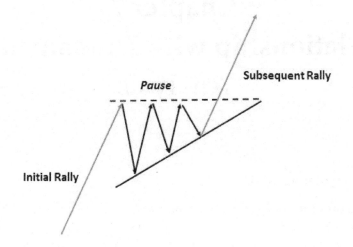

Chapter 7
Relationship with Fundamental Analysis

Fundamental Analysis

I n order to trade in the forex market successfully, one of the most important things you can learn is the most reliable way to spot a trade that is going to end up being reliably profitable from one that blows up in your face. This is where proper analysis comes in handy, whether technical or fundamental. Fundamental analysis is easier to learn, though it is more time consuming to use properly, while technical analysis can be more difficult to wrap your mind around but can be done quite quickly once you get the hang of it. While both will help you to find the information you are looking for, they go about doing so in different ways; fundamental analysis concerns itself with looking at the big picture while technical analysis focuses on the price of a given currency in the moment to the exclusion of all else.

This divide when it comes to information means that fundamental analysis will always be useful when it comes to determining currencies that are currently undervalued based on current market forces. The information that is crucial to fundamental analysis is generated by external sources which means there won't always be new information available at all times.

Generally speaking, fundamental analysis allows you a likely glimpse at the future of the currency in question based on a variety of different variables such as publicized changes to the monetary policy that the countries you are interested in might affect. Fundamental analysis is always made up of the same set of steps which are described in detail below.

Start by determining the baseline: When it comes to considering the fundamental aspects of a pair of currencies, the first thing that you are going to want to do is to determine a baseline from which those currencies tend to return to time and again compared to the other commonly traded currency pairs. This will allow you to determine when it is time to make a move as you will be able to easily pinpoint changes to the pair that are important enough to warrant further consideration.

In order to accurately determine the baseline, the first thing you will need to do is to look into any relevant macroeconomic policies that are currently affecting your currency of choice. You will also want to look into the available historical data as past behavior is one of the best indicators of future events. While this part of the process can certainly prove tedious, their importance cannot be overstated.

After you have determined the historical precedent of the currency pair you are curious about, the next thing you will want to consider is the phase the currency is currently in and how likely it is going to remain in that phase for the foreseeable future. Every currency goes through phases on a regular basis as part of the natural market cycle. The first phase is known as the boom phase which can be easily identified by its low volatility and high liquidity. The opposite of this phase is known as the bust phase wherein volatility is extremely high, and liquidity is extremely low. There are also pre and post versions of both phases that can be used to determine how much time the phase in question has before it is on its way out. Determining the right phase is a key part of knowing when you are on the right track regarding a particular trading pair.

In order to determine the current major or minor phase, the easiest thing to do is to start by checking the current rates of defaults along with banks loans as well as the accumulated reserve levels of the currencies in question. If numbers are relatively low them a boom phase is likely to be on its way, if not already in full swing. If the current numbers have already overstayed their welcome, then you can be fairly confident that a post-boom phase is likely to start at any time. Alternatively, if the numbers in question are higher than the baseline you have already established then you know that the currency in question is either due for a bust phase or is already experiencing it.

You can make money from either of the major phases as long as you are aware of them early on enough to turn a profit before things start to swing back in the opposite direction. Generally speaking, this means that the faster you can pinpoint what the next phase is going to be, the greater your dividends of any related trades will be.

Broaden your scope: After you have a general idea of the baseline for your favored currencies, as well as their current phases, the next thing you will need to do is look at the state of the global market as a whole to determine how it could possibly affect your trading pair. To ensure this part of the process is as effective as possible you are going to need to look beyond the obvious signs that everyone can see to find the indicators that you know will surely make waves as soon as they make it into the public consciousness.

One of the best places to start looking for this information is in the technology sector as emerging technologies can turn entire economies around in a relatively short period of time.

Technological indicators are often a great way to take advantage of a boom phase by getting in on the ground floor as, once it starts, it is likely to continue for as long as it takes for the technology to be fully integrated into the mainstream. Once it reaches the point of complete saturation then a bust phase is likely going to be on the horizon, and sooner rather than later. If you feel as though the countries responsible for the currencies in question are soon going to be in a post-boom or post-bust phase, then you are going to want to be very careful in any speculative market as the drop-off is sure to be coming and it is difficult to pinpoint exactly when.

If you know that a phase shift is coming, but you aren't quite sure when, then it is a good idea to focus on smaller leverage amounts than during other phases as they are more likely to pay off in the short-term. At the same time, you are also going to want to keep any eye out for long-term positions that are likely to pay out if a phase shift does occur. On the other hand, if the phase you are in currently is just starting out, you can make trades that have a higher potential for risk as the time concerns aren't going to be nearly serious enough to warrant the additional caution.

Look to global currency policy: While regional concerns are often going to be able to provide you with an insight into some long-reaching changes a given currency might experience in the near future, you are also going to want to broaden your search, even more, to include relevant global policies as well. While determining where you are going to start can be difficult at first, all you really need to do is to provide the same level of analysis that you used at the micro level on a macro basis instead. The best place to start with this sort of thing is going to be with the interest rates of the major players including the Federal Reserve, the European Central Bank, the Bank of Japan, the Bank of England and any other banks that may affect the currencies you are considering trading.

You will also need to consider any relevant legal mandates or policy biases that are currently in play to make sure that you aren't blindsided by these sorts of things when the times actually comes to stop doing research and actually make a move. While certainly time consuming, understanding every side of all the major issues will make it far easier to determine if certain currencies are flush with supply where the next emerging markets are likely to appear and what worldwide expectations are when it comes to future interest rate changes as well as market volatility.

Don't forget the past: Those who forget the past are doomed to repeat it and that goes double for forex traders. Once you have a solid grasp on the current events of the day, you are going to want to dig deeper and look for scenarios in the past that match what is currently going on today. This level of understanding will ultimately lead to a greater understanding of the current strength of your respective currencies while also giving you an opportunity to accurately determine the length of the current phase as well.

In order to ensure you are able to capitalize on your knowledge as effectively as possible, the ideal time to jump onto a new trade is going to be when one of the currency pairs is entering a post-boom phase while the other is entering the post-bust phase. This will ensure that the traditional credit channels are not exhausted completely, and you will thus have access to the maximum amount of allowable risk of any market state. This level of risk is going to start dropping as soon as the market conditions hit an ideal state and will continue until the situation with the currencies is reversed so getting in and making a profit when the time is right is crucial to your long-term success.

Don't forget volatility: Keeping the current level of volatility in mind is crucial when it comes to ensuring that the investments you are making are actually going to pay off in a reasonable period of time. Luckily, it is relatively easy to determine the current level of volatility in a given market, all you need to do is to look to that country's stock market. The greater the level of stability the market in question is experiencing, the more confident those who are investing in it are going to remain when means the more stable the forex market is going to remain as well.

Additionally, it is important to keep in mind that, no matter what the current level of volatility may be, the market is never truly stable. As such, the best traders are those who prepare for the worst while at the same time hoping for the best. Generally speaking, the more robust a boom phase is, the lower the overall level of volatility is going to be.

Think outside the box on currency pairs: All of the information that you gather throughout the process should give you a decent idea regarding the current state of the currency pairs you are keeping tabs on.

Chapter 8
Range Trading or Channel Trading

ange bound strategy is also known as the average accurate range indicator (ATR). This is one of the favorite indicators with so many users. Range bounder strategy is an indicator that measures volatility in the forex market. You need to know that the ATR indicator DOES not tell you the direction of the trend. Meaning that the market value may be higher; however, the ATR value may below.

ATR indicators only measure volatility; thus, it focuses more on the range of the candles. So as the scope of the candles gets smaller, the indicator values will decrease.

You, therefore, need to find explosive breakout trade before. You need to know that the market is always changing so it will move. It will run from a period of low volatility to a period of high volatility. It will then move from a period of high volatility to a period of low volatility. Thus a range bond strategy is more of a cycle, and it continues. This is how the market will move. Therefore if you have noticed that the market is in a low volatility environment, then there is a good chance that volatility could expand soon.

Once you have learned the circle, then it's time to pull out your ATR indicators by paying attention to your ATR value. Especially the multi-year ATR low value. You will notice that there is a point when the market is weak, and the volatility will be as well when the market breaks down, volatility picks up. You need to note that when a market breaks down, there may be a big move that may follow. This is a powerful trading technique that helps understand your market.

You also need to know how to set up a proper trade loss. This is where the trade indicator becomes so useful. Often traders will look at price rejection level help them know how much buffer they should put as your stop loss to prevent you from being stopped out prematurely. Once this is done, you need to know how to ride massive trends in the market using the ATR indicator. Get your ATR value and make sure that you use the multiple of that value to trailing your stop loss.

An ATR indicator should also help predict market reversal. You need to note that an ATR indicator is a potential energy tool. Thus, if you look at the indicator and it tells that throughout the past three weeks its 300 pips, based on the prior period. So the energy that has been stocked for a week has been used up. Thus the market could show signs of reversing from there. Accordingly, this value will alert you of what to expect.

Sometimes a stock will repeatedly swing between two pricing levels for a relatively extended period of time. That is, it is trading within a range. The range can be estimated by drawing levels of support and resistance on the same chart.

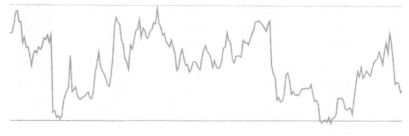

In the above chart, the price level of resistance is indicated by the upper red line. The price level for support is indicated by the lower, purple line. Ranges can last for any length of time, and can even go on for months. The key to finding a trading range is that it lasts over a time frame that is of interest in your particular case. Remember that trade ranges don't last forever, at some point there will be a breakout to the upside or the downside, and the stock will settle in with a new level of support and/or resistance. These are guidelines only.

Trading Strategy for Ranges

However, notice that the price fluctuations within the range offer opportunities for profit. Once you have established a level of support, you can use that as your price level to enter the position.

It's possible that you will miss out on the upside, but a smart trader takes a methodical approach. Rather than being greedy or waiting around to see if the price might continue increasing, the smart trader sets up rules for their trade beforehand, and they stick to their rules. It's better to ensure a limited profit and duplicate the process, than it is to wait too long hoping for higher highs and find yourself losing money. Unfortunately that happens all too often.

Chapter 9
News Trading

N ews Trading. Again, this is where you will want to be paying attention to the happenings of the financial world. When big news hits regarding a stock that you are informed enough about that you are able to generally predict its market moves, take advantage of the moment by buying or selling. This should usually be done very early in the day, shortly after the market opens up since that is when the news usually will first come out. If you wait until later in the day, everyone will have gotten a feel for how the market is reacting and thus may not be so eager to sell or buy. The day trader's objective, however, is to take advantage of small, yet drastic moves within the market, and so buying or selling when the market is at its most volatile may be of the most use to you. It is important to remember not to get ahead of yourself though. Be sure to think through each trade calmly and rationally, avoiding making any passionate decisions that you may later pay through the teeth for.

A word of warning however: there is a difference between news trading, which is legal, and trading on information that you already know ahead of the market. If, for example, a friend tells you that tomorrow morning company XYZ is going to file for bankruptcy, you would be tempted to immediately sell your stock for a hefty profit before it collapses. But to do so before the company announced it would indicate illegal activity. Similarly, if you decide to scalp (different from the first strategy), then you are purposely talking up or down a particular security causing the market to change and then taking advantage of it. That would also be viewed as unfavorable by authorities. Don't do it.

Other Trading Strategies

Since you have now learned the basics of day trading, let us take a look at some of the more artistic aspects. These strategies are only a few of those available and will work differently for each individual depending upon mindset, experience, and confidence. Some of these strategies are old and time-proven, but as always, they can be subject to change in order to fit a specific trader. Peruse these few options and take into consideration which ones might be the best fit for you in terms of capital, how much daily time you can commit to trading, and your current comfort level.

Scalping. This is probably the easiest for traders who don't want to put any significant amount of money on the line, but it requires a lot of patience and fast work. Essentially, scalping involves acquiring very small increments of cash, usually in pence, and slowly accumulating it by making numerous small trades a day. It relies upon the bid-ask spread, in which the bid is how much buyers are willing to pay for a security and then ask is how much sellers require for someone else to purchase it. In order to make a profit, traders are looking for when the gap between the bid and ask is slightly wider or narrower than usual. In the case of a wider spread, there will be a higher demand to buy than sell, and so traders will attempt to sell off their securities for slightly more pence than the normal ask price.

If the bid-ask spread is narrower, there is a greater demand to sell than buy, so that the prices will be slightly lower to buy a security. In this case, a trader will purchase a security at a lower price and then sell it again when the bid-ask spread has returned to normal levels.

Be sure to speak with your broker and ensure you are making enough money scalping so that you don't end up spending all of your profits paying commission.

Momentum Trading. This is where all of the constant reviewing of the financial world will come in hand. Momentum trading is when a trader buys or sells a stock that is on an extremely volatile upswing or downswing. Where all of the research comes in is that you need to be absolutely sure that your stock is truly on a momentum and will not reverse itself after you have already made your move. Confirm this by reviewing charts and finding where that stock has hit its highest and lowest points. If the stock you are looking at is not going to make a move more sufficient than it's normal peaks and valleys then it is not worth your time. In addition to this, reading financial news about changes in companies and emerging partnerships will also be good indicators of a stock entering a period of high volatility. To complete a momentum trade, you will need to chart the trends of the particular stock you are interested in and, when you believe it is going to hit momentum, wait for a gap and then enter your trade. Give the stock most of the day to breathe so that you can reap all of the benefits of the momentum (and your game plan for this particular stock and strategy should reflect that) before exiting. As always, don't forget to place your stop-loss order as soon as you enter the trade.

Pivot Points. With the help of an abundance of charts, this particular strategy is a fairly easy one to grasp. Essentially, pivot points take advantage of the highs and lows of the day. Since you should be dealing with most of the same stocks day in and day out, you will be able to chart the highs and lows of each particular stock over the long term. However, you will not have this added advantage when you begin day trading, so it is advisable to review past daily charts.

In order to take advantage of this strategy, mark out the highs and lows and then watch the daily charts like a hawk to find where you believe the lowest or highest point is. Once you have identified that point, buy or sell as is appropriate in order to gain a profit. In the case of buying, your profit will come from an exceptionally low price. In the case of selling, you will want to sell a stock for an astronomically higher price than you bought it. Take a look at the graph above to get an idea of when to buy a stock. Note that the "R's" labelled on the graph represent resistance within the market (typed in green) and the "S's" represent support (typed in red). Although this is actually a depiction of the first 8 months on the Dow Jones in 2009, it is easy to see how looking at a daily, monthly, or yearly chart would help you to determine the average highs and lows of a particular stock. Theoretically, in this case you would have wanted to buy the stock at the very lowest point on the chart and then sell it at the highest point, which may or may not be represented on this graph. However, since this is day trading and you are only dealing in the short-term, you will want to close out your position by the end of the day.

As you can see, the strategies involved in day trading really aren't that difficult to grasp. Unlike options trading, they rely on a few basic principles and are flexible to almost everyone's needs. Where they get difficult is when traders must keep track of multiple trades at the same time and not get them confused. Doing so can often lead to disaster in which the trader forgets to make his or her exit and then loses money on what would have otherwise been a profitable trade. Avoid this by keeping a proper log of your trades in your journal and don't take on more than you can handle. Study up on more strategies, as these are just the top of the iceberg, and find which works with best with your trading style and will reap you the greatest reward.

Chapter 10
Pairs Trading

Currency Pairs

I n the Forex, the value of one currency is only relevant when compared to another, which is why we talk about currency pairs.

The currency that is used as the reference is called the base currency; the money that is quoted, concerning the base currency, is instead called "quoted" or "secondary."

In the case of the Euro/Dollar pair, written Eur/Usd, the currency on the left is the Base currency, so in this case, the Euro, and the quoted currency is on the right, in this example the Dollar.

Therefore, the price of the Eur/Usd quotation tells us how many units of the quoted currency are needed to buy one unit of the base currency.

Let's see a quick example:

Very simply, if the current price of Eur/Usd is 1.10897, it means that 1€ corresponds to 1.10897$.

The term *Long* or *Buy* indicates the purchase of a pair of currencies in which we assume a rise in prices, thus focusing on the increase in the value of the base currency and therefore on a weakening of the currency quoted.

With the term *Short* or *Sell*, we mean instead the sale of a currency pair, in which we assume a fall in prices, so we expect a decline from the base currency.

Let us take a case where the Euro/Dollar pair's current quotation price is 1.10. This means that 1€ equals 1.10$.

If at this point we open a Buy operation, and the price subsequently rises from 1.10 to 1.20, it means that at this point 1€ is equivalent to

1.20$, so the value of the Euro against the dollar has increased: you need more dollars to have 1€ and, consequently, we are in profit because we have opened a bullish operation, called Buy or Long.

On the contrary, always assuming the quotation 1.10 as the current starting price, we decide to open a transaction Sell: then, betting on a fall in prices, *i.e.* a devaluation of the base currency, we will gain if the price goes down from 1.10.

If then the price goes down to 1.05, we will be in profit. Conversely, if the price should rise above the threshold of 1.10 (for example to 1.15), we would better be selling or we will be losing money.

Further, we will see how profit is calculated based on price movements.

In the meantime, I hope we have understood that the relationship between two currencies is called currency pair. These pairs can be divided into three macro-categories:

- Major Pairs.
- Minor Pairs (or Cross).
- Exotic Pairs.

Major Pairs

Major or significant pairs are all major currency pairs that contain the US dollar, either as a base currency or as a quoted currency.

These pairs generate the most trading activity on the currency market. The main features of these significant pairs are higher liquidity and lower spreads.

The most frequent pair traded in absolute is the Euro/Dollar with 28% of total transactions, followed immediately by the pair Dollar/Yen with 14% of the transactions.

Minor Pairs

Minor pairs, also called cross currency pairs, are all those currency pairs that do not contain the U.S. dollar.

Exotic Pairs

Exotic currency pairs are all those in which there is the dollar combined with other international currencies that are not among the top 7. These pairs are much less traded: they have low liquidity and therefore involve a high spread.

Asset Class

There are different perspectives you can take when classifying asset classes. It would be perfectly valid for instance to say that the main asset classes are stocks, bonds, currencies and commodities. For most market participants, that way of looking at asset classes makes the most sense.

But for systematic, quantitative traders, another definition may be more practical. When looking at the various markets we have available to us, we can group them in different ways. One way to group asset classes would be to look at the type of instruments used to trade them. The type of instrument is, for a systematic trader, often more important than the properties of the underlying market.

This becomes particularly clear with futures, as we will soon see, where you can trade just about anything in a uniform manner. Futures behave quite differently than stocks, from a mechanical point of view, and that's important when building trading models.

The currency space is an interesting demonstration of this concept. You can trade spot currencies, or you can trade currency futures. It's really the same underlying asset, but the mechanics of the two types of instruments is very different and would need to be modeled in different ways.

Chapter 11
Intraday Scalping

Intraday and Multiday Operations

W e have seen before that the principal trades are: scalper, day trading (or intraday), multiday, and position.

We are mainly interested in intraday and multiday trading: this is because, usually, we retailers do not have tools advanced enough that we can operate in the scalping world with a certain speed of execution, and we cannot open a trade and wait for months before closing it. If you want to try these two transactions on your own, of course, I have nothing to object to.

So, we're going to analyze the intraday and multiday trades. We choose above all these two because, given my quantitative analyses, there are a higher number of cases to be investigated and therefore data closer to expectations.

Let's use an example: if I analyze the past ten years of the Euro Dollar (EurUsd), studying an intraday strategy, I can have thousands of executed trades to explain the trends; unlike a "position" strategy in which there would be much fewer trades, consequently, this means less statistical predictability.

Intraday

As we have said, intraday or day trading includes all those transactions that are opened, managed, and closed in a day.

This means that if I open a Long operation (i.e., assuming a rise in prices) at 10:00 in the morning, then I will manage it and usually close it within 24 hours.

My automatic systems are mainly intraday or at the closest after 24/48h: this is because I like seeing activities open, managed, and closed within the day.

I prefer this type of operation also because I can use quantitative analyses; there is a need to study past years' strategies with a good number of trades.

Let's take, for example, the time frame of the last ten years: in the case of position strategies, we could hypothetically have 20 to 50 trades to analyze. How do I know, then, whether this is a real statistical advantage or whether it is mere luck?

It is a different ballgame to have 1,000/2,000/3,000 trades to analyze: with a larger pool of data you can better evaluate the strategy and type of operation. You will never be sure that past studies will be reflected identically in the future, but yes, you can rely on a more accurate analysis.

But it is not enough to have a large number of trades to analyze: an ad hoc procedure is also needed to avoid significant assessment errors. All of which I will explain in more detail in the training courses I have created and which I will tell you about later.

Another advantage of closing trades within the day is to avoid sudden increases in spreads in the transition from the current stock exchange day to the next day, when there is a transfer of liquidity that involves an increase in ranges and that risks going to hit a Stop Loss set, thus creating the potential of finding unpleasant losses on your account. We will see in more detail what is meant by Stop Loss and Take Profit.

A small disadvantage of the intraday operation is having daily "costs of management." For daily costs, we mean the spread and the commissions managed from the broker that we use: but we will see this in detail.

In addition to this, it must be said that, obviously, in intraday transactions, the gain is "limited." Limited in the sense that, objectively, we cannot make significant gains from a single intraday trade, as it could happen for a long-term trade kept open for months. This is because price movements are usually never so large as to allow for high pay-outs, except for the case of macroeconomic news that have a significant impact on the market and make prices jump enormously. But these events are now quite rare.

Multiday

Multiday trading is a fair trade-off between intraday and long-term trading.

The main advantage of this operation is, above all, being able to ride the trend for several days when we are in position, and the market is giving us reason to: this, therefore, turns into a higher gain, a cold pressing of the asset of reference.

All this with the help of techniques such as breakeven or trailing profit (trade management tools in progress), which allow you to make the operation safe by setting a minimum level of profit.

However, I would advise you to close your operations on Friday evening, before the market closes. This is because on Monday, at the reopening of the trading sessions, you can find yourself in front of significant gaps in the market and very high spreads, which can also result in premature closures of operations caused by the activation of the stop loss. I mean, you could end up with unpleasant surprises.

At the end of this paragraph, dedicated to the various operations, I can undoubtedly say that none excludes the other and that on an excellent diversification, any type of trading can be used, except scalping.

With a long-term analysis, you can include position strategies in your portfolio: for example, if you believe that Amazon will grow in the next few years, devote a portion of your capital to this, wait for a retracement of prices and purchases assuming a rise.

For intraday and multiday trading, you can use trading systems, both for analysis and for live trading after adequate studies, and with the right methodology and useful tools.

Chapter 12
Breakout

reak out is known to be one of the most straightforward approaches to use in forex trading. It is easy to note when you are wrong. You can tell when the price goes higher the range or lower your range. Break up is defined either by the swing high or swing lows or characterized by support or resistance. Swing low is a mini version of support and resistance. They are not of significance, but they are pretty evident on the chats when you identify swing highs or lows in the market. Resistance in the market is where there will be potential sellers coming into the market. Resistance is much more respectable and is vary obviously in your chat.

There is a period that you should avoid trading breakouts. You need to know that you should not trade breakouts against the trends as you know that the trend is not your "friend" until it bends. It is not much you can gain if you are trading against the trend. You should also not trade breakouts when the market is far much from the stricture. The problem of going longs in the structure is that you will never know where to put your stop loss as there will know structure to guide you.

To trade breakouts like a pro, you need to:

- Trade with the trend
- Trade near the stricture
- Trade breakouts with the buildups. Buildups are the congested area in your chat where the sellers are not making any pressure. Maybe it is due to sellers not being there, or there are a good number of buyers who are willing to buy at higher prices. These are signs of strengths that you need to look up to.

Breakout Strategy

This is a common strategy employed by traders new and old. The main idea behind this strategy is that you chose a price point for a given stock that, once hit, will indicate enough of a positive swing to justify buying more of the stock. When using this method, it is important to consider a price point as well as the amount of time you are willing to give the stock in order for it to reach that price point. This is a strong strategy to employ if the market is moving in a certain direction and ensures you will always know when to jump on the bandwagon.

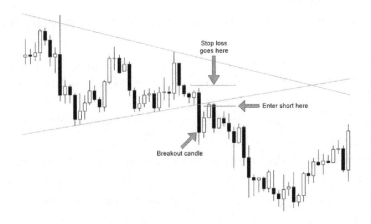

This strategy is an effective choice if the market is currently or was recently at either a drastic high or low. To complete this strategy properly, all you need to do is set an order that is either above the high or slightly above the low and then play the averages. If the market is not moving strongly in one direction or another, then this strategy can easily backfire as prices are more likely to stick to prescribed ranges. If there are no strong signs of trending use with caution.

Retracement strategy

To properly implement this strategy, it is important that you are able to determine a likely pattern for the price of the stock to continue trending towards. To take advantage of this fact, you wait for each price increase before the inevitable decrease which comes as some people sell and others try and trade the opposite. You sell on the high and use the profits to buy back in at an increase of shares under the assumption that it will rise again. Then you simply repeat until you are no longer sure of the increase.

This strategy will only work effectively when there is something major enough to cause ripples across the market that are not felt all at once. This strategy will become less effective the unsure you are about additional jumps in price and should therefore always be used carefully. You may be tempted after seeing a single large jump from a stock to try and employ this strategy but beware of using it flippantly. Stay strong and you will turn a profit.

Pivot points

In order to take advantage of this strategy, it is important that you first become extremely familiar with the specific securities that you prefer to work with day in and day out so that you have a general understanding of their high and low points, thus making it easier to predict where it is likely they are going to go next.

If you don't have access to this type of first-hand information, then you can use existing historical charts to make do, as long as you can clearly determine the highs and lows for the security in question. In order to ensure this strategy works as well as possible, you will need to have a clear top and bottom determined. You will then simply buy or sell based on not where the security is currently going, but where it is likely to go once it rounds the pivot point and starts back the other way.

Essentially, you are going to look at these charts and try to figure out where the lowest and the highest points are. When the stock gets to the lowest point, it is time to enter the market and purchase the stock at a lower price, hopefully, lower than market value. You will then hold onto the stock for a bit, waiting for it to reach the high point on the chart, or at least higher than where you started so that you can make a profit when it's time to sell.

Pairs trading

As the name implies, pairs trading is a strategy wherein you choose a general category of stocks, tech stocks, for example, and then go short on one stock in the sector while going long on the other. Making these trades at the same time will bolster your odds of ensuring one of them actually turns a profit while also ensuring that you are able to turn a profit regardless of the conditions in the market. You will also be able to see movement on all sides more easily including sideways movement, downtrends, and uptrends and then bet on a few different options within the market. Since you are betting on both sides, you are more likely to make some money compared to just picking one kind of stock.

Contrarian trading

Day traders that use momentum to trade will buy bonds and stocks when their prices are going up and selling them when the prices begin to go down. These people believe that if something is going up in its price, it will continue to do so for a while and that something that is falling will continue to fall. Momentum trading is only one trading strategy, and, for most traders, it works well, especially with a strong bull market.

Contrarian trading, though, is the exact opposite of those momentum traders, and it also has the possibility to work very well. The belief in the contrarian strategy is that things aren't going to continue to rise forever and that nothing will fall forever.

The contrarian investment style goes against the market trends that are currently prevailing by purchasing assets that are performing poorly, and sell them once they are performing well. This type of investor believes that when another person says that the market is moving up, does so when they are completely invested and aren't planning on purchasing more. This means the market is at its peak, which means a downturn is about to happen, and the contrarian investor has already sold.

A trader that uses the contrarian strategy will look for assets that have been on the rise and will sell them, and they prefer to buy stocks that have been falling in price. It doesn't mean that you should buy cheap or sell but instead look for things that appear to be overpriced and to buy what looks to be a bargain. Contrarian investment also places emphasis on out-of-favor securities that have a low P/E ratio.

This investment style is distinguished from others in that they buy and sell against the grain of what other investors believe at a given time. These investors will enter the market when others feel pessimistic about it, and its value is a lot lower than the intrinsic value. When there is such a largely pessimistic view about a stock, the chances of the price lowering so low that the risks and downfalls of the stock are overblown. Finding out which of the distressed stocks to purchase and then sell it after the company has recovered will boost the value of the stock. This is the main play of the contrarian investor.

Chapter 13
Application on the Options Market

Very successful investor says that research makes all the difference not only in options trading but trading in general. The better resources you have the more knowledge you will acquire. This is especially significant for learning as much as you can about underlying securities for example or to find as many details about the market that is constantly changing. Significance of the right source of information eventually becomes the key to your progress, even more, if the world of options trading is still new to you. We can say that there are two types of relevant resources for options trading. The first one includes traditional resources such as magazines, newsletters, and newspapers. The second type is newer, it has a variety of options and these kinds of resources are mostly referred to as online resources.

The Internet offers a variety of free content, which is why many investors see it as their first stop whenever they need some kind of information. Further technology development also had a huge impact on the amount of information, tools, and possibilities that a person can access so using apps for education and trading, in general, has become a common thing. In the following text, we will list some of the most relevant option trading resources divided into the categories we explained above.

Even though they are considered to be more traditional, magazines, newspapers, newsletters, are still popular for research, for both experienced investors and beginners on the market. It is useful to know that many newsletters offer paid services such as recommendations, picks, research of certain categories and other relevant information.

We will start with the magazines. Some of them such as Forbes is still one of the greatest and strongest magazines in the world for this matter. So, we have Fortune, Forbes, Consumer Money Adviser, Bloomberg BusinessWeek, Kiplinger's, and Fast Company as some of the most relevant magazines today.

Newspapers that you might find useful are the Financial Times, the Wall Street Journal, The Washington Post, Value Line, and Barron's. Some of the most recommended ones are ETF Trader, Market Watch Options Trader, The Proactive Fund Investor, Hulbert Interactive, The Technical Indicator, The Prudent Speculator, Dow Theory Forecasts, and Global Resources Trading

When it comes to online resources, they are probably the most frequent source of information for everything, not only for options trading. However, it is possible to find numerous websites that offer research that is up to date. Many of these analyses and other useful data can be found for free.

Technology development made many things easier with trading. Many apps have emerged and enabled investors to keep a close track of their investments at all times. It is important to know that there are apps that are not only for investment but for brokerage companies too. In the following text, you can find some of the investment apps that are most frequently used and that have excellent feedback.

How to avoid costly mistakes

Losing profit is not something that you want as an investor since the main purpose of options trading is to make money not the other way around. To do so, some tips can help you avoid mistakes that can be costly.

First of all, don't invest more capital than you are ready to lose. Keep in mind that trading options don't go without risks. There aren't any guarantees that the propositions that you'll face with will gain you anything and your decisions are based on the hunch. Furthermore, if you don't have good timing and your hunch isn't right, you can lose the entire investment, not only the cash you were expecting to earn.

The best way to avoid this kind of scenario is to start small. It is recommended that you use no more than 15 percent of your total portfolio on options trading.

The second tip that you should be aware of at all times is that good research gets the job done. If somebody says that it is a good idea to invest in options and you rush in and make an order without thinking it through, once more, you can lose more than you could earn. You should make your own research and decide based on facts before you start trading.

There is another thing that you should be mindful of. No matter the strategy you choose for options trading, you should always try to adjust it to the current condition on the market. Not all strategies work in all environments which is why you must be up to date with circumstances in the world of finance and you have to adapt accordingly.

Without a proper exit strategy, it is useless to talk about successful business in options trading. You need to make a plan that you will follow through regardless of your emotions. Rational decisions are the main factor in trade, being emotional and making fast decisions out of rage or spite or feeling of insecurity can only make things worse. Stick to the plan you figured before you started trading because it should have both downside and upside points along with the timeframe for its execution. Just like you shouldn't let negative feelings influence your decision making, you shouldn't allow the feeling of over-confidence in gaining large profits pull you back from the path you have set for yourself.

When it comes to risks, there is no need to take more risks than necessary, which means that the level of risk should be as big as your comfort with it. Level of risk tolerance is different for everyone; it is an individual think and only the investor himself can set its limit. Try to estimate that level and then choose all further actions accordingly. It is the safest premise to base your decisions on without being too insecure about every choice you make.

Chapter 14
Analyzing Mood Swing in the Market

T he market is a chaotic place with a number of traders vying for dominance over one another. There are a countless number of strategies and time frames in play and at any point, it is close to impossible to determine who will emerge with the upper hand. In such an environment, how is it then possible to make any money? After all, if everything is unpredictable, how can you get your picks right?

Well, this is where thinking in terms of probabilities comes into play. While you cannot get every single bet right, as long as you get enough right and make enough money on those to offset your losses, you will make money in the long run.

It's not about getting one or two right. It's about executing the strategy with the best odds of winning over and over again and ensuring that your math works out with regards to the relationship between your win rate and average win.

So, it really comes down to finding patterns which repeat themselves over time in the markets. What causes these patterns? Well, the other traders of course! To put it more accurately, the orders that the other traders place in the market are what creates patterns that repeat themselves over time.

The first step to understanding these patterns is to understand what trends and ranges are. Identifying them and learning to spot when they transition into one another will give you a massive leg up not only with your options trading but also with directional trading.

Trends

In theory spotting a trend is simple enough. Look left to right and if the price is headed up or down, it's a trend. Well, sometimes it is really that simple. However, for the majority of the time you have both with and counter-trend forces operating in the market. It is possible to have long counter trend reactions within a larger trend and sometimes, depending on the time frame you're in, these counter-trend reactions take up the majority of your screen space.

Trend vs. Range

This is a chart of the UK100 CFD, which mimics the FTSE 100, on the four-hour time frame. Three-quarters of the chart is a downtrend and the last quarter is a wild uptrend. Using the looking left to right guideline, we'd conclude that this instrument is in a range. Is that really true though?

Just looking at that chart, you can clearly see that short-term momentum is bullish. So, if you were considering taking a trade on this, would you implement a range strategy or a trending one? This is exactly the sort of thing that catches traders up.

The key to deciphering trends is to watch for two things: counter trend participation quality and turning points. Let's tackle counter trend participation first.

Counter Trend Participation

When a new trend begins, the market experiences extremely imbalanced order flow which is tilted towards one side. There's isn't much counter trend participation against this seeming tidal wave of with trend orders. Price marches on without any opposition and experiences only a few hiccups.

As time goes on though, the trend forces run out of steam and have to take breaks to gather themselves. This is where counter trend traders start testing the trend and trying to see how far back into the trend they can go. While it is unrealistic to expect a full reversal at this point, the quality of the correction or pushback tells us a lot about the strength distribution between the with and counter-trend forces. Eventually, the counter-trend players manage to push so far back against the trend that a stalemate results in the market. The counter-trend forces are equally balanced and thus the trend comes to an end. After all, you need an imbalance for the market to tip one way or another and a balanced order flow is only going to result in a sideways market.

While all this is going on behind the scenes, the price chart is what records the push and pull between these two forces. Using the price chart, we can not only anticipate when a trend is coming to an end but also how long it could potentially take before it does. This second factor, which helps us estimate the time it could take, is invaluable from an options perspective, especially if you're using a horizontal spread strategy.

In all cases, the greater the number of them, the greater the counter-trend participation in the market. The closer a trend is to ending, the greater the counter-trend participation. Thus, the minute you begin to see price move into a large, sideways move with an equal number of buyers and sellers in it, you can be sure that some form of redistribution is going on.

Mind you, the trend might continue or reverse. Either way, it doesn't matter. What matters is that you know the trend is weak and that now is probably not the time to be banking on trend strategies.

Starting from the left, we can see that there is close to no counter trend bars, bearish in this case, and the bulls make easy progress. Note the angle with which the bulls proceed upwards.

Then comes the first major correction and the counter-trend players push back against the last third of the bull move. Notice how strong the bearish bars are and note their character compared to the bullish bars.

The bulls recover and push the price higher at the original angle and without any bearish presence, which seems odd. This is soon explained as the bears slam price back down and for a while, it looks as if they've managed to form a V top reversal in the trend, which is an extremely rare occurrence.

The price action that follows is a more accurate reflection of the power in the market, with both bulls and bears sharing chunks of the order flow, with overall order flow in the bull's favor but only just. Price here is certainly in an uptrend but looking at the extent of the bearish pushbacks, perhaps we should be on our guard for a bearish reversal. After all order flow is looking pretty sideways at this point. So how would we approach an options strategy with the chart in the state it is in at the extreme right? Well, for one, any strategy that requires an option beyond the near month is out of the question, given the probability of it turning. Secondly, looking at the order flow, it does seem to be following a channel, doesn't it?

While the channel isn't very clean, if you were aggressive enough, you could consider deploying a collar with the strike prices above and below this channel to take advantage of the price movement. You could also employ some moderately bullish strategies as price approaches the bottom of this channel and figuring out the extent of the bull move is easier thanks to you being able to reference the top of the channel.

As price moves in this channel, it's all well and good. Eventually though, we know that the trend has to flip. How do we know when this happens?

Turning Points

As bulls and bears struggle over who gets to control the order flow, price swings up and down. You will notice that every time price comes back into the 6427-6349 zone, the bulls seem to step in masse and repulse the bears.

This tells us that the bulls are willing to defend this level in large numbers and strongly at that. Given the number of times the bears have tested this level, we can safely assume that above this level, bullish strength is a bit weak. However, at this level, it is as if the bulls have retreated and are treating this as a sort of last resort, for the trend to be maintained. You can see where I'm going with this.

If this level were to be breached by the bears, it is a good bet that a large number of bulls will be taken out. In martial terms, the largest army of bulls has been marshaled at this level. If this force is defeated, it is unlikely that there's going to be too much resistance to the bears below this level.

This zone, in short, is a turning point. If price breaches this zone decisively, we can safely assume that the bears have moved in and control the majority if the order flow.

Turning Point Breached

The decisive turning point zone is marked by the two horizontal lines and the price touches this level twice more and is repulsed by the bulls. Notice how the last bounce before the level breaks produces an extremely weak bullish bounce and price simply caves through this. Notice the strength with which the bears break through.

The FTSE was in a longer uptrend on the weekly chart, so the bulls aren't completely done yet. However, as far as the daily timeframe is concerned, notice how price retests that same level but this time around, it acts as resistance instead of support.

For now, we can conclude that as long as the price remains below the turning point, we are bearishly biased. You can see this by looking at the angle with which bulls push back as well as, the lack of strong bearish participation on the push upwards.

This doesn't mean we go ahead and pencil in a bull move and start implementing strategies that take advantage of the upcoming bullish move. Remember, nothing is for certain in the markets. Don't change your bias or strategy until the turning point decisively breaks.

Some key things to note here are that a turning point is always a major S/R level. It is usually a swing point where a large number of with trend forces gather to support the trend. This will not always be the case, so don't make the mistake of hanging on to older turning points.

The current order flow and price action are what matters the most, so pay attention to that above all else. Also, note how the candles that test this level all have wicks on top of them.

This indicates that the bears are quite strong here and that any subsequent attack will be handled the same way until the level breaks. Do we know when the level will break? Well, we can't say with any accuracy. However, we can estimate the probability of it breaking.

The latest upswing has seen very little bearish pushback, comparatively speaking, and the push into the level is strong. Instinct would say that there's one more rejection left here. However, who knows? Until the level breaks, we stay bearish. When the level breaks, we switch to the bullish side.

Putting it all Together

So now we're ready to put all of this together into one coherent package. Your analysis should always begin with determining the current state of the market. Ranges are pretty straightforward to spot, and they occur either within big pullbacks in trends or at the end of trends.

Chapter 15
Options Trading Strategies

Options Strategies

We are now going to leave the world of selling options and go back to the one that most people are interested in, which is the world of trading options. We are going to have a look at strategies that can be used to increase the odds of profits when trading options. In reality, some of these strategies involve buying and selling options at the same time. Keep in mind that these techniques will require a higher-level designation from your broker. So, it might not be something you can use right away if you are a beginner.

Strangles

One of the simplest strategies that go beyond simply buying options, hoping to profit on moves of the underlying share price, is called a strangle. This strategy involves buying a call option and a put option simultaneously. They will have the same expiration dates, but different strike prices. If the price of the stock rises the put option will expire worthless (but of course it may still hold a small amount of value when you closed your position, and you can sell it and recoup some of the loss). But you will make a profit off the call option. On the other hand, if the stock price declines, the call option will expire worthlessly, but you can make a profit from the put option.

In this case, you can make substantial profits no matter which way the stock moves, but the larger the move, the more profits. On the upside, the profit potential is theoretically unlimited. On the downside, the stock could theoretically fall to zero, so there is a limit, but potential gains are substantial.

The breakeven price on the upside is the strike price of the call plus the amount of the two premiums settled for the options.

If the stock price declines the breakeven price would be the difference between the strike value of the put option and the sum of the two premiums paid for the options.

Straddles

When you purchase a call and a put option with similar strike amounts and expiration dates, this is called a straddle. The idea here is that the trader is hoping the share price will either rise or fall by a significant amount. It won't matter which way the price moves. Again, if the price rises the put option will expire worthless, if the price falls the call option will expire worthlessly. For example, suppose a stock is trading at $100 a share. We can buy at the money call and put options that expire in 30 days. The price of the call and put options would be $344 and $342 respectively, for a total investment of $686.

With 20 days left to expiration, suppose the share price rises to $107. Then the call is priced at $766, and the put is at $65. We can sell them both at this time, for $831 and make a profit of $145.

Suppose that, instead of at 20 days to expiration, the share price dropped to $92. In that case, the call is priced at $39, and the put is priced at $837. We can sell them for $876, making a profit of $190.

So, although the profits are modest compared to a situation where we had speculated correctly on the directional move of the stock and bought only calls or puts, this way we profit no matter which way the share price moves. The downside to this strategy is that the share price may not move in a big enough way to make profits possible. Remember that extrinsic value will be declining for both the call and the put options.

Selling covered calls against LEAPS and other LEAPS Strategies

A LEAP is a long-term option that is an option that expires at a date that is two years in the future. They are regular options otherwise, but you can do some interesting things with LEAPS. Because the expiration date is so far away, they cost a lot more. Looking at Apple, call options with a $195 strike price that expires in two years are selling for $28.28 (for a total price of $2,828). While that seems expensive, consider that 100 shares of Apple would cost $19,422 at the time of writing.

If you buy in the money LEAPS, then you can use them to sell covered calls. This is an interesting strategy that lets you earn premium income without having actually to buy the shares of stock. LEAPS can also be used for other investing strategies. For example, if Apple is trading at $194, we can buy a LEAP option for $3,479 with a strike price of $190 that expires in two years. If, at some point during that two-year period, the share price rose to $200 we could exercise the option and buy the shares at $190, saving $10 a share. Also, at the same time, we could have been selling covered calls against the LEAPS.

Buying Put Options as Insurance

A put option gives you the right to sell shares of stock at a certain price. Suppose that you wanted to ensure your investment in Apple stock, and you had purchased 100 shares at $191 a share, for a total investment of $19,000. You are worried that the share price is going to drop and so you could buy a put option as a kind of insurance. Looking ahead, you see a put option with a $190 strike price for $4.10. So, you spend $410 and buy the put option.

Should the price of Apple shares suddenly tumble you could exercise your right under the put option to dispose of your shares by selling at the strike price to minimize your losses. Suppose you wake up one morning and the share price has dropped to $170 for some reason. Had you not bought the option you could have tried to get rid of your shares now and take a loss of $21 a share. But, since you bought the put option, you can sell your shares for $190 a share. That is a $1 loss since you purchased the shares at $191. However, you also have to take into account the premium paid for the put options contract, which was $4.10. So, your total loss would be $5.10 a share, but that is still less than the loss of $21 a share that you would have suffered selling the shares on the market at the $170 price. When investors buy stock and a put at the same time, it is called a married put.

Spreads

Spreads involve buying and selling options simultaneously. This is a more complicated options strategy that is only used by advanced traders. You will have to get a high-level designation with your brokerage in order to use this type of strategy. We won't go into details because these methods are beyond the scope of junior options traders, but we will briefly mention some of the more popular methods so that you can have some awareness.

One of the interesting things about spreads is they can be used by level 3 traders to earn a regular income from options. If you think the price of a stock is going to stay the same or rise, you sell a put credit spread. You sell a higher-priced option and buy a lower-priced option at the same time. The difference in option prices is your profit. There is a chance of loss if the price drops to the strike price of the puts (and you could get assigned if it goes below the strike price of the put option you sold). You can buy back the spread, in that case, to avoid getting assigned.

If you think that the price of a stock is going to drop you can sell to open a credit spread. In this case, you are hoping the price of the stock is going to stay the same or drop. You sell a call with a low strike price and buy a call with a high strike price (both out of the money). The difference in price is your profit, and losses are capped.

We can also consider more complicated spreads.

For example, you can use a diagonal spread with calls. This means you buy a call that has a shorter expiration date but a strike amount that is higher, and then you sell a call with a longer expiration date and a lower strike price. This is done in such a way that you earn more, from selling the call, than you spend on buying the call for a considerable strike amount, and so you get a net credit to your account.

Spreads can become quite complicated, and there are many different types of spreads. If a trader thinks that the price of a stock will only go up a small amount, they can do a bull call spread. Profit and loss are capped in this case. The two options would have the same expiration date.

If you sell a call with a lower strike price and simultaneously buy a call with a high strike price, this is called a bear call spread. You seek to profit if the underlying stock drops in price. This can also be done by using two put options. In that case, you buy a put option that has a higher strike and sell a put option with a lower strike price.

A bull spread involves attempting to profit when the price of the stock rises by a small amount. In this case, you can also use either two call options or two put options. You buy an option with a lower strike price while selling an option with a higher strike price.

Spreads can be combined in more complicated ways. An iron butterfly combines a bear call spread with a bear put spread. The purpose of doing this is to generate steady income while minimizing the risk of loss.

An iron condor uses a put spread, and a call spread together. There would be four options simultaneously, with the same expiration dates but different strike prices. It involves selling both sides (calls and puts).

Chapter 16
Application on the Futures Market

W hat actually happens when you buy futures? – is actually one of the most frequent questions in relation to futures trading. The answer to this question can be summarized in a sentence that states: when you buy futures, you are actually accepting to buy products or services that the company from which you bought futures has not produced yet.

In comparison to stock trading, futures trading is much riskier because you deal with products and services that are not yet produced. With such characteristics, future trading is very popular not only among the producing companies and individuals and customers but also among speculators as well.

While stocks or shares are being traded on stock markets, futures are being traded on futures markets. The idea of future markets developed from the needs of agricultural producers in the mid-nineteenth century where often happened that the demand was much bigger than supply.

The difference between the futures markets and futures markets today is that today's futures markets have crossed the borders of agricultural production and entered many other sectors such as financial. As such, future markets today are used for buying and selling currencies as well as some other financial instruments. What future markets made possible is the opportunity for a farmer to be able to participate in the goods with customers on the other end of the world. One of the biggest and most important future markets is the International Monetary Market (IMM) that was established in 1972.

Futures are financial derivatives that obtain their value from the movement in the price of another asset. It means that the price of futures is not dependent on its inherent value, but on the price of the asset, the futures contract is tracking.

One of the advantages of the futures market is that is centralized and that people from around the world electronically are able to make future contracts. These futures contracts will specify the price of the merchandise and the time of delivery. Besides that, every future contract contains information about the quality and the quantity of the sold goods, specific price and the method in which the goods are to be delivered to the buyers.

A person who buys or sells a futures contract does not pay for the whole value of the contract. He pays a small upfront fee to trigger an open position. For example, if the value of the futures contract is $350,000 when the S&P 500 is 1400, he only pays $21,875 as its initial margin. The exchange sets this margin and may change anytime.

If the S&P 500 moved up to 1500, the futures contract will be worth $375,000. Thus, the person will earn $25,000 in profit. However, if the index fell to 1390 from its original 1400, he will lose $2,500 because the futures contract will now be worth $347,500. This $2,500 is not a realized loss yet. The broker will also not require the individual to add more cash to his trading account.

However, if the index fell to 1300, the futures contract will be worth $325,000. The individual loses $50,000. The broker will require him to add more money to his trading account because his initial margin of $21,875 is no longer enough to cover his losses.

Futures Market Categories

There are similarities in all futures contracts. However, each contract may track different assets. As such, it is important to study the various markets that exist.

You can trade futures contracts on different categories and assets. However, if you are still a new trader, it is important to trade assets that you know. For example, if you are into stock trading for a few years already, you must start with futures contracts using stock indexes. This way, you won't have a hard time understanding the underlying asset. You only need to understand how the futures market works.

After choosing a category, decide on the asset that you want to trade. For example, you want to trade futures contracts in the energy category. Focus on coal, natural gas, crude oil or heating oil. The markets trade at various levels, so you must understand relevant things, like the nuances, liquidity, margin requirements, contract sizes and volatility. Do the necessary research before trading in futures contracts.

Types of Trade

A basis trade allows you to go long or short on a futures contract and go short or long on the cash market. It is a wager that the difference in price between the two markets will fluctuate. For example, you decide to buy a 10-year US Treasury bond futures then sell a physical 10-year US Treasury bond.

A spread trade allows you to go short and long on two futures contracts. It is a wager that the difference in price between the futures contracts will change. For example, you buy an S&P 500 futures contract for August delivery and sell an S&P 500 futures contract for November delivery.

A hedging trade allows you to sell a futures contract to offset a position you hold in the current market. For example, a stock trader does not want to sell his shares for tax reasons. However, he is fearful of a sharp decline in the stock market so he sells S&P 500 futures contract as a hedge.

An important issue that must be mention in regards to futures and futures contracts is the notion of prices and the limits of future contracts. In future contracts, prices are expressed in classical currencies such as US dollars. The prices in the aspect of future contracts also have the minimum amount of money for which the price of the product may go up or go down. This minimum in the context of futures contracts is referred to as "ticks".

These tricks are very important for an investor who is investing huge sums of money or is buying a huge number of products because the fluctuation of prices can have enormous influence on the amount of money spent on certain products. It must also be noted that these "ticks" are not the same for each merchandise. Every commodity in the trading of futures has its own "ticks", the minimum for price fluctuation and it depends on the type of commodity.

How Can We Make a Profit on the Futures Markets?

One thing to remember, is, that even if you buy and sell futures contracts in commodities, you don't actually take delivery of the underlying commodity. You would close out your contracts before the delivery date.

Let's take a simple example and relate that to a futures contract. You saw a house for sale for $300 000. You believe that in the next year its value will appreciate by about 10% but the downside is you don't have enough money to buy the house outright so you decide to put down a deposit of $30 000. One year later the property has appreciated in value, as expected, by 10% and is now worth $330 000. You decide to sell the property and make a profit of $30 000. Your initial investment was $30 000 and you sold the house at a profit of $30 000, which gives you a 100% profit on your investment.

Commodity trading works very similarly. Let's take an example. You've been analyzing the corn market and you expect the prices to increase, so you decide to buy the September contract which is presently trading at $2.40 per bushel. There are 5000 bushels in a corn contract. You pay a $500 deposit or margin as required by the exchange.

After four weeks the price has increased to $3.40 a bushel, as expected. This means the contract value is now $3.40 X 5000 = $17000. You bought the contract at $12000 ($2.40 X 5000) four weeks ago and you made a profit of $5000 ($17000 -$14000). The return on your investment of $500 is 1000% in just 4 weeks.

You can also make profits when market prices drop. Let's say you anticipate a drop in the soybeans price from its current level of $5.00 per bushel. There are also 5000 bushels in a soybean contract. You decide to sell one September contract at the current level. You pay a $1000 deposit or margin. Six weeks later the price has dropped considerably, as expected, to $3.50 per bushel. You decide to close your position and take your profits. You do this by buying a contract to offset the contract you sold six weeks earlier. The difference between the price you sold and the price bought back is your profit. $25000($5.00 X 5000) − $17500($3.5 X 5000) = $7500 profit for an investment of $1000. 750% profit in six weeks.

Selling Short - How does it work?

How can one make money when the market is dropping? This is something that happens around us every day of our lives. Let's say you are a car dealer and you sell brand new cars. The factory-supplied you with a couple of cars on consignment that you can display on your showroom floor and you don't have to pay for them right away because the factory allows you some time to sell them. After a while, you sell one of the cars for $50 000 and now you have to pay the factory, but only $30 000, which is the cost price to you that leaves you with a profit of $20 000. What did you actually do? You borrowed the car from the factory and sold it to your client at a higher price than the factory charges you and that way you made money. You sold first and bought it later. When we sell futures we do the same thing, we sell high because we anticipate the market will trade down and we can buy back or close our position at a lower price and make a profit. Just like the car dealer.

There Must Be Risks?

With any business you have risks. When you open a business you have to invest huge amounts of capital upfront to set up your business. You have to rent offices, buy stock and pay salaries, etc. before the first customer walks through your door. You have no idea how many customers will walk in or whether you will generate enough business to even recover your capital expenses. With the speculative markets it's the same but how you manage your risk will determine your success.

Let's compare the stock market with the futures market, you can diversify your risk in the stock market by investing in different non-correlated stock and under normal circumstances it will work well but sudden political changes or news regarding the economy can affect all share prices overnight, even if you did spread your investments across a number of companies, all your profits can be wiped in extreme situations, as we have seen in recent years.

Comparing this to futures markets where you can spread your investments across a diverse range of commodity markets like corn, silver, oil, sugar, wheat or cotton, it's impossible to imagine any situation affecting all these markets at the same time. Economic disasters, droughts, war, floods, and political events will always happen and they also affect certain commodity markets, but spreading your investment not only minimizes your losses but also puts you in a position to benefit from any price move.

Chapter 17
Which Market to Trade and with which Broker

here is a huge array of products to trade with on offer but for scalping you need products with large volumes exchanged and volatility. I find these in the mini DAX and the e-mini Dow futures. The volatility, *i.e.* daily range (distance between the low of the day and the high of the day) is wide. In addition, and this point is very important, these products are traded on regulated and centralized markets: Eurex for the DAX futures and CME for the e-mini Dow; as opposed to CFDs which are OTC products; *i.e.* your broker is the counterpart of your trade. When you buy, your broker is your seller and when you sell, your broker is buying from you. On the other hand, on a centralized market, your order is routed and executed when someone else's order matches yours (buyers' and sellers' prices meet). In addition, on the future markets you can see the volume of transactions, while on the CFD, your broker may show no volume at all or only the volumes exchanged on their platform.

And more importantly, in the future markets you see the prices offered by other market participants while on CFDs, you only get the prices offered by your broker. To illustrate, this I have just taken below a snapshot of prices offered by two different CFD brokers at the same time.

Ticket order

Which broker offers the right price?
In case of high volatility, CFDs do not react the same way as futures: the prices may adjust at a different pace and the spread offered by

the broker may increase. A market order may even be repriced if the market is moving very quickly. Stop orders may incur slippage which means you will lose few points to your broker as the price you are paid is few points away from your stop order.

I like to compare CFDs and futures to the current trends in grocery consumption. People like to consume fresh products that come directly from the farm, without any middlemen and wholesalers that make their margin in the process. Well, trading futures is similar. You get the prices directly from the market while CFDs are products offered by your broker who gets their revenue through the spreads. Moreover, CFD providers hedge their positions or some part of them using futures and options.

So, I can only recommend that you trade with future or mini future contracts. However, CFDs can be useful to trade small positions when you make your first steps in trading as you can trade products at only one euro per point instead of 5 euros on a mini future contract or even 25 euros per points on the DAX future. Note that CFDs are not available in all countries due to local laws and financial regulation.

But if you can and want to trade CFDs, make sure you look at the spreads offered by different brokers before choosing who to trade with. Half a point is not much difference, but in scalping it means a lot. After 20 trades, paying half a point more on each trade at one euro per point will result in an extra 10 euros wasted in commissions; and so on, after 40 trades, you will have wasted 20 euros. Let's say in a month if you perform 600 to 800 trades, you will then have wasted 300 to 400 euros in extra commissions.

How to choose your broker:

In order to be able to scalp in good conditions, you need to look out for the following points when choosing your broker:

- Tight spreads if you choose to work with CFDs. One euro or dollar per point is the maximum you should pay as you don't want to be working just for your broker;
- Real time data flux is essential. The subscription to the Eurex data flux (DAX and mini DAX) will cost you about 20 euros per month and another 25 euros for a

subscription to CME CBOT (e-mini Dow) data. Your broker collects the fees for the data supplier; you don't need to pay the supplier directly. If you just want to trade CFDs you won't have to pay these fees, but you will have only access to the data provided by your broker.

- Most of the platforms will let you place simple orders such as buy limit or sell limit orders, with the option to set up an automated take profit and stop loss orders. But some go even further by letting you set up an automated order for part of the position and another one for the second part of the position and so on if you want to set up 3 different targets. I

- Be aware that some brokers operate with a first in first out rule which means that they won't let you have opposite positions on the same product run separately, a.k.a. hedging. A new executed sell order may not open a position but offset or close an already opened buy position. On the other hand, CFD brokers may let you trade, hedge and operate your positions separately from one another. While short and long positions of equivalent quantities and on the same product offset each other in theory, your broker may still calculate a margin cover for each position separately. So, keep an eye on your margin usage.

- If you are starting with a small account, *i.e.* with less than € 5,000 look for brokers that will let you trade on small quantities, as small as 1/100th of one lot. That way you can start trading taking minimum risk until you build confidence in your trading.

- Being able to trade from a smartphone, an iPad or similar. I certainly cannot recommend that you use these devices for your scalping, but they shall be used as part of plan B if a problem comes up with your computer while you are trading or if your internet broadband suddenly shuts down or resets itself. Your smartphone connected to a mobile phone network will be your back up device to modify or close some orders if necessary, until your computer and the internet are back up and running. Most brokers offer mobile technology in today's world.

- This was the plan B. The plan C is that you should be able to call your broker's trading desk as a last resort, in case of emergency, if your computer and your mobile application don't let you perform an action that needs to be done.

- Lastly, you absolutely need to work with a minimum of two brokers because if for any reason there is a technical problem on one of your brokers' platforms, you need to able to act swiftly on your second broker's platform. Let's say you need to close a position but broker A's platform for some reason is not working. Then you can always open an opposite order on broker's B platform. For instance, you need to close a long position with broker A, but a technical problem doesn't let you do so. Then you should open a short position with broker B, until everything is back up and running. Then you can work on closing these positions simultaneously afterwards.

Once you are ready to trade with the mini futures, I recommend that you have at least 12,000 euros to be able to scalp with 2 lots when the occasion occurs. For the most accurate information, choose the tick by tick data flux if you can choose a data provider. Some data providers offer market data sent to your computer on a second by second basis while others have their data refreshed on a tick by tick basis, which is every time a transaction occurs on the market, showing you the latest price exchanged.

You may want to explore and trade some additional markets, but I recommend not trading more than two markets at a time because scalping requires concentration and prompt action in your trades.

Chapter 18
Application on the Stocks Market

A stock is a form of security that suggests proportional ownership in a company. Stocks are acquired and sold predominantly on stock exchanges, however, there can be private arrangements as well. These exchanges/trades need to fit within government laws which are expected to shield investors from misleading practices. Stocks can be obtained from a large number of online platforms. Businesses issue (offer) stock to raise capital. The holder of stock (a shareholder) has now acquired a portion of the company and share its profit and loss. Therefore, a shareholder is considered an owner of the company. Ownership is constrained by the amount of shares an individual owns in regard to the amount of shares the company is divided into. For example, if a company has 1,000 shares of stock and one individual owns 100 shares, that individual would receive 10% of the company's capital and profits.

Financial experts don't own companies as such; instead, they sell shares offered by companies. Under the law, there are different types of companies and some are viewed as independent because of how they have set up their businesses. Regardless of the type of company, ultimately, they must report costs, income, changes in structure, etc., or they can be sued. A business set up as an "independent," known as a sole proprietorship, suggests that the owner assumes all responsibilities and is liable for all financial aspects of the business. A business set up as a company of any sort means that the business is separate from its owners and the owners aren't personally responsible for the financial aspects of the business.

This separation is of extreme importance; it limits the commitment of both the company and the shareholder/owner. If the business comes up short, a judge may rule for the company to be liquidated – however, your very own assets will not come under threat. The court can't demand that you sell your shares, though the value of your shares will have fallen significantly.

Trading is the basic idea of exchanging one thing for another. In this regard it is buying or selling, where compensation is paid by a buyer to a seller. Trade can happen inside an economy among sellers and buyers. Overall, trade allows countries to develop markets for the exchange of goods and services that for the most part wouldn't have been available otherwise. It is the reason why an American purchaser can choose between a Japanese, German, or American conduit. Due to overall trade, the market contains progressively significant competition which makes it possible for buyers to get products and services at affordable costs.

In fiscal markets, trading implies the buying and selling of insurances, for instance, the purchase of stock on the New York Stock Exchange (NYSE).

Fundamentals of stock/securities exchange

The exchange of stocks and securities happen on platforms like the New York Stock Exchange and Nasdaq. Stocks are recorded on a specific exchange, which links buyers and sellers, allowing them to trade those stocks. The trade is tracked in the market and allows buyers to get company stocks at fair prices. The value of these stocks move – up or down – depending on many factors in the market. Investors are able to look at these factors and make a decision on whether or not they want to purchase these stocks.

A market record tracks the value of a stock, which either addresses the market with everything taken into account or a specific fragments of the market. You're likely going to hear most about the S&P 500, the Nasdaq composite and the Dow Jones Industrial Average in this regard.

Financial advisors use data to benchmark the value of their own portfolios and, some of the time, to shed light on their stock exchanging decisions. You can also put your assets into an entire portfolio based on the data available in the market.

Stock exchanging information

Most financial experts would be well-taught to build a portfolio with a variety of different financial assets. However, experts who prefer a greater degree of movement take more interest in stock exchanging. This type of investment incorporates the buying and selling of stocks. The goal of people who trade in stock is to use market data and things happening in the market to either sell stock for a profit, or buy stocks at low prices to make a profit later. Some stock traders are occasional investors, which means they buy and sell every now and then. Others are serious investors, making as little as twelve exchanges for every month.

Financial experts who exchange stocks do wide research, as often as possible, devoting hours day by day tracking the market. They rely upon particular audits, using instruments to chart a stock's advancements attempting to find trading openings and examples. Various online middlemen offer stock exchanging information, including expert reports, stock research, and charting tools.

What is a bear market?

A bear market means stock prices are falling — limits move to 20% or more — based on data referenced previously.

Progressive financial experts may be alright with the term bear market. Profiting in the trade business will always far outlasts the typical bear market; which is why in a bear market, smart investors will hold their shares until the market recovers. This has been seen time and time again. The S&P 500, which holds around 500 of the greatest stocks in the U.S., has consistently maintained an average of around 7% consistently, when you factor in reinvested profits and varied growth. That suggests that if you invested $1,000 30 years ago, you could have around $7,600 today.

Stock market crash versus correction

A crash happens when the commercial value prices fall by 10% or more. It is an unexpected, incredibly sharp fall in stock prices; for example, in October 1987, when stocks dove 23% in a single day.

The stock market tends to be affected longer by crashes in the market and can last from two to nine years.

The criticalness of improvement

You can't avoid the possibility of bear markets or the economy crashing, or even losing money while trading. What you can do, however, is limit the effects these types of market will have on your investment by maintaining a diversified portfolio.

Diversification shields your portfolio from unavoidable market risks. If you dump a large portion of your cash into one means of investment, you're betting on growth that can rapidly turn to loss by a large number of factors.

To cushion risks, financial specialists expand by pooling different types of stocks together, offsetting the inevitable possibility that one stock will crash and your entire portfolio will be affected or you lose everything.

You can put together individual stocks and assets in a single portfolio. One recommendation: dedicate 10% or less of your portfolio to a few stocks you believe in each time you decide to invest.

Ways to invest

There are different ways for new investors to purchase stocks. If you need to pay very low fees, you will need to invest additional time making your own trades. If you wish to beat the market, however, you'll pay higher charges by getting someone to trade on your behalf. If you don't have the time or interest, you may need to make do with lower results.

Most stock purchasers get anxious when the market is doing well. Incredibly, this makes them purchase stocks when they are the most volatile. Obviously, business share that is not performing well triggers fear. That makes most investors sell when the costs are low.

Choosing what amount to invest is an individual decision. It depends upon your comfort with risk. It depends upon your ability and capacity to invest energy into getting some answers concerning the stock exchange.

Purchase Stocks Online

Purchasing stocks online costs the least, yet gives little encouragement. You are charged a set price, or a percent of your purchase, for every trade. It very well may be the least secure. It expects you to teach yourself altogether on the best way to invest. Consequently, it additionally takes the most time. It's a smart idea to check the top web based trading sites before you begin.

Investment Groups

Joining an investment group gives you more data at a sensible price. However, it takes a great deal of effort to meet with the other group members. They all have different degrees of expertise. You might be required to pool a portion of your assets into a group account before trading. Once more, it's a smart idea to examine the better investment groups before you begin.

Full-time Brokers

A full-time broker is costly on the grounds that you'll pay higher fees. Nevertheless, you get more data and assistance and that shields you from greed and fear. You should search around to choose a decent broker that you can trust. The Securities and Trade Commission shares helpful tips on the best ways to choose a broker.

Money Manager

Money managers select and purchase the stocks for you. You pay them a weighty charge, typically 1-2 percent of your complete portfolio. If the chief progresses admirably, it takes minimal amount of time. That is on the grounds that you can simply meet with them more than once per year. Ensure you realize how to choose a decent financial advisor.

File Fund

Otherwise called market traded assets, record assets can be a cheap and safe approach to benefit from stocks. They essentially track the stocks in a file. Models incorporate the MSCI developing business sector record. The reserve rises and falls alongside the file. There is no yearly cost. However, it's difficult to outflank the market along these lines since record supports just track the market. All things being equal, there are a great deal of valid justifications why you ought to put resources into a file funds.

Common Funds

Common assets are a generally more secure approach to benefit from stocks. The company supervisor will purchase a gathering of stocks for you. You don't possess the stock, yet a portion of the investment. Most assets have a yearly cost, between 0.5 percent to 3 percent. They guarantee to outflank the S&P 500, or other equivalent file reserves. For additional information, see 16 Best Tips on Mutual Fund Basics and Before You Buy a Mutual Fund.

Theories of stock investments

Theories of stock investments look like basic resources. Both of them pool all of their investors' dollars into one viably supervised hold. In any case, theories stock investments put assets into ensnared fiscal instruments known as subordinates. They guarantee to win the normal resources with these significantly used theories.

Theoretical stock investments are private companies, not open organizations. That suggests they aren't coordinated by the SEC. They are risky, yet various investors acknowledge this higher danger prompts a better yield.

Selling Your Stocks

As important as buying stocks is knowing when to sell them. Most financial experts buy when the stock exchange is rising and sell when it's falling. Regardless, a clever money marketer seeks after a strategy subject to their financial needs.

You should reliably watch out for the noteworthy market records. The three greatest U.S. records are the Dow Jones Industrial Average, the S&P 500, and the Nasdaq. In any case, don't solidify in case they enter a modification or a mishap. Those events don't prop up long.

Chapter 19
How Does The Stock Market Work?

T he stock market is not like your neighborhood grocery store: you can only buy and sell through licensed brokers who make trades on major indexes like NASDAQ and S&P 100. This is where investors meet up to buy and sell stocks or other financial investments like bonds. The stock market is made up of so many exchanges, like the NASDAQ or the New York Exchange. These exchanges are not open all through the day. Most exchanges like the NASDAQ and NYSE are open from 9:30 am to 4 pm. EST. Although premarket and trading after closing time now exist, not all brokers do this.

Companies list their stocks on an exchange in a bid to raise money for their business, and investors buy those shares. In addition to this, investors can trade shares among themselves, and the exchange keeps track of the rate of supply and demand of each listed stock. The rate of supply and demand for stocks determines the price. If there's a high demand for a particular stock, its price tends to rise. On the other hand, the price of a stock goes down when there's less demand for it. The stock market computer algorithm handles these varying fluctuations in prices.

How Does The Stock Market Work?

A Stock market analysis definitely looks like gibberish to beginners and average investors. However, you should know that the way this market works is actually quite simple. Just imagine a typical auction house or an online auction website. This market works in the same way - it allows buyers and sellers to negotiate prices and carry out successful trades. The first stock market took place in a physical marketplace, however, these days, trades happen electronically via the internet and online stockbrokers. From the comfort of your homes, you can easily bid and negotiate for the prices of stocks with online stockbrokers.

Furthermore, you might come across news headlines that say the stock market has crashed or gone up. Once again, don't fret or get all excited when you come across such news. Most often than not, this means a stock market index has gone up or down. In other words, the stocks in a market index have gone down. Before we proceed, let's explore the meaning of market indexes.

Stock Market Indexes

Market indexes track the performance of a group of stocks in a particular sector like manufacturing or technology. The value of the stocks featured in an index is representative of all the stocks in that sector. It is very important to take note of what stocks each market index represents. In addition to this, giant market indexes like the Dow Jones Industrial Average, the NASDAQ composite, and the Standard & Poor's 500, are often used as proxies for the performance of the stock market as a whole. You can choose to invest in an entire index through the exchange-traded funds and index funds, as it can track a specific sector or index of the stock market.

Bullish and Bearish Markets

Talking about the bullish outlook of the stock market is guaranteed to get beginners looking astonished. Yes, it sounds ridiculous at first, but with time, you get to appreciate the ingenuity of these descriptions. Let's start with the bearish market. A bear is an animal you would never want to meet on a hike; it strikes fear into your heart, and that's the effect you will get from a bearish market. The threshold for a bearish market varies within a 20 percent loss or more. Most young investors unfamiliar with a bear market as we've been in a bull market since the first quarter of 2019. In fact, this makes it the second-longest bull market in history. Just as you have probably guessed by now, a bull market indicates that stock prices are rising. You should know that the market is continually changing from bull to bear and vice versa. From the Great Recession to the global market crash, these changing market prices indicate the start of larger economic patterns. For instance, a bull market shows that investors are investing heavily and that the economy is doing extremely well. On the other hand, a bear market shows investors are scared and pulling back, with the economy on the brink of collapsing. If this made you paranoid about the next bear market, don't fret. Business analysts have shown that the average bull market generally outlasts the average bear market by a large margin. This is why you can grow your money in stocks over an extended period of time.

Stock Market Corrections and Crash

A stock market crash is every investor's nightmare. It is usually extremely difficult to watch stocks that you've spent so many years accumulating diminish before your very eyes. Yes, this is how volatile the stock market is. Stock market crashes usually include a very sudden and sharp drop in stock prices, and it might herald the beginning of a bear market. On the other hand, stock market corrections occur when the market drops by 10 percent - this is just the market's way of balancing itself. The current bull market has gone through 5 market corrections.

Analyzing the Stock Market

You are not psychic. It is nearly impossible to accurately predict the outcome of your stock to the last detail. However, you can become near perfect at reading the stock market by learning how to properly analyze the components of this market. There are two basic types of analyses: technical analysis and fundamental analysis.

Fundamental Market Analysis

Fundamental analysis involves getting data about a company's stocks or a particular sector in the stock market, via financial records, company assets, economic reports, and market share. Analysts and investors can conduct fundamental analysis via the metrics on a corporation's financial statement. These metrics include cash flow statements, balance sheet statements, footnotes, and income statements. Most times, you can get a company's financial statement through a 10-k report in the database. In addition to this, the SEC's EDGAR is a good place to get the financial statement of the company you are interested in. With the financial statement, you can deduce the revenues, expenses, and profits a company has made.

What's more? By looking at the financial statement, you will have a measure of a company's growth trajectory, leverage, liquidity, and solvency. Analysts utilize different ratios to make an accurate prediction about stocks. For example, the quick ratio and current ratio are useful in determining if a company will be able to pay its short-term liabilities with the current asset. If the current ratio is less than 1, the company is in poor financial health and may not be able to recover from its short-term debt. Here's another example: a stock analyst can use the debt ratio to measure the current level of debt taken on by the company. If the debt ratio is above 1, it means the company has more debt than assets and it's only a matter of time before it goes under.

Technical Market Analysis

This is the second part of stock market analysis and it revolves around studying past market actions to predict the stock price direction. Technical analysts put more focus on the price and volume of shares. Additionally, they analyze the market as a whole and study the supply and demand factors that dictate market movement. In technical analyses, charts are of inestimable value. Charts are a vital tool as they show the graphical representation of a stock's trend within a set time frame. What's more? Technical investors are able to identify and mark certain areas as resistance or support levels on a chart. The resistance level is a previous high stock price before the current price. On the other hand, support levels are represented by a previous low before the current stock price. Therefore, a break below the support levels marks the beginning of a bearish trend. Alternatively, a break above the resistance level marks the beginning of a bullish market trend. Technical analysis is only effective when the rise and fall of stock prices are influenced by supply and demand forces. However, technical analysis is mostly rendered ineffective in the face of outside forces that affect stock prices such as stock splits, dividend announcements, scandals, changes in management, mergers, and so on. Investors can make use of both types of analyses to get an accurate prediction of their stock values.

Why You Need To Diversify

According to research by Ned Davis, a bear market occurs every 3.5 years and has an average lifespan of 15 months. One thing is clear, though: you can't avoid bear markets. You can, however, avoid the risks that come with investing in a single investment portfolio. Let's look at a common mistake that new investors typically make. Research points to the fact that individual stocks dwindle to a loss of 100 percent. By throwing in your lot with one company, you are exposing yourself to many setbacks. For example, you can lose your money if a corporation is embroiled in a scandal, poor leadership, and regulatory issues. So, how can you balance out your losses? By investing in therefore mentioned index fund or ETF fund, as these indexes hold many different stocks, as by doing this, you've automatically diversified your investment. Here's a nugget to cherish: put 90 percent of your investment funds in an index fund, and put the remaining 10 percent in an individual stock that you trust.

When to Sell Your Stocks

One thing is sure - you are not going to hold your stocks forever. All our investment advice and energies are directed towards buying. Yes, it is the buying of stocks that kick-start the whole investment when chasing your dream concept. However, just as every beginning has an end, you will eventually sell every stock you buy. It is the natural order. Even so, selling off stock is not an easy decision. Heck! It's even harder to determine the right time to sell. This is the point where greed and human emotions start to battle with pragmatism. Many investors try to make sensible selling decisions solely based on price movements. However, this is not a sure strategy, as it is still sensible to hold onto a stock that has fallen in value. Conversely, selling a stock when it has reached your target is seen as prudent. So, how can you navigate around this dilemma?

Why Selling Is So Hard

Do you know why it's so hard to let go of your stocks even when you have a fixed strategy to follow? The answer lies in human greed. When making decisions, it's an innate human tendency to be greedy.

Chapter 20
Application on the Forex Market

Trading Platforms

If there's something essentially needed to trade Forex, it is a trading platform! If you are assuming that trading is ideal for absolute beginners, I'd say yes, but you are not going to make millions overnight. If you look at Forex trading like gambling, you will not be able to become a profitable trader because greed will invade you. If you want to become a great trader, you must have skills and patience. Also, you must keep practicing trading as it helps to shape up your trading style into a better version. Once you do your homework, you'd feel as if you are good to go. But then, Forex trading knowledge can't be accumulated into a few pages or days. It is a continuous learning process. If you have just started with the basics of Forex trading, you have a lot more to learn. A beginner should have access to a user-friendly platform that can be easily handled when trading.

A beginner's journey is already complex, so when the trader doesn't select the right platform, the difficulties increase. When the trading platform is easy to understand, you will not have difficulties when trying out new strategies and techniques on the demo account. There are many reliable brokers that you can select when you are trading Forex, but the problem is finding the ideal broker. To earn extra income, Forex is a good choice. But it doesn't mean Forex can be traded as the main source of income. However, either main income or part-time income, you must find the ideal broker and an excellent platform to keep going in trading. Even though there are many good brokers, you must do your research to find the right one that offers the most straightforward trading platform. I know, you will encounter difficulties when selecting the right broker, so let me help you.

Before you settle for an ideal platform check whether the platform is reliable; it is one of the most crucial factors that you must consider when selecting a trading platform. You don't want to lose all the money that you collected, so make sure to find a platform that you can rely on. If you're going to deposit and withdraw your cash without facing any issues, the trading platform must be reliable.

Another important factor is charges related to the platform. You must consider the charges because your profits will disappear even before you know it if the charges are high. Besides, you are just starting your journey so your income will not be massive. The smaller income that you gain must be protected, so for that, you must consider the charges related to the trading platform.

You must next consider the licensing factor of the Forex platforms. If the relevant authorities monitor the platform, they are unlikely to fool you. The trading platforms will work according to terms and conditions, so you don't have to worry when you are trading through it. But to find whether the platform is licensed, you must do some research even if it is tough. Along with these, you must consider the simplicity in the Forex trading platform, but due to the software used, eventually, almost all the trading platforms have become easier to handle. In the meantime, don't forget to consider the leverage, margin, and other requirements that generally should be considered when selecting a trading platform. Once you select the ideal platform, you will be able to trade in a hassle-free way. However, there's more to learn about Forex trading platforms. So, keep reading!

There are two types of platforms, such as commercial and prop platforms. Before you pick any, you must ensure to understand the types in detail. Thus, prop platforms are designed by Forex brokers, and specialized companies develop commercial platforms. However, there are unique features for both the trading platforms. Even though the prop platforms are considerable, there are times when you might want to change the broker. But when you try to do it, you have to learn the new platform from scratch.

Basically, prop platforms are not suitable for naïve traders because you might have to struggle a lot to understand the sophisticated features. But, why do these trading platforms include complex features? Well, a Forex broker's main duty is not to create and manage trading platforms. Hence, they don't spend much time to introduce better trading tools and features to prop platforms. For example, if you consider Aplari or FXCM you might find it difficult to handle because brokers develop these. Beginners like you need a lot of time to get adjusted with the trading platform. But, I don't say trade execution speed is terrible because it is excellent in prop platforms, yet beginners will have a tough time understanding this platform.

So, beginners like you can consider the platforms designed by professional companies. One of the most common trading software is Metatrader. This is a user-friendly and high standard platform that you can consider even if you don't have experience. But if you are looking for a platform that includes broker feeds, then this is not going to help because the commercial platform has poor customization. These companies sell commercial platforms to Forex brokers so the benefits may be biased towards the broker, but not the trader. Yet, as beginners, you are not going to find anything better than commercial platforms because they are extremely user-friendly and flexible.

So that's about the types of platforms that you will come across. But, I'm pretty sure you'll have some doubts related to selecting the right trading platform. Hence, I'll solve some of the common questions below.

What to consider when selecting the right platform?

You already know this, yet let me provide a brief answer. But, before you make a decision, it is better to read some reviews about the platform so that you will make a solid decision.

Which Forex software will be ideal?

A technical trader must consider a comfortable charting platform. The platform that you have selected must have all the necessary tools. Only if you select the right trading platform will you be able to enjoy trading. A fundamental trader must consider the news and analysis factor and check whether it is accessible by the Forex software that the trader has selected.

Should you trust the platforms that provide exclusive offers?

You already know when something is too good to be true, we shouldn't rely on it. Just like that, if a platform is providing exclusive things that you cannot fathom, then you must think twice before considering that platform. If they are offering so much, they should have massive profits. If yes, then from where do they get so much profit? Instead of falling for exclusive offers, you can find a platform that is reliable and reasonable.

I hope these questions and answers cleared most doubts that you had about trading platforms. However, it is better to get some idea about the famous trading platforms. Let's get started!

MetaTrader 5

Both MT4 and MT5 were introduced by one company some time back. The best thing about MetaTrader 5 is that you can use it to trade options and stock trading. Most traders who trade on the stock market along with the Forex market consider MT5 because it is simple and beneficial.

MetaTrader 4

Currently, a higher percentage of traders use MetaTrader 4 to trade Forex. Even brokers recommend MT4 as the best trading platform. Yet, certain fund managers and professional traders don't prefer MT4. Beginners like you can benefit immensely from this platform because it is user-friendly. If you have selected the right broker who offers MT4, you will be able to enjoy comparatively cheap prices. Also, this is an old platform provided to Forex traders. You must also note that this platform has a great team to solve issues related to trading. But sadly, fund managers believe that trade execution is not as fast as they want.

NinjaTrader

This is the oldest platform remaining in the industry. Even now, some traders prefer using this trading platform because it is easy to handle. Also, this platform has special features that can be enjoyed by traders.

TradeStation

This is for fund managers and professional traders because this platform has speed and high-end technology required by professional traders and managers. This platform has some issues with the user-friendly option, but fund managers and professional traders don't worry about it.

Finally, you must understand that the trading platform is all about how comfortable you are with the platform. It should provide an easy path to enter and exit trades while providing a user-friendly feature. If you select the right platform, you will be able to make a solid trading decision. But, making profits will depend on your skill, so you can't entirely depend on the trading platform. Of course, it is a supporting factor, but it is not a reason to make profits. If you want to reach success in trading, you must not think twice to get help from Forex mentors and professionals. Anyway, let me provide some insights into some other factors as well.

Opening an Account

You must be excited about Forex trading. But, without learning the ways to open an account, how will you even trade? With online Forex trading, the excitement to trade Forex has increased immensely. However, to start trading Forex, you must find a broker, select a trading platform, and then open an account. But the part of opening an account is pretty easy. To open an account, you need certain things including name, email, address, contact number, account type, a password for the account, citizenship, date of birth, employment details, Tax ID, and a few more financial questions. The steps of opening an account will differ from one broker to another, yet the following are the general procedures to open an account:

Sometimes, you might have to fill the application with the details related to the trading experience.

Select the broker and check for the suitable and available account. After completing the application, register with your username, and then you'll receive the credentials to your Forex trading account. Now, you'll have access to the broker's client portal.

And then, transfer the deposit funds through any of the possible payment methods to your trading account. But remember, you might have to bear charges as per the payment method.

Once the funding procedure is complete, you can then trade Forex. But, your broker will provide necessary guidance and ideas before you enter into live trading.

Once you complete these procedures, you are good to begin your journey. But, are you wondering why you have to follow all these hectic rules and regulations? Well, the Forex market wasn't filled with rules and regulations, but once the market allowed retail trading, the rules and regulations became compulsory. If the market wasn't strict, it would be easy for the market participants to gamble on the market. The factor of reliability will become questionable. Also, you will not find brokers who don't require these details. On the other hand, if you find brokers who don't ask these questions, then you have to think about opening an account.

Well, an important thing about opening an account is risk disclosure. As a beginner, you are likely to be mindless about this factor, but remember, this is very important

Chapter 21
Application on the Commodities Market

T rading in the commodity markets based on fundamental news and analysis differs dramatically from the quick-natured technical analysis, which often requires traders to shift from bullish to bearish in the blink of an eye. Fundamental analysis provides slow-handed guidance to traders. In general, the practice of entering or exiting trades based on market fundamentals is a dawdling and tedious process, demanding massively deep pockets and patience. Imagine being a fundamentalist who identified oil as being overvalued near $100 per barrel in 2008, or on the multiple occasion's oil moved above $100 from 2011 to 2013. Initially, a trader selling a futures contract solely on fundamentals would have either blown out his trading account, given up on the trade before it paid off, or suffered a roughly $50,000 drawdown before having an opportunity to profit from the correct analysis. This is because each dollar of crude oil price change equals a profit or loss of $1,000 to a one-lot futures trader. In 2008, the price of oil reached $150 per barrel before suffering from a steep decline. On subsequent occasions, the suffering would have been limited to about $10,000 to $15,000, but still a painful endeavor.

If you are familiar with the popular commodity trading book *Hot Commodities*, written by Jim Rogers, this slow-paced fundamental approach is exactly what he writes about. Not all of us have the capital to employ such a longterm view in the leveraged world of commodities, as Mr. Rogers does. Accordingly, before assuming commodity trading is as "easy" as that particular book implies, you must consider the vast financial difference in the reality of most commodity traders and the author.

Other than obtaining a big-picture consensus of the market makeup, relying on fundamental analysis alone can be a daunting task for the average trader. After all, it can take months, or even years, for traders to get their hands on absolutely accurate fundamental information. By then, the markets have already moved. Alternatively, during times in which markets are ignoring fundamentals, it can take months, or years, for prices to revert to a more equilibrium price.

What Is Fundamental Analysis?

Fundamental analysis of the commodity markets involves the study of the interaction between supply and demand; with this analysis, traders attempt to predict future price movement. Specifically, the entire concept of fundamental analysis is built upon the following equations:

Demand > Supply = Higher prices

Supply > Demand = Low prices

Most analysts agree that commodity market supply and demand figures are quantifiable, yet even the diehard fundamentalists will admit accurate statistics are not available in real time. Thus, any numbers plugged into the simple and neat formulas given are relatively meaningless. If you input garbage data into the formula, the result will also be garbage. Accordingly, when an analyst runs the numbers she is almost certainly working with either outdated or inaccurate data. Fundamental analysts waiting for confirmed government supply and demand data will be calculating months after the fact. Alternatively, if they are calculating based on estimates (whether they are government or personally derived), it is nothing more than a guess.

Most recall the simple supply and demand cross charts taught in high school and college economic courses; unfortunately, this academic practice erroneously simplifies a concept that is actually highly complex. In my opinion, what appears to be the most straightforward form of commodity market analysis—fundamental—is actually the most difficult in practice.

Because of the massive complexity that comes with estimating current supply and demand details of any given commodity, the seemingly simple mathematical equation fundamentalists use to speculate on prices can be confusing at best, but misleading at worst. In addition, regardless of the time dedicated to deciphering the market's fundamental code, it can be extremely problematic for a trader to succeed using this method of analysis alone.

In order to understand the place of the commodity markets, one needs to consider the bigger picture.

Asset classes are certainly not limited to these five groups, but these are the most common categories. Obviously, any classification is rather arbitrary or, at least, subjective. Even wine or art can be seen as specific asset classes, as much as volatility or weather. On the basis of any assets, including the latter, derivatives or structured products can be developed and traded.

Classification of commodities

Zooming in on the asset class commodities could lead to identify subcategories.

At further detailed level, more subclasses can be identified. Metals can be split into precious and non-precious metals.

Indirect investments

Nowadays, the ownership of shares, bonds or currencies is registered digitally.

Consequently, the transfer of title takes place without physical hassle. The physical process, however, is unavoidable with commodities. As they are consumed physically they also have to be transported materially. Analogously, storage of commodities requires physical storage capacity. Nevertheless, investors and financial traders who would like to be exposed to commodity prices typically dislike to purchase commodities physically, because then they must store the actual products. However, most of these market participants do not hold tangible storage capacity. Moreover, most of them do not want to be involved with the relevant concrete matters at all. This is why investments are made indirectly. Luckily for them, exposures can be created in many ways.

Indirect investments in commodities can be made by placing capital in equity.

One could, for instance, buy shares of mining firms, oil and gas companies or corporates which produce or process agricultural products. However, this brings risk beyond commodity prices. After all, a stock price is not just influenced by the relevant commodity price. Moreover, a corporate share price is impacted by numerous drivers, amongst which are the management, logistical success or failures and operational performance, but also the management and possibly even accounting scandals. This often leads to a discrepancy between the stock price development and the underlying commodity price development. This basis risk could work two ways, namely in favour or adversely. One could profit from leverage but, on the other side, one may want to avoid underperformance. Therefore, investors often seek an alternative indirect investment opportunity, with a more direct relationship. Commodity derivatives provide such an alternative. A commodity derivatives contract is an agreement whereby the underlying value typically concerns a commodity or commodity index. Examples of commodity derivatives are commodity futures, commodity options and commodity swaps.

Commodity markets are complex systems

Before taking a position in commodities, an investor or market participant has to realise that the commodity markets are much more complex than capital markets, FX markets or money markets. After all, commodity markets face most elements that drive and influence typical financial markets, but on top of that, commodity markets are severely impacted by many more driving forces, such as politics, weather circumstances and the availability plus utilisation of production, consumption, transport and storage capacity. For this reason, one requires in-depth knowledge about technical aspects. A background in engineering or physics would be quite helpful to understand the commodity supply chains and, hence, the commodity markets. Compared to the money markets, commodity markets are relatively new, and thus far from mature. In addition, they face relatively many fundamental price driving factors, they are significantly impacted by economic cycles and they are typically exposed to a relatively large number of events. As a consequence of the latter, commodity prices face relatively high volatility, especially in the spot markets. Moreover, some commodity markets can even show negative prices. In addition, commodity markets, compared to money markets, are characterised by a relatively weak relationship between spot and forward prices, have to deal with strong seasonality, show fragmented markets instead of centralisation and face relatively complex derivatives.

Chapter 22
Application on the Crypto Value Market

T he query whether crypto-currencies follow structured chart behaviors similar to the normal economic markets has been presented by several traders. Admittedly, crypto-currencies similar to Bitcoin and Ethereum act very well owing to the dearth of elementary players whose supposition can be opposite to the actual behavior of crypto-currency prices. These charts are unpredictable when it comes to fluctuation of price but can be effective as far as the prediction of the potential behavior of price is concerned.

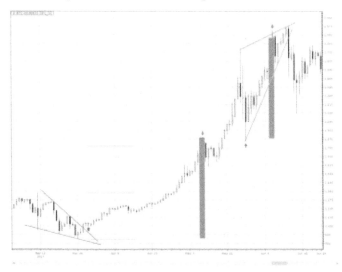

The effective representation of basic graphical patterns across this period is evident from left to right side of the graph.

The upper points on the graph show the breakout of a falling wedge to determine the initial point of the wedge.

The breakout of the consolidation zone is directed upwards. The target is labeled thus stopping the move.

The upper target estimated by the block keeps the trend moving upwards leading to fulfillment and beginning of a stronger pullback.

The breakout of the rising wedge is directed towards the downside. The results are indicated in the next chart.

The breakout of the rising wedge is followed by the pullback from an extended move.

A measured move target that is ready is likely to bring about the multi down leg.

The measured move target can also be achieved by the tagged wedge break target. This eliminates the need to go low.

As the falling wedge is considered unusual pattern of topping, there was an expectation of year-high test.

The step by step explanation is given to facilitate your understanding.

The fundamental graphical pattern will represent the reasonable forecasting power on near-term price movements, as long as a standardized market exists for the trading of any instrument. In other words, if the trader is only focused on his profits, the graph pattern will depict the expected outcomes of market behavior. Since different types of people are engaged in crypto-currency trade and financial markets, it's obvious that the fluctuation of price will also be different for both types of trades.

Due to the introduction of futures contracts on Bitcoin, however this situation is changing. This enables the experienced trade firm employees to trade crypto-currencies under the protective regulations offered by various exchanges such as Chicago Board of Trade and the Chicago Mercantile Exchange. It is expected that the huge financial organizations will shortly take over the current crypto-currency players.

To sum it up, Bitcoin is expected to act similar to a developing regulated derivatives market. Due to the possible use of arbitrage algorithms for trading Bitcoin with financial institutes, greater correspondence is seen between the price actions of the bitcoin and other financial markets. Contrary to the claims of bitcoin promoters, bitcoin is now becoming the financial tool intended to serve a particular purpose.

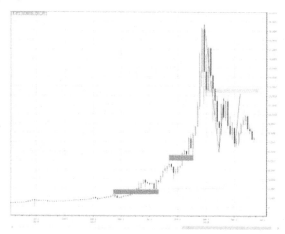

The next move of the bitcoin is still the main query forwarded by many after it deviated from the ever-high of 19666. It must amaze many that the stock market bottom with S&P 500 is printing a low of 666. The main thing here is not if there is any conspiracy involved behind this and we will only focus on the facts depicted from charts.

The chart shown above shows the Bitcoin details.

In year 2017, a couple of pockets were left behind by the massive upwards movement towards the blow-off. It was expected that the higher one will be tagged; however, it did not occur till now. This implies that Bitcoin is still expected to trade between 5500 and 5600 prior to trading over 12600 which was its level at 2017 closing.

The movement of the bitcoin to the 2017 closure of 12600 from the existing level of trading over 7000 (May 2018) will be considered as the complex multiple leg move. This movement is expected to be followed with immediate selling most probably targeting the low pockets.

Considering the time taken by the bitcoin to move above 19000, it is logical to expect the bitcoin to require similar time period to grasp this move.

It is appropriate to check the bottoming of the bitcoin as long as there is no formation of weekly level bottom pattern. Although it may require a lot of patience by Perma bulls to wait for the bottoming of bitcoin, it is worth waiting since it may fell down boundlessly.

Ethereum

The peak of the bitcoin was followed by the peak of various other crypto-currencies particularly Ethereum which showed a rise to maximum position in January 2018. This may be attributed to the hype created by Bitcoin at that time. More interesting is the fact that Ethereum doubled even after the fall of bitcoin. Such a movement was new for the Ethereum however; bitcoin has seen this up and down many times.

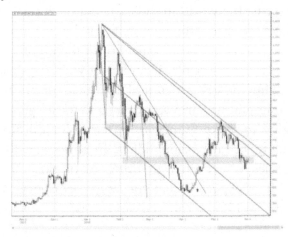

Three downside pushes are evident from the Ethereum's pullback structure. The Ethereum put an end to this move prior to reaching the third downside target. This was done through the resistance trend line's breakout shown by an upward arrow.

The breakout lead to an upwards move towards the peak of the channel due to the swing lows developed in the pullback process.

It resulted in a situation where second swing held more importance. Currently, Ethereum is being traded at this zone (as at end of May 2018). In case of maintenance of this level, we can expect an upward move towards the start of the pullback as per the indication of the three pushes down pattern. The highest-ever level of Ethereum is the start of pullback. The potential situation of the bitcoin is different from this situation of Ethereum.

However, this is not that simple. The daily charts still reveal a downtrend with a strong resistance being shown by the down channel top. Ethereum will not move upwards and will be kept low as long as the channel top is not cleared. The channel top will cause the Ethereum to break the record of the lowest level made in May 2018. Keeping the channel midpoint as the main target, even lower prices are expected. Currently (as of end of May 2018), the mid-channel level is almost 300.

Crypto-Currency is Not Money

In my opinion I must clarify the fact that crypto-currencies would not be able to rule the world in their current position as claimed by their promoters. They are not a valuable source or a monetary form. Although the concept of the significance of the crypto-currency for restoring trust was reasonable, it could not yield the desired results because of technological issues and issues in practical execution. However, no significant harm was caused to the assets.

The longing to make money from technological advancements led to the emergence of various ideas. In particular, the advent of crypto-currencies is expected to bring revolutions in the future transactions. It is expected that the crypto-currency concept will bring about technological advancements causing massive revolutions in all aspects.

It is not easy to determine the crypto-currency that can endure the current bearish market trends. Even if one determines the right kind of crypto-currency, it is expected to lose its significance with the technological advancements in the similar manner in which the advent of Facebook rendered the previous social media platforms as obsolete.

Trading in crypto-currencies must involve a lot of caution on part of the trader since it is a hazardous play. It is better to understand the risky nature of crypto-currencies so that you don't put the amount you cannot afford to lose for betting. This statement is right for all types of trades. There is no emphasis on the management of risk to be the only factor of concern for the survival of a trader in this market.

Chapter 23
Top Day Trading Tools

Software Tools

Retail traders, in particular, can already access almost the same kinds of programs used by institutional traders. Moreover, many of these tools are either available online or downloadable in the computer. In fact, with the growing popularity of mobile devices such as tablets and smart phones, some of these programs can also be downloaded in these devices. This way, you can trade anytime and anywhere even when you're on a holiday or commuting.

These software tools can include:

Stock Screeners

A stock screener is a tool that allows you to compare company stocks against a set of criteria, which can include share price, market capitalization, dividend yield, volatility, valuation ratios, and analyst estimates.

What I like about stock screeners is they are very easy to use since the parameters can already be provided for you. All you have to do is to choose.

Now I can get more information on every company or narrow my search some more so I have fewer but hopefully better-choice stocks to consider.

Stock screeners can be an excellent tool too to begin your research. In fact, it guides you on what kind of information to look for as you can see in the MORE INFO column. You can save more time as well. Note, though, that not all stock screeners have the same features. Some are pretty basic while others are comprehensive they can also let you run screening for other types of securities like bonds and mutual funds, like Yahoo Finance.

Auto Traders

Also known as automatic trading systems, these are programs that execute buys and sells on your behalf. Normally, you just set certain parameters, and they do the rest. One of the biggest advantages of auto trading is you don't have to constantly keep track of your trading literally as the system does it for you. In fact, over the years, it has become more sophisticated that it can already "read" historical data and provide you with recommendations or information so you can make more correct decisions. Also, you can execute the same commands multiple times in any given day and trade several accounts or orders at any given time.

However, there are downsides. First, there's disruption of the markets. In 2014 over 70% of trading is due to these automated systems. Now imagine if every trader executes huge orders every single time. Market movements can then become incredibly erratic. Moreover, even if these systems are designed to work more powerfully than any trader's thinking and analytical capacity, they are still prone to glitches, and these glitches can be disastrous. For example, it can place large orders that you don't want to in the first place.

Streaming Quotes

You can also consider this as your equivalent to a ticker tape. The only difference is that you'll get more information from streaming quotes.

Now streaming quotes are quotes displayed in real time, so don't be surprised if the numbers tend to change very fast for certain stocks. It only goes to show that the market is definitely active. For a day trader, streaming quotes are a valuable tool as they can help you make decisions including corrections on the fly. You can spot emerging buying and selling trends and analyze real-time charts. NASDAQ has an example of a streaming quote, although it's much simpler than the others like Quotestream or Scottrader.

Live Market Analysis

Although technical analysis is essential in day trading, you should also not neglect fundamental analysis as the latter can even dictate the results of the former. For this reason, I also use Live Market Analysis.

Live Market Analysis is simply a collection of any information, news, press releases, and reports pertaining to the companies that are being traded. They may not be directly related to finance (e.g., news about mergers or acquisitions) but they can influence stock price movement within the day.

You can source the analysis online such as Yahoo or Google Finance.

Stop Loss Management

I hope I've already established the fact that stop loss is incredibly important as part of your risk management strategy.

Learning Markets gives us two more options. These are the support and moving average methods.

Support levels refer to the level in which stock price dips the lowest before it goes high up. When you look at a fall below the uptrend is the support level. In the support method, your stop loss can be placed just a bit below than the previous support level as this assumes that going below the stop-loss price means a continuous or longer downtrend for the stock.

Investopedia, on the other hand, has a good definition of moving averages. One of the benefits of this is that it cancels out "noise" or fluctuations that may not be that consistent. In other words, it gives you a clear picture of the possible movement of stock prices. For the stop loss setup, you can determine the moving average and have it just below the moving average.

Penny Stock Level 2 Quotes

Once in a while, day traders look for a penny stock, although the name can be a misnomer since, according to the Securities and Exchange Commission (SEC), these stocks are those that have less than $5 per share value.

Some traders like penny stocks because there's a lot of room for appreciation, which means opportunities for massive return. Moreover, a person's capital can go a long way with penny stocks. For example, if a person has $5,000, he can allocate $1,000 for penny stocks worth $3 each. This means he gets 300 shares (rounded off to the nearest hundreds). Compare that if he uses the same amount to buy shares worth $5.

However, there are several downsides with penny stocks. One, they are hard to come by and they are thinly traded. Therefore, there's not much technical information you can use to make good decisions about them. Second, they are usually not found in major exchanges because they have failed to meet some of the requirements or criteria. You may also have issues with liquidity, which means you may not be able to sell the stock quickly simply because penny stocks themselves are not that liquid.

Nevertheless, if you want to give penny stocks a try, you can use Level 2 Quotes, which is obviously higher than the level 1 quote, which includes the streaming quote. An important data available in level 2 quote is that of the market maker or those who have significant control of the market, including the brokerage firms. They are the ones who have massive volumes of order sizes, which they are going to trade. Market makers meant to earn a profit, so orders may be hold off until they know they can make a gain. Traders in level 1, however, wouldn't know that. In level 2 quotes, traders can observe movements of money makers and see what stocks they have the most interest.

Chapter 24
Momentum Trading

M omentum is at the heart of all-day trading as finding trades with the right amount of momentum is the only way you can reliably guarantee a profit on your trades. Luckily, it is not unrealistic to expect to find at least one underlying asset that is likely to move as much as 30 percent each day due to the fact that all underlying assets with this much momentum all tend to share a few common technical indicators.

Momentum stock anatomy

While it might seem difficult to understand how anyone could expect to pick a stock with the right momentum out of the thousands of possible choices, the fact of the matter is that all high momentum stocks typically have several things in common.

In fact, if you were given a list of 5,000 stocks, using the factors below you could likely come up with a list of 10 or less.

Float: The first thing you are going to want to keep in mind is that the stocks with the highest momentum are generally going to have a float that is less than 100 million shares. Float refers to the total number of shares that are currently available and can be found by taking the total number of outstanding shares and subtracting out all those that are restricted or are, functionally speaking, no longer traded. Restricted shares are those that are currently in the midst of a lockup period or other, similar restriction. The less float a stock has, the more volatility it is going to contain. Stocks with smaller float tend to have low liquidity and a higher bid/ask spread.

Daily charts: The next thing you are going to want to look for is stocks that are consistently beating their moving average and trending away from either the support or resistance depending on if you following a positive or negative trend.

Relative volume: You are also going to want to ensure that the stocks you are considering have a high amount of relative volume, with the minimum being twice what the current average is.

The average you should consider in this case would be the current volume compared to the historical average for the stock in question. The standard volume is going to reset every night at midnight which means this is a great indicator when it comes to stocks that are seeing a higher than average amount of action right now.

Catalyst: While not, strictly speaking, required, you may still find it helpful to look for stocks that are currently having their momentum boosted by external sources. This can include things like activist investors, FDA announcements, and PR campaigns and earnings reports.

Exit indicators to watch

Besides knowing what a potentially profitable momentum trade looks like, you are also going to need to know what to look for to ensure that you can successfully get while the getting is good. Keep the following in mind and you will always be able to get out without having to sacrifice any of your hard earned profits.

Don't get greedy: It is important to set profit targets before you go into any trade, and then follow through on them when the trade turns in your favor. If you find yourself riding a stronger trend than you initially anticipated, the best choice is to instead sell off half of your holdings before setting a new and improved price target for the rest, allowing you to have your cake and eat it too.

Red candles: If you are not quite at your price target and you come across a candle that closes in the red then this is a strong indicator that you should take what you have and exit ASAP. If you have already sold off half of your holdings at this point, however, then you are going to want to go ahead and hold through the first red candle as long as it doesn't go so far as to actively trigger your stop loss.

Extension bar: An extension bar is a candle with a spike that causes dramatically increased profits. If this occurs you want to lock in your profits as quickly as possible as it is unlikely to last very long. This is your lucky day and it is important to capitalize on it.

Choosing a screener

Another important aspect of using a momentum strategy correctly is using a quality stock screen in order to find stocks that are trending towards the extreme ends of the market based on the criteria outlined above. A good screener is a virtually indispensable tool when it comes to narrowing down the field of potential options on any given day, the best of the best even let you generate your own unique filters that display a list of stocks that meet a variety of different criteria. What follows is a list of some of the most popular screeners on the market today.

StockFetchter: StockFetcher is one of the more complicated screeners out there, but all that complexity comes with a degree of power that is difficult to beat. Its power comes from a virtually unlimited number of parameters that its users can add to filter, ensuring that you only see exactly the types of stocks you are looking for. It offers a free as well as a paid version, the free version allows you to see the top five stocks that match your parameters while the paid version, $8.95 per month, shows you unlimited results.

Finviz: This site offers a wide variety of different premade filters that are designed to return results on the most promising stocks for a given day. It is extremely user friendly as well and functions from three drop-down menus based on the type of indicator, technical, fundamental or descriptive, and lets you choose the criteria for each. The results can then be sorted in a myriad of different ways to make it as easy to find the types of stocks you are looking for as possible.

The biggest downside to Finviz is that it uses delayed data which means it is going to be most effective for those who run evening screens so they are ready to go when the market opens.

Chartmill: This site allows users to filter stocks based on a number of predetermined criteria including things like price, performance, volume, technical indicators and candlestick patterns. It also offers up a number of more specialized indicators including things like squeeze plays, intensity, trend and pocket pivots. This site works based on a credit system, and every user is given 6,000 credits each month for free. Every scan costs a few hundred credits so you should be able to take advantage of a variety of their tools virtually free of charge. Additional credits then cost $10 per 10,000 or they have an unlimited option available for about $30 per month.

Stockrover^l: This tool is specifically designed to cater to the Canadian market in addition to the US stock market. It offers up a variety of fundamental filters in addition to technical and performance-based options. This tool also allows you to track stocks that are near their established lows and high, those that may be gaining momentum and even those that are seeing a lot of love from various hedge funds. Users also have the ability to create custom screens as well as unique equations for even more advanced screening. Users can also backtest their ideas to make sure that everything is working as intended. While their basic options are free to use, the more complex choices are gated behind a paywall that costs $250 for a year's subscription.

Know your filters

Day trading is about more than finding stocks that are high in volume, it is also about finding those that are currently experiencing a higher than average degree of movement as well. The following filters will help ensure that the stocks you find have plenty of both.

Steady volatility: In order to trade stocks that are extremely volatile with as little research as possible, the following criterion is a good place to start.

While additional research is always going to be preferable in the long run, you can find success if you run this scan once a week and pay close attention to the results.

This list should ideally return stocks that have moved at least 5 percent every day for the past 50 days. It is important to use a minimum of 50 days, though 75 or 100 will produce even more reliable results overall. Results of this magnitude will show that the stock in question has moved a significant amount over the past few months which means it is likely to continue to do so for the near future. The second criterion will determine the amount you should be willing to pay per share and can be altered based on your personal preferences.

The third criterion will determine the level of volume that you find acceptable for the given timeframe. The example will look for volume that is greater than four million shares within the past month. From there, it will eliminate leverage ETFs from the results which can be eliminated if you are interested in trading ETFs. Finally, the add column will show the list of stocks with the largest amount of volume and the greatest overall amount of movement. Selecting these columns will then rank the results from least to greatest based on the criteria provided.

Monitor regularly: Alternately, you may want to do a daily search to determine the stocks that will experience the greatest range of movement in the coming hours. To do so, you will want to create a new list of stocks every evening to ensure that you will be ready to go when the market opens. This list can then be made up of stocks that have shown a higher volatility in the previous day either in terms of gains or in terms of losses. Adding in volume to these criteria will then help to make sure the results will likely continue to generate the kind of volume that day trading successfully requires. Useful filters for this search include an average volume that is greater than one million and the more you increase the minimum volume the fewer results you'll see.

When using this strategy, it is especially important to pick out any stocks that are likely to see major news releases before the next day as these are almost guaranteed to make the price move in a number of random directions before ultimately settling down. As such, it is often best to wait until after the details of the release are known and you can more accurately determine what the response is, though not so long that you miss out on the combination of high volume and high volatility. If you don't already have an earnings calendar bookmarked, the one available for free from Yahoo Finance! Is well respected.

Monitor intraday volatility: Another option that is worth considering is doing your researching during the day as a means of determining which stocks are experiencing the greatest overall amount of movement at the moment.

Chapter 25
Common Day Trading Mistakes to Avoid

A side from doing the right things, you'll also need to refrain from certain things to succeed as a day trader. Here are some of the most common day trading mistakes you should avoid committing.

Excessive Day Trading

By excessive, I mean executing too many day trades. One of the most common mistakes many newbie day traders make is assuming that they can become day trading ninjas in just a couple of weeks if they trade often enough to get it right. But while more practice can eventually translate into day trading mastery later on, it doesn't mean you can cram all that practice in a very short period of time via very frequent day trading. The adage "the more, the merrier" doesn't necessarily apply to day trading.

Remember, timing is crucial for day trading success. And timing is dependent on how the market is doing during the day. There will be days when day trading opportunities are few and far between and there'll be days when day trading opportunities abound. Don't force trades for the sake of getting enough day trades under your belt.

Even in the midst of a plethora of profitable day trading opportunities, the more the merrier still doesn't apply. Why? If you're a newbie trader, your best bet at becoming a day trading ninja at the soonest possible time is to concentrate on one or two day trades per day only. By limiting your day trades, to just one or two, you have the opportunity to closely monitor and learn from your trades. Can you imagine executing 5 or more trades daily as a newbie and monitor all those positions simultaneously? You'll only get confused and overwhelmed and worse, you may even miss day trading triggers and signals and fail to profitably close your positions.

Winging It

If you want to succeed as a day trader, you need to hold each trading day in reverence and high esteem. How do you do that? By planning your day trading strategies for the day and executing those strategies instead of just winging it.

As cliché as it may sound, failing to plan really is planning to fail. And considering the financial stakes involved in day trading, you shouldn't go through your trading days without any plan on hand. Luck favors those who are prepared and planning can convince lady luck that you are prepared.

Expecting Too Much Too Soon

This much is true about day trading: it's one of the most exciting and exhilarating jobs in the world! And stories many day traders tell of riches accumulated through this economic activity add more excitement, desire, and urgency for many to get into it.

However, too much excitement and desire resulting from many day trading success stories can be very detrimental to newbie day traders. Let me correct myself: it is detrimental to newbie day traders. Why? Such stories, many of which are probably urban legends, give newbies unrealistic expectations of quick and easy day trading riches. Many beginner day traders get the impression that day trading is a get-rich-quick scheme!

It's not. What many day traders hardly brag about are the times they also lost money and how long it took them to master the craft enough to quit their jobs and do it full time. And even rarer are stories of the myriad number of people who've attempted day trading and failed. It's the dearth of such stories that tend to make day trading neophytes have unrealistic expectations about day trading.

What's the problem with lofty day trading expectations? Here's the problem: if you have very unrealistic expectations, it's almost certain that you'll fail. It's because unrealistic expectations can't be met and therefore, there's zero chances for success.

One of the most unrealistic expectations surrounding day trading is being able to double one's initial trading capital in a couple of months, at most. Similar to such expectations is that of being able to quit one's day job and live an abundant life in just a few months via day trading. Successful day traders went through numerous failures, too, before they succeeded at day trading and were able to do it for a living.

If you decide to give day trading a shot, have realistic expectations. In fact, don't even expect to profit soon. Instead take the initial losses as they come, limiting them through sensible stop-loss limits, and learning from them. Eventually, you'll get the hang of it and your day trading profits will start eclipsing your day trading losses.

Changing Strategies Frequently

Do you know how to ride a bike? If not, do you know someone who does? Whether it's you or somebody you know, learning how to ride a bike wasn't instant. It took time and a couple of falls and bruises along the way.

But despite falls, scratches and bruises, you or that person you know stuck to learning how to ride a bike and with enough time and practice, succeeded in doing so. It was because you or the other person knew that initial failures mean that riding a bike was impossible. It's just challenging at first.

It's the same with learning how to day trade profitably. You'll need to give yourself enough time and practice to master it. Just because you suffered trading losses in the beginning doesn't mean it's not working or it's not for you. It probably means you haven't really mastered it yet.

But if you quit and shift to a new trading strategy or plan quickly, you'll have to start again from scratch, extend your learning time, and possibly lose more money than you would've if you stuck around to your initial strategy long enough to give yourself a shot at day trading successfully or concluding with certainty that it's not working for you.

If you frequently change your day trading strategies, i.e., you don't give yourself enough time to learn day trading strategies, your chances of mastering them become much lower. In which case, your chances of succeeding in day trading becomes much lower, too.

Not Analyzing Past Trades

Those who don't learn history are doomed to repeat it, said writer and philosopher George Santayana. We can paraphrase it to apply to day traders, too: Those who don't learn from their day trading mistakes will be doomed to repeat them.

If you don't keep a day trading journal containing records of all your trades and more importantly, analyze them, you'll be doomed to repeat your losing day trades. It's because by not doing so, you won't be able to determine what you're doing wrong and what you should be doing instead in order to have more profitable day trades than losing ones.

As another saying goes: if you always do what you always did, you'll always get what you always got. Unless you analyze your past day trades on a regular basis, you'll be doomed to repeating the same mistakes and continue losing money on them.

Ditching Correlations

We can define correlations as a relationship where one thing influences the outcome or behavior of another. A positive correlation means that both tend to move in the same direction or exhibit similar behaviors, i.e., when one goes up, the other goes up, too, and vice versa.

Correlations abound in the stock market. For example, returns on the stock market are usually negatively correlated with the Federal Reserve's interest rates, i.e., when the Feds increase interest rates, returns on stock market investments go down and vice versa.

Correlations exist across industries in the stock market, too. For example, property development stocks are positively correlated to steel and cement manufacturing stocks. This is because when the property development's booming, it buys more steel and cement from manufacturing companies, which in turn also increase their income.

Ignoring correlations during day trading increase your risks for erroneous position taking and exiting. You may take a short position on a steel manufacturer's stock while taking a long position on a property development company's stock and if they have a positive correlation, one of those two positions will most likely end up in a loss.

But caution must be exercised with using correlations in your day trades. Don't establish correlations where there's none. Your job is to simply identify if there are observable correlations, what those correlations are, and how strong they are.

Being Greedy

Remember the story of the goose that lay golden eggs? Because the goose's owner was so greedy and couldn't wait for the goose to lay more eggs immediately, he killed the goose and cut it open.

Sadly for the owner, there were no golden eggs inside the goose because it only created and laid one golden egg every day. His greed caused him to destroy his only wealth-generating asset.

When it comes to day trading, greed can have the same negative financial impact. Greed can make a day trader hold on to an already profitable position longer than needed and result in smaller profits later on or worse, trading losses.

If you remember my story, that was greed in action. Had I been content with the very good returns I already had and closed my position, my paper gains could've become actual gains. I let my greed control my trading and chose to hold on to that stock much longer than I needed to. That trade turned into a losing one eventually.

That's why you must be disciplined enough to stick to your day trading stop-loss and profit-taking limits. And that's why you should program those limits on your platform, too. Doing so minimizes the risks of greed hijacking your otherwise profitable day trades.

Chapter 26
Portfolio Diversification

D ay traders generally execute trades in the course of a single trading day while investors buy and hold stocks for days, weeks, months, and sometimes even a couple of years. In between these two extremes are other forms of trading. These include swing trading and position trading, among others.

Swing trading is where a trader buys an interest in a commodity or stock and holds the position for a couple of days before disposing of it. Position trading, on the other hand, is where a trader buys a stake in a commodity or stock for a number of weeks or even several months. While all these trades carry a certain element of risk, day trading carries the biggest risk.

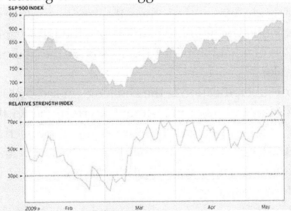

A trader with the necessary skills and access to all the important resources is bound to succeed and will encounter a steep learning curve. Professional day traders work full time, whether working for themselves or for large institutions. They often set a schedule which they always adhere to. It is never wise to be a part-time day trader, a hobby trader, or a gambler. To succeed, you have to trade on a fulltime basis and be as disciplined as possible.

Introduction to Diversification

Diversification is considered an effective risk management technique. It is widely used by both traders and investors. The gist behind this approach is that investing funds in just single security is extremely risky as the entire trade could potentially go up in smoke or incur significant losses.

An ideal portfolio of securities is expected to fetch a much higher return compared to a no-diversified portfolio. This is true even when compared to the returns of lower risk investments like bonds. Generally, diversification is advisable not only because it yields better returns but also because it offers protection against losses.

Diversification Basics

Traders and investors put their funds in securities at the securities markets. One of the dangers of investing in the markets is that traders are likely to hold onto only one or two stocks at a time. This is risky because if a trade was to fail, then the trader could experience a catastrophe. However, with diversification, the risk is spread out so that regardless of what happens to some stocks, the trader still stands to be profitable.

At the core of diversification is the challenge posed by unsystematic risks. When some stocks or investments perform better than others, these risks are neutralized. Therefore, for a perfectly balanced portfolio, a trader should ensure that they only deal with assets that are non-correlated. This means that the assets respond in opposite ways or differently to market forces.

The ideal portfolio should contain between 25 and 30 different securities. This is the perfect way of ensuring that the risk levels are drastically reduced and the only expected outcomes are profitability. In summary, diversification is a popular strategy that is used by both traders and investors. It makes use of a wide variety of securities in order to improve yield and mitigate against inherent and potential risks.

It is advisable to invest or trade in a variety of assets and not all from one class. For instance, a properly diversified portfolio should include assets such as currencies, options, stocks, bonds, and so on. This approach will increase the chances of profitability and minimize risks and exposure. Diversification is even better if assets are acquired across geographical regions as well.

Best Diversification Approach

Diversification focuses on asset allocation. It consists of a plan that endeavors to allocate funds or assets appropriately across a variety of investments. When an investor diversifies his or her portfolio, then there is some level of risk that has to be accepted. However, it is also advisable to devise an exit strategy so that the investor is able to let go of the asset and recoup their funds. This becomes necessary when a specific asset class is not yielding any worthwhile returns compared to others.

If an investor is able to create an aptly diversified portfolio, their investment will be adequately covered. An adequately diversified portfolio also allows room for growth. Appropriate asset allocation is highly recommended as it allows investors a chance to leverage risk and manage any possible portfolio volatility because different assets have varying reactions to adverse market conditions.

Investor opinions on diversifications

Different investors have varying opinions regarding the type of investment scenarios they consider being ideal. Numerous investors believe that a properly diversified portfolio will likely bring in a double-digit return despite prevailing market conditions. They also agree that in the worst case situation will be simply a general decrease in the value of the different assets. Yet with all this information out there, very few investors are actually able to achieve portfolio diversification.

So why are investors unable to simply diversify their portfolios appropriately? The answers are varied and diverse. The challenges encountered by investors in diversification include weighting imbalance, hidden correlation, underlying devaluation, and false returns, among others. While these challenges sound rather technical, they can easily be solved. The solution is also rather simple. By hacking these challenges, an investor will then be able to benefit from an aptly diversified platform.

The Process of Asset Class Allocation

There are different ways of allocating investments to assets. According to studies, most investors, including professional investors, portfolio managers, and seasoned traders actually rarely beat the indexes within their preferred asset class. It is also important to note that there is a visible correlation between the performance of an underlying asset class and the returns that an investor receives. In general, professional investors tend to perform more or less the same as an index within the same class asset.

Investment returns from a diversified portfolio can generally be expected to closely imitate the related asset class. Therefore, asset class choice is considered an extremely crucial aspect of an investment. In fact, it is the single more crucial aspect for the success of a particular asset class. Other factors, such as individual asset selection and market timing, only contribute about 6% of the variance in investment outcomes.

Wide Diversifications between Various Asset Classes

Diversification to numerous investors simply implies spreading their funds through a wide variety of stocks in different sectors such as health care, financial, energy, as well as medium caps, small, and large-cap companies. This is the opinion of your average investor. However, a closer look at this approach reveals that investors are simply putting their money in different sectors of stocks class. These asset classes can very easily fall and rise when the markets do.

A reliably diversified portfolio is one where the investor or even the manager is watchful and alert because of the hidden correlation that exists between different asset classes. This correlation can easily change with time, and there are several reasons for this. One reason is international markets. Many investors often choose to diversify their portfolios with international stocks.

However, there is also a noticeable correlation across the different global financial markets. This correlation is clearly visible not just across European markets but also emerging markets from around the world. There is also a clear correlation between equities and fixed income markets, which are generally the hallmarks of diversification. This correlation is actually a challenge and is probably a result of the relationship between structured financing and investment banking. Another factor that contributes to this correlation is the rapid growth and popularity of hedge funds. Take the case where a large international organization such as a hedge fund suffers losses in a particular asset class.

Should this happen, then the firm may have to dispose of some assets across the different asset classes. This will have a multiplier effect as numerous other investments, and other investors will, therefore, be affected even though they had diversified their portfolios appropriately. This is a challenge that affects numerous investors who are probably unaware of its existence. They are also probably unaware of how it should be rectified or avoided.

Realignment of Asset Classes

One of the best approaches to solving the correlation challenge is to focus on class realignment. Basically, asset allocation should not be considered as a static process. Asset class imbalance is a phenomenon that occurs when the securities markets develop, and different asset classes exhibit varied performance.

After a while, investors should assess their investments then diversify out of underperforming assets and instead shift this investment to other asset classes that are performing well and are profitable in the long term. Even then, it is advisable to be vigilant so that no one single asset class is overweighted as other standard risks are still inherent. Also, a prolonged bullish market can result in overweighting one of the different asset classes which could be ready for a correction. There are a couple of approaches that an investor can focus on, and these are discussed below.

Diversification and the Relative Value

Investors sometimes find asset returns to be misleading, including veteran investors. As such, it is advisable to interpret asset returns in relation to the specific asset class performance. The interpretation should also take into consideration the risks that this asset class is exposed to and even the underlying currency.

When diversifying investments, it is important to think about diversifying into asset classes that come with different risk profiles. These should also be held in a variety of currencies. You should not expect to enjoy the same outcomes when investing in government bonds and technology stocks. However, it is recommended to endeavor to understand how each suits the larger investment objective.

Using such an approach, it will be possible to benefit more from a small gain from an asset within a market where the currency is increasing in value. This is as compared to a large gain from an asset within a market where the currency is in decline. As such, huge gains can translate into losses when the gains are reverted back to the stronger currency. This is the reason why it is advisable to ensure that proper research and evaluation of different asset classes are conducted.

Currencies should be considered

Currency considerations are crucial when selecting asset classes to diversify in. take the Swiss franc for instance. It is one of the world's most stable currencies and has been that way since the 1940s. Because of this reason, this particular currency can be safely and reliably used to measure the performance of other currencies.

However, private investors sometimes take too long choosing and trading stocks. Such activities are both overwhelming and time-consuming. This is why, in such instances, it is advisable to approach this differently and focus more on the asset class. With this kind of approach, it is possible to be even more profitable. Proper asset allocation is crucial to successful investing. It enables investors to mitigate any investment risks as well as portfolio volatility. The reason is that different asset classes have different reactions to all the different market conditions.

Constructing a well-thought out and aptly diversified portfolio, it is possible to have a stable and profitable portfolio that even outperforms the index of assets. Investors also have the opportunity to leverage against any potential risks because of different reactions by the different market conditions.

Chapter 27
Options Day Trading Rules for Success

T here is more to options day trading to just having a style or a strategy. If that was all it took, then you could just adopt those that are proven to work and just stick with them. Yes, options day trading styles and strategy are important but they are not the end-all-be-all of this career.

The winning factor is the options day trader himself or herself. *You* are the factor that determines whether or not you will win or lose in this career. Only taking the time to develop your expertise, seeking guidance when necessary and being totally dedicated allows a person to move from a novice options day trader to an experienced one that is successful and hitting his or her target goals.

To develop into the options day trader you want to be, being disciplined is necessary. There are options day trading rules that can help you develop that necessary discipline. You will make mistakes. Every beginner in any niche does and even experienced options day traders are human and thus, have bad days too.

Knowing common mistakes helps you avoid many of these mistakes and takes away much of the guesswork. Having rules to abide by helps you avoid these mistakes as well.

Below, I have listed 11 rules that every options day trader must know. Following them is entirely up to you but know that they are proven to help beginner options day trader turn into winning options day traders.

Rule for Success #1 – Have Realistic Expectations

It is sad to say that many people who enter the options trading industry are doing so to make a quick buck. Options trading is not a get-rich-quick scheme. It is a reputable career that has made many people rich but that is only because these people have put in the time, effort, study and dedication to learning the craft and mastering it. Mastery does not happen overnight and beginner options day traders need to be prepared for that learning curve and to have the fortitude to stick with day trading options even when it becomes tough.

Losses are also part of the game. No trading style or strategy will guarantee gains all the time. In fact, the best options traders have a winning percentage of about 80% and a losing average of approximately 20%. That is why an options day trader needs to be a good money manager and a good risk manager. Be prepared for eventual losses and be prepared to minimize those losses.

Rule for Success #2 – Start Small to Grow a Big Portfolio

Caution is the name of the game when you just get started with day trading options. Remember that you are still learning options trading and developing an understanding of the financial market. Do not jump the gun even if you are eager. After you have practiced paper trading, start with smaller options positions and steadily grow your standing as you get a lay of the options day trading land. This strategy allows you to keep your losses to a minimum and to develop a systematic way of entering positions.

Rule for Success #3 – Know Your Limits

You may be tempted to trade as much as possible to develop a winning monthly average but that strategy will have the opposite effect and land you with a losing average. Remember that every options trader needs careful consideration before that contract is set up. Never overtrade and tie up your investment fund.

Rule for Success #4 – Be Mentally, Physically and Emotionally Prepared Every Day

This is a mentally, physically and emotionally tasking career and you need to be able to meet the demands of this career. That means keeping your body, mind and heart in good health at all times. Ensure that you schedule time for self-care every day. That can be as simple as taking the time to read for recreation to having elaborate self-care routine carved out in the evenings.

Not keeping your mind, heart and head in optimum health means that they are more likely to fail you. Signs that you need to buckle up and care for yourself more diligently include being constantly tired, being short-tempered, feeling preoccupied and being easily distracted.

To ensure you perform your best every day, here a few tasks that you need to perform:

- Get the recommended amount of sleep daily. This is between 7 and 9 hours for an adult.
- Practice a balanced diet. The brain and body need adequate nutrition to work their best. Include fruits, complex carbs and veggies in this diet and reduce the consumption of processed foods.
- Eat breakfast lunch and dinner every day. Fuel your mind and body with the main meals. Eating a healthy breakfast is especially important because it helps set the tone for the rest of the day.
- Exercise regularly. Being inactive increases your risk of developing chronic diseases like heart disease, certain cancers and other terrible health consequences. Adding just a few minutes of exercise to your daily routine not only reduces those risks but also allows your brain to function better, which is a huge advantage for an options day trader.
- Drink alcohol in moderation or not at all.
- Stop smoking.
- Reduce stress contributors in your environment.

Rule for Success #5 – Do Your Homework Daily

Get up early and study the financial environment before the market opens and look at the news. This allows you to develop a daily options trading plan. The process of analyzing the financial climate before the market opens is called pre-market preparation. It is a necessary task that needs to be performed every day to asset competition and to align your overall strategy with the short-term conditions of that day.

An easy way to do this is to develop a pre-market checklist. An example of a pre-market checklist includes but is not limited to:

- Checking the individual markets that you frequently trade options in or plan to trade options in to evaluate support and resistance.
- Checking the news to assess whether events that could affect the market developed overnight.
- Assessing what other options traders are doing to determined volume and competition.
- Determining what safe exits for losing positions are.
- Considering the seasonality of certain markets are some as affected by the day of the week, the month of the year, *etc.*

Rule for Success #6 – Analyze Your Daily Performance

To determine if the options day trading style and strategies that you have adopted are working for you, you need to track your performance. At the most basic, this needs to be done on a daily basis by virtue of the fact that you are trading options daily. This will allow you to notice patterns in your profit and loss. This can lead to you determining the why and how of these gains and losses. These determinations lead to fine tuning your daily processes for maximum returns. These daily performance reviews allow you to also make determinations on the long-term activity of your options day trading career.

Rule for Success #7 – Do Not Be Greedy

If you are fortunate enough to make a 100% return on your investment, do not be greedy and try to reap more benefit from the position. You might have the position turn on you and you can lose everything. When and if such a rare circumstance happens to you, sell your position and take the profits.

Rule for Success #8 – Pay Attention to Volatility

Volatility speaks to how likely a price change will occur over a specific amount of time on the financial market. Volatility can work for an options day trader or against the options day trader. It all depends on what the options day trader is trying to accomplish and what his or her current position is.

There are many external factors that affect volatility and such factors include the economic climate, global events and news reports. Strangles and straddles strategies are great for use in volatile markets.

There are different types of volatility and they include:
- Price volatility, which describes how the price of an asset increases or decreases based on the supply and demand of that asset.
- Historical volatility, which is a measure of how an asset has performed over the last 12 months.
- Implied volatility, which is a measure of how an asset will perform in the future.

Rule for Success #9 – Use the Greeks

Greeks are a collection of measures that provide a gage of an option's price sensitivity in relation to other factors. Each Greek is represented by a letter from the Greek alphabet. These Greeks use complex formulas to be determined but they are the system that option pricing is based on. Even though these calculations can be complex, they can be done quickly and efficiently so that options day traders can use them as a method of advancing their trades for the most profitable position.

Chapter 28
Trading With the Trend

Buying Calls

S o let's get started by considering the most basic strategy of all, and that is buying a call option because you believe that the price of the stock is going to increase in the near future. Therefore the goal was buying a call option would be to purchase it at the right moment and then hope that the stock will go up so much that we are able to sell the option for a profit. This all sounds simple enough almost like something that you could never miss. Unfortunately, in practice, it's actually a lot more challenging than it sounds on paper.

The first consideration is going to be whether or not you purchase an option that is in the money or out of the money. If this strategy works maybe that is not really an important consideration provided that it's not too far out of the money. The reason that people decide to purchase out of the money options is that they are cheaper as compared to in the money options. It's also a fact that if the stock is moving in the right direction out of the money options will gain at price as well.

So if someone tells you that you can't make profits from out of the money options they are not being completely honest with you. In fact, you can make profits but it's always going to depend on how the stock is moving and the distance between your strike price and the share price.

The best strategy to use when going with out of the money options is to purchase them slightly out of the money by a dollar or two. What this does is it ensures the price of the option is going to be significantly impacted by changes in the stock price. Second, you wouldn't be purchasing a call unless there was a good chance that the share price would be moving up. So if you are close in price to the market price, and there is a reasonable amount of time until expiration, there would be a good chance that the share price would actually rise above your strike price. If that happens it could mean significant profits for you.

Of course, you can always take the risk of putting it a little bit more money upfront and investing in a call option that is already in the money. If the stock price rises, that is only going to solidify your position. You also have a little bit of insurance there. That comes from the fact that if you choose a decent strike price there is a solid chance it will stay in the money and so even if it doesn't gain much value you will be able to sell it and either not lose that much, or still make a profit.

So what are we hoping for with this strategy? The main hope would be that there is a large trend that takes off so that we can write the trend and earn a healthy profit. Since options are so sensitive to the price of the stock if such a trend occurs it's pretty easy to make decent money. The key, of course, is getting in the trend at the right time and knowing when to get out of the position.

Market Awareness

The first thing to keep in mind is what I call market awareness. This involves being aware of everything that could possibly impact the price of the underlying stock. This can mean not only paying attention to the chart of the stock, but you also need to be paying attention to the news and not just financial news. So let's take a recent example by looking at Facebook. In recent months Facebook has been constantly in the news. Some of the news has been good such as a decent earnings report. On the other hand, Facebook has been receiving some pushback from governments around the world. One of the issues that have been raised is privacy concerns. Facebook is also catching a lot of flak over its plan to create a cryptocurrency.

So here is the point. Every time one of these news items comes out, it's a potential for a trend. But there are a couple of problems with this. In many cases, you simply don't know when dramatic news is going to come out. So you have to be paying attention at all times and have your money ready to go. The best-case scenario is purchasing an option for the day before some large event. People are often reacting strongly in the markets when there is a good or bad jobs report or the GDP number is about to come out. So what you would want to do in that case is first of all pay attention to the news and see what the expectations are of all the market watchers that everyone pays attention to. Of course, they are often off the mark but it gives you some kind of idea where things might be heading. If a good jobs report is expected, then you might want to invest in an index fund such as DIA which is for the Dow Jones industrial average. One thing you know is that a good jobs report is going to send the Dow and the S&P 500 up by large amounts. So the key is to be prepared by purchasing your options the day before. But on the other hand you might be wrong with your guess, which could be costly.

You could wait until the news actually comes out. But I have to say from my experience trading this is a difficult proposition. The reason is you would be surprised how quickly the price rises when dramatic news comes out either way. So when one sense is a safer way to approach things but the price might be rising so fast that you find it nearly impossible to actually purchase the options. That you can execute a trade the trend might even be over. But if you're there in the middle of the action you might as well try and then you can ride it out and probably make pretty good profits.

Some people like to sit around and study stock market charts. During the course of everyday trading when there hasn't been any dramatic news announcement or something like that which will massively impact the price of the underlying stock, looking at candlesticks charts along with moving averages can give you a good idea of went to enter or exit trades. However, it's fair to say that there is a little bit of hype surrounding these tools. The fact is they don't always work because they are easily misled or maybe it's the human mind that is misled by short term changes that go against the main trend but is temporary. So you can make the mistake while following candlesticks and moving averages of seeing evidence of the sudden downtrend and then selling your position, only to find out that the downtrend wasn't real and it was only a temporary setback soon followed by a resumption of the main trend. So that is something to be careful about.

Setting Profit Goals

If you were going to trade this way probably the best thing to do is to set a specific level of modest profit to use as a goal. One that I use is $50 per options contract. Some people may be more conservative so you could set a goal of $30 profit. Some people might be more risk-oriented. I would honestly discourage that kind of thinking because sitting there hoping for $100 dollars profit per contract, while it is possible, you may also find yourself in a situation more often than not where you lose money. What might happen is you have to sit around waiting too long to hit that magic number and it never materializes. Options can quickly turn from winners into losers because they magnify the changes in the underlying stock price by 100. So it's very easy to lose money quickly.

In my experience, the $50 price level is pretty good. The only time that this value has hurt me is when I see the $50 profit hit and I failed to sell my positions because I got greedy watching the upward trend and hoped for even more money. So that is something you should avoid it's better to stick to your law, whatever you happen to pick, and then always implemented no matter what the situation is. Remember that there is always another day to trade. You're trading career never depends on a single trade or a single days trading. The bottom line is that it's better to take a small profit her option contract and per trade and then go back and trade some more, then it is to hope for large profits that may never materialize. Also, you can always magnify small profits by trading multiple options at once. So if you trade 10 options and you're only going to accept a $30 profit on the trade, which means in total you could make $300. It doesn't really matter what specific number you pick, but you should pick a value and stick to it. If I have a regret from trading the only regret is that I didn't stick to the rules that I have set for myself.

Day Trading?

For those who are not aware, if you are labeled a patterned day trader, you need to have $25,000 in your account, and you need to open a margin account. So for most individual traders with small accounts, the last thing you want is to be labeled as a day trader. However, since options lose a lot of value from time decay, and many trends are short-lived, you may find yourself in situations where you have to enter a day trade. But if you are doing this make sure that you only do three per five day trading period. That way you will avoid getting the designation and all the problems that might come about with it. In this case, if you buy a lot of several options that have the same strike price and the same expiration date, those are going to count as the same security. That may result in problems if you need to unload them all on the same day. One way to get around this is to purchase call options with slightly different strike prices instead of getting a bunch with all the same strike price. Of course, if you were going to hold your positions overnight and risk the loss from time decay having to do that may not be something to worry about.

Trading Puts

Trading puts using these techniques is going to be basically the same, with the only difference being that you would be looking for downward trends. This is actually a little bit different because people are accustomed to thinking in terms of rising stock prices means profits. So it might be hard to wrap your mind around the idea of profiting from stock market declines.

Conclusion

Thank you for making it through to the end of *Day Trading Strategies*, let's hope it was informative and able to provide you with all of the tools and information you need to manage your journey in the market trade.

Day trading is described as the process of speculation of risks and either buying or selling of financial instruments on the same day of trading. The financial instruments are bought at a lower price and later sold at a higher price. People who participate in this form of trade are mostly referred to as speculators. Day trading is the different form of trading known as swing trading. Swing trading involves selling of financial instruments and latter buying them at a lower price. It is a form of trade that has several people have invested their time and capital in. The potential for making profits is very high. However, it is also accompanied by the high potential of making huge percentages of loss. People who are terms as high-risk takers have the potential to realize good amounts of profits or huge losses. It is because of the nature of the trade. The losses are experienced because of several variables that are always present in trading. The gains and individual experiences are brought to light by margin buying.

There as a big difference between swing trade and day trade. The difference hails from their definitions, it goes a mile ahead to time spent in and risks involvement in both forms of trade. Day trade has lower risk involvement but one has to spend more of his or her time, unlike swing trade. Day traders are prone to participating in two forms of trade which are long trades or short trades. Long trade involves an individual purchasing the financial instruments and selling them after them increasing in value. On the other hand, short trade involves selling financial instruments and later purchasing them after their prices have dropped.

The trading market has undergone through several advancements. The major change was witnessed during the deregulation process. There was the creation of electronic financial markets during this period. One of the major innovations was the high-frequency trading index. It uses heavy algorithms to enable huge financial firms in stock trading to perform numerous orders in seconds. It is advantageous because it can also predict market trends.

The process of day trading has several challenges. An individual is supposed to be able to make a good decision during two important moments. The first moment is during a good streak and the other is during moments an individual has a poor run. At this point risk management and trading, psychology comes in handy to help an individual in the trade. One is not supposed to panic or make hasty decisions during these moments. It is important for an individual to have an effective watchlist. A good watchlist built by a trader is supposed to be able to understand the modern trading markets. This is made possible when it features stocks in play, float and market capital, pre-market grippers, real-time intraday scans, and planning trade based on scanners. The success of day trading is also incumbent on effective strategies. The common strategies include ABCD patterns, bag flag momentum, reversal trading, movie average trading, and opening range breakouts.

There are also advanced strategies that can be used to ensure the success of day trading. Three of these strategies are one stock in play, bull flag, and a fallen angel. With the use of these strategies, a successful trader builds his or her trading business step by step. The common steps involve building a watchlist, having a trading plan and knowing how to execute.

Create Automatic Income for Life Immediately!

Forex Signals.

High Conversions Verified Forex Results.

https://1e503-r5sjod5kcm4z3ggybs8j.hop.clickbank.net

OR

BOTS Live Trading Room

https://db240ys-r9r60z39q8rgnkuklg.hop.clickbank.net

Made in the USA
Las Vegas, NV
18 December 2024

14744136R00390